Product Liability

Jurisdictional comparisons **First edition 2014**

General Editors:
Annette Hughes, Corrs Chambers Westgarth
& Rod Freeman, Hogan Lovells International LLP

THOMSON REUTERS

General Editors
Annette Hughes, Corrs Chambers Westgarth
& Rod Freeman, Hogan Lovells International LLP

Commercial Director
Katie Burrington

Commissioning Editor
Emily Kyriacou

Senior Editor
Caroline Pearce

Design and Production
Dawn McGovern

Editorial Assistant
Nicola Pender

Published in June 2014 by European Lawyer Reference Series,
100 Avenue Road, London NW3 3PF
part of Thomson Reuters (Professional) UK Limited
(Registered in England & Wales, Company No 1679046.
Registered Office and address for service:
Aldgate House, 33 Aldgate High Street, London EC3N 1DL)

A CIP catalogue record for this book is available from the British Library.

ISBN: 978-0-414031-93-7

Contents

Foreword

Annette Hughes Partner, Corrs Chambers Westgarth;
President, Australian National Product Liability Association

Product liability is an ever-growing area of legal practice, and area of risk for companies involved in the manufacture and supply of products, particularly consumer goods, all around the world.

In today's international economy, product liability issues are necessarily cross border. It is common for companies that manufacture products to export those products across the globe. It is also common for component parts of products to be sourced from the far reaches of the globe, creating a complex web which can be difficult to unravel when things go wrong. It is critical for such companies to have a working knowledge of the laws on product liability across the jurisdictions into which their products or component parts reach.

Product liability laws or the practical application of those laws can vary greatly across jurisdictions – even across jurisdictions one would ordinarily expect to be aligned or coordinated. Add to this the differences in the operation of the courts and civil procedure (including discovery processes) across jurisdictions, and it is easy to see the need for an understanding of cross-border issues. Further, governments around the world continue to grapple with the challenges posed by and regulation required around class actions and litigation funding, balancing the interests of plaintiffs to be compensated for their loss and damage, and the interests of manufacturers and suppliers, for whom awards of damages (never mind the costs of conducting such actions) may be devastating.

Finally, the regulatory schemes for addressing product liability issues vary around the world, and despite efforts at coordination and information sharing (for example, between regulators as well as by public databases such as the Global Recalls portal maintained by the Organisation for Economic Cooperation and Development), understanding the interplay between them and how to manage cross-border product manufacture and supply, let alone a repair or recall, can be a daunting task.

I hope this publication provides an informative and accessible guide to legal practitioners, in-house counsel and students on the laws governing product liability and product liability litigation in the jurisdictions covered.

I am extremely grateful to each of the preeminent product liability legal practitioners from across the globe who have donated their precious time to contribute a chapter on the laws of their country to this publication. Without their assistance, this publication would not have been possible.

I am particularly grateful to Rod Freeman of Hogan Lovells, who served as co-editor, and contributed the England & Wales and European Union chapters. Thanks also must go to Katie Burrington, Dawn McGovern, Caroline Pearce, Nicola Pender and the rest of the Thomson Reuters team for their tireless efforts on this important project.

Finally, on a personal note, I would like to thank my colleagues at Corrs Chambers Westgarth for their support of this project, including Barbara Bell and Simon Frauenfelder, who assisted with the Australia chapter.

Annette Hughes,
Melbourne, May 2014

Argentina

Marval, O'Farrell & Mairal
Leandro M. Castelli & Alejo M. Gascón

1. LIABILITY

1.1 What are the principal sources of law and regulation relating to product liability?

Product liability is governed by the general regime for damages in Argentina, which has its legal source in the Civil Code and under the Consumer Protection Law 24,240 as amended.

The general regime

Liability may be: (i) contractual; or (ii) non-contractual.

(i) Contractual liability

The liability of the supplier is based on the contract entered into with the purchaser. The supplier undertakes a safety obligation which consists of a guarantee that the product involved will not harm the purchaser due to defects which could make it dangerous. This safety obligation is deemed implicit in every purchase agreement, even if it is not expressly referred to in the contract.

As noted, the supplier is deemed to undertake an outcome obligation towards the purchaser, because the product involved in the contract is aimed to satisfy a given purpose. The supplier is also liable for hidden defects existing at the time of the purchase.

(ii) Non-contractual liability

Product liability may also arise when no contract exists between the plaintiff and the manufacturer because there is an obligation not to harm another person and to indemnify whenever such harm is done. Additionally, such obligations also arise from the defects of the product or from the risk of introducing a defective product into the market. Accordingly, when the damage has been caused by a fault or risk inherent to the product the manufacturer will be strictly liable.

The Consumer Protection Law (CPL)

Product liability was originally governed exclusively by the Civil Code. However, in the 1990s, an increasing idea of protection of consumer rights arose. As a result, the Argentine Congress passed the Consumer Protection Law (CPL) which provides further protection when consumers are involved in a consumer contract or relationship.

Consumers are individuals or companies that acquire or use goods or services as end-users, for free or not, and for their own benefit or for the benefit of their family or social group. Any person who is not part of a consumer relationship, but acquires or uses products as a consequence of a consumer relationship, will also be considered to be a consumer.

The CPL sets forth the strict, joint and several liability of the producer, manufacturer, distributor, supplier, retailer and/or anyone using its brand or trademark on the product or service, for damages arising from the risk or defect of products or services.

The carrier will be responsible for damages caused to the product as a consequence or on the occasion of the service.

Consumers are further protected by the fair trade laws which establish rules for the labelling and advertisement of products. Lastly, in principle, antitrust laws make provisions for protecting consumers from the abuses of market manipulation and anti-competitive behaviour.

1.2 What is required to establish causation under the most common causes of action available?

In order to establish civil liability there must be a causation link between the act or omission and the damage arising.

Causation is established by testing for 'adequate cause'. Therefore, an act or omission resulting in damage will be attributed to a person if such act or omission regularly or commonly leads to the production of such result. An abstract or objective foreseeability test is thus required to establish whether or not a given result is the consequence of a given act or omission.

The cause should never be just a mere condition of the damage. It has to contribute effectively to the harm suffered.

Traditionally it was necessary to meet these four strict requirements in order to impose civil liability on a defendant.

(i) an act that is against the law. Here, law means any kind of regulations;
(ii) a harm suffered by the victim of the illegal act;
(iii) the existence of a causal relation between the illegal act and the loss; and
(iv) that the harm can be attributed to a person, based on an objective or a subjective criteria. Subjective would be when the wrong-doer has behaved with negligence or wilful misconduct. Objective is in cases of strict liability, without consideration on the wrongdoer's fault.

Currently, these requirements are considered to be more flexible.

1.3 Is strict liability available and, if so, in what circumstances?

Yes, strict liability is available; however, it is the exception to the rule that liability is based on fault or negligence.

Under Article 1113 of the Civil Code, owners and custodians are liable for:

(i) the damages caused by their things;
(ii) the damages caused by virtue of the risk or defect inherent in their things.

In order to avoid liability in the first case, the owners or custodians must show that they have not been incurred in negligence. This would be more a case of change in the burden of proof than a case of strict liability (ie, negligence is in principle inferred).

In the second case, the owners or custodians of the risky or defective thing may only avoid strict liability in full or in part by showing negligence in the victim or in a third party for whom they are not liable. Although not specifically mentioned in Article 1113 of the Civil Code, an external *force majeure* event would also exonerate liability.

Also if the thing were used against the express or inferred will of its owner or custodians, they would in principle not be held liable (Article 1113, last paragraph, Civil Code).

Finally, the CPL also contemplates a broad strict liability provision in the event that a consumer is injured by virtue of the defect or risk of a product or of a service.

1.4 Are guarantees or warranties as to quality implied by law?

The consumer and successive purchasers are entitled to a legal warranty affording protection against defects or faults of any kind whatsoever, even though they might have been visible or apparent at the time of the agreement, when they affect the identity between what was offered and what was delivered, as well as proper operation thereof.

Manufacturers, distributors, importers and suppliers are jointly and severally liable for granting and complying with the legal warranty. The legal warranty will be in force for three months as from delivery in the case of second-hand movable property and for six months as from delivery in all remaining cases, and the parties may agree on a longer term. In the event that the product shall be carried to the manufacturing plant or to the authorised repair shop, the party liable for the warranty will be responsible for transportation as well as freight and insurance costs and any other cost due to transportation thereof.

Manufacturers, distributors, importers and suppliers shall repair the product under warranty covering the shipping charges (ie, insurance, freight, etc.) and replacement part expenses, and furthermore provide the consumer with a document containing: (i) the nature of the reparation; (ii) the list of replaced or repaired pieces; (iii) the date the consumer delivered the product to the warrantor; and (iv) the date the product was returned to the consumer.

1.5 How is a product 'defect' defined?

The law does not provide a definition of product 'defect'. However, Argentine scholars' opinions refer to the European Council Directive 85/374/EEC of 25 July, 1985 which states that 'A product is defective when it does not provide the safety which a person is entitled to expect, taking all circumstances into account, including: (i) the presentation of the product; (ii) the use to which it could reasonably be expected that the product would be put; (iii) the time when the product was put into circulation' and that 'A product shall not be considered defective for the sole reason that a better product is subsequently put into circulation'.

In fact, it is said, that the European Directive does not contain a 'defect' definition, but points out when a product may be defective. In this respect, the law's intention is to avoid the analysis of the causes or origins of the defect which produces damage, and to emphasise the circumstances which occur for a product not to fulfil the security conditions, which ultimately will be judged by courts in each case.

The outcome measure of the defectiveness of the product is the lack of security; this is the composition of the set of tools of prevention of harm that can reasonably be expected.

Consumers should expect that products provide security that is reasonably foreseeable.

As said, Argentine Law does not provide for a product 'defect' definition. In any case, a terminology related with Article 1113 of the Civil Code is used: the damages caused by virtue of the risk or defect inherent in their things.

1.6 Who in the supply chain has obligations or duties for defective products? What obligations or duties do they owe and to whom?

When a consumer is injured by virtue of the defect or risk of a product or of a service, the producer, manufacturer, importer, distributor, supplier, vendor and whoever may have placed their brand in the product or service, will be held liable.

In addition, the carrier will be held liable under this provision for the damages resulting by virtue of or on the occasion of its service. In all these cases liability is joint and several, notwithstanding the corresponding recovery actions that may be available.

Producers and suppliers must provide consumers with truthful, objective and adequate information, which must be detailed, efficacious and sufficient on the essential features of the goods and services supplied and their marketing conditions. Such information should be free for consumers and provided with the necessary clarity that allows for full understanding.

The CPL also provides that products shall be supplied or rendered in a way that their use under regular conditions does not represent a danger for a consumer's health. Those products or services that imply a risk to a consumer's health must be sold according to the applicable rules (or reasonable rules if there are no applicable regulations), mechanisms and instructions to ensure safeness, and attaching a user's manual including safety rules.

Producers and suppliers have a duty to comply with labelling and packaging requirements, providing information to consumers from the time the products are introduced to the market. Additionally, those producers and suppliers who become aware that a product is dangerous after having introduced it to the market must immediately inform this circumstance to the competent authorities and to consumers through the appropriate media.

1.7 By what means can a supplier limit its liability for defective products?

In order to be fully or partially exonerated from liability, the supplier must show that the cause of the damage is alien to such supplier. This, however, has generally been construed as requiring proof that the cause of the damage is alien to the whole marketing chain. (CNCiv., panel I, *Mirás v Grupo 3 Servicios S.A.*, (2003), JA 2003-IV-323)

1.8 Are there particular goods or services which have specific obligations or duties attached to them?

Producers and suppliers have a duty to comply with labelling and packaging requirements, providing information to consumers for every good or service that is introduced to the market. Additionally, the products or services which may entail a risk to health or personal safety of consumers or users must be marketed in conformity with pre-established or reasonable mechanisms, instructions and standards that guarantee their safeness.

Pre-established or reasonable mechanisms are set forth by specific authorities depending on the service or product (eg, National Administration of Drugs, Food and Medical Technology (ANMAT – after its acronym in Spanish) is the national health authority for food, medical and pharmaceutical products).

2. DEFENCES

2.1 What are the possible defences to a product liability claim?

In strict liability cases the defendant may prove:

(i) that there is no causation between the damage and the product;
(ii) force majeure;
(iii) that the plaintiff was responsible for the damage; or
(iv) that the damage was caused by a third person and that the defendant has no duty to respond for that person.

2.2 Is there a limit on the time in which proceedings may be brought (limitations and repose)?

The statute of limitations for damages resulting from non-contractual obligations (ie, torts) is two years and for damages resulting from contractual obligations is 10 years. In the case of consumer claims, the minimum statute of limitations is three years.

The statute of limitation provision is generally computed from the date of the event upon which the plaintiff is suing to the date the complaint is filed.

3. LITIGATION OF PRODUCT LIABILITY DISPUTES

3.1 In which courts are product liability proceedings brought?

Product liability disputes are generally heard either before the National/Provincial Commercial Courts or the Federal Civil and Commercial Courts, depending on the federal or non-federal nature of the matter.

Argentina is a federal republic, comprising 23 provinces and a federal capital (the City of Buenos Aires). Justice is administered by federal and provincial courts. A distinction is drawn between federal and national courts in the City of Buenos Aires.

The provincial court system is organised in three tiers: lower courts, courts of appeal and the Provincial Supreme Court. Provincial courts deal with cases based either on local laws or on non-federal laws. Within the territory of each province, there are also federal courts.

Within the City of Buenos Aires there are two types of courts: federal courts and national courts. Federal courts deal with federal law matters while national courts deal with non-federal law matters.

3.2 How are proceedings commenced?

Prior to the filing of the complaint, disputes to be tried in the City of Buenos Aires and many other provinces must be submitted to a pre-trial mandatory mediation proceeding.

This rule is not applicable to criminal, labour, bankruptcy, hereditary, non-patrimonial family cases, interim measures and cases involving the Federal State.

The proceeding may last up to 60 days and parties, in the case of individuals, must personally attend the hearings accompanied by their attorneys.

Settlements agreed in mediation processes are binding and may be enforced as judicial judgments.

If no agreement is reached, once the mediator formally closes the proceeding the claimant is entitled to file their complaint before the courts within the statute of limitation term applicable to the complaint.

The Argentine court procedure is mainly written rather than oral.

Under the federal system, the introductory stage of the fact finding proceeding begins with the filing of the complaint with the court and service of process on the defendant.

The Procedural Code states that the complaint must include the name and domicile of both the claimant and the defendant, a thorough description of all the circumstances of fact that the claimant wishes to rely on to sustain the claim with a brief explanation of the applicable legal arguments. The claimant must also clearly identify the relief sought.

All documentary evidence must be attached to the complaint or duly identified if the party is not in possession of the document and all other types of evidence must be offered in the complaint.

The complaint may be amended or extended before it is served to the defendant.

New facts or documents can only be invoked or attached to the docket if they are dated after the filing of the complaint or the response, or if they were unknown to the party at the time of filing the complaint or the response.

3.3 Are disputed issues decided by a judge or a jury?

Argentine law does not provide for lay juries. Cases are decided exclusively by professional judges.

3.4 Who has the burden of proof and to what standard?

As a general rule, the burden of proof lies with the party that alleges the existence of a controverted fact upon which it bases its case.

In recent years, courts have started to modify this principle holding that evidence must be produced by the party in the best position to do so. This principle, for instance, is usually followed in medical malpractice cases where the doctor or hospital is expected to prove that they acted without negligence.

Courts do not decide in advance which party must provide the evidence.

Moreover, in some cases substantive law imposes the burden of proof on specific litigants (eg, CPL on the owner of goods that caused injuries and the manufacturer or seller of products that harmed consumers, etc.).

3.5 How is evidence given in proceedings and are witnesses cross-examined?

Parties must produce all relevant documentary evidence on which they wish to rely submitting their claim or their response and a list of specific documents that they wish the court to order the opposing party or third party to produce. They must also indicate all the other means of evidence they intend to rely upon.

The Procedural Code identifies and regulates certain types of admissible evidence in detail, which includes the following:

(i) requests for information from third parties;
(ii) declaration of the parties;
(iii) deposition of fact witnesses;
(iv) expert witnesses' reports; and
(v) judicial inspection.

It also grants judges the power of ordering the production of other kinds of evidence, if deemed appropriate for the solution of the case.

In principle, fact witnesses give oral evidence. Oral testimony is received at one or more hearings. Witnesses must testify under oath and criminal sanctions may apply for perjury.

The party who proposes the witness can submit, in writing, a list of questions to the judge, who may amend them or ask additional questions. The parties can also orally propose questions at the hearing. The judge has discretion in relation to the admissibility of the questions.

Fact witnesses can be cross-examined. However, the judge has discretion in relation to the admissibility of the questions.

3.6 Are the parties able to rely on expert opinion evidence and, if so, are there any special rules or procedures for expert opinion evidence?

Expert witnesses are only appointed by the court at the parties' request. However, in most jurisdictions the parties can appoint consultants to attend all proceedings conducted by the court-appointed expert and produce a report together with the court-appointed expert or separately.

Court-appointed experts provide independent advice and answer the questions admitted by the courts. The parties can propose questions which may be amended by the courts.

Once the court-appointed expert has produced their report, the parties can challenge it or require clarifications.

3.7 Is pre-trial discovery permitted? If so, in what circumstances? If not, what other mechanisms, if any, are available for obtaining evidence from a party or a third party?

The procedure for the discovery of documents as it exists in other countries, does not exist in the Argentine legal system. Parties have the right to produce only the documents upon which they intend to base their case.

The only exception to this principle is the right that a party has to request from its opponent or a third party the production of specifically identified documents which are relevant to the dispute. In this case, if the required party does not produce the documents the judge may draw a negative inference against such party at the time of rendering the final decision.

It must be noted that when Argentina ratified the 1970 Hague Convention on the Taking of Evidence Abroad in Civil or Commercial Matters, it filed a reservation stating that it would not execute Letters of Request issued for the purpose of obtaining pre-trial discovery of documents as known in the common law countries.

Additionally, expert witnesses may demand access to documents that the parties have not attached. Although these documents are not incorporated to the file, the information they contain is analysed by the expert and may be included in their report if it is relevant. If the access to documents that is requested by the expert is not granted, the court may draw a negative inference.

Private investigation (different from the review of public records) is a very rare practice in Argentina and, as such, would probably not yield useful results. Private investigation improperly conducted (or depicted as such) may raise objections and even criminal accusations.

3.8 Is there liability for spoliation of evidence/a remedy for destruction of or failure to preserve evidence (most relevantly, the product)?

In principle, there is no liability for spoliation of evidence. However, civil and commercial judges may draw a negative inference regarding any destruction of evidence or failure to preserve evidence.

3.9 Is interlocutory or interim relief available prior to the full trial of a proceeding? If so, in what circumstances?

Yes, interlocutory or interim relief is available prior to the full trial of a proceeding. In principle these interlocutory reliefs should be decided by the court before dealing with the substance of the dispute. However, judges generally decide them when rendering the decision.

Some of the preliminary motions admitted by the procedural codes in this line are as follows:

(i) statute of limitations;
(ii) lack of jurisdiction;
(iii) lack of legal capacity (or authorisation) to take part in an action or of insufficient powers;
(iv) lack of standing to sue or to be sued, when this is evident;

(v) *lis pendens;*
(vi) deficiencies in the way the claim has been presented; and
(vii) *res judicata.*

However, as the CPL allows cases to be tried through summary proceedings, some of these defences may not be admitted as preliminary motions.

3.10 Can the winning party recover its costs?

Argentina is a losing-party-pays jurisdiction. Consequently, the winning party can recover court fees from the losing party and other incidental expenses as well as their own costs.

3.11 What avenues of appeal are available?

Appeals may be of different types depending on the decision against which they are filed, the court that issued the decision and whether the decision is a final judgment or whether it is an interlocutory order of the court.

There are basically two stages when judgments may be challenged:
(i) appeals to the Courts of Appeals in respect of decisions by first instance judges; and
(ii) appeals to the Supreme Court in respect of decisions of the Courts of Appeals.

Interlocutory decisions made by trial courts after hearing both parties or after hearing only one party, but which cause an irreparable damage to the other party, may be appealed in the same way as a final judgment. Decisions regarding evidence in principle are not subject to appeal.

In summary proceedings only the final judgment and decisions granting or rejecting interim measures may be appealed.

4. CLASS ACTIONS/REPRESENTATIVE PROCEEDINGS

4.1 Is there a mechanism for class actions or representative proceedings, or co-ordinated proceedings for product liability claims? If so, what are the basic mechanics?

The law does not provide for a mechanism for class actions or representative proceedings. However, it must be noted that the CPL entitles non-governmental organisations (NGOs) and consumer associations to file collective actions in defence of a group of affected consumers. This law also provides for an opt-out system and allows the representative associations to litigate without having to bear the court tax (and, according to some case law, other legal expenses).

Class action admissibility rules and proceeding guidelines were provided by the Supreme Court while ruling *Halabi v Executive Power* (2009), H. 270. XLII. REX. Such ruling describes the main characteristics of class actions for the enforcement of individual and homogeneous rights; thus implying a difference from those rights which protect collective rights and are individual by nature.

The Supreme Court classified rights under three categories:
(i) individual;

(ii) rights of collective impact that concern collective assets; and
(iii) rights of collective impact that concern individuals but homogeneous assets.

It finally set the following requirements in order to admit the actions for claiming the rights mentioned in item (iii):

- there must be a sole detrimental fact that affects an important number of individual rights;
- the action must be focused on the common effects and not on the claims of each particular person;
- each individual interest, individually considered, must not justify the filing of a lawsuit which could compromise access to justice.

Notwithstanding the above, the ruling expressly states that the class action will be admitted even if the requirements are not strictly complied with, whenever there is a matter of extreme importance involved, such as the environment, consumer rights, health, or if it is affecting groups that have been traditionally ignored, or less protected.

Likewise, the Supreme Court also explained that the formal admission of any class action requires the verification of certain elemental requirements which are of the essence and affect its feasibility; such requirements are:

- the precise identification of the affected collective group;
- the competence/capability of the person who will be representing such group;
- the existence of common arguments related to facts and rights;
- the proper notification to all the people who may have an interest in the result of the trial, thus ensuring them the possibility of opting in or out;
- the proper publicity of the case to avoid multiplication or superposition of class actions on the same matter.

The Supreme Court granted *erga omnes* effects to the judgment in *re Halabi*.

5. LITIGATION FUNDING

5.1 Is litigation funding by third parties permissible in your country? If so, is it common?

Litigation funding does not exist. Claimants who are not able to afford litigation costs may request authorisation to litigate *in forma pauperis*. The authorised party is exempt from the payment of the court tax and winners' attorney's fees. The CPL also provides a similar procedure if requested.

5.2 Are contingency fee or 'no win no fee' arrangements permissible?

Fees are fixed by the courts and in principle are borne by the unsuccessful party. However, parties are free to negotiate fees with their own lawyers.

6. REMEDIES

6.1 What remedies are available to a party who successfully pursues a product liability claim?

Consumers who successfully pursue a product liability claim may choose to:

(i) request specific performance of the obligation provided if such performance were possible;
(ii) accept another product or the rendering of equivalent services;
(iii) rescind the agreement with a right to reimbursement of any amount paid irrespective of the effects already verified and considering the agreement in its entirety.

In addition to these remedies, consumers may claim damages.

6.2 How are damages calculated/are there limitations on available damages?

There is no rule or proceeding in order to calculate damages. The general principle applicable to damages states that the award shall provide full compensation for all the damages caused to the victim that are not too remote. Therefore, the relief sought may include:

(i) compensatory damages, which may include bodily injury, mental damage, aesthetic damage and damage to property;
(ii) loss of profit;
(iii) moral damages, which may be recovered when hurt feelings cause physical pain, suffering or spiritual anxiety; and
(iv) punitive damages as described below.

Argentine case law has also awarded damages for the 'loss of opportunity'.

6.3 Are punitive or exemplary damages available and in what circumstances?

Punitive damages may be available under the CPL. Under Article 52 *bis* of the CPL, the court may impose, at the request of the injured party, punitive damages to the suppliers in breach of legal or contractual duties. Pursuant to this provision, the amount of punitive damages will be imposed according to the 'seriousness and other circumstances of the case' and regardless of other applicable indemnifications available to the consumer. Punitive damages may not exceed the amount of ARS 5,000,000 (approximately US$756,000 at current exchange rates).

6.4 Is liability joint and several/how does apportionment of liability work, including where a partially responsible entity is not a party to the proceeding?

When more than one supplier is liable for the breach, all sued suppliers are held jointly and severally liable in respect of the consumer, notwithstanding their recovery rights.

7. ROLE OF REGULATORS

7.1 Please explain the role, responsibilities and powers of the regulators in your country which have jurisdiction over product liability issues.

The Domestic Trade Secretary (DTS – an agency of the Ministry of Economy) through the Consumer Protection Undersecretary (CPU) is the national implementing authority for the CPL. The provinces and the City of Buenos

Aires are the local implementing authorities.

The CPL empowered the DTS as the control agency to:

(i) develop policies to the consumer advocacy for a sustainable consumption and environmental protection;
(ii) maintain a national register of associations of consumers and users;
(iii) receive and act on the concerns and complaints of consumers or users;
(iv) arrange for inspections related to the application of the CPL;
(v) request reports and reviews to public and private entities regarding the matters of the CPL; and
(vi) dispose *ex officio* or by request from hearings involving complainants' victims, suspected offenders, witnesses and experts.

Additionally, the DTS managed the National System of Arbitration of Consumer Affairs. This Arbitration System provides for an administrative alternative dispute resolution for consumers and suppliers issues.

On a lower administrative level the CPU complies with the following directives:

(i) understanding on the implementation of policies and regulatory frameworks needed to strengthen consumer rights;
(ii) advice, orientation and broadcasting of information to consumers and suppliers;
(iii) processing of consumer complaints, monitoring, and establishing sanctions if deemed applicable;
(iv) monitoring and control over suppliers' illegal or harmful behaviours;
(v) training to teachers, education entities as well as provincial and/or municipal agencies and civil, social, community, professional and/or business organisations agencies;
(vi) organisation, maintenance and promotion of the national register of associations of consumers and users.

Additionally, authorities that have approved the commercialisation of the product shall monitor product's compliance with specific regulations including safety matters.

7.2 Are there any mandatory reporting requirements related to product safety issues?

Pursuant to Section 4 of Decree 1798/94, which regulates the CPL, those suppliers who become aware that a product is dangerous after having introduced it into the market must notify this circumstance immediately to the competent authorities and to consumers through the appropriate media. In practice this means that as soon as possible suppliers should notify the Consumer Protection Agencies and any other authorities that have approved the commercialisation of the product involved, as well as the consumers.

7.3 Do the regulators have the power to:

(i) ban certain goods or services?

Yes, both the DTS and the authorities involved in the authorisation of the product have the power to ban certain goods or services.

(ii) require a supplier to recall a product?

Yes, both the DTS and the authorities involved in the authorisation of the product have the power to require a supplier to recall a product.

(iii) prescribe standards in respect of certain goods or services and require that the goods or services meet those standards?

Yes, both the DTS and the authorities involved in the authorisation of the product have the power.

(iv) require production of information without court process?

Yes, both the DTS and the authorities involved in the authorisation of the product have the power to require production of information without court process, through an administrative proceeding.

If so, broadly explain the circumstances in which the regulator can exercise the power and any penalties that apply if a supplier fails to comply.

The regulator may ban certain goods or services or require a supplier to recall a product whenever the damage or the defects of the products or services has been verified. In order to verify such standards the regulator is empowered to require production of information through an administrative proceeding and where necessary apply the following penalties to those liable suppliers:

(i) warning;

(ii) fine in an amount equivalent to between ARS 100 (approximately US$12 at current rates) and ARS 5,000,000;

(iii) seizure of goods and products that are the subject matter of the infringement;

(iv) shutdown of premises or suspension of the impaired service for a term of up to 30 days;

(v) suspension of registration in the registers of suppliers required to contract with the government, for up to five years;

(vi) forfeiture of concessions, privileges and special tax or credit systems granted in their favour.

The CPL provides for administrative sanctions even if the damage did not occur (in order to prevent future harmful behaviour to consumer rights).

8. VOLUNTARY CONDUCT

8.1 Are there regulations pertaining to the voluntary conduct of a product repair or recall by a supplier?

There is no express legal obligation pertaining to the voluntary conduct of a product repair or recall by supplier. However, if the product is considered risky or dangerous, the recall could be considered necessary as part of the general duty to prevent damages and the duty of suppliers to sell safe products. Also, it is likely to be taken into consideration for the graduation of sanctions and the imposition of liability, as it could be considered as a measure to reduce risks or damages.

It must be noted that those suppliers that become aware that a product is dangerous after having introduced it into the market must notify this circumstance immediately to the competent authorities and to consumers through the appropriate media.

9. EMERGING ISSUES AND LAW REFORM

9.1 Are there important developing and emerging issues or trends in product liability law in your country? If so, please broadly identify them.

An emerging issue arises with regard to the illicit act requirement mentioned in answer 1.2 (i).

We can define 'illicit act' as one consisting of a breach of law that causes harm to another and gives rise to an obligation to redress by the party responsible by virtue of a sufficient attribution factor.

No voluntary act is to be deemed illicit if it is not expressly prohibited by the law; and no illicit act may be sanctioned without such sanction being imposed by law. Likewise, any person who may cause harm to another by virtue of an omission shall be held liable only to the extent that a provision in the law imposed a duty to fulfil such omitted act. Basically, any act against the law or against a valid agreement is illicit. Articles 1066 and 1074 of the Civil Code provide for: (i) a duty not to do what is forbidden by law; and (ii) a duty to do what law orders. It is generally understood that the term 'law', in these provisions, is used in its broad sense.

As a general rule, however, any harm or injury caused by the negligence or fault of a person must be repaired, even if there were no breach to a specific provision of the law. This general rule is said to tacitly impose a duty to act in a fashion that causes no harm to others, ie, prudently and diligently, such general duty being supplemented by the more specific duties not to do what is forbidden by law and to do what the law orders.

Notwithstanding the above, recently there has been a line of case law arguing that, when a person has suffered an unjust harm, civil liability may be established even if the existence of an illicit act could not be established. In this regard, many authors sustain that any act that causes harm is illegal *per se*, or that any harm suffered by an innocent person or unjustified should be redressed.

9.2 Please describe any proposed important law reform in the area of product liability in your country.

Chief Justice Ricardo Lorenzetti, together with more than 100 specialists and university professors, has prepared the Civil and Commercial Unification Bill (Unification Bill), a single body of rules regulating the principal institutions of private law.

The Unification Bill has been considered by both Chambers of Congress by means of the intervention of a bicameral commission which collected all comments and remarks from a range of sectors of civil society. On 28 November, 2013 the Argentine Senate approved the Unification Bill which must now be considered by the Lower House during the 2014 ordinary sessions.

Were it to be enacted into law (it seems that this will be its fate in the short term), the two codes most extensively applied in Argentina, with a total of approximately 5000 sections currently regulating civil and commercial matters (including their amendments) on a separate basis will be replaced by a single code containing 2,671 sections. Moreover, the new Code applies a different methodology, which is closer to the one that has been used for many years at universities.

Its priority is given to general and community interest by means of the protection of collective incidence rights, public order rules within the framework of contracts and consumer rights, and the restrictive interpretation of adhesion contracts.

A noteworthy reform is projected in connection with civil liability. The distinction between contractual and tort liability is eliminated and stress is made not only on damage compensation but on the prevention thereof. For this purpose judges are empowered to issue preventive measures and also dissuasive penalties where collective incidence rights are at stake.

It is also acknowledged that liability for property risk includes those who obtain a profit therefrom and whether the activity generating the damages may have been recognised by the administrative authority is irrelevant.

The last volume of the draft regulates the expiry of obligations upon the running of a statute of limitations, setting forth as a general rule a shorter period (five years), and considers the forfeiture of rights on a separate basis.

10. REGULATORY WEBSITES/INFORMATION

10.1 Please identify any useful regulatory references relating to product liability law in your country, for example, a product safety/consumer law website maintained by the main regulator.

- *www.jus.gob.ar/atencion-al-ciudadano/guia-de-derivaciones/defensa-del-consumidor.aspx*
- *www.consumidor.gov.ar/*
- *www.buenosaires.gob.ar/defensaconsumidor*

Australia

Corrs Chambers Westgarth Annette Hughes

1. LIABILITY

1.1 What are the principal sources of law and regulation relating to product liability?

Product liability is regulated by statute and common law in Australia. As a federal system, Australia has relevant legislation at both the state and national level.

At the national level, the Australian Consumer Law (ACL) (which is Schedule 2 to the Competition and Consumer Act 2010 (Cth) (CCA)) provides a broad set of statutory standards, the breach of which will see manufacturers and suppliers of goods and services liable to compensate consumers for loss and damage suffered. In addition, manufacturers and suppliers of goods which breach the provisions of the ACL may face enforcement action and pecuniary penalties from the regulator that administers the ACL, the Australian Competition and Consumer Commission (ACCC).

In addition, manufacturers and suppliers may be liable under other provisions, including:

- under state fair trading laws, which largely mirror the provisions of the ACL;
- in tort, for the negligent manufacture or supply of goods and services; and
- under contract law for the supply of goods in breach of express or implied warranties, both in business to consumer transactions and business to business transactions.

Product liability proceedings most commonly involve allegations of both breaches of the ACL and negligence, while contract claims tend to be relied on where other provisions don't apply, or where they are very clear and helpful to the claimant (which is more rare).

There are a wider array of regulations and laws regarding other aspects of product liability – we have focused on the product safety provisions.

1.2 What is required to establish causation under the most common causes of action available?

Under the main statutory cause of action in the ACL for the supply of defective goods, a manufacturer will be liable where:

- that manufacturer supplies goods in trade or commerce; and
- the goods have a safety defect; and
- *because of* that defect an individual suffers injuries (s138 of the ACL).

In this context, the words 'because of' require that there be a causal connection between the defect and the injury suffered.

Under common law causes of action such as negligence, it is generally necessary to show that there was some negligent aspect of the manufacturer's conduct, which, in fact, on the balance of probabilities caused the loss or damage suffered by the plaintiff. However, the fact that a safety defect exists in the product will go far to ground an inference that there has been the requisite negligent conduct.

Under contract, liability will depend on establishing that the product supplied breached an express or implied term as to the quality or safety of the product. The causation test is the same for breach of contract as it is for negligence.

1.3 Is strict liability available and, if so, in what circumstances?

Strict liability is available under the ACL, such that a manufacturer will be liable where it is established that:

- the manufacturer has supplied goods in trade or commerce; and
- the goods have a safety defect; and
- because of that defect an individual has suffered an injury or injuries (s138 of the ACL).

Under this statutory cause of action, there is no additional requirement that the manufacturer has acted negligently or recklessly in supplying the defective product.

1.4 Are guarantees or warranties as to quality implied by law?

Yes, both the statute and general law imply guarantees as to quality of goods or services, however, the ACL implies much broader and much stricter requirements than would apply at general law.

The key implied guarantee is one that all goods are of 'acceptable quality' (s54 of the ACL), which includes warranties that goods are as:

- fit for all the purposes for which goods of that kind are commonly supplied;
- acceptable in appearance and finish;
- free from defects;
- safe; and
- durable,

as a reasonable consumer fully acquainted with the state and condition of the goods would regard as acceptable. Whether goods meet the guaranteed standard is judged by reference to a number of factors, including the nature and price of the goods, as well as any marketing or information statements used in conjunction with the goods (s54(3)).

Division 1 of Part 3-2 of the ACL also contains other implied guarantees as they relate to goods and services, including guarantees as to:

- good title to goods (s51);
- fitness for purpose (s55);
- true supply of goods by their description (s56) or by reference to a sample or demonstrator model (s57);

- reasonable action to ensure provision of repairs and spare parts (s58); and
- use of due care and skill in providing services (s60).

Importantly, these guarantees cannot be excluded or limited by agreement (s64). Any term of a contract that purports to 'exclude, restrict, or modify' these consumer guarantees, or limit liability below that available under the ACL (s64A) is deemed to be void to the extent it attempts to do so.

1.5 How is a product 'defect' defined?

Under s9 of the ACL, goods will have a 'safety defect' if their 'safety is not such as persons generally are entitled to expect' having regard to factors such as:

- the marketing of the goods;
- their packaging or any mark use in relation to them;
- instructions for their use;
- what might reasonably be expected to be done with them; and
- the time they were supplied by the manufacturer.

The ACL also provides that an inference cannot be drawn that goods have a safety defect merely because safer goods were later supplied (s9(3)) or the goods complied with a mandatory standard and the standard was not the safest possible standard having regard to the latest state of scientific or technical knowledge (s9(4)).

Accordingly, manufacturers have significant control over ensuring their products do not have 'safety defects' by ensuring the products are labelled, marketed and supplied in compliance with safe practices.

1.6 Who in the supply chain has obligations or duties for defective products? What obligations or duties do they owe and to whom?

The ACL imposes obligations primarily on 'manufacturers' and, in some circumstances, 'suppliers' of goods or services. The definition of manufacturer in s7 of the ACL is broad, and includes a person or business that:

- makes or assembles goods;
- holds themselves out as the manufacturer of the goods;
- has brand name applied to or included in the goods; or
- imports the goods if the actual importer does not have an office in Australia.

A person who supplies goods, but is not also the manufacturer of those goods will be 'deemed' to be the manufacturer unless that supplier:

- identifies the person who manufactured or supplied them with the goods; and
- that identified person is available as a defendant in Australia.

Under tort law, the manufacturer and supplier will owe a duty of care to those who are supplied with their goods, in accordance with general duty of care principles.

1.7 By what means can a supplier limit its liability for defective products?

There are limited means by which suppliers can limit their liability for the supply of defective goods. However, there are steps that suppliers may take to limit their exposure, especially as between those in the chain of supply (in contrast with exposure directly to consumers). Contractual terms limiting liability can be effective as between suppliers (including manufacturers).

Importantly, suppliers cannot exclude or limit the consumer protections provided by the ACL. Under s64 of the ACL, any contractual term that purports to limit these rights is void to the extent that it seeks to exclude or limit rights to a level below that available under the ACL.

In addition, attempts to exclude statutory rights by posting notices inconsistent with the ACL may result in a manufacturer being prosecuted by the ACCC for misleading or deceptive conduct, which may result in fines or orders requiring corrective advertising.

As noted above, whether a product has a 'safety defect' depends in part upon its marketing, labelling, and intended uses. Accordingly, careful attention to providing clear and detailed warnings and labels and information will go some way to protect against liability. However, as noted, this can provide only so much protection. It is also important to take appropriate care in product design and manufacture, as well as to knowledge regarding product use patters.

1.8 Are there particular goods or services which have specific obligations or duties attached to them?

Yes, there are some goods and services which are regulated entirely outside the ACL and the general law principles discussed here. The following are of particular note:

- pharmaceuticals, medical devices and other therapeutic goods are regulated under the Therapeutic Goods Act 1989 (Cth);
- food is regulated under separate Australia New Zealand Food Standards Code and other state and territory legislation;
- poisons and medicines are regulated under the Poisons Standard (and some also under the Therapeutic Goods Act 1989 (Cth);
- dangerous goods (particularly, transportation of) are addressed under the Australian Dangerous Goods Code and the state and territory legislation that implements it;
- weapons are addressed under the National Firearms Safety Code;
- veterinary and agricultural products are regulated under the Agricultural and Veterinary Chemicals Code;
- hazardous substances and industrial machinery are addressed under national and state workplace health and safety laws; and
- motor vehicles are regulated under the Motor Vehicles Standards Act 1989 (Cth) as well as other state and territory legislation.

2. DEFENCES

2.1 What are the possible defences to a product liability claim?

There are defences to actions under the ACL, but they are of limited application and cannot often be relied upon. Under ss142 and 148 of the ACL, a supplier may avoid liability for actions based on defective goods if the safety defect:

- did not exist when goods were supplied;
- came about because of compliance with a mandatory standard;
- at the time the goods were supplied, the defect could not be discovered based on scientific or technical knowledge; or
- is only attributable to the design, markings or instructions of other goods in which the goods were contained.

In practice, it is rare that these defences will apply, and liability to pay compensation often follows closely if a 'safety defect' can be linked to an injury.

There are additional defences available at general law, but these defences will not protect against liability for breaches of the ACL. For instance, in tort, suppliers may rely upon defences such as the consumer's voluntary assumption of risk or contributory negligence. It is common to plead matters under the consumer laws in part to avoid these defences.

2.2 Is there a limit on the time in which proceedings may be brought (limitations and repose)?

Yes, but the time limits differ between actions under the ACL and actions under the general law.

The ACL contains a number of overlapping periods for defective goods actions. The general rule is that a defective goods action – other than one including damages for personal injury – must be commenced within 10 years of the supply of the goods by the manufacturer (s143(2) the ACL).

However, there are special rules for actions in which a plaintiff claims damages for personal injury. Under the ACL and CCA, a person cannot bring any defective goods action in which they claim damages for personal injury:

- if three years have elapsed since they have become aware, or ought to have become aware of all of the following:
- the loss suffered;
- the defect in the goods; and
- the identity of person who manufactured the goods; or
- if 12 years have elapsed since the date of the act or omission causing death or injury (ss87F and 87H CCA).

Limitation periods for tort and contract are governed by state legislation. In all jurisdictions except the Northern Territory, no plaintiff may bring an action in contract or tort after the expiration of six years from when the cause of action arose. In the Northern Territory, the period is three years.

In tort, the cause of action is taken to arise once damage has been suffered. For breach of contract, the cause of action arises once the contract has in fact been breached.

Finally, courts generally have a broad discretion to extend limitations periods in order to serve justice.

3. LITIGATION OF PRODUCT LIABILITY DISPUTES

3.1 In which courts are product liability proceedings brought?

Product liability proceedings may be litigated in any level or branch of the Australian court hierarchy, from inferior and superior state courts to the federal courts. The appropriate court is typically chosen depending on the laws relied on (eg, federal or state) and the amount in controversy.

3.2 How are proceedings commenced?

Proceedings are commenced by filing with the appropriate court a form of originating process, known either as a writ or an originating application depending upon the court in which proceedings are filed. This originating process will be accompanied by an affidavit or statement of claim that sets out all of the commencing parties' allegations and the material facts that support them.

3.3 Are disputed issues decided by a judge or a jury?

Almost all civil trials in Australia are decided by a judge sitting alone.

However, court rules in all jurisdictions except South Australia and the Australian Capital Territory allow for a plaintiff to apply for the case to be heard before a jury, subject to the payment of additional jury fees. In some jurisdictions, legislation and court rules preclude trial of a civil action by jury if the trial requires prolonged examination of documents or scientific investigation, and these issues cannot conveniently be dealt with by a jury.

3.4 Who has the burden of proof and to what standard?

In civil trials, the plaintiff has the burden of proof with respect to liability and must prove facts to the 'balance of probabilities', a lower standard than the criminal standard of 'beyond reasonable doubt.' In practice, this means that the plaintiff must show that a fact is on the evidence 'more likely than not'.

However, once a plaintiff has proved the facts necessary for a defendant's liability, the burden of proof shifts to the defendant to establish any defence, also to the balance of probabilities.

3.5 How is evidence given in proceedings and are witnesses cross-examined?

Evidence in chief in civil trials can be given either orally or by affidavit. In most courts, evidence will be given orally unless the court gives leave for affidavit evidence to be used. Accordingly, in most proceedings, evidence will be given orally but witness statements or outlines of evidence will be served in advance.

A person giving evidence may be cross-examined irrespective of whether they give evidence orally or by affidavit. Court rules in most jurisdictions prevent parties relying upon affidavit evidence unless the maker of the affidavit is available for cross-examination, subject to some exceptions.

3.6 Are the parties able to rely on expert opinion evidence and, if so, are there any special rules or procedures for expert opinion evidence?

Yes, the parties are able to rely upon expert opinion evidence. In all Australian jurisdictions, the evidence of persons with 'specialised knowledge' gleaned from specialised skill, training or experience is an exception to the general prohibition on opinion evidence.

Experts must, prior to giving evidence, agree to abide by expert 'codes of conduct', which impress upon experts their role to act impartially and assist the court, rather than act as advocate for a party's position – see, eg, Federal Court of Australia, Practice Note CM 7, 'Expert Witnesses in Proceedings in the Federal Court of Australia'.

3.7 Is pre-trial discovery permitted? If so, in what circumstances? If not, what other mechanisms, if any, are available for obtaining evidence from an party or a third party?

Pre-trial discovery of documents is generally permitted, but Australian courts are increasingly reticent to order broad-based and voluminous discovery. For instance, in the Federal Court of Australia, a party is not entitled to discovery unless the making of the order 'will facilitate the just resolution of the proceeding as quickly, inexpensively, and efficiently as possible': Federal Court Rules 2001 (Cth) r20.11.

Parties may also serve notices to produce documents during trials. If the documents sought are not produced by the party to whom the notice is addressed, then the party serving the notice may lead secondary evidence of the contents or nature of the document.

It should be noted that 'discovery' in Australia is generally limited to the provision of documents, and there is no provision for compulsory interviewing of another party's witnesses (depositions).

In addition to conventional discovery, parties may obtain documents by:

- applications for preliminary discovery, where discovery is given even before proceedings are commenced to allow a party to either establish they have a cause of action, or establish against whom they have a cause of action;
- third party discovery and subpoenas, which may be directed to persons or entities that are not parties to the dispute.

Finally, interrogatories are not commonly used and will require leave of court.

3.8 Is there liability for spoliation of evidence/a remedy for destruction of or failure to preserve evidence (most relevantly, the product)?

All Australian jurisdictions impose harsh penalties for the destruction of any evidence, including products themselves. For instance, in the State of Victoria, s254 of the Crimes Act 1958 (Vic) makes it a criminal offence to destroy, conceal, or render illegible or unusable any evidence that 'is, or is reasonably likely to be, required in evidence in a legal proceeding' – an offence punishable by up to six years imprisonment or a fine of more than A$400,000.

Furthermore, once proceedings have commenced or they are clearly anticipated, all parties are under an obligation to take positive steps to prevent the destruction of any documents. Failure to comply with this obligation may involve costs sanctions, the striking out of pleadings, issue sanctions, or even fines and imprisonment.

3.9 Is interlocutory or interim relief available prior to the full trial of a proceeding? If so, in what circumstances?

Yes, forms of interlocutory or interim relief, including injunctions, are available where:

- a party can show there is a 'serious question to be tried', in that they have a cause of action that has some likelihood of success; and
- the 'balance of convenience' favours granting the relief.

The 'balance of convenience' compares the harm likely to be suffered by each party if particular relief is granted. For instance, the harm that the public may suffer because of an allegedly defective product would be balanced against the financial impact of the relief on the manufacturer.

A party seeking interlocutory or interim injunctive relief must, as a matter of course, give an 'undertaking to damages'. This undertaking requires the party seeking relief to compensate the party subject to the injunction for loss or damage they suffer, if the first-named party does not obtain the final relief on which the injunction is based.

In the product liability context, it is likely that such relief will be granted if there is some appreciable risk of danger to the community.

In addition, orders may be made to freeze the assets of a party to a proceeding if there is a demonstrable risk that they will seek to shift those assets out of the jurisdiction in order to frustrate any award against them.

3.10 Can the winning party recover its costs?

Yes. In Australia, the usual rule is that 'costs follow the event', such that a successful defendant or plaintiff will be able to recover its costs from the other party depending on who is ultimately successful in the proceedings. If the parties are both successful in part, courts will often apportion costs on an issue-by-issue or percentage basis.

However, the usual costs order will usually only cover between 60% and 70% of the actual fees and expenses incurred in litigation because parties recover their fees in accordance with court fee 'scales', which are likely not to cover the entire cost of litigation.

Furthermore, if a party has engaged in delaying or obstructive tactics, they may either:

- if they were unsuccessful, be ordered to pay 'indemnity costs' which equates to a much higher proportion of the other side's costs; or
- if they were successful, lose their prima facie entitlement to receive costs or even be required to pay the unsuccessful side's costs, depending on the severity of the conduct.

3.11 What avenues of appeal are available?

Actions heard in State Courts may be appealed to State Courts of Appeal. Actions heard in the Federal Court may be appealed to the Full Bench of the Federal Court, sitting as an appellate court. Such appeals may or may not be as of right.

From there, parties may apply to the High Court of Australia for special leave to have their further appeal heard in that court, irrespective of whether the action came from a State Court of Appeal or the Full Bench of the Federal Court. However, special leave is not granted as of right, and the High Court will generally only grant leave to cases that involve questions of law of 'public importance' or where there is a difference of opinion between different state and federal courts.

There are no further avenues of appeal from the High Court.

4. CLASS ACTIONS/REPRESENTATIVE PROCEEDINGS

4.1 Is there a mechanism for class actions or representative proceedings, or coordinated proceedings for product liability claims? If so, what are the basic mechanics?

Yes. Legislation and court rules in each jurisdiction allow for actions to be brought as representative proceedings. However, the regime in Part IVA of the Federal Court of Australia Act 1976 (Cth) is the most used. Victoria has a similarly prescriptive statutory regime, but class actions in other jurisdictions rely upon existing — and less developed — court rules about representative proceedings.

Australian jurisdictions have embraced the opt-out model of representative proceedings, such that one or a few named plaintiffs will bring an action in the name of a nominal class of plaintiffs. The class of applicable plaintiffs is then defined within the proceeding and persons or entities within that class are given the opportunity to give notice of opting-out to allow them to pursue their own actions against the class action defendant. This 'opt out' process happens relatively early in the proceeding. If persons do not opt-out by a date fixed by the court, they will be bound by the court's judgment in the proceeding.

The Australian representative proceeding model protects class members who do not participate in the action by providing that costs orders may only be levied against the representative plaintiffs who have brought the suit.

Threshold requirements for a representative proceeding include:

- the claims must arise out of the 'same, or similar, circumstances' or transactions;
- seven or more people must have claims against the same defendant; and
- claims must involve at least one common substantial issue of law.

Importantly, in Australia, the onus is on a defendant to disprove that these threshold requirements have not been met.

In addition to the representative proceeding model, multiple similar actions may be consolidated together into a single action, but this mechanism does not provide the same cost protection to non-representative plaintiffs.

5. LITIGATION FUNDING

5.1 Is litigation funding by third parties permissible in your country? If so, is it common?

Yes. Litigation funding is both permissible and common in Australia, and is particularly common in respect of class action-type litigation. To date, litigation funding has financed a number of large consumer and shareholder class actions, most particularly with respect to corporate disclosure obligations, directors' and officers' duties and financial services.

At this stage, litigation funding remains a largely unregulated aspect of Australia's financial services industry, however, the recently-elected government seemingly has an appetite to impose stricter regulation on the industry.

5.2 Are contingency fee or 'no win no fee' arrangements permissible?

Contingency fees are prohibited in all Australian jurisdictions and lawyers are prohibited from charging on the basis of a percentage fee of any amount awarded to their client.

However, litigation funders are <u>not</u> prohibited from charging contingency fees, which sees an arrangement whereby the litigation funder provides the funding directly to the plaintiff or class or plaintiff, and pays the lawyers' legal bills often irrespective of whether the action is ultimately successful. In this way, it is often the litigation funder and not the lawyers who bear the risk of unsuccessful actions in Australia.

'No win no fee' arrangements are permitted in all Australian jurisdictions. Under these arrangements, lawyers provide the same costs disclosures and charge fees on the same basis as they would for other professional services, but only charge the client those fees if the matter is successful. Lawyers may still claim for disbursements outlaid and the client themselves will have to pay any costs order levied against them.

There are recent reform moves afoot to allow contingency fees to be charged by lawyers directly.

6. REMEDIES

6.1 What remedies are available to a party who successfully pursues a product liability claim?

Under the ACL, the key remedy available is damage for loss or damage suffered because of the defective product. A person affected may claim the costs of medical treatments, lost past and future wages, or where the damage is to goods or property, the cost of repairing or replacing that property (ss138-141).

In addition, the court may:

- order injunctions prohibiting repeated contraventions of the ACL, in an action brought by the ACCC (s232);
- make other orders requiring that a manufacturer perform community services, implement compliance programmes, or conduct corrective advertising or awareness raising campaigns.

Under the general law, the court may order a manufacturer to pay damages and may, in some circumstances, order injunctions to prevent repeated negligent conduct or supply.

6.2 How are damages calculated/are there limitations on available damages?

Damages are calculated on the basis of actual loss suffered, or likely to be suffered, by a plaintiff because of the conduct of the defendant. These losses are likely to include:

- actual incurred or future losses caused by injury caused by the defect, such as the cost of medical treatment and loss of earnings;
- non-economic losses that arise from any above injury, such as pain and suffering, loss of amenities of life, loss of expectation of life and permanent disfigurement;
- losses arising from damage to the defective goods themselves, or the cost of repair or replacement of the goods; and
- losses for damage to land or fixtures associated with the defect.

The only limit on damages available under the ACL for the supply of defective goods is a $250,000 cap on non-economic loss (s87M). Other losses are not capped and must be paid if they are suffered.

Similarly, for general law liability in tort, the total amount of compensation that may be awarded for non-economic loss is capped, but at different levels in each jurisdiction. Currently, the amounts of these caps stand at between approximately $450,000 and $550,000.

6.3 Are punitive or exemplary damages available and in what circumstances?

Punitive damages are not available under the ACL, but they are available at general law.

However, punitive damages are rarely awarded unless there is some special feature of the defendants' approach that shows they have acted with 'contumelious disregard of another's rights'.

Furthermore, tort reform in some state jurisdictions has placed limitations on the availability of punitive and exemplary damages in some proceedings — for instance, s21 of the Civil Liability Act 2002 (NSW) excludes punitive damages for negligence claims for personal injury.

Aggravated damages may also be awarded where the defendant's conduct has actually exacerbated the harm suffered by the plaintiff — for example, where undue rough treatment of the plaintiff during the litigation process has exacerbated mental harm caused by the defendant. Because these form part of the harm actually suffered by the plaintiff, they may be claimed under the ACL.

6.4 Is liability joint and several/how does apportionment of liability work, including where a partially responsible entity is not a party to the proceeding?

If a claim relates to personal injury, a defendant can be liable for a plaintiff's entire loss even if they have only contributed to that loss. To avoid this situation, defendants in Australia must join other parties responsible for that loss to proceedings.

Proportionate liability regimes may be available where the damage caused by a defective good is limited to damage to property. Under these regimes, a defendant cannot be held liable for, or be forced to pay, a proportion of the loss greater than that which is just and reasonable, having regard to that defendant's responsibility for the loss. This would often involve the court ascribing a percentage responsibility level to respective parties and requiring them to pay that proportion of any final damages award.

7. ROLE OF REGULATORS

7.1 Please explain the role, responsibilities and powers of the regulators in your country which have jurisdiction over product liability issues.

The ACCC is the key national regulator responsible for administering the ACL. The ACCC is an independent federal statutory authority which has a broad regulatory role, including to enforce the CCA (which includes Australia's competition laws) and the ACL. The ACCC has wide ranging investigative and enforcement powers. As discussed below, the ACCC plays an important role in the regulation of the product safety provisions of the ACL.

The ACCC is supported by state- and territory-based fair trading regulators, such as Consumer Affairs Victoria and New South Wales Fair Trading.

7.2 Are there any mandatory reporting requirements related to product safety issues?

Under the ACL, a report must be lodged with the ACCC if a supplier of a consumer good becomes aware of the death, serious injury or illness of a person and considers that the death, serious injury or illness was caused, or may have been caused, by the use or foreseeable use of their consumer good. The report must be lodged within two days of the supplier becoming aware of that death, injury or illness (s131). This obligation is triggered unless it is 'clear' that the good was not involved, or 'very unlikely' that it was involved (s131(2)).

A 'consumer good' is defined as goods that are intended to be used for 'person, domestic, or household use' (s2). There is no upper monetary limit on this definition.

Reports will be kept confidential except in 'exceptional circumstances' such as disclosure being in the public interest, or disclosure being necessary for the ACCC to bring enforcement action against a supplier (s132A).

Failure to comply with this obligation is a criminal offence of strict liability, punishable by fine (s202). Accordingly, it is prudent for a supplier to report any death, serious injury or illness they become aware of that is connected with their consumer goods, even if the supplier doubts that their consumer goods caused the death, serious injury or illness.

7.3 Do the regulators have the power to:
(i) ban certain goods or services?
(ii) require a supplier to recall a product?
(iii) prescribe standards in respect of certain goods or services and require that the goods or services meet those standards?
(iv) require production of information without court process?
If so, broadly explain the circumstances in which the regulator can exercise the power and any penalties that apply if a supplier fails to comply.

The key regulatory powers are exercised by the relevant state or federal minister, acting on the advice of the ACCC or the state regulator, as applicable. Below is a summary of these key powers and how they are operated.

Bans

The Federal Government minister responsible for product safety may issue either an interim or permanent ban that applies throughout Australia where it appears to the Minister that 'goods of that kind will or may cause injury to a person'. Bans may be imposed urgently and without notice if there is an 'imminent risk of death, serious illness, or serious injury' to consumers (s132J CCA). Once a product is banned, it is an offence to then supply that product (s114 ACL).

In addition, the minister responsible for product safety in each state and territory government may also impose interim bans on products, but those bans only have effect within that state or territory and cannot be made permanent (ss110 and 114 of the ACL)

Compulsory recalls

Both state and federal ministers may initiate a compulsory recall by issuing a recall notice to a supplier, in circumstances where:

- it appears to the minister that goods, including when reasonably misused, may cause injury;
- the goods do not comply with a safety standard that is in force; or
- an interim or permanent ban is in force in respect of the goods (s122(1) ACL).

The recall notice can require the supplier to do any or all of the following:

- recall the goods;
- disclose to the public or consumers of a defect or dangerous with respect to the good;
- repair or replace the goods; or
- refund amounts paid for the good (s124 of the ACL).

Once a recall notice is in place, it becomes an offence to supply a product of that kind.

There are also compulsory notification procedures in place where a supplier decides to voluntarily recall a product.

Standards

The Federal Government minister, on the advice of the ACCC, has the power under the ACL to impose safety standards on particular classes of goods or services that pose particular risks to consumers. These standards impose substantive requirements on the construction and composition of products themselves and are highly prescriptive in the level of detail they contain. It is an offence not to comply with these standards (s106 ACL).

In addition to safety standards, ministers may impose 'information standards' that require suppliers to provide specific information when supplying particular goods or services (s134 ACL). It is also an offence not to provide the information specified (s136 ACL).

Helpfully, the details of all products subject to safety standards are provided on the ACCC website: *www.productsafety.gov.au/content/index.phtml/tag/mandatorystandards*.

Production of information

The ACCC has a number of compulsory evidence gathering processes, the most significant of which is the power to issue a notice under s155 of the CCA. This section empowers the ACCC to require any person to provide documents and information if the ACCC has reason to believe that the person is capable of furnishing information about the contravention of the CCA. The ACCC can also compel a person to appear at a specified time and place to give oral or written evidence (s155(1)(c)).

8. VOLUNTARY CONDUCT

8.1 Are there regulations pertaining to the voluntary conduct of a product repair or recall by a supplier?

Yes. A supplier that initiates a voluntary recall must, within two days of 'taking action' to recall consumer goods, notify the ACCC of that recall (s128 ACL). Section 128 of the ACL sets out a prescriptive set of criteria that requires the supplier to give the ACCC detailed information about the product, the recall process, and where it has been sold, but most importantly, about any defects in the product or risks that the product poses to consumers (s128(7)). The notice will then be published on the ACCC website.

Once this voluntary recall notice has been issued, the ACCC may take further action, including directing further compliance steps or advising the minister to issue a compulsory recall notice of broader application. This means that, in practice, it is best for suppliers to actively engage with the ACCC by seeking input on the supplier's recall plan to reduce the likelihood that the ACCC and the minister will impose a mandatory recall.

9. EMERGING ISSUES AND LAW REFORM

9.1 Are there important developing and emerging issues or trends in product liability law in your country?

A key issue facing the product liability sphere is the possible tightening of regulation regarding litigation funding. Up to this point, litigation funders have avoided much of the regulation that ordinarily attends the provision of other financial products to consumers. At this stage, the official engagement with reform pushes has been limited to:

- comments by the now Federal Attorney General, George Brandis QC, that the litigation funding is 'under active review right now'; and
- a 15-month public inquiry by the Federal Government's Productivity Commission into access to justice and the role of litigation funders, which is due to present its findings in 2015.

9.2 Please describe any proposed important law reform in the area of product liability in your country.

In addition, the Federal Government is undertaking a 'root and branch review' of the CCA as a whole, including the ACL. However, the terms of reference for this review, released in March 2014, are focused almost exclusively on the competition provisions contained in the CCA, rather than the consumer protections provided in the ACL.

10. REGULATORY WEBSITES/INFORMATION

10.1 Please identify any useful regulatory references relating to product liability law in your country, for example, a product safety/consumer law website maintained by the main regulator.

- ACCC website: *www.accc.gov.au/*
- ACCC Safe Product website: *www.accc.gov.au/consumers/consumer-protection/buying-safe-products*
- Australian Consumer Law website: *www.consumerlaw.gov.au/content/Content.aspx?doc=home.htm*
- Product Safety specialised website maintained by the ACCC: *www.productsafety.gov.au/content/index.phtml/itemId/970225*
- ACCC compliance and enforcement policy: *www.accc.gov.au/about-us/australian-competition-consumer-commission/compliance-enforcement-policy*

The author gratefully acknowledges the assistance of Barbara Bell and Simon Frauenfelder in the compilation of this chapter.

Brazil

Zingales & Pagotto Sociedade de Advogados (ZISP Law)
Leopoldo Pagotto & Marina Esposito

1. LIABILITY

1.1 What are the principal sources of law and regulation relating to product liability?

The main source of law regarding product liability is Law No. 8.078/1990, also known as *Código de Defesa do Consumidor* (Consumer Protection Code).

Other important sources of law relating to product liability can be listed as follows:

- Law No. 10.406/2002 (Civil Code);
- Law No. 5.869/1973 (Code of Civil Procedure).

Moreover, a wide range of regulations are issued by some public agencies which directly or indirectly perform activities relating to product liability. Three main agencies must be mentioned:

- *Secretaria Nacional de Defesa do Consumidor* (SENACON – National Bureau of Consumer Protection), which is a branch of the Ministry of Justice in charge of coordinating the national, state and municipal agencies relating to consumer protection. Its website in Portuguese can be found at *http://portal.mj.gov.br/data/Pages/MJ5E813CF3PTBRNN.htm*
- The *Conselho Nacional de Metrologia, Normalização e Qualidade Industrial* (National Council of Metrology, Standardisation and Industrial Quality – CONMETRO) and the *Instituto Nacional de Metrologia, Normalização e Qualidade* Industrial (INMETRO – National Institute of Metrology, Quality and Technology). These are government-sponsored standard-setting agencies which enjoy a great deal of credibility to decide whether products are subject to defects or not – quite often, they carry out preventive investigations about certain products and the outcome of their surveys is widely publicised. Their website in Portuguese can be found at *https://www.inmetro.gov.br.* An English website with some limited resources is also available at *www.inmetro.gov.br/english/index.asp*
- State and municipal agencies generically called PROCON (acronym for Consumer Protection in Portuguese). There is a wide range of legal entities called PROCON in Brazil. They may be linked to the Prosecutor's Office, to the State government and/or to the local government. In the State of São Paulo, Fundação PROCON is a public foundation empowered for the protection of consumer rights. A Portuguese website can be found at *www.procon.sp.gov.br/*

1.2 What is required to establish causation under the most common causes of action available?

In order to establish causation, damages (of either material or moral nature) must be originated from a defect in the product or service.

1.3 Is strict liability available and, if so, in what circumstances?

The Consumer Protection Code regulates several details in the relationship between consumer and suppliers – it was built based upon the concept of strict liability. If the Consumer Protection Code is applicable, then strict liability usually also applies.

The Consumer Protection Code brings a broad definition to the term 'supplier', which includes the natural person or legal entity which produces, supplies, imports or even sells the product or service. On the other hand, 'consumer' is the natural person or legal entity, who acquires or uses a product or a service as its ultimate receiver, ie, the final player in the supply chain.

1.4 Are guarantees or warranties as to quality implied by law?

Yes, guarantees and warranties as to quality are implied by the Consumer Protection Code. It rules that actual quality of the product and service advertised by the supplier must meet its actual characteristics. It is risky to use a different picture of the product and add a small notice saying that the 'picture does not correspond to the product'.

INMETRO and other standard-setting agencies may set specific warranties and guarantees relating to the products that fall under their jurisdiction.

1.5 How is a product 'defect' defined?

The concept of a product defect is closely connected to the idea of the level of safety that the general consumer society would expect from that specific product. It is related to the potential hazard that may be generated from that product, taking into account the relevant circumstances brought by Article 12 of the Consumer Protection Code, which are:

(i) the product's presentation;
(ii) the use and the risks that one may reasonably expect from that product; and
(iii) the time period when the product was made available for the general market or put into circulation.

As one may observe, not only are the intrinsic characteristics of the merchandise taken into account when analysing whether a product is defective, but its presentation also plays an important role in defining what a defect is. For example, the lack of or insufficient information about how to use the product, as well as its potential risks, are also part of the general concept of defect.

Defect does not exclusively refer to whether the product serves its purpose or not: it also concerns its potential collateral damages and side effects. For instance, MER-29 is a very efficient anti-cholesterol drug that may cause serious eye problems as side effect.

According to the doctrine, there are three types of defect:

(i) defectively manufactured products: In a large-scale production, this type of defect is nearly unavoidable. A defectively manufactured product is flawed, because of some error in making it. Under normal circumstances, it should appear only in a limited number of samples of the product, not in the whole stock;
(ii) defectively designed products: Under this circumstance, a product's design is inherently dangerous or defective, since there was an error in the conception of the product. Therefore, not just a few samples are defective, but the entire line is considered defective;
(iii) failure to provide adequate warnings or instructions/inadequate exposure, presentation: This type of defect involves the failure to provide adequate warnings or instructions about the product's proper use. Moreover, it also regards how the product is presented to the consumers, the premises where it is stocked and under which conditions (climate, temperature etc.) it is maintained and so forth.

Whichever the type of defect, it is important to bear in mind that in order to have a product liability claim, one must establish causation between the injury-causing product and its defect. In other words, this means that the injury or the damage must arise from the defect of the product. For example, if a person buys a defective product and it falls on the person's foot, causing an injury due to the weight of this defective product, there is no causation between the defect and the injury and as a result of that, no product liability claim arises. Of course, in this case, the consumer is not bound to keep the defective product, but the remedy to be sought is not a product liability claim, because it is not related to the safety of the product.

1.6 Who in the supply chain has obligations or duties for defective products? What obligations or duties do they owe and to whom?

All players in the supply chain are jointly liable for the defective products. At the consumer's will, he or she may prosecute the manufacturer, the producer, the importer, the builder or the seller at the same time or just one of them.

However, according to Articles 12 and 13 of the Consumer Protection Code, manufacturer, producer, importer and builder are strictly liable for their products/services, whereas the seller's responsibility is subsidiary (for more information see section 1.7 below).

Once the lawsuit is over, the party which was held liable for the defective product is entitled to mutual indemnification.

1.7 By what means can a supplier limit its liability for defective products?

The term 'supplier' is broadly defined by the Consumer Protection Code as *'every natural person or legal entity, public or private, domestic or foreign, as well as subjects without legal entity that carry on activities of production, assembly, creation, construction, processing, import, export, distribution or marketing of products or services'.*

As a rule, the supplier is strictly liable for damages caused to consumers by defects relating to the provision of services, as well as insufficient or inadequate information about its use and risks.

The merchant or seller is subject to subsidiary liability whenever any of those parties cannot be identified or whenever the supplied product does not have clear information regarding its manufacturer, producer, importer and/or builder. The merchant or seller is strictly liable whenever the defect is caused by poor storage and conservation of the product.

Considering these provisions are stated by the legislation, from the consumer point of view, any contract clause limiting the liability of any party of the supply chain will be null and void.

Therefore, the only possibility for a supplier to limit its responsibility is by assuring that all relevant information regarding the product/service is disclosed to the consumer and checking how the products are being handled/stored. Nevertheless, from a legal perspective, it does not matter how the contract is drafted – adding a clause in a sale and purchase contract limiting liability will not lead to an enforceable defence and judges will consider such a clause as abusive.

1.8 Are there particular goods or services which have specific obligations or duties attached to them?

Many particular goods have obligations or duties attached to them, such as drugs, food and chemical products. These obligations are very specific, since they are subject to specific regulatory commissions and standard-setting agencies.

2. DEFENCES

2.1 What are the possible defences to a product liability claim?

As a rule, as explained above, the supplier is strictly liable for damages caused to consumers by defects relating to the supply of products and services, as well as insufficient or inadequate information about its use and risks. The only exception to this rule is provided by Article 14, paragraph 3, which determines that there are only two hypotheses in which the supplier will not be held responsible:

(a) when the supplier who provided the service proves that the defect does not exist; or

(b) when the supplier proves that the defect was caused by the sole fault of the consumer or third party.

2.2 Is there a limit on the time in which proceedings may be brought (limitations and repose)?

Yes, according to Article 27 of the Code a claim for compensation must be made within five years. The term initiates when the consumer identifies the product/service defect and the person responsible for it.

3. LITIGATION OF PRODUCT LIABILITY DISPUTES

3.1 In which courts are product liability proceedings brought?

In general, product liability proceedings are brought in civil courts. Most cases are brought before the Small Claims Court. Cases with the value of up to 20 minimum wages can be brought before the Small Claims Court without the need of a lawyer. Cases with the value of up to 40 minimum wages can be brought before the Small Claims Court with the assistance of a lawyer. Cases with any value may be brought before the regular State Courts.

Another common alternative dispute resolution takes place before the PROCONs, which are quite famous among the population. The PROCONs are administrative agencies and as such, they have limited jurisdiction. What the PROCONs normally do is to notify the seller or merchant and invite it to come to a conciliatory meeting. If no agreement is reached, PROCONs have nothing to do. Normally, copies of the case filing as well as proper guidance are provided for the consumer, who must go to court.

3.2 How are proceedings commenced?

Proceedings are commenced by a motion similar to a statement claim or a complaint.

3.3 Are disputed issues decided by a judge or a jury?

The disputed issues are decided by a judge. There is no jury trial for civil cases in Brazil.

3.4 Who has the burden of proof and to what standard?

In Brazil, the general rule about evidence is 'he who alleges must prove'. In other words, like most civil claims, the plaintiff sets forth its allegations in a complaint, petition or other pleading and he must prove it. On the other hand, the Consumer Protection Code breaks the general rule with the purpose of protecting the consumer, who usually has less economic power and technical information regarding the product/service than its supplier. Therefore, if the consumer proves that he/she is in this position of vulnerability in relation to the supplier, the complainant may request the reversal of the burden of proof. In practice, judges take the reversal of the burden of proof for granted and in almost every case the burden of evidence lays on the supplier.

3.5 How is evidence given in proceedings and are witnesses cross-examined?

Every kind of evidence that is not forbidden may be used, such as documents, testimonials, video and audio recordings, reports given by experts, among others. The legislation does not rule that a certain type of evidence is more valuable than another. The judge must analyse all evidence brought to the proceedings and decide which piece is deemed to be more convincing and relevant for the case under review.

Regarding witness cross-examination, it is important to explain that in Brazil the judge is the one who leads the examination of witnesses. This means that the attorneys are not allowed to ask direct questions of the witness, so that their questions must be directed to the judge who will redirect them to the witness.

3.6 Are the parties able to rely on expert opinion evidence and, if so, are there any special rules or procedures for expert opinion evidence?

The parties are able to rely on expert opinion. They may either request that the court appoint an official expert or may present a report given by an expert retained by them. The value of the evidence will be different: the expert opinion evidence produced under the auspices of the court tend to be stronger than the ones produced unilaterally by the parties. These pieces of evidence are not binding on the judge though.

3.7 Is pre-trial discovery permitted? If so, in what circumstances? If not, what other mechanisms, if any, are available for obtaining evidence from a party or a third party?

There is no pre-trial discovery. Incidentally, evidence gathering is quite different from the one that exists in common law countries. There is no discovery phase in Brazil and the parties enjoy self-incriminating privilege: in other words, no party can be forced to produce evidence against himself or herself, even if the court requests so. This makes evidence gathering in Brazil much less pervasive than in common law countries.

3.8 Is there liability for spoliation of evidence/a remedy for destruction of or failure to preserve evidence (most relevantly, the product)?

If a party believes that a piece of evidence is in danger, there are precautionary measures available in order to preserve it. For example, the party may request a judicial order determining that the piece of evidence be put under judicial custody.

When the complaint has already been filed or when it is proved that the party intended to destroy/spoil a piece of evidence, the responsible party may be held liable for his/her conduct before the civil and criminal courts.

3.9 Is interlocutory or interim relief available prior to the full trial of a proceeding?

Yes, they are available. Generally speaking, an interlocutory injunction is permitted when the party proves that there is '*fumus bonis iuris*' and '*periculum in mora*'. In other words, the party must prove that his or her allegation is very likely to be truthful and that a potential danger may arise from the delay in providing him/her with the requested measure.

3.10 Can the winning party recover its costs?

If the claim is brought before the Small Claim Courts, it is not possible for the winning party to recover its costs. On the other hand, if the claim is brought before the regular State Courts, it is possible, since the losing party will have to compensate the winning party for the amount determined by the judge, plus attorney's fees and judicial costs.

3.11 What avenues of appeal are available?

If the case is brought before the regular State Courts, the losing party may file an appeal before the Court of Justice, which is a higher court. The trial in the Court of Justice will consist of a collegiate body, in which three judges review and decide on the matter – eventually, if they do not reach a unanimous decision, two other judges may cast their votes. The parties are entitled to have the full review of the case (merits and law) before the Court of Justice, even though no additional evidence gathering is allowed.

After the trial of the Court of Justice, it is possible to file appeal to two other higher courts, even though only formal aspects relating to the applicable law of the case are subject to review. No discussion on the fact-finding will be allowed. The two higher courts are the following:

- the *Superior Tribunal de Justiça* (STJ – Superior Tribunal of Justice), which has jurisdiction over issues relating to the federal infra-constitutional legislation. To put it simply, the appealed decision contradicts a Federal Act or interprets it in a way that diverges from other courts.
- the *Supremo Tribunal Federal* (STF – Supreme Court), which has jurisdiction over issues related to the federal constitution.

4. CLASS ACTIONS/REPRESENTATIVE PROCEEDINGS

4.1 Is there a mechanism for class actions or representative proceedings, or coordinated proceedings for product liability claims? If so, what are the basic mechanics?

Yes, there are. Pursuant to Articles 81 and 82 of the Consumer Protection Code, a collective suit may be filed whenever the claim involves diffuse, transindividual or collective interests. The following ones have standing to submit the collective suit:

(a) the Public Prosecutor;
(b) the Union, the States, the Municipalities and the Federal District;
(c) the entities and the public authorities with specific jurisdiction over the interests and rights relating to the Consumer Protection Code; and
(d) the associations legally incorporated for at least one year with the institutional purpose of protecting the interests and rights relating to the Consumer Protection Code.

5. LITIGATION FUNDING

5.1 Is litigation funding by third parties permissible in your country? If so, is it common?

There is no clear legal prohibition to litigation funding, even though there may be some legal issues threatening such a possibility. However, to the best of our knowledge, it has not yet been tried so far in any kind of litigation.

5.2 Are contingency fee or 'no win no fee' arrangements permissible?

Although contingency fees are only permitted under certain circumstances, they are rare in complex cases in practice. The Brazilian Bar Association does neither appreciate, nor recommend this type of arrangement.

6. REMEDIES

6.1 What remedies are available to a party that successfully pursues a product liability claim?

The party that successfully pursues a product liability claim may enforce its award in courts.

6.2 How are damages calculated/are there limitations on available damages?

Damages can be either material or moral.

Material damages are calculated based on both the actual economic losses (eg, property damage and medical) as well as the reasonably expected profits that were not incurred as a result of the damage, if any.

Moral damages are very loosely defined. Neither the legislation nor the case law have established clear limits and grounds to calculating the damages. The suffering, pain and emotional distress on the victim, among others, are taken into account on a very subjective basis. Although the value of the moral damages has been increasing over recent years, they are still comparatively low compared with what is awarded in the United States of America.

Please see item 6.3 below for more information.

6.3 Are punitive or exemplary damages available and in what circumstances?

There is a great deal of controversy about the punitive damages doctrine.

There are books of doctrine in favour of and against the existence of punitive damages. The same applies in relation to the judicial precedents. Both understandings are based on solid legal arguments and the courts are unlikely to agree on the topic in the near future.

Those who are supportive of the existence of punitive damages argue that there is still not a clear definition in legislation regarding the criteria to set the amount of moral damages to be awarded. As a result, a judge should take into consideration the economic power of the liable party, which could be a large corporation. If this is the case, the payment of a small amount would not be an effective measure to prevent the condemned supplier from continuing with its abusive practices.

On the other hand, those who are not supportive of the punitive damages argue that awarding a large pecuniary amount to a victim would characterise unjust/illicit enrichment, which is prohibited by the Civil Procedure Code. So far, this has been the prevailing decision endorsed by the *Superior Tribunal de Justiça* (Superior Tribunal of Justice).

6.4 Is liability joint and several/how does apportionment of liability work, including where a partially responsible entity is not a party to the proceeding?

The suppliers are jointly and severally liable for the product defects. In any consumer protection case, the courts will not consider allegations that one party was more liable than the other as a defence to minimise the portion of the indemnification. Such a discussion will be subject to possible law suits involving the suppliers.

Please see sections 1.6 and 1.7 above.

7. ROLE OF REGULATORS

7.1 Please explain the role, responsibilities and powers of the regulators in your country which have jurisdiction over product liability issues.

Many regulatory agencies have jurisdiction over product liability issues, depending on the category of the product. For instance, food, drugs and cosmetics are regulated by a specific agency, which is the *Agência Nacional de Vigilância Sanitária* (ANVISA – National Agency of Sanitary Surveillance).

There are some agencies which are responsible for Consumer Protection in general, such as the INMETRO, CONMETRO and the Bureau of Consumer Protection (please see section 1.1 above).

The Bureau of Consumer Protection focuses on the planning, development, coordination and implementation of the National Policy for Consumer Relations. Its objectives are the following:

(i) ensure the protection and exercise of the consumers rights;

(ii) promote harmonisation in consumer relations; and

(iii) encourage the integration and joint action by members of national system of consumer protection.

CONMETRO and INMETRO are the authorities responsible for issuing, fiscalising and applying all technical regulations with which all goods sold in Brazil, inputs, final products and services must comply. Their standard-setting jurisdiction is very broadly defined.

7.2 Are there any mandatory reporting requirements related to product safety issues?

Yes, there are. Pursuant to Article 10 of the Consumer Protection Code, whenever the supplier offers a defective product or service that creates a danger for consumers, it must immediately report the fact to the agencies with jurisdiction over the product. Portaria No. 487, dated 12 March, 2012, issued by the Ministry of Justice, regulates the proceedings to be complied with.

7.3 Do the regulators have the power to:
(i) ban certain goods or services?
(ii) require a supplier to recall a product?
(iii) prescribe standards in respect of certain goods or services and require that the goods or services meet those standards?
(iv) require production of information without court process?
If so, broadly explain the circumstances in which the regulator can exercise the power and any penalties that apply if a supplier fails to comply.

Generally speaking, the regulators have power to perform all the measures listed above. The circumstances will vary from agency to agency, depending on the category of the product. For instance, the *Agência Nacional de*

Vigilância Sanitária (ANVISA – National Agency of Sanitary Surveillance) is entrusted with the power to ban any substance which is dangerous to consumers.

Since most of these agencies are independent administrative authorities, they are empowered to conduct administrative proceedings relating to issues that are under their competence. Therefore, they may require production of information without court process, as well as apply penalties.

8. VOLUNTARY CONDUCT

8.1 Are there regulations pertaining to the voluntary conduct of a product repair or recall by a supplier?

Product repair or recall of a defective product is a legal obligation of the supplier that should apply the measure as soon as the defect is detected. Portaria No. 487, dated 12 March, 2012, issued by the Ministry of Justice, regulates the proceedings to be complied with.

When a defect is identified after the product/service has been put into circulation, its supplier must immediately inform the *Departamento de Proteção e Defesa do Consumidor* (Department of Consumer Protection) (DPDC), the PROCON as well as the agency/ administrative authority, which holds jurisdiction over the product scope.

This communication must thoroughly inform about the product and its manufacturer/producer (eg, information on the company, such as name, address, administrators etc, as well as product information such as brand, time of fabrication etc). The defect and its potential hazards must also be described in detail. The company must submit a 'media plan' describing measures to be adopted in order to inform the general population about the recall and the risks on continuing on using the defective product must also accompany the recall informative.

The supplier will be solely responsible for the costs generated by the recall and repair of the product.

9. EMERGING ISSUES AND LAW REFORM

9.1 Are there important developing and emerging issues or trends in product liability law in your country?

No, there is not any imminent law change.

9.2 Please describe any proposed important law reform in the area of product liability in your country.

The House of the Representatives has recently passed a new piece of legislation about the internet, also known as the *Marco Civil da Internet* (Civil Landmark of the Internet). Currently, the Bill is under review of the Senate. If sanctioned by the President of the Republic, the new piece of law will impact on e-commerce with indirect effect on the regulations about product liability of products and services sold by the internet.

10. REGULATORY WEBSITES/INFORMATION

10.1 Please identify any useful regulatory references relating to product liability law in your country, for example, a product safety/ consumer law website maintained by the main regulator.

- Fundação Procon: *www.portaldoconsumidor.gov.br/procon.asp?acao=buscar*
- INMETRO: *https://www.inmetro.gov.br/*
- Bureau of Consumer Protection: *http://portal.mj.gov.br/data/Pages/MJ5E813CF3PTBRNN.htm*

Canada

Fasken Martineau DuMoulin LLP
Peter Pliszka, Michael Parrish, Enrico Forlini & Robin Roddey

1. LIABILITY

1.1 What are the principal sources of law and regulation relating to product liability?

In common law Canada (comprising all provinces and territories with the exception of the province of Quebec) a manufacturer or supplier of a defective product may be liable to a consumer or other party injured by a product on the basis of either contract or tort law principles. The basis for holding a manufacturer or seller liable in contract is that the defendant breached a warranty or other term in the contract with respect to the quality or attributes of the product. Such terms will often be expressly agreed to through the words and conduct of the parties. Furthermore, sale of goods legislation in each common law province provides that a seller of goods impliedly warrants their quality. In many common law provinces, these implied obligations of product quality cannot be excluded in consumer contracts.

In addition to (or in the absence of) a contractual relationship, a consumer may also rely on the tort of negligence. Such a claim in tort is founded on the rationale that parties that design, manufacture and sell products owe a general duty to exercise reasonable care in order that those products do not create unreasonable risk of injury to users and others.

The province of Quebec distinguishes itself from the rest of Canada in that its private law is governed not by the common law, but by a Civil Code containing a comprehensive set of legal principles covering all aspects of civil law, including the law of product liability. Provincial statutes complete this legal framework. The general principles of Quebec product liability law are contained in the Civil Code of Quebec (LRQ, c C-1991) (CCQ), specifically in Articles 1726 to 1731 of the Code for contractual claims and Articles 1468, 1469 and 1473 of the Code for extra-contractual claims. These provisions contain the rules relating to the 'warranty of quality'. In contracts entered into by a consumer, the Consumer Protection Act (RSQ, c P-40.1) (CPA) and the Regulation respecting the application of the CPA (RRQ, c P-40.1, r 3) supplement the warranty of quality or product liability regime of the CCQ.

1.2 What is required to establish causation under the most common causes of action available?

For contractual liability to be established, a consumer must prove the following:

(a) there was an enforceable contract between the consumer and the manufacturer or distributor;
(b) the manufacturer or distributor breached a term of the contract, eg, the product failed to meet express or implied warranties of quality or durability; and
(c) the damages claimed are a reasonably foreseeable consequence of the breach.

As a matter of tort law, there are three main ways in which a manufacturer or seller may be negligent:

(i) negligent manufacture;
(ii) negligent design; and
(iii) failure to give reasonable warnings concerning the product's potential risks.

To prove negligence, the plaintiff must plead and establish the following elements:

(a) the defendant owed a duty of care to the plaintiff with respect to the product;
(b) the defendant's conduct fell below the standard of reasonable care; and
(c) the defendant's breach of the standard of care (ie, the resulting product defect or insufficient warning) caused or contributed to the plaintiff's loss or injury.

Canadian courts normally apply a 'but for' test for causation of loss or injury. The plaintiff must establish on a balance of probabilities that, but for the defendant's negligence, the loss or injury would not have been suffered. In other words, the plaintiff bears the burden of proving that, had the defendant met the standard of reasonable care, it is more likely than not that the loss or injury would have been avoided.

1.3 Is strict liability available and, if so, in what circumstances?

Liability for breach of contractual conditions or warranties is strict. If the seller has expressly or impliedly contracted to deliver a product free of defects, and the product is shown to have been defective, the degree of care exercised by the seller, or the reasonableness of the seller's actions, is irrelevant.

While courts in Canada's common law provinces have adopted a high standard of care for the design and manufacture of products, they have repeatedly rejected the doctrine of strict liability for tort claims respecting product defects: *Phillips v Ford Motor Co. of Canada Ltd.* (1971), 18 D.L.R. (3d) 641 (Ont. C.A.). As a result, Canadian common law courts require that a plaintiff prove that a manufacturer is 'at fault'; that is, the manufacturer's conduct fell below the standard of reasonableness. While plaintiffs have sought to advance strict liability claims in a number of recent proposed class actions, these arguments have been consistently rejected: *Andersen v St. Jude Medical Inc.*, [2002] O.J. No. 260 (S.C.J.).

In contrast, in Quebec, the law of product liability under the CCQ does not require proof of fault or negligence. It is irrelevant whether the manufacturer or supplier exercised great care; if there is a defect in the product that causes harm, he or she will be liable for it. In other words, in a

recourse based on a contract, if the buyer proves that:
(i) the product is defective;
(ii) the defect existed at the time of the sale;
(iii) the defect was not apparent; and
(iv) the defect was unknown to the buyer,
then the seller as well as the manufacturer, distributor, wholesaler and importer will be liable under the law of product liability (Articles 1726 & 1731 CCQ). Where the product is purchased from a 'professional seller' and the product malfunctions or deteriorates prematurely as compared with similar products, Article 1729 CCQ prescribes a rebuttable presumption that the defect existed at the time of sale.

That said, the negligence or fault of the seller is still material in a suit which asserts a product defect. Indeed, if the buyer is able to prove, in addition to the four conditions which give rise to liability for a defective product, that the seller was or ought to have been aware of the hidden defect, then the seller is bound not only to restore the purchase price, but to pay all damages suffered by the buyer. In other words, the knowledge (presumed or actual) of the defect is considered a fault or negligence of the seller and opens the door to consequential damages (Article 1728 CCQ). Where the buyer is unable to prove such fault, the seller's liability or exposure is limited to reimbursing the purchase price or an amount which corresponds to the cost to remedy the defect.

In terms of extra-contractual recourses under Quebec law, the victim need only prove that there exists a safety defect, that he/she suffered injury and that there is a causal link between the defect and the injury, and the manufacturer will be presumed liable.

1.4 Are guarantees or warranties as to quality implied by law?

Contracts for the sale of goods in Canadian common law provinces are typically governed by provincial legislation based on the original English Sale of Goods Act. This legislation provides for implied conditions with respect to fitness for purpose, merchantability and durability. While commercial parties can vary or waive these implied conditions by agreement, consumer protection legislation in many provinces prohibits any contractual waiver or exclusion of these warranties in consumer contracts. Generally speaking, these obligations are owed only by the seller with whom the purchaser of the product has a direct contractual relationship. While manufacturers who do not sell directly to consumers may choose to provide a manufacturer's warranty, it is open to the manufacturer to define the terms of such warranty; generally, the terms of such a warranty are not implied either by statute or the common law.

In Quebec, both the CCQ and CPA contain implied warranties of quality. Pursuant to Article 1726 CCQ, the seller is statutorily held to warrant that the products he sells are exempt from latent defects, except where the defect is known to the buyer or is apparent. The implied statutory terms relevant in the consumer context also provide for warranties of quality, fitness and durability (Articles 37 and 38 CPA).

1.5 How is a product 'defect' defined?

Under Canadian common law, a product is generally considered to be 'defective' if it poses an unreasonable risk of harm to person or property when foreseeably used. However, simply because a product is defective does not, by itself, establish negligence. Rather, the plaintiff must establish that the defect arose as a result of the manufacturer's negligence. In order to prove a manufacturing defect, the plaintiff must show that: (i) the product was not manufactured according to its design and specifications; (ii) the non-conformance resulted in the defect; (iii) the non-conformance and defect arose as a result of the manufacturer's breach of the standard of care; and (iv) the defect caused the plaintiff's loss. Where a design defect is alleged, the plaintiff must establish that: (i) the design of the product posed an unreasonable risk to users; (ii) the design did not meet the standard of care in that it was not reasonable in all of the circumstances; and (iii) the defect caused the plaintiff's loss. In determining whether the design was reasonable, Canadian courts generally apply a 'risk-utility analysis' under which the court will weigh a number of factors including the availability of alternative designs, the degree of safety improvement they represent, their cost, and their impact upon the product's usefulness and availability: *Tabrizi v Whallon Machine Inc.* (1996). 29 C.C.L.T. (2d) 176 at 185 (B.C.S.C.).

Not every product that causes damage is necessarily defective or a source of liability. It has been held that 'the law does not require a manufacturer to produce articles which are accident-proof, or incapable of doing harm. A manufacturer is not 'an insurer' of anyone who suffers injury while using, or misusing, the product': *Stiles v Beckett* (1996), 17 B.C.L.R. (3d) 144 (C.A.), Rather, there must be a determination that the product itself falls short of reasonable standards. The onus is on the plaintiff to prove on the balance of probabilities that the product, as designed, manufactured or labelled, fell below reasonable standards considering all of the circumstances. Defects in design or manufacture that are benign or cosmetic will not normally give rise to tort liability, but may be regarded as a breach of an express or implied contractual warranty.

Generally, the reasonableness of a product design will be judged by the standard existing at the time the product entered the marketplace, not when the product caused the injury: *Brunski v Dominion Stores Ltd.* (1981), 20 C.C.L.T. 14 (Ont. H.C.). However, where a manufacturer becomes aware of a danger unknown at the time of sale, the manufacturer may have a duty to take measures to warn current users of the product: *Rivtow Marine Ltd. v Washington Iron Works,* [1974] S.C.R. 1189. This duty will apply even where the product is no longer being manufactured or sold.

While product 'defect' is not defined *per se* in Quebec legislation, Article 1726 of the CCQ provides the essence of the legal warranty of quality incumbent on sellers and describes the notion of 'latent defects' as follows:

'The seller is bound to warrant the buyer that the property and its accessories are, at the time of the sale, free of latent defects which render it unfit for the use for which it was intended or which so diminish its usefulness that the buyer would not have bought it or paid so high a price if he had been aware of them.'

To give rise to liability, therefore, the product at issue must be affected by a defect that is: (a) serious; (b) hidden; (c) unknown to the buyer; and (d) existing at the time of the sale.

In *ABB v Domtar* 2007 SCC 50, the Supreme Court of Canada defined three types of latent defects under the product liability law of Quebec: (a) the material defect, which relates to a specific good; (b) the functional defect, which relates to the good's design; and (c) the conventional defect, which arises where the buyer has disclosed that the good is to be put to a particular use. Material and functional defects are assessed in light of the normal use to which buyers put the good, whereas a conventional defect is assessed in light of the particular use indicated by the buyer to the seller. In extra-contractual product liability, the notion of 'safety defect' is defined at Article 1469 CCQ.

1.6 Who in the supply chain has obligations or duties for defective products? What obligations or duties do they owe and to whom?

Canadian common law courts have held that a duty of care can potentially be owed by almost any participant in the chain of product distribution, including:

(i) manufacturers;
(ii) product designers;
(iii) importers, wholesalers, distributors and retailers;
(iv) repairers and installers;
(v) inspectors and certifiers; and
(vi) users of the product.

However, the standard that such parties must meet will vary depending upon the functions that each performs with respect to the product and its distribution. For example, a wholesale distributor may have limited obligations because it has no practical control over the design or manufacture of the product, nor any practical ability to provide product warnings to the consumer. Since liability depends upon proof of negligence, it is necessary to show that the defendant acted unreasonably and that the plaintiff's loss would have been avoided had the defendant acted reasonably.

The duty of care owed by a manufacturer is very broad and is most often not disputed. Canadian common law courts have found that the duty of care owed by manufacturers extends beyond the original purchaser of a product and is also owed to other persons who could foreseeably suffer injury as a consequence of a defect in the product. The other parties in the supply chain may also be found to owe a duty of care to persons beyond the original purchaser. Generally speaking, if it is reasonably foreseeable that a party's careless conduct in respect of the product could result in personal injury or property damage, a duty of care will be owed.

In Quebec, all sellers, whether professional or not, are bound by the legal warranty of quality (Article 1726 CCQ). Moreover, by exception to the principle of privity of contract, manufacturers, any persons who distribute products under their name or as their own, and suppliers of a product, including wholesalers and importers, are also bound to warrant the buyer in the same manner as the seller (Article 1730 CCQ). Quebec Courts have defined a 'manufacturer' as any person whose transformation activities allow the product to be used for its intended purpose (*Horecki v Beaver Lumber co.*, [1991] R.R.A. 234 (C.S.); confirmed by [1992] R.J.Q. 1763 (C.A.)). Therefore, whereas in the common law provinces, the liability of intermediate parties in the supply chain must generally be framed in negligence and requires proof of fault, in Quebec such parties are made contractually responsible.

Therefore, unlike the case in the common law provinces, where the liability of intermediate parties in the supply chain must generally be framed in negligence, the buyer of a defective product in Quebec has a 'contractual' recourse against anyone involved in the manufacturing and sales of the product, even if his or her contractual relationship is with the seller only. The seller, manufacturer and anyone else held to the warranty are joint and several co-debtors of the warranty obligations, by operation of law. Likewise, Articles 53 and 54 of Quebec's CPA provide that the buyer of a defective product has a 'contractual' recourse against the merchant or the manufacturer, even if his or her contractual relationship is with the seller only.

1.7 By what means can a supplier limit their liability for defective products?

Common methods used by Canadian suppliers to try to limit their liability for defective products include:

(a) expressly limiting or excluding such liability in the contract between the supplier and the purchaser of the product. As noted, however, consumer protection statutes in some provinces may prohibit the exclusion of implied warranties of fitness or quality. In Quebec, a limitation of liability clause is illegal and unenforceable in a contract governed by the CPA;

(b) negotiating contractual protections from the party above the supplier in the supply chain, such as a promise to defend and indemnify the supplier for any claims by third parties alleging a product defect;

(c) in the event of litigation, adding other parties in the supply chain as third party defendants on the basis that: (i) they owed and breached a duty of care to the plaintiff directly and thus caused or contributed to the plaintiff's damages; or (ii) they owed the supplier an independent contractual or tort duty with respect to the distribution of the product, and breached such contract or tort duty; and

(d) claiming contributory negligence against the plaintiff, on the grounds that some unreasonable conduct on the plaintiff's part caused, contributed to or exacerbated the damages suffered.

However, the law of Quebec imposes significant limitations on the availability of the first of these mechanisms. While Quebec law generally considers limitation of liability clauses as valid and enforceable in regards to hidden defects (Article 1732 CCQ), the ability to limit liability through such provisions is subject to the following limitations. Firstly, a limitation of liability clause purporting to shield a seller or manufacturer from a product defect is not enforceable as it relates to bodily or moral injury (Article 1474 CCQ). Secondly, such a clause is likewise unenforceable where the injury results from intentional or gross fault (Article 1474 CCQ). Thirdly, a 'professional seller' cannot exclude or limit its liability for latent defects that it knew or is presumed to have known about and that were not disclosed to the buyer at the time of the sale (Article 1733 CCQ).

1.8 Are there particular goods or services which have specific obligations or duties attached to them?

As regards civil liability for product defects, neither Canadian common law nor statute law in the common law provinces imposes any specific obligations in respect of particular products or types of products. There is simply a general requirement of reasonableness; that is, for every person that is found to owe a duty of care, the standard of care is 'to use reasonable care in the circumstances and nothing more': *Stewart v Pettie* (1995), 121 D.L.R. (4th) 222 (S.C.C.). In practice, this means that the degree of care to be exercised will vary with the nature of the product and the nature and severity of the risks that the product potentially poses. For example, there is a very high standard of care demanded of manufacturers of food and medical products because such products have a capacity to cause significant injury to consumers if care is not exercised.

In terms of product liability under Quebec law, it is equally the case that there are no specific obligations or duties attaching to particular goods or services.

There are, however, a number of statutes and regulations that prescribe product standards and requirements for a wide variety of goods; these are discussed below. These standards are promulgated for regulatory purposes, prescribing the attributes that a product must exhibit before it may lawfully be manufactured, imported or sold in Canada. In themselves, these standards do not define a manufacturer's or seller's duty of care for purposes of civil liability. While the failure to meet these regulatory standards would likely be treated as persuasive evidence of negligence, satisfying the statutory standards will not necessarily constitute proof that the defendant has met the standard of care, as the court may find that the common law standard of care is more exacting than the regulatory standard.

2. DEFENCES

2.1 What are the possible defences to a product liability claim?

There are a number of available defences in Canada which may be raised by a defendant in a product liability claim. In addition to asserting that the plaintiff has not established the requisite elements of the claim, a defendant may also advance one or more of the following defences:

(i) the plaintiff knew of and accepted the risk of injury;
(ii) the plaintiff improperly used the product;
(iii) the plaintiff modified the product in an unforeseeable way;
(iv) there was an unforeseeable intervening act or event which caused or contributed to the plaintiff's injuries; and

(v) the plaintiff contractually waived his or her right to sue.
The availability of these defences is very fact-specific.

Where a defendant is able to prove that the plaintiff knew of the defect or risk in question and continued to use the product, the plaintiff may be held to have voluntarily assumed the risk of injury. Where this defence is available, the defendant will be completely exonerated. Because of this harsh result, this common law defence has been virtually repealed in Canadian law; only in the most exceptional circumstances will a court be prepared to find that the plaintiff has knowingly agreed to assume all risk and agreed that he or she would not look to the defendant. Consequently, carelessness on the part of the plaintiff, if sufficient to support a defence at all, will generally result in a finding that the plaintiff negligently contributed to the injury, rather than a complete defence. Such contributory negligence may take the form of failing to observe defects that ought to have been observed, underestimating the significance of what was observed, not reading instructions for use or by misusing the product: *Smith v Inglis Ltd.* (1978), 83 D.L.R. (3d) 215 (N.S.C.A.).

Further, while a manufacturer will not be responsible for every occurrence where its product is misused, in some circumstances, foreseeable misuse may give rise to a duty to provide additional warnings, or a duty to design the product so that damage or injury is reasonably minimised in circumstances of misuse. For example, collisions are not an intended use of motor vehicles, but because automobile accidents are foreseeable events, automobiles must be manufactured with a reasonable degree of 'crashworthiness': *Baker v Suzuki Motors Co.,* [1993] 8 WWR 1 (Alta. Q.B.).

In a case where it is alleged that the manufacturer failed to provide the consumer with adequate warnings, liability can be avoided where it is shown that the manufacture has adequately warned a 'learned intermediary' between the manufacturer and the user of the product, where it can reasonably be expected that that intermediary will ensure that the product is used safely: *Hollis v Dow Corning Corp.,* [1995] 4 S.C.R. 634 (S.C.C.).

Canadian courts in the common law provinces will generally give effect to contractual waiver, exclusion or limitation clauses that exclude or limit liability of the manufacturer or vendor. However, courts have traditionally been reluctant to give full effect of such clauses and will interpret them narrowly against the party invoking their protection. As a result, waiver, exclusion and limitation clauses in Canada must be drafted very precisely in order to ensure their enforceability, particularly where the clause is intended to exclude or limit liability for negligence: *Hunter Engineering Co. v Syncrude Canada Ltd.* (1989), 57 D.L.R. (4th) 321 (S.C.C.). The court may also refuse to give effect to such clauses if they were not adequately brought to the purchaser's attention, and therefore cannot be said to form part of the contract terms that the purchaser agreed to. This may be the case, for example, in a consumer contract, where the exclusion of liability is expressed in 'fine print' terms that the consumer likely will not have read: *Tetaka v BMW Canada Inc.,* 2007), 28 BLR (4th) 327 (Ont. Div. Ct.).

The defences available in Quebec are generally the same as those in the common law provinces, although, as discussed above, Quebec law imposes more restrictive rules respecting limitation of liability clauses.

2.2 Is there a limit on the time in which proceedings may be brought (limitations and repose)?

The time for bringing an action in Canada is generally governed by provincial and territorial limitation period legislation. Therefore the periods within which an action for compensation may be commenced will vary from province to province and may vary depending on the nature of the loss or damage for which compensation is claimed, and the legal cause of action relied upon to assert such a claim. In certain provinces the limitation period may differ in product liability cases depending upon the damage that the product defect is alleged to have caused (whether personal injury or damage to other tangible property), or whether the claim is asserted in negligence or breach of contract.

However, in the majority of common law provinces and territories, all such claims must be commenced within two years from the date on which the claimant discovered the claim. While in many cases, this discovery date will be the date upon which the product fails and causes injury, this period may be extended if, for example, the claimant is not aware of the identities of potential defendants at that time. Therefore, the claim must be brought within two years from the date upon which the claimant would, through the exercise of reasonable diligence, have discovered that he or she had a claim against the particular defendant.

In Quebec, the limitation period applicable to a buyer's recourse for breach of legal warranty of quality, pursuant to both the CCQ and CPA, is three years from the time the buyer becomes aware of the defect.

3. LITIGATION OF PRODUCT LIABILITY DISPUTES

3.1 In which courts are product liability proceedings brought?

Product liability claims for personal injury or damage to property are generally brought in the superior court of the province which has the greatest connection to the claim. Typically, this will be where the accident occurred. Several provinces have specialised 'small claims courts' which follow a more streamlined procedure for claims below a certain value; in Ontario, the Small Claims Court can hear cases involves claims for up to C$25,000. However, the vast majority of product liability claims are brought in the provincial superior courts.

In Quebec, proceedings can be brought before three different courts depending of the amount at issue. Matters where the sum claimed is C$7,000 or below are brought before the Court of Quebec, Small Claims Division. Matters where the sum claimed is between C$7,001 and C$69,999 are brought before the Court of Quebec and matters where the sum claimed is C$70,000 and over are brought before the Superior Court.

Where a product liability claim fundamentally relates to a matter of federal jurisdiction, for example, maritime law, it may be possible to bring such a claim to the Federal Court of Canada. However, such cases are exceptional.

3.2 How are proceedings commenced?

Product liability suits in common law Canada are primarily commenced by a document known as a statement of claim or notice of civil claim. This document will set out the identity of the parties and the facts and legal basis underlying the complaint. The complaint is filed with the registry of the superior court with jurisdiction and then served on each defendant according to the applicable rules of court.

In Quebec, the document initiating proceedings is referred to as a Motion to Institute Proceedings.

3.3 Are disputed issues decided by a judge or a jury?

Product liability claims are normally determined by a judge alone. However, in certain provinces, product liability cases may be determined before a judge and jury where the case does not raise complex scientific matters.

3.4 Who has the burden of proof and to what standard?

The plaintiff has the burden of proof to establish on the balance of probabilities all of the elements necessary for the court to determine liability and damages.

The plaintiff also bears the burden of proof in proceedings in Quebec, although, as discussed above, the law prescribes certain evidentiary presumptions in favour of the plaintiff.

3.5 How is evidence given in proceedings and are witnesses cross-examined?

Evidence is normally given by live testimony of witnesses in court. The party calling the witness will conduct direct examination and the opposing party will then have an opportunity to cross-examine the witness. Additionally, evidence may be adduced in certain circumstances by *affidavit* or through pre-trial deposition.

Canadian courts are generally reluctant to limit the number of witnesses, length of witness testimony and the length of trials generally. As a result, product liability trials in Canada can often be very lengthy.

3.6 Are the parties able to rely on expert opinion evidence and, if so, are there any special rules or procedures for expert opinion evidence?

Expert evidence is commonly accepted by Canadian courts in product liability cases. Indeed, in most such cases, where it alleged that the manufacturer has failed to exercise reasonable care in designing or manufacturing the product, it will be necessary to introduce expert evidence to establish the relevant standard of care.

In order for expert evidence to qualify for admissibility, it must be:

(i) relevant;
(ii) necessary to assist the trier of fact;
(iii) not barred by an exclusionary rule; and
(iv) given by a properly-qualified expert.

Even where expert evidence may satisfy these criteria, the court retains the discretion to exclude expert evidence that is marginal in its probative value in relation to its potential prejudicial effects.

Generally, expert evidence is adduced through both written reports and testimony at trial. In most provinces, it is a procedural requirement that the expert's written report be served on the other party in advance of trial.

3.7 Is pre-trial discovery permitted? If so, in what circumstances? If not, what other mechanisms, if any, are available for obtaining evidence from an party or a third party?

Document production obligations in Canadian common law civil cases are very broad. While the exact scope of document production will vary from province to province, parties are generally required to list and produce all documents in their possession or control which may be relevant to matters in issue in the litigation. In the common law provinces, it is not necessary for an opposing party to seek production of documents; rather, the rules of court impose the obligation on each party in the litigation. In Quebec, the obligation to make documentary production is not automatic, but must be requested, either by motion to the court or as a request made in the course of oral discovery.

The rules of civil procedure in each province normally allow oral discovery in all superior court cases, although certain exceptions exist for claims involving smaller amounts. Examinations for discovery are normally taken under oath and transcribed by court reporter. Generally, each party is entitled to examine under oath one representative of each of the other parties that are adverse in interest. Where the party is a corporation, the company will be required to produce one representative knowledgeable about the issues in the litigation. Even though a typical product liability lawsuit will involve issues about which numerous employees of the defendant manufacturer may have relevant knowledge, the plaintiff is entitled to examine only one of these employees unless the court orders otherwise. Other than in Alberta and Nova Scotia, there is no general right to conduct depositions of parties or non-party witnesses without court order. The right to depose or examine non-party witnesses before trial is generally restricted to situations where the evidence possessed by the non-party witness is not available from any other source.

3.8 Is there liability for spoliation of evidence/a remedy for destruction of or failure to preserve evidence (most relevantly, the product)?

In Canadian common law provinces, spoliation is not recognised as an independent tort. Rather, spoliation remains a principle of evidence. Specifically, the court may draw an inference that the missing evidence would have been unhelpful to a party's case if:

(i) the evidence was destroyed by that party;
(ii) it was relevant to the matters in the action;
(iii) legal proceedings were contemplated or pending; and
(iv) the destruction of the evidence was carried out intentionally.

Therefore, a party can avoid the inference by demonstrating that the destruction of the evidence was accidental or inadvertent, or was carried out for reasons other than to affect the litigation: *Topp v Costco Wholesale Canada Ltd.,* 2012 ONSC 3354.

In Quebec, under Article 1739 CCQ, a buyer who ascertains that a product is defective must give notice in writing of the defect to the seller within a reasonable time after discovering it. Reasonable notice is a substantive condition and failure to provide it can result in the dismissal of the action. However, courts will only dismiss the case if the failure to notify the seller resulted in the inability of the seller to inspect the defect. In practice, the destruction of evidence before a notice is sent can affect the weight given to a plaintiff's evidence, but will usually not deprive the plaintiff of its right of action.

3.9 Is interlocutory or interim relief available prior to the full trial of a proceeding?

Interlocutory or interim relief is not normally sought or granted in Canadian product liability litigation. In certain circumstances, the court may make interim orders such as injunctions or preservation orders to compel parties to preserve evidence pending the litigation. Normally, a claimant cannot obtain any type of advance or interim award with respect to damages or costs until liability is established at trial.

3.10 Can the winning party recover its costs?

Canadian common law courts have the jurisdiction to award 'costs' of the litigation to a party. Although costs awards are ultimately in the discretion of the trial judge, the default practice among Canadian common law courts is to award costs to the successful party in the lawsuit. Typically, this means that the unsuccessful party must pay some percentage of the successful party's legal fees and reasonable disbursements. The specific quantum of costs and disbursements recovered depends upon the rules of procedure of the particular province and will vary from province to province. Special costs approaching full indemnification may be awarded where a party's conduct in the litigation has been reprehensible and deserving of rebuke. Conversely, if the successful part is found to have misconducted itself in the litigation, costs may be reduced or denied altogether.

In Quebec, the winning party can usually recover its disbursements and court costs, including judicial fees based on a tariff, and expert witness fees. However, the winning party cannot recover fees paid to its own attorney unless the party is able to prove abuse of process on the part of the defendant; in practice, it is difficult to meet this standard.

3.11 What avenues of appeal are available?

Provincial superior court trial judgments may generally be appealed as of right to provincial courts of appeal. However, in several provinces special rules apply to appeal rights where the amount of the judgment is below a prescribed sum. Security may be ordered before an appeal may proceed.

The ultimate right of appeal in civil matters is to the Supreme Court of Canada, although leave must be granted on application by the would-be appellant. Such leave is rarely granted since the Supreme Court of Canada will generally only agree to hear a case if it raises legal issues of sufficient importance. Product liability cases in the Supreme Court of Canada are uncommon.

Appellate courts will generally be highly deferential to the findings of fact made by the trial judge, and will intervene on such findings only if it is shown that the judge made some palpable and overriding error in his or her appreciation of the evidence. By contrast, on pure questions of law, the appellate court will review the decision below on a standard of correctness: *Housen v Nikolaisen,* 2002 SCC 33.

4. CLASS ACTIONS/REPRESENTATIVE PROCEEDINGS

4.1 Is there a mechanism for class actions or representative proceedings, or coordinated proceedings for product liability claims? If so, what are the basic mechanics?

Class actions are permitted in nine of the 10 Canadian provinces (the one exception being Prince Edward Island) pursuant to class proceedings legislation in each of the provinces. The fundamental components of a class action proceeding in Canada are certification, trial of common issues, and (if the common issues are resolved in favour of the plaintiff), adjudication of individual issues and damages.

In order for an action to proceed as a class proceeding, it must be certified by the court as a class action. Generally, the test for certification in Canada comprises five elements:

(i) the pleading discloses a cause of action;
(ii) there is an identifiable class of two or more persons;
(iii) the claims or defences of the class members raise one or more issues that are common among all of the class members;
(iv) there is no other procedure preferable to a class proceeding for the resolution of the common issues; and
(v) the representative plaintiff will fairly represent the interests of the class.

5. LITIGATION FUNDING

5.1 Is litigation funding by third parties permissible in your country? If so, is it common?

Historically, third party funding for litigation proceedings was generally prohibited by common law rules against champerty and maintenance. However, in recent years, Canadian courts in some provinces have accepted the role of litigation funding by third parties, particularly in class actions where other sources of funding are likely to be unavailable. Generally, such funding arrangements must be disclosed and are subject to approval by the court. Court supervision is regarded as necessary to ensure that the interests of the class members are not compromised in favour of the interests of those financing the litigation: *Fehr v Sun Life Assurance Company of Canada,* 2012 ONSC 2715. Canadian law is unsettled on the question of whether a plaintiff can recover as damages interest paid on funds borrowed to finance the litigation.

5.2 Are contingency fee or 'no win no fee' arrangements permissible?

Historically, contingency fee arrangements in civil litigation in Canada were also contrary to the rules respecting champerty and maintenance because they also involved the litigation being financed by someone other than the plaintiff; specifically, plaintiff's counsel. Once again, the introduction of class actions legislation in Canada has resulted in a relaxation of these principles. It is now the case that in product liability actions, contingency fee arrangements are permitted in both class actions and individual actions. However, such arrangements must comply with the rules prescribed by the bar association regulating the legal profession in each province, and their enforcement remains subject to court supervision.

6. REMEDIES

6.1 What remedies are available to a party who successfully pursues a product liability claim?

While both the common law remedy of damages and various equitable remedies are theoretically available as remedies in any civil action in Canada, the remedy generally sought and granted in a product liability lawsuit is an award of compensatory damages.

An alternative remedy that in some circumstances may be available in a breach of contract action is the remedy of rescission of the contract. Rescission is available where the defective product can be returned to the vendor in exchange for the return of the purchase price. In the vast majority of defective product cases, however, the claim will be for damage or injury beyond the product itself.

In principle, the purchaser of a product that proves to be defective could seek an order of specific performance, requiring the seller to deliver a non-defective product. However, such relief is rarely sought or granted, since it is presumed that an award of damages will adequately compensate the purchaser.

In brief, the types of damages generally recognised by Canadian courts in product liability lawsuits are:

(a) the cost of remedying the defect in the product or, alternatively, the differential between the value of the defective product and a non-defective product;
(b) damage to property caused by the defective product;
(c) personal injury caused by the defective product;
(d) liabilities incurred by the plaintiff as a result of the defect; and
(e) loss of profits and damage to reputation.

Personal injury damages are typically divided into two categories: pecuniary general damages and non-pecuniary general damages. Pecuniary damages comprise the expenses incurred by the injured plaintiff such as cost of future care, lost earning capacity, etc. Non-pecuniary general damages comprise pain and suffering, loss of life expectancy and loss of enjoyment of life.

6.2 How are damages calculated/are there limitations on available damages?

Non-pecuniary general damages are subject to a court-made cap. In three decisions rendered in 1978, the Supreme Court of Canada capped non-pecuniary general damages in personal injury cases at C$100,000. Indexed for inflation, that cap is now approximately C$348,000.

There is no cap on damages for such pecuniary items as cost of future care or loss of future income. Rather, these damages are whatever the evidence shows such loss to be. Typically, expert evidence is adduced by the parties to establish the amount of pecuniary loss, particularly in catastrophic injury cases where the cost of future care may be substantial.

6.3 Are punitive or exemplary damages available and in what circumstances?

Although Canadian courts may award punitive damages, such awards are very uncommon. Punitive damages will only be awarded in circumstances where the defendant's conduct is regarded by the court as unduly harsh, high-handed, vindictive, reprehensible, oppressive and/or malicious, or otherwise deserving of the court's condemnation. While there is no explicit cap on punitive damages, a 2002 decision of the Supreme Court of Canada indicated that the upper range, even in the most egregious circumstances, would be C$1,000,000.

Punitive damages may be more readily available in Quebec. Under the CPA, a consumer may seek punitive damages even if the merchant was unaware of the defect. This is true even if no compensatory damages are granted and there is no bad faith on the part of the manufacturer: *Brault & Martineau v Riendeau,* 2010 QCCA 366 (C.A.).

6.4 Is liability joint and several/how does apportionment of liability work, including where a partially responsible entity is not a party to the proceeding?

Typically, where multiple defendants are found liable in a product liability lawsuit the court will apportion liability among them in proportion to the respective wrongfulness of their conduct. This apportionment is often pursuant to provincial statute. Such defendants are jointly and severally liable to the plaintiff, but as among themselves are liable to make contribution in accordance with their respective allocations. In practice, this means that a defendant may be liable to the plaintiff for an amount greater than the portion allocated by the court, if other defendants are insolvent or otherwise judgment-proof. In certain provinces, the court may sever joint liability where the plaintiff has been contributorily negligent.

Ordinarily, a court will not apportion any liability to a person who is alleged to have contributed to the plaintiff's loss, but who is not a party to the proceeding. If a defendant seeks to reduce its ultimate liability by demonstrating that some other person also contributed to the plaintiff's loss, it is expected that that other person be added to the proceeding by way of a third party claim. If, however, the plaintiff chooses to expressly limit his or her claim to a particular defendant's proportionate liability (as is sometimes done after an action is commenced, in order to facilitate a settlement with some, but not all, defendants), the court has authority to quantify that proportionate share of liability by notionally allocating liability to an absent party.

7. ROLE OF REGULATORS

7.1 Please explain the role, responsibilities and powers of the regulators in your country which have jurisdiction over product liability issues.

Although there is no single government entity that regulates all products in Canada, certain products are subject to product-specific regulators. The most prominent examples are Health Canada (which regulates drugs, medical devices, cosmetics,and food) and Transport Canada (which regulates motor vehicles and certain motor vehicle components). Beyond that, the Consumer Product Safety Directorate of Health Canada regulates most other types of consumer products pursuant to the Canada Consumer Product Safety Act.

These regulators do not, however, deal with product liability *per se*. Proceedings to obtain compensation for injury or loss by reason of a defective product must be initiated by the injured person and pursued in the civil courts. However, complaints to and findings of regulators may be used in subsequent civil proceedings as, for example, evidence that the manufacturer was aware of complaints and problems with the product.

7.2 Are there any mandatory reporting requirements related to product safety issues?

The enabling legislation which prescribes the role and responsibilities of each of the above-noted regulators requires suppliers of those products to report to the regulator safety-related incidents involving the product, or safety-related defects in the product. The form and manner of reporting varies among the different regulators.

7.3 Do the regulators have the power to:

(i) ban certain goods or services?

Yes, most Canadian regulators have the power to immediately order, or seek court order, that a manufacturer stop selling a product in Canada.

(ii) require a supplier to recall a product?

The Canadian Food Inspection Agency has the power to direct the recall of food products, and the Consumer Product Safety Directorate of Health Canada has the power to order a supplier to recall other consumer products that are believed to have a safety-related defect. Industry Canada has the power to seek court order for the recall of certain electronic telecommunication devices. Additionally, provincial regulators such as the British Columbia Safety Authority have the power to order the stop-sale and recall of certain products.

(iii) prescribe standards in respect of certain goods or services and require that the goods or services meet those standards?

The regulators identified above may prescribe product standards, and may enforce those standards.

(iv) require production of information without court process?

Most of the regulators of consumer products in Canada have the power to require a company to disclose information to the regulator, without having to apply to a court for an order for such disclosure. Generally, the only threshold that typically needs to be met by the regulator is that it has reasonable grounds to believe that the information it seeks is relevant to determining whether a violation of a regulation has occurred.

The potential penalties for failure to comply with a requirement imposed by the legislation or by the order of the regulator vary depending upon the particular type of product and nature of the offence. Generally, the supplier may be subject to a penalty involving incarceration and/or a monetary fine. Furthermore, in respect of recalls under the Canada Consumer Product and Safety Act, where a supplier fails to comply with an order to conduct a recall, Health Canada is authorised to conduct the recall itself and charge the expense of doing so to the supplier.

8. VOLUNTARY CONDUCT

8.1 Are there regulations pertaining to the voluntary conduct of a product repair or recall by a supplier?

The product regulations in Canada do not state the manner in which a recall, or other corrective action such as repair campaign, is to be conducted. However, some of the regulators in Canada have publicly issued guidelines to their industry constituents setting out recommended 'best practices' for the manner in which a recall should be performed. Such guidelines address matters such as the creation of a 'recall team', appropriate methods for gathering information from the field, appropriate methods for seeking to retrieve products from the marketplace, and recommendations for storing and ultimately disposing of the recalled products.

9. EMERGING ISSUES AND LAW REFORM

9.1 Are there important developing and emerging issues or trends in product liability law in your country?

Developing and emerging issues include:

- impact of increased consumer protection legislation and regulation;
- development of a national class action regime;
- judicial clarification of whether waiver of tort is an independent cause of action.

9.2 Please describe any proposed important law reform in the area of product liability in your country.

Proposed or potential areas for statutory or common law reform include:

(i) Protocols for potential judicial comity and cooperation to facilitate a national class action regime;

(ii) increased consumer protection legislation; and

(iii) reform of wrongful death legislation in some provinces.

10. REGULATORY WEBSITES/INFORMATION

10.1 Please identify any useful regulatory references relating to product liability law in your country, for example, a product safety/consumer law website maintained by the main regulator.

The primary federal product safety regulators in Canada, and their websites, are as follows:

- Health Canada (drugs and health products): *www.hc-sc.gc.ca/dhp-mps/index-eng.php*
- Health Canada, Consumer Product Safety Directorate: *www.hc-sc.gc.ca/cps-spc/index-eng.php*
- Canada Food Inspection Agency (food products): *www.inspection.gc.ca/*
- Transport Canada (motor vehicles): *www.tc.gc.ca/eng/roadsafety/menu.htm*

China

Dacheng Law Offices Wu Feng

1. LIABILITY

1.1 What are the principal sources of law and regulation relating to product liability?

In China, the laws relevant to product liability are listed as follows: the General Principles of the Civil Law of the People's Republic of China enacted on 1 January 1987, the Contract Law of the People's Republic of China enacted on 1 October 1999 (hereinafter referred to as 'Contract Law'), the Tort Law of the People's Republic of China enacted on 1 July 2010 (hereinafter referred to as 'Tort Law'), the Product Liability Law of the People's Republic of China enacted in 1993 and amended in 2000 (hereinafter referred to as 'Product Liability Law'), the Law of the People's Republic of China on the Protection of Consumer Rights and Interests enacted on 1 January 1994 (hereinafter referred to as 'Law on the Protection of Consumer Rights and Interests'), and the Civil Procedure Law of the People's Republic of China enacted in 1991 and amended in 2012 (hereinafter referred to as 'Civil Procedure Law').

1.2 What is required to establish causation under the most common causes of action available?

If the plaintiff brings a lawsuit regarding product liability, the following conditions shall be met:

(i) the plaintiff shall be citizens, legal persons or other organisations whose, person or property damage is due to the defect of products;
(ii) the defendant shall be the producer or the seller of the defective products;
(iii) the plaintiff shall have specific claims, facts and reasons; and
(iv) claims shall be within the scope of the court's acceptance of civil litigations and shall be under the jurisdiction of the accepting court.

1.3 Is strict liability available and, if so, in what circumstances?

Pursuant to Article 41 of Tort Law, where a defective product causes any harm to any person, the producer shall assume tort liability. Chinese law regards the producer's liability as strict liability, which means that the producer shall assume tort liability without taking fault into account. However, the seller, carrier and warehouseman, shall be responsible for compensation for the damage only if the defect of a product is caused by their fault.

1.4 Are guarantees or warranties as to quality implied by law?

The producer shall be liable for the quality of the products they produce. Products shall meet the following quality requirements:

(i) products shall be free from any unreasonable dangers threatening the safety of people and property. If there are State standards or trade standards for ensuring the health of the human body and safety of lives and property, the products shall conform to such standards;

(ii) products shall have the property they are due to have, except cases in which there are explanations about the defects of the property of the products;

(iii) products shall tally with the standards prescribed or specified on the packages and with the quality specified in the instructions for use or shown in the samples provided.

Sellers shall adopt measures to maintain the quality of products for sale.

1.5 How is a product 'defect' defined?

Pursuant to Article 46 of Product Liability Law, there are two standards aiming to determine the defect of a product. One is a *de facto* standard, which defines a defect as the unreasonable dangers existing in the products that threaten the safety of person or properties. The other is the legal standard, which defines a defect as failure to conform to the standards set by the State or the specific trade if there is any.

1.6 Who in the supply chain has obligations or duties for defective products? What obligations or duties do they owe and to whom?

(i) The producer's compensatory liability

A producer shall be liable for compensation if his defective product causes damage to human life or property other than the defective product itself.

(ii) The seller's compensatory fault liability.

If damage to human life or property of others is due to a product's defect, which is attributable to the fault of a seller, the seller shall be liable for compensation. Where the seller can identify neither the producer of the defective product nor the supplier thereof, the seller shall be liable for compensation.

(iii) The carrier, warehouseman and other third parties' compensatory fault liability.

Where any harm is caused to another person by a defective product and the defect is caused by the fault of a carrier or a warehouseman, a producer or seller of the product that has paid the compensation shall be entitled to be reimbursed by the third party.

1.7 By what means can a supplier limit their liability for defective products?

Chinese law forbids the producer or the seller from limiting their liability for defective products by any means.

1.8 Are there particular goods or services which have specific obligations or duties attached to them?

Yes. We could take mobile telephones and household automobile products as an example. Pursuant to Regulations on the Liability of Repairing, Replacing and Returning Mobile Telephone Commodities and the Regulations on the Liability of Repairing, Replacing and Returning Household Automobile Products, producers and sellers of mobile telephones or household automobile products shall assume special legal liabilities such as repairing, replacing and returning.

2. DEFENCES

2.1 What are the possible defences to a product liability claim?

The general possible defence grounds regarding product liability suits include, but are not limited to, the following points:

(i) the defendant against whom the plaintiff brings a lawsuit is not proper;
(ii) the plaintiff is not able to prove the defect of a product and the causation between such defect and the damage;
(iii) the defendant cites evidence to prove the existence of legal exemptions;
(iv) the damage suffered by the plaintiff is caused by various reasons;
(v) the damage suffered by the plaintiff has already been compensated in full or in part by other legal means;
(vi) the suit brought by the plaintiff has exceeded the limitation of action.

2.2 Is there a limit on the time in which proceedings may be brought (limitations and repose)?

Pursuant to Article 45 of Product Liability Law: (i) the limitation of action for claiming for compensation for damages due to defects of products is two years, starting from the date when the parties concerned is notified or should have known the matter; (ii) the right of request for compensation claim for damages done due to defects of products shall lose effect after the tenth year after the products with defects that caused damage was first delivered to the users or consumers. However, cases in which the specified safe use period has not been exceeded are exceptions.

3. LITIGATION OF PRODUCT LIABILITY DISPUTES

3.1 In which courts are product liability proceedings brought?

There is no judging body specifically that hears product liability litigation under Chinese law. The judging court shall be determined based on the general principles as follows:

(i) In terms of territorial jurisdiction, pursuant to Civil Procedure Law, as a lawsuit brought on an infringing act, the product liability litigation shall be under the jurisdiction of the court in the place where the infringing act took place or where the defendant has his domicile. Moreover, the place where the tort is committed includes the location where the tortious act is performed and where the damage caused by the tortious act occurs.
(ii) In terms of jurisdiction by level, the plaintiff shall bring a suit to a

court of corresponding level according to factors such as the region of litigation, the litigation amount and whether the case has major impact in an area or the State or not. Generally, the plaintiff files suits in a Chinese basic people's court.

3.2 How are proceedings commenced?

Pursuant to Chinese law, the litigation procedure begins once the People's Court having jurisdiction registers the case.

3.3 Are disputed issues decided by a judge or a jury?

Generally, in Chinese law product liability cases of first instance shall be tried in a People's Court by a collegial panel consisting of both judges and assessors or of judges alone.

However, if both parties concerned have reached an arbitration agreement, an arbitration tribunal decides the award.

3.4 Who has the burden of proof and to what standard?

The general rule established by Chinese law in order to allocate the burden of proof in civil litigation is the 'person who alleges adduces evidence'.

In terms of the allocation of the burden of proof in product liability litigation, the plaintiff, as a victim, shall bear the burden of proof to prove the facts as follows:

(i) the product is defective. If the victim is not able to prove the defectiveness of the product first, the victim shall bear the risk of losing the suit;
(ii) the damages, including death, personal injury other loss of property other than the defective product and any other serious losses;
(iii) that causation exists between the defect of the product and the damages of the victim.

The standard for judging whether the victim fulfils the above burden of proof requires its compliance with the standard of high probability required in civil litigation.

If the victim fulfils the burden of proof as proving the facts mentioned above, it is the producer's or seller's duty to prove the existence of grounds for exemption from liability. If the producer or seller is unable to fulfil this burden of proof, they shall bear the risk of losing the suit.

3.5 How is evidence given in proceedings and are witnesses cross-examined?

Cross-examination shall be conducted in the following order:

(i) the plaintiff presents evidence, and the defendant and the third party cross-examine the plaintiff;
(ii) the defendant presents evidence, and the plaintiff and the third party cross-examine the defendant;
(iii) the third party presents evidence, and the plaintiff and defendant cross-examine the third party.

The evidence investigated and collected by the People's Court in line with the application of a concerned party shall be deemed as evidence provided by the applying party.

The People's Court shall present evidence investigated and collected in line with its responsibilities during the court hearing and listen to the concerned parties' reactions. They may also disclose information regarding the investigation and collection of evidence.

When inquiry of a witness is made, other witnesses shall not be present. The People's Court may have witnesses cross-examine each other when it is deemed necessary.

3.6 Are the parties able to rely on expert opinion evidence and, if so, are there any special rules or procedures for expert opinion evidence?

A concerned party may apply to the People's Court to allow one or two person(s) with expertise to appear in court and give explanations on specific issues involved in the lawsuit. Where the People's Court assents to such application, the applying party shall bear relevant expenses.

The judicial personnel and parties concerned may make inquiries of the persons with expertise appearing in court.

Subject to approval by the People's Court, persons with expertise appearing in court on behalf of respective parties may cross-examine each other in respect of issues involved in the lawsuit.

Persons with expertise may make inquiry of an expert examiner.

3.7 Is pre-trial discovery permitted? If so, in what circumstances? If not, what other mechanisms, if any, are available for obtaining evidence from a party or a third party?

The exchange of evidence before trial is allowed.

Upon application by a concerned party, the People's Court may organise the exchange of evidence by parties prior to the sitting of the court.

In the event of a complicated case or a case involving large amounts of evidence, the People's Court shall organise the exchange of evidence by parties after the expiry of the time limit for defence but before the sitting of the court.

3.8 Is there liability for spoliation of evidence/a remedy for destruction of or failure to preserve evidence (most relevantly, the product)?

The resulting legal liabilities are as follows:

(i) The negative legal consequence is losing the suit. Where there is evidence proving that a party concerned refuses to provide without any justifiable reason the evidence that he actually has, and the opposite party alleges that the contents of such evidence are disadvantageous to the evidence holder, such allegation can be construed as justifiable. If evidence such as the product itself is damaged or lost because of one party's deliberate intention or negligence, resulting in the impossibility of finding out whether the product is defective or not, that party shall bear the legal responsibility of losing the case.

(ii) Pursuant to Article 111 of Civil Procedure Law, if a participant or any other person in the court proceedings forges or destroys important evidence, thereby obstructing the trial of a case by the People's Court, the court shall, according to the seriousness of the act, impose a fine on or detain that person; if the act constitutes a crime, the offender shall be investigated for criminal responsibility according to the law.

3.9 Is interlocutory or interim relief available prior to the full trial of a proceeding? If so, in what circumstances?

Pursuant to Article 100 of Civil Procedure Law, if the execution of a judgment becomes difficult or damage has been caused to the parties possibly because of the acts of one party or for other reasons, the court may, at the application of the other party, rule to adopt measures for the preservation of property and order it to conduct or not to conduct certain acts. In the absence of such application, the court may of itself, when necessary, order the adoption of measures for such preservation. This is the first time Chinese law has made provisions for pre-trial injunctions, which can also be applied to product liability litigation when the statutory requirements are met.

3.10 Can the winning party recover its costs?

In practice, the Chinese court is generally not in favour of claims proposed by prevailing parties in order to obtain retainer fees and fees relevant to the litigation that he has already paid.

3.11 What avenues of appeal are available?

If a party refuses to accept the judgment of first instance of the local People's Court, he shall have the right to file an appeal with the People's Court at the next higher level within 15 days after the date on which the written judgment is served.

4. CLASS ACTIONS/REPRESENTATIVE PROCEEDINGS

4.1 Is there a mechanism for class actions or representative proceedings, or coordinated proceedings for product liability claims? If so, what are the basic mechanics?

The prevailing Chinese law system provides 'representative proceedings' instead of 'class action' such as in the Anglo-American legal system.

Pursuant to Article 53 of Civil Procedure Law

A joint lawsuit in which one party is numerous may be brought by representatives selected by and from the party. The act of litigation of such representatives shall be effective for all members of the party they represent. However, confirmation, modification or waiver of claims of action or confirmation of the claims of the other party or institution of a compromise by the representatives shall be subject to the approval of the party they represent.

Pursuant to Article 54 of Civil Procedure Law:
With respect to a case in which the object of action is of the same category and one party is numerous and of an uncertain number upon institution of the lawsuit, the people's court may issue a public notice, stating the particulars and claims of the case and informing claimants to file at the people's court within a fixed period of time.

Claimants who have filed at the people's court may select representatives from among themselves to engage in litigation; if such representatives cannot be created through selection, they may be decided by the people's court through negotiation with the claimants who have filed at the court. The act of litigation of such representatives shall be effective for the party they represent. However, modification or waiver of claims of action or confirmation of the claims of the other party or institution of a compromise by the representatives shall be subject to the approval of the party they represent.

The judgments or orders rendered by the people's court shall be effective for all the claimants who have filed at the court. The same judgments or orders shall be binding on the claimants who have not filed at the court but instituted legal proceedings during the limitation of action.

5. LITIGATION FUNDING

5.1 Is litigation funding by third parties permissible in your country? If so, is it common?

No.

5.2 Are contingency fee or 'no win no fee' arrangements permissible?

No.

6. COMPENSATION

6.1 What remedies are available to a party who successfully pursues a product liability claim?

Pursuant to Article 16 of Tort Law, where an infringement act causes any personal injury to another person, the tortfeasor shall compensate the victim for reasonable expenses for treatment and rehabilitation, such as medical treatment expenses, nursing fees and travel expenses, as well as lost wages. If the victim suffers any disability, the tortfeasor shall also pay the costs of disability assistance equipment for the living of the victim and the disability indemnity. If it causes the death of the victim, the tortfeasor shall also pay the funeral service fees and compensation for death.

Pursuant to Article 44 of Product Liability Law, where personal injury and property loss are caused by a product due to its defectiveness, the offender shall restore the damaged property to its original state, or reimburse its estimated price. Where the victim suffers any other serious losses, the offender shall also compensate for such losses.

6.2 How are damages calculated/are there limitations on available damages?

The damages covered under product liability can be divided into three categories. The first is property damage compensation, meaning property losses other than the defective product itself. The second is personal injury compensation, meaning the personal injury to the victim. The third is compensation for the infliction of mental distress. Pursuant to Article 22 of the Tort Law, where any harm caused by a tort to a personal right or interest of another person inflicts serious mental distress on the victim of the tort, the victim of the tort may require compensation for the infliction of mental distress.

Generally, in terms of the limitation of the amount of compensation in product liability litigation, the principle of 'filling up', meaning the amount of compensation equal to the actual damage, shall be followed. However, pursuant to Article 47 of the Tort Law, where a producer or seller knowing of any defect of a product continues to manufacture or sell the product and the defect causes a death or serious damage to the health of another person, the victim shall be entitled to require the corresponding punitive compensation. Consequently, in special circumstances, the amount of compensation may exceed the actual damage.

6.3 Are punitive or exemplary damages available and in what circumstances?

Punitive compensation is possible in product liability litigation according to Chinese law.

Pursuant to Article 47 of the Tort Law, where a producer or seller knowing of any defect of a product continues to manufacture or sell the product and the defect causes a death or serious damage to the health of another person, the victim shall be entitled to require corresponding punitive compensation. The conditions that apply to punitive compensation are listed as follows: firstly, the tortfeasor shall have subjective intention, meaning the tortfeasor knowing about the defect continues manufacturing or selling the product; secondly, it gives rise to significant damages, meaning the death or serious bodily harm of others; thirdly, there is a causation between the defect and damages, meaning the death or serious bodily harm of the victim was caused by the offender's manufacture or sale of the defective product.

6.4 Is liability joint and several/how does apportionment of liability work, including where a partially responsible entity is not a party to the proceeding?

Pursuant to Article 43 of the Tort Law, where any harm is caused by a defective product, the victim may require compensation to be made by the producer or seller of the product. If the defect of the product is caused by the producer and the seller has made compensation for the defect, the seller shall be entitled to be reimbursed by the producer. If the defect of the product is caused by the fault of the seller and the producer has made compensation for the defect, the producer shall be entitled to be reimbursed by the seller. Therefore, instead of bearing joint and several liabilities, the liability between the producer and the seller shall be defined as unreal joint and several liabilities, meaning either the producer or the seller may assume the entire liability in product liability litigation. However, if there exists evidence that the defect of the product is caused solely by the producer or the seller, a party that had formerly assumed sole liability may seek compensation from the party responsible for the defect.

7. ROLE OF REGULATORS

7.1 Please explain the role, responsibilities and powers of the regulators in your country which have jurisdiction over product liability issues.

The court has jurisdiction over product liability disputes without arbitration agreement.

The arbitration institution has jurisdiction over product liability disputes where an arbitration agreement is reached and the concerned parties apply for arbitration proceedings. The arbitration award shall be final and binding.

The General Administration of Quality Supervision, Inspection and Quarantine of the People's Republic of China (AQSIQ) is the organisation in charge of national quality management, management of standardisation and the supervision and management of certification and accreditation of the import and export of the products. Moreover, it is also responsible for enforcing the relevant laws and regulations regarding quality inspection and quarantine clearance, for implementing defective product recall systems and exercising the responsibilities of administrative enforcement of law.

The State Administration for Industry & Commerce of the People's Republic of China (SAIC) assumes responsibility for supervising and managing commodity quality and food safety in circulation, deals with complaints, claims and reports posed by consumers regarding product liability issues and makes decisions regarding administrative penalties.

7.2 Are there any mandatory reporting requirements related to product safety issues?

There are stipulations concerning the mandatory reporting of some product safety issues in Chinese law.

The food safety incident reporting system

Pursuant to Article 71 of the Food Safety Law of the People's Republic of China, the organisation where a food safety incident has occurred shall take immediate action to prevent the incident from spreading. The organisation where the incident has occurred and the institution that receives and treats the patients, shall immediately report to the administrative department of health in the county of jurisdiction.

Reporting system for potential danger and accidents of special equipment

Pursuant to Article 63 of the Special Equipment Safety Law of the People's Republic of China, where, in performing its duties, a department responsible for special equipment safety supervision and administration discovers any serious illegal action or special equipment with serious potential accident risks, it shall immediately report its findings to the superior department responsible for special equipment safety.

Pursuant to Article 70 of the Special Equipment Safety Law of the People's Republic of China, after a special equipment accident occurs, the entity where the accident occurs shall carry out the measures detailed in its emergency response plan, organise rescue, prevent expansion of the accident, reduce casualties and property damage, protect the scene of the accident and relevant evidence, and promptly report to the department responsible for special equipment safety supervision and administration and other relevant departments of the People's Government at or above the county level at the place of accident.

Reporting system for the recall of automobile products

Pursuant to Article 12 of the Regulations on the Administration of Recall of Defective Automobile Products, upon being aware of the possible defects in automobile products, producers involved shall promptly organise investigation and analysis, and truthfully report the conclusion of such investigation and analysis to the Product Quality Supervision Department of the State Council.

Reporting system for the recall of children's toys

Pursuant to Article 21 of the Provisions on the Administration of Recall of Children's Toys, after a toy defect is confirmed, the producer shall immediately stop manufacturing and distributing the defective toys, release all information regarding the defectiveness of the toys according to law to the public, alert distributors to stop selling the defective toys, alert consumers to stop purchasing the defective toys and make a voluntary recall of the defective toys.

7.3 Do the regulators have the power to:

(i) ban certain goods or services?

Yes. The commodities and services forbidden from trade are generally items or transactions forbidden to circulate freely under Chinese law, such as guns, ammunition, drugs, historical relics, valuable and rare animals and plant life.

(ii) require a supplier to recall a product?

Yes. As of August 2013, the regulations regarding the recall of specific products in China include the Regulations on the Administration of Recall of Defective Automobile Products and Provisions on the Administration of Recall of Children's Toys.

In addition, pursuant to Article 46 of Tort Law, where any defect of a product is found after the product is put into circulation, the producer or seller shall promptly enact remedial measures including warning and recall.

(iii) prescribe standards in respect of certain goods or services and require that the goods or services meet those standards?

Yes, such standards exist.

In terms of products, Measures for the Administration of Alcohol Circulation, effective from 1 January 2006, requires alcohol merchants to follow specific standards and rules during operation.

In terms of services, the Evaluation System for After-Sales Service of Commodities, effective from 1 October 2006, applies to the evaluation of the level of after-sales service of manufacturing enterprises and sales and service enterprises within the territory of the People's Republic of China.

(iv) require production of information without court process?

According to several specific laws, government agencies with authorisations may require producers to disclose some information without standard trial procedures. For example, pursuant to Article 14 of the Regulation on the Administration of Recall of Defective Automobile Products, during investigation of a defect, the Product Quality Supervision Department of the State Council may enter the business premises of a producer or dealer to conduct on-site investigation, consult or copy relevant information and records, and interview relevant entities and individuals regarding possible defects in automobile products. A producer shall cooperate in the investigation of a defect and provide relevant information, products and special equipment necessary for the investigation.

If so, broadly explain the circumstances in which the regulator can exercise the power and any penalties that apply if a supplier fails to comply.

Pursuant to Article 23 of the Provisions on the Administration of Recall of Defective Automobile Products, where a producer or dealer refuses to coordinate the investigations by the product quality supervision department, the product quality supervision department shall order it to make corrections; otherwise, the product quality supervision department will impose a fine of not less than RMB 500,000 but not more than RMB 1 million, as well as confiscate the illegal income of the producer or dealer, if any. The licensing authority shall also revoke relevant licences if the circumstances of violation are serious.

8. VOLUNTARY CONDUCT

8.1 Are there regulations pertaining to the voluntary conduct of a product repair or recall by a supplier?

Yes. In terms of automobile products, there are the Provisions on the Administration of Recall of Defective Auto Products, which focus on the recall system, and the Provisions on the Liability for the Repair, Replacement and Return of Household Automotive Products, which focus on the repair of the product.

The purpose of the Provisions on the Administration of Recall of Defective Auto Products is to strengthen administration on matters concerning the recall of defective automobile products, eliminate the danger caused by defective automobile products to the safety of the body and property of their users and the general public, and maintain public security, public interests and social economic order.

Drawing on the experience of the Lemon Law of the United States, China enacted the Provisions on the Liability for the Repair, Replacement and Return of Household Automotive Products in order to protect the lawful rights and interests of consumers of household automotive products and confirm the legal liability for the repair, replacement and return of the household automotive products assumed by the seller of the automobile product.

9. EMERGING ISSUES AND LAW REFORM

9.1 Are there important developing and emerging issues or trends in product liability law in your country?

Tort Law, effective from 1 July 2010, specifically stipulates regulations regarding product liability in its fifth chapter, which reflect the important trends and developments in the field of product liability in China. There are six main aspects as follows:

(i) The nature of the product liability is confirmed as tort liability.

Pursuant to Article 41 of the Tort Law, where a defective product causes any harm to another person, the producer shall assume tort liability. Additionally, Article 42 further states that where a product with any defect caused by the fault of the seller causes any harm to another person, the seller shall assume tort liability. Where a seller can specify neither the producer nor supplier of a defective product, the seller shall assume tort liability.

(ii) Reimbursement may be pursued where the defect of a product is caused by the fault of a third party.

Pursuant to Article 44 of the Tort Law, where any harm is caused to another person by a defective product and the defect is caused by the fault of a third party such as carrier or warehouseman, the producer or seller of the product that has already paid compensation shall be entitled to be reimbursed by the third party.

(iii) The danger of the defect of the product may be intervened in advance.

Pursuant to Article 45 of Tort Law, where the defect of a product endangers the personal or property safety of another person, the victim shall be entitled to require the producer or seller to assume tort liabilities by removing the obstruction or eliminating the danger.

(iv) Punitive compensation applies to the product liability.

Pursuant to Article 47 of Tort Law, where a producer or seller knowing of any defect of a product continues manufacturing or selling the product and the defect causes a death or any serious damage to the health of another person, the victim shall be entitled to require the corresponding punitive compensation.

(v) Product liability, as tort liability, should be regarded as a priority.
Pursuant to Article 4 of the Tort Law, where the assets of a tortfeasor are not adequate for payments of the tort liabilities and the administrative or criminal liabilities for the same act, the tortfeasor shall first assume the tort liability.

(vi) Compensation for the infliction of mental distress is applicable to product liability.
Pursuant to Article 22 of the Tort Law, where any harm caused by a tort to a personal right or interest of another person inflicts serious mental distress on the victim of the tort, the victim may require compensation for the infliction of mental distress.

9.2 Please describe any proposed important law reform in the area of product liability in your country.

The Law of the People's Republic of China on the Protection of Consumer Rights and Interests has been implemented for more than 20 years since its enactment in 1993. The NPC Law Committee published the draft of its amendment in April 2013, soliciting public reaction.

This draft of the amendment to the Law of the People's Republic of China on the Protection of Consumer Rights and Interests has proposed the following important tendencies of law reform:

(i) A shifting of the burden of proof regarding some product quality disputes was proposed for the first time.
(ii) Consumers of some products will be able to make unconditional returns within seven days of receiving the product.
(iii) The Consumer's Association is able to file a suit on behalf of large numbers of consumers.

10. REGULATORY WEBSITES/INFORMATION

10.1 Please identify any useful regulatory references relating to product liability law in your country, for example, a product safety/consumer law website maintained by the main regulator.

- The National People's Congress of People's Republic of China: *www.npc.gov.cn/*
- General Administration of Quality Supervision, Inspection and Quarantine of the People's Republic of China: *www.aqsiq.gov.cn/*
- The Quality Examination Website of China: *www.cqn.com.cn/*
- China Product Quality Association: *www.21315.org/*
- China Consumer's Association: *www.cca.org.cn*

Croatia

Bogdanović, Dolički & Partners
Nina Iličić & Olga Bogdanović

1. LIABILITY

1.1 What are the principal sources of law and regulation relating to product liability?

The principal source of law relating to product liability is the Obligations Act (Official Gazette nos. 35/05, 41/08,125/11), ie, its Articles 1073-1080. The provisions are consistent with the European Union Council Directive of 25 July 1985 on the Approximation of the Laws, Regulations and Administrative Provisions of the Member States Concerning Liability for Defective Products (85/374/EEC). Product liability provisions define: products, defective products, producers, presumptions for liability and burden of proof, prohibition of contractual exclusion or restriction of liability, extent of damage, amount of compensation, reasons for exemption from liability, periods for the exercise of right to compensation of damage and cumulative application of rules concerning other types of liability for damage. The existing defective product liability system provides protection of injured persons (consumers) against harmful consequences of a defective product, but also protection of producers against excessively strict liability since the liability is restricted both in terms of quantity and quality (*Klub pravnika Grada Zagreba*, Tribina 23.02.2006, Odgovornost za neispravan proizvod, page 6, *https://www.pravo.unizg.hr/_...*/ODGOVORNOST_ZA..., 04.02.2014*)*.

1.2 What is required to establish causation under the most common causes of action available?

The conditions to be cumulatively fulfilled for the liability for damage caused by defective products are: defectiveness of product, resulting damage and causal link between the defectiveness of the product and the damage suffered. The burden of proof rests entirely on the injured person and the injured person has to prove both the defectiveness of the product, the damage and the causal link. The causality is not presumed.

1.3 Is strict liability available and, if so, in what circumstances?

Strict liability is prescribed since the Obligations Act expressly defines that the producer putting products into circulation is responsible for the damage caused by the defectiveness of that product regardless of fault. Hence, fault is not a prerequisite for liability and producers do not have to be in contractual relationship with the injured person (purchaser etc.) (*Mlikotin Tomić, D.:*

Odgovornost za naknadu štete bez krivnje prema novom hrvatskom i europskom pravu, Zbornik Pravnog fakulteta u Zagrebu, 56: Posebni broj /2006, page 443).

Still, the Obligations Act prescribes a number of reasons for exemption from and restriction of liability. For a producer to free himself from the liability, any of the following circumstances must be proved:

- that he did not put the product into circulation;
- that, having regard to circumstances of the case, it is probable that neither the defectiveness nor its cause existed at the time when the product was put into circulation;
- that the product was neither manufactured for sale, lease or any other economic purpose, nor manufactured or put into circulation in the course of his business;
- that the defectiveness is due to compliance of the product with mandatory regulations in force at the time when the product was put into circulation;
- that the state of scientific and technical knowledge at the time when the product was put into circulation was not such as to enable the existence of the defect to be discovered;
- that the damage was caused exclusively by an act of the injured person or any person for whom the injured person is responsible, ie, by an act of a third party which could not have been foreseen by the producer and whose consequences he could not have avoided or removed. If the injured person (or any person for whom the injured person is responsible) only partially contributed to the occurrence of damage, the producer is partially released from the liability, and if the occurrence of damage was contributed to partially by a third party, such third party is jointly and severally liable with the producer.

Furthermore, the producer of a raw material or a component of the product can raise a defence that he followed the design of the finished product or instructions given by the producer of the finished product and prove that the defect of a part of the product resulted therefrom.

1.4 Are guarantees or warranties as to quality implied by law?

Products have to fulfil safety and technical requirements as well as standards which are governed by the General Product Safety Act (Official Gazette nos.158/03, 107/07, 30/90, 139/10, 14/14), the Act on Technical Requirements for Products and on Conformity Assessment (Official Gazette no. 80/13,14/14) and the Standardisation Act (Official Gazette no.80/13).

The General Product Safety Act is the main source of law governing general safety requirements for all products and the duties of producers and distributors in placing safe products on the market. The General Product Safety Act is applied if there is no special law regulating safety requirements for certain products. The producer has to place only safe products on the market. Safe products are products which, under normal or reasonably foreseeable conditions of use, do not present a risk, or present only the minimum risk compatible to the usage of the product considered to be acceptable and consistent with a high level of protection of human health and safety. Attention is paid to the characteristics of the product; the effect on other products with which it is used; instructions and warnings; the categories of consumers at risk when using it (children and elderly persons). Products need to comply with applicable European Union provisions on safety and Croatian standards adopting the European Union harmonised standards. If there are no such provisions, the conformity of products is determined based on Croatian standards transposing the pertinent European standards different from the already mentioned ones; other Croatian standards; recommendations of the European Commission; best practices in the field of product safety; the current level of science and technology and the level of safety objectively expected by consumers.

The Act on Technical Requirements for Products and on Conformity Assessment regulates the way of prescribing technical requirements for products and the conformity assessment procedure and obligations of economic operators who place products on the market or make them available on the market. This Act is applied if there is no special law regulating the way of prescribing of special technical requirements and the conformity assessment procedure for products. When compliance is proven, producers shall draw up conformity declarations and affix the conformity marking when required.

The Standardisation Act governs preparation and issuance of Croatian standards which aim is to increase product safety. Croatian standards are issued by a national standardisation institute.

1.5 How is a product 'defect' defined?

In order to define a product defect, the product itself should be defined first.

According to the law, the product is any movable. Hence, defective product liability rules relate to all types of movables. Immovables are excluded, but independent parts installed in movables or immovables are included. The definition of product includes also electricity and other forms of energy.

The Obligations Act does not contain any special definition of movables. Therefore, a general definition of a thing, stipulated in the Law on Property and Other Proprietary Rights (Official Gazette nos. 91/96, 68/98, 137/99, 22/00, 73/00, 129/00, 114/01, 79/06, 141/06, 146/08, 38/09, 153/09, 143/12) applies, according to which things are corporeal parts of nature, other than people, serving for use by people. Things are also deemed anything equalised with things by law. Movables are things which can be moved from one place to another without harming their substance. Things which are by their nature movable are in the legal sense deemed immovables if they are accessories to immovable things or are equalised with immovable things by law. Non-corporeal entities could also be things, provided that they should be subordinated to human power, eg, wind is not a thing until it is not subordinated to human power. (*Gorenc, V.: Komentar Zakona o obveznim odnosima, Zagreb,* 2005, page 1670).

Legal science took an attitude that software as well as blood and human organs are products in the sense of legal definition, but only when severed

(*Klub pravnika Grada Zagreba, Tribina 23.02.2006, Odgovornost za neispravan proizvod,* page 6, *https://www.pravo.unizg.hr/_...*/ODGOVORNOST_ZA..., 04.02.2014).

With regard to a defective product, a general definition was accepted that covers all possible types of product defects. A product is defective if it does not provide the safety which is reasonably expected from such product. When assessing the defectiveness, the following should also be considered: all circumstances of the case, especially the manner of presentation of the product to the public, the use to which it could reasonably be expected that the product would be put, the time when the product was put into circulation. The producer is expected to foresee that his product could sometimes be used other than basically intended (eg, a child can put a toy in his mouth) and that in such case he ensures his harmlessness for health and property of the user (*Klarić, P., Vedriš, M.: Građansko pravo, Zagreb,* 2009, page 619).

The safety which is reasonably expected from products is a basic criteria of distinction to safe and unsafe. Consumer expectations should be evaluated on the basis of objective criteria. Hence, it does not matter what a particular consumer expected, it matters what is normally expected from such a product (*Klub pravnika Grada Zagreba, Tribina 23.02.2006, Odgovornost za neispravan proizvod,* page 6, *https://www.pravo.unizg.hr/_...*/ODGOVORNOST_ZA..., 04.02.2014).

1.6 Who in the supply chain has obligations or duties for defective products? What obligations or duties do they owe and to whom?

The law determines a wide number of responsible persons who potentially have obligations for defective products, ie, against whom a claim for damages may be raised, and it practically includes all who are a part of the supply chain (producer, agent, wholesaler, retailer).

Primarily liable is the producer, being the person: who made the finished product; who manufactured the raw material, independent or dependent component installed in the finished product; as well as who, by labelling the product with his name, trademark or other distinction mark, presents himself as its producer.

Secondly, if the product is imported for sale, lease or any other form of putting the product into circulation, the importer of the product is also liable. The importer is liable jointly and severally with the producer and a person presenting himself as producer.

If it is not possible to identify the producer or importer, a subordinate liability of each person putting the product into circulation, ie, distributor, exists. The distributor can, however, free himself from liability if he informs the injured person, within a reasonable time, of the identity of the person who supplied the product. Similarly, the distributor can be released from liability when it is not possible to identify the importer of the product, even if the name, company name or other identification of the producer is indicated on the product. This being so, the injured person is obliged to request the information from the distributor in order to identify the primary responsible producer or his supplier. It is not specified what is deemed a reasonable period, thus causing a certain degree of legal uncertainty (*Bevanda, M.: Odgovornost za štetu izazvanu neispravnim proizvodom u hrvatskom i bosanskohercegovačkom pravu, Zbornik Pravnog fakulteta Sveučilišta Rijeka,* 28:1/2007, page 23-24).

If several persons are liable for the damage resulting from the defective product, they are liable jointly and severally. This rule is *in favorem* of the injured person who does not have to prove who is responsible for damages and to what extent since all of them are joint and several debtors.

A damaging act is deemed an act of putting the defective product into circulation. A product is deemed put into circulation when it is voluntarily transferred to another person for sale or distribution for economic purpose. (*Bevanda, M.: Odgovornost za štetu izazvanu neispravnim proizvodom u hrvatskom i bosanskohercegovačkom pravu, Zbornik Pravnog fakulteta Sveučilišta Rijeka,* 28:1/2007, page 34).

A person entitled to damages for a defective product is a natural person who suffered damage due to the defective product. The liability rules apply to relations accruing between the producer and the injured person regardless of whether the injured person is in contractual relation with the producer (purchaser) or not.

In case of liability for damage for a defective product, a material damage is compensated only and not just any material damage, but only:

- material damage caused by death or bodily injury of the user of the defective product. To the scope of damage special Articles 1093-1097 of the Obligations Act apply governing material damage in case of death, bodily injury and health damage (eg, costs of funeral, medical treatment, lost profit, loss of alimony)
- material damage caused by damage of the injured party's property other than the defective product, provided the property was only intended for personal use and if used by the injured party mainly for his personal use. Such liability is further limited by amount, so that the injured person is only entitled to the amount of damage exceeding €500.

It is not possible to claim recovery of damage on the defective product itself or claim recovery of non-material damage. The injured person will be able to have the damage recovered under different liability rules rooted in law, for which the law prescribes different, more stringent requirements for the injured person (*Gorenc, V.: Komentar Zakona o obveznim odnosima, Zagreb,* 2005, pages 1665-1666).

The product liability for damage caused by nuclear catastrophe is fully excluded.

1.7 By what means can a supplier limit their liability for defective products?

The law prohibits contractual preclusion or restriction of producer's liability for defective products. If such provision is nonetheless agreed, it would be null and void. However, the injured person can upon occurrence of damage waive his right (fully or partially) to compensation for damage (*Bevanda,*

M.: Odgovornost za štetu izazvanu neispravnim proizvodom u hrvatskom i bosanskohercegovačkom pravu, Zbornik Pravnog fakulteta Sveučilišta Rijeka, 28:1/2007, page 39).

It is advisable for producers to make sure their products comply with the safety requirements as laid down in legislation, to carefully formulate instructions for use, to make contractual arrangements with their suppliers of components to seek indemnity from other in the event of liability and to conclude appropriate insurance coverage regarding product liability.

1.8 Are there particular goods or services which have specific obligations or duties attached to them?

Defective product liability is uniformly governed by the Obligations Act, which applies to all types of defective products. Currently there are no specific product liability rules for particular goods, and product liability rules do not cover liability for services.

However, there are different rules on safety requirements that certain products have to meet (eg, safety requirements for toys), regulated in different laws and by-laws (see section 1.4 above). Failure to respect these rules can represent an offence, which could be useful in product liability litigations.

The injured person may cumulatively also claim compensation under some other liability rules defined in the Obligations Act imposing different, less favourable requirements for the injured person. The injured person can so claim: compensation for damage under liability rules for the damage caused by hazardous substances or hazardous activity; compensation for damage caused by material deficiency of a product and under general rules governing contractual and non-contractual liability.

2. DEFENCES

2.1 What are the possible defences to a product liability claim?

Even though strict liability of the producer putting a defective product into circulation is prescribed, the law prescribes a number of reasons for release and restriction of liability, which are all stated under section 1.3. The burden of proof for any of these reasons lies with the producer (ie, other persons responsible in the supply chain).

2.2 Is there a limit on the time in which proceedings may be brought (limitations and repose)?

The injured person has to bring an action for assertion of claims for recovery of damage within a (subjective) limitation period of three years from the day the damage, product defectiveness and identity of the producer became known or should have become known to him.

The right to recovery of the damage by defective product is extinguished within 10 years from the putting of the product in circulation (preclusion period), unless if in that period an action is brought against the producer for recovery of damage.

3. LITIGATION OF PRODUCT LIABILITY DISPUTES

3.1 In which courts are product liability proceedings brought?

Injured parties can obtain compensation for damage caused by a defective product by bringing court action. Under the Civil Procedure Act (Official Gazette nos. 53/91, 91/92, 58/93, 112/99, 88/01, 117/03, 88/05, 02/07, 84/08, 123/08, 57/11, 148/11, 25/13), the subject matter jurisdiction for compensation claims for damage caused by a defective product lies with the Croatian Municipal Courts as the courts of first instance. The Croatian County Courts sitting as the courts of second instance hear the appeals against the first-instance rulings.

3.2 How are proceedings commenced?

The injured person commences the proceeding by filing a complaint which must include a claim against the defendant (a claim for compensation of damage caused by the defective product), a statement of facts relied upon in support of the plaintiff's claim for relief, and a statement of proposed evidence supporting those facts (proof of defectiveness of the product, proof of damage and proof of causal link between the damage suffered and the defective product).

3.3 Are disputed issues decided by a judge or a jury?

Disputed issues are decided by a professional judge.

3.4 Who has the burden of proof and to what standard?

The entire burden of proof lies with the plaintiff (injured party), meaning the plaintiff has to prove all three: defectiveness of the product, damage incurred, and the causal link between the defect of the product and the damage suffered. The guilt of the defendant does not have to be proved.

The law provides that the liability of the defendant (producer or other persons responsible in the supply chain) may be released or reduced for the reasons stated in section 1.3 above, which have to be proven by the defendant.

3.5 How is evidence given in proceedings and are witnesses cross-examined?

The basic rule is that each party to the proceeding presents the facts of their case and proposes evidence to support their contentions or to refute the counterparty's contentions and evidence. Consequently, the court generally hears only the evidence proposed by the parties. The plaintiff and the defendant must in the complaint, ie, in the response to the complaint, state all material facts and propose all the evidence in support of their contentions and refuting the contentions proposed by the counterparty.

The court proceeding is divided into two stages: preliminary proceeding and trial. In the preliminary proceeding the parties must present all the facts and proposals of evidence. At the preliminary proceeding, the court decides which evidence will be heard at the trial, and rejects other evidence that is, in the opinion of the court, not relevant to the decision. At the end of the preliminary proceeding, the court sets the date for the trial, which is reduced to the role of evidence hearing. The parties have a right to present new facts and evidence at the stage of the trial only if such new facts and evidence could not have been presented at the preliminary proceeding through no fault of their own.

Evidentiary means include witnesses and expert witness testimony, documents, on-site inspection and testimonies of the parties to the proceeding. Witness examination consists of three stages: the judge first allows the witnesses to freely testify, afterwards the judge asks questions but keeps them within the existing submissions of the parties for the purpose of clarifying or supplementing the parties statements, if necessary, and finally the parties themselves ask questions, with the party that proposed the witness being the first to ask questions.

3.6 Are the parties able to rely on expert opinion evidence and, if so, are there any special rules or procedures for expert opinion evidence?

The parties are able to rely on expert opinion evidence. The party proposing the expert opinion evidence may propose the expert, while the counterparty may challenge the proposed expert witness. In case of a challenge by the counterparty, the expert witness will be appointed by the court. In practice, expert witnesses are professionals appointed primarily from the permanent court experts. In order to ensure neutrality of expert witnesses, the Civil Procedure Act provides grounds for their excusal from a specific case (eg, he/she is related to the parties, the expert was already appointed in the same case before). The parties have the right to ask questions, request supplements and make objections against the expert opinion if they are unclear, incomplete or contradictory or there is reasonable doubt about their accuracy. If the irregularities cannot be resolved by examining the expert, the court can order a renewal of the opinions either by the same or different expert.

The court's evaluation of evidence is not limited by any rules on the quality for specific evidence, ie, the rule of free evaluation of evidence applies. Therefore the expert opinion must formally be regarded as no more or less of an important piece of evidence as any other. However, the practical impact of the expert opinion lies with the fact that the judge does not have the specific knowledge and skills required to evaluate the relevant facts of the case and therefore must rely on the expert. Therefore, it may very well be that the judge will use the expert opinion as the basis on which all other evidence will be evaluated.

3.7 Is pre-trial discovery permitted? If so, in what circumstances? If not, what other mechanisms, if any, are available for obtaining evidence from a party or a third party?

There is no pre-trial discovery in Croatian civil litigation procedure, only in Croatian criminal procedure.

The Civil Procedure Act lays down the rules for obtaining evidence from a party to the proceeding or a third party, depending on the type of evidentiary means.

Documents and on-site inspection

Each party has an obligation to present the document it proposes to be admitted in evidence. Also, the party must surrender documents when such surrender is required under the law (eg, a document entrusted to it for safekeeping) and if the content of the document is considered to be common to both parties to the proceeding. However, the court cannot use coercion against the party in possession of the document in order to ensure access to it.

When a document is in possession of the counterparty, the court will call upon the counterparty to surrender the document. However, if the counterparty denies possession or withholds presentation of the document, the court may not use coercive means against them. Also, the counterparty may withhold production of the document for the same reasons for which witnesses may withhold their testimony (please see below).

The court will exercise its discretionary power to assess the relevance of the fact that a party to the proceeding is withholding production of a document.

A third party, who is not a party to the proceeding, must produce the documents that have to be produced under the law and if the content of the document is considered to be common to both parties to the proceeding. Otherwise, the court will issue an enforcement order against the third party for production of the document. Third parties must also surrender to the court other documents (which they are not required to surrender under the law and the content of which is not considered to be common to both parties), but they have a right to withhold production of documents for the same reasons for which witnesses may refrain from testifying.

If a document is in possession of a government body or a public person, and the party cannot ensure that the document will be surrendered or produced, such document will be obtained by the court.

If an item in possession of one of the parties, a third party, a government body or another public person, should be examined on site, the above rules for obtaining documents from such persons will apply.

Witnesses

Any witness summoned by the court must appear before the court, but he or she has the right to refrain from testifying for just cause (eg, because by testifying they would disclose the facts received by them in the course of their professional employment covered by professional privilege, or because by testifying they would expose themselves or their relatives to a considerable economic loss or criminal prosecution). The court will force a witness to appear/sanction him or her with a fine in case of failure to appear before the court without good cause. The court will sanction a witness with a fine or imprisonment (of up to one month duration) when testimony is withheld without just cause.

Expert witnesses

The court will sanction an expert witness with a fine in case of failure to appear before the court without good cause or refusal to testify without good cause.

Examination of parties

The testimony given by the parties may be used as evidence. However, if parties do not wish to give testimony, the court cannot use any coercive means against them. The court will use its discretionary power to assess the relevance of the fact that a certain party to the proceeding has not testified.

3.8 Is there liability for spoliation of evidence/a remedy for destruction of or failure to preserve evidence (most relevantly, the product)?

The Civil Procedure Act does not regulate liability for spoliation of evidence/a remedy for destruction of or failure to preserve evidence. However, the Croatian Penal Code (Official Gazette nos. 125/11, 144/12) recognises obstruction of evidence as a criminal offence punishable with imprisonment of up to eight years. Obstruction of evidence entails actions such as leading a witness or an expert witness to give false evidence in court by using force, threat or by bestowing gifts. It also includes concealing, damaging or destroying material objects or documents to be used in evidence, and falsifying evidence in a proceeding before court.

The Civil Procedure Act does, however, prescribe the possibility of preserving the evidence. If there is justified concern that subsequent presentation of evidence might not be possible or that presentation will be more difficult, the court may, even before the commencement of litigation, decide to have the evidence presented. Motions to secure evidence must be filed by the parties to the proceeding, and they must be supported by arguments as to why presentation of evidence is deemed necessary and why subsequent presentation will be impossible or difficult.

3.9 Is interlocutory or interim relief available prior to the full trial of a proceeding? If so, in what circumstances?

Interlocutory or interim relief is not applicable in Croatian law.

However, Croatian law recognises temporary injunctions, which aim to remove immediate danger in order to protect certain good or value, prevention of further damage caused by breach of regulation or illicit conduct, need to act urgently to ensure unhindered course of the proceeding (*Kapural, M.: Privremene mjere u pravu tržišnog natjecanja,* page 3, *www.aztn.hr/uploads/.../o.../mirta_kapural/6_mk.pdf,* 04.02.2014). Under the Civil Procedure Act, the court may grant temporary injunctions according to the rules of the Enforcement Act (Official Gazette nos. 112/12, 25/13), with the aim of removing imminent danger of illicit damage or preventing violence or removing irreparable damage. Under the Enforcement Act a temporary injunction may be sought from the court before the commencement, during, and even after the end of the court proceedings, for as long as the enforcement is not executed. Both monetary and non-monetary claims can be secured by temporary injunctions. In the case of a monetary claim, the court must be convinced that both the existence of the claim, and the danger of the counterparty's preventing or considerably hampering collection of the claim by selling, concealing or otherwise disposing of its assets, are probable. In the case of a non-monetary claim, the court must find it probable both that the claim exists and that without such an injunction, the counterparty would prevent or significantly hamper collection of the claim (eg, by changing the current state of affairs) or that an injunction is necessary in order to prevent violence or occurrence of irreparable damage. Temporary injunctions may include any measure that accomplishes the purpose of security, eg, prohibiting all sales of the counterparty's assets, ordering the counterparty to take certain actions that are necessary to preserve the current state of affairs etc.

3.10 Can the winning party recover their costs?

A party that is entirely unsuccessful in the action is obliged to pay the costs of the counterparty.

If a party is partially successful, the court may, taking into consideration the success achieved, order that each party bears their own costs or that one party pays the other a proportionate amount.

The court may decide that one party should pay all the costs incurred by the counterparty if the counterparty was unsuccessful but only in a relatively insignificant part of its claim and provided no special costs arose in relation to that insignificant part.

3.11 What avenues of appeal are available?

There are ordinary and extraordinary legal remedies.

Appeal is an ordinary remedy for relief against first-instance judgments. A timely filing of an appeal prevents the judgment from becoming final. Appeals are heard by second-instance courts. If the appellate court determines that the appeal has merit, it may: set aside the first-instance judgment and send the case back to the first-instance court for retrial; set aside the first-instance judgment and dismiss the complaint; or amended the first-instance judgment by itself.

Extraordinary legal remedies are used when seeking relief from final court judgments. Extraordinary legal remedies are: judicial review and motion for retrial.

The power of judicial review lies with the Supreme Court of the Republic of Croatia. The review does not stay the enforcement of decision against which it was granted. The review is a limited legal remedy since it cannot be used against all second-instance judgments but only against, among other, second-instance judgments in cases with a value exceeding HRK 200,000 or in cases where the second-instance court itself held the hearings, ie, admitted evidence, or amended first-instance judgment based on the current state of the file (ordinary review).

In cases where it is not possible to petition for ordinary review due to the above reasons, the parties can file a petition for the extraordinary review against the second-instance judgment if the resolution of the dispute depends on resolution of a substantive or procedural law issue which is important for uniform application of law and equal justice to all. The review is also limited from the point of view of reasons for which it may be sought. As a rule, the review may be sought for breach of procedural rules in the proceedings conducted at lower courts or for breach of substantive law, but it cannot be sought for erroneous factual determination. If the Supreme Court finds the review on the merits, then it will: set aside the second-instance or the first-instance judgment, and send the case back to the competent court for retrial; set aside the first-instance and the second-instance judgments and dismiss the complaint; or amend the first-instance and the second-instance judgments by itself.

Motion for retrial is an extraordinary legal remedy for relief against final judgments under which any final judgment can be challenged. The reasons for retrial are explicitly listed: if a judge that, under the law, ought to have been recused, took part in the judgment; if a party was unlawfully denied an opportunity to be heard in court; if the party did not have legal representation; if the court decision is based on a false testimony given by a witness or an expert witness; if the decision is based on a counterfeit document; if the decision was the result of a criminal offence by a judge, a legal representative for any of the parties; if the court decision is based on another court decision or decision issued by another body, and such decision has been effectively amended or annulled; if the preliminary issue, which was the basis of the court decision, has been effectively decided by a competent body; if a party gains an opportunity to use a final court decision rendered earlier among the same parties and upon the same claim; if a party learns of any new facts or gains an opportunity to use new evidence based on which a more favourable decision for the party may have been reached if these facts or evidence had been used in the prior proceeding. The time limit to file a motion for retrial is 30 days counting from the moment the party learned of any reason to file a motion (subjective deadline). The right to file a motion for retrial is extinguished within five years after the date when the challenged decision became final.

Motions for retrial are heard by the same court that issued a ruling in the first-instance process, unless the reason for retrial relates to the procedure before a higher court. If the motion is granted, the previous judgment is repealed and a new trial is set to re-deliberate the main issue.

4. CLASS ACTIONS/REPRESENTATIVE PROCEEDINGS

4.1 Is there a mechanism for class actions or representative proceedings, or coordinated proceedings for product liability claims? If so, what are the basic mechanics?

In Croatian law, it is not possible to bring class actions or representative proceedings for product liability claims. Proceedings must be brought by individuals who have suffered damage.

The Civil Procedure Act only provides for the possibility to bring action for protection of collective interests and rights. However, such action can be brought only by certain associations or other legal entities, and only if this right is granted to them under a special law (*Menđušić Škugor, E.: Udružna tužba kao mehanizam zaštite kolektivnih prava i interesa", Sveučilište u Zagrebu, Pravni fakultet,* 2012, page 16, *www.unizg.hr/.../Udru%C5%BEna+...doc,* 04.02.2014). So, for instance, under the Consumer Protection Act (Official Gazette 41/14), as a *lex specialis,* consumer protection organisations and competent government bodies may bring action for protection of collective consumer interests, where in case of success by the plaintiff, the court will order the defendant to cease the conduct that breaches consumer protection regulations, and to desist from such conduct in the future. Such court judgment has a preventive character in relation to individual claims for product liability because it is binding on other courts in those individual proceedings instituted by consumers for compensation of damage caused by defendant's illicit conduct *(Baretić, M.: Zaštita potrošača u Republici Hrvatskoj nakon ulaska u Europsku uniju - jesmo li implementacijom europskog prava izgradili sustav zaštite potrošača, Strengthening Consumer Protection in Serbia, Pravni fakultet Univerziteta u Beogradu,* page 94).

5. LITIGATION FUNDING

5.1 Is litigation funding by third parties permissible in your country? If so, is it common?

Third party funding is not regulated by Croatian law.

5.2 Are contingency fee or 'no win no fee' arrangements permissible?

'No win no fee' arrangements are not permissible under Croatian law. A 'contingency fee' is generally not permissible, however, there is an exception in property disputes whereby attorneys have a right to make an arrangement with the party whereby the attorney's remuneration will be proportionate to the party's success in the proceeding, limited to up to 30% of the total success achieved.

6. REMEDIES

6.1 What remedies are available to a party who successfully pursues a product liability claim?

In case of liability for damage caused by a defective product, only material damage is compensated, and not just any material damage, but only:

- material damage caused by death or personal injury of the user of the defective product. Compensation may include reimbursement of funeral costs, medical costs, loss of earnings caused by disability of the injured person during treatment or after the treatment, loss of alimony for persons who were the deceased's dependants, indemnity for permanently increased needs of the injured party after injury.
- material damage caused by damage to an asset owned by the injured party other than the defective product itself, provided such asset is intended for personal use and provided it had been used by the injured party mainly for personal needs. Such liability is further limited by amount, so that the injured person is only entitled to the amount of damage exceeding €500.

Repairs of damage to the defective product itself or compensation of non-material damage cannot be claimed for (the injured person might be entitled to those under different liability rules rooted in law, for which more stringent requirements for the injured person are prescribed).

6.2 How are damages calculated/are there limitations on available damages?

In general, existence of damage and its proportions will be assessed by expert witness since the court does not have the specific knowledge and skills required to evaluate the relevant facts and therefore must rely on the expert.

There is a lower limit for awarded damages when damage is caused to an asset of the injured party intended for private use, meaning that the injured party can claim only for that portion of the loss that exceeds the value of €500.

As a rule, there is no upper limit for maximum awarded damages, however, in case of compensation of damage caused by death and suffered by the deceased's dependants, the amount of annuity awarded cannot be higher than the amount that dependents would have been receiving from the deceased person had he or she been still alive.

6.3 Are punitive or exemplary damages available and in what circumstances?

Punitive or exemplary damages are not available. The main principle in Croatian law is that the damages awarded must put the claimant into the same position the claimant would have occupied had the damage not occurred, ie, not better and not worse.

6.4 Is liability joint and several/how does apportionment of liability work, including where a partially responsible entity is not a party to the proceeding?

If several persons are liable for the same damage caused by a defective product, their liability is joint and several. The injured party can make a claim against any of them for the full amount of damage. The injurer who paid full amount of damage to the claimant is entitled to seek financial reimbursement from the remaining injurers, depending on their respective contributions to the damage.

7. ROLE OF REGULATORS

7.1 Please explain the role, responsibilities and powers of the regulators in your country which have jurisdiction over product liability issues.

Various entities have powers related to product liability issues.

The Consumer Protection Act governs the protection of the rights of consumers when buying goods and services. As entities competent for consumer protection defined are:

- the Croatian Parliament adopts the National Consumer Protection Programme proposed by Croatian Government;

- the National Consumer Protection Council as an advisory body to the Government participates in drafting of consumer protection regulations and reports;
- the Government informs the Parliament on the realisation of the consumer protection policy;
- the competent Ministry performs consumer protection policy implementation and coordinates entities competent for consumer protection;
- consumer protection associations;
- and others.

The Croatian Government prescribes by a special decree which of the above entities are entitled to bring an action for protection of collective interests and rights of consumers.

The role of business associations the Croatian Chamber of Economy and the Croatian Chamber of Crafts is also of importance since it is possible to file applications to their Courts of Honour or mediation proposals in case of disputes between consumers and traders.

Furthermore, state inspectors have an important role in the field of product safety, conformity and consumer protection. They provide inspection services *ex officio* or based on complaints of consumers. They act within competent ministries whereby the Ministry of Economy is in charge of consumer protection and product safety. Their powers are defined by law (see below section 7.3).

7.2 Are there any mandatory reporting requirements related to product safety issues?

There are mandatory reporting requirements related to product safety issues.

Traders and producers have to inform consumers about safe usage of the products by delivery of documents prepared by producers (warranties, usage instructions, authorised repair shops, warnings about possible risks, product conformity statements).

Producers and distributors must immediately notify the competent authorities about incompatibility with general safety requirements and the risks that products they have placed on the market pose to consumers. They have to indicate: data that enable identification of the product; a description of the risk; information needed for products' follow-ups; the description of actions undertaken to limit the risk. Additionally, the competent authority will publicise information on product identification, the nature of the risk and the measures taken, unless it is considered professional secrecy.

Producers, importers and distributors are obliged to notify without delay the competent authority on incompatibility of products with applicable provisions regulating technical requirements and undertaken measures if these products pose a risk. If products pose a risk, but have not yet been placed on the market, distributors and importers have to notify the producer, too.

Competent authorities have to exchange information on products posing a risk in order to inform the public. According to the Regulation on Rapid

Information Exchange System Relating to Products Posing a Risk to the Health and Safety of Consumers (Official Gazette no. 5/11), the competent authority receives and transmits notifications on dangerous products to the European Commission and other Croatian authorities (RAPEX alert system).

7.3 Do the regulators have the power to:
(i) ban certain goods or services?
(ii) require a supplier to recall a product?
(iii) prescribe standards in respect of certain goods or services and require that the goods or services meet those standards?
(iv) require production of information without court process?
If so, broadly explain the circumstances in which the regulator can exercise the power and any penalties that apply if a supplier fails to comply.

State inspectors' powers are defined by law. They may by resolution impose measures to economic operators who place products or make products available on the market and, when necessary, to other persons or entities in order to ensure cooperation in carrying out measures for avoidance and limitation of risks.

State inspectors have the following powers:

- to prohibit the placing of dangerous and incompatible products on the market. If products are dangerous or it is doubtful that products fulfil technical requirements, they are entitled to temporarily prohibit supply of products until test and safety assessments have been completed;
- to withdraw dangerous products already placed on the market and alert consumers about their risks. If other measures are not sufficient, state inspectors may order the recall of affected products from consumers and their destruction;
- to order the fulfilment of conditions for placing products on the market and marking them with warnings if products pose risks in certain conditions;
- to request necessary information from the parties concerned for any product (not only a hazardous one) and information on conformity of products with prescribed technical requirements. Producers, importers and distributors have to cooperate and make available, upon the justified request of the state inspector, information needed for proving conformity of products.

Additionally, state inspectors may check: safety characteristics of products and carry out conformity assessment procedures; take product samples to check their safety and conformity with technical requirements; order removal of non-compliance with technical requirements in good time; order the delivery of the product having caused damage to a consumer in correct condition and impose other proscribed measures.

Failing to comply with obligations prescribed by law or a decision of the state inspector represents an offence of responsible persons punishable by fines.

8. VOLUNTARY CONDUCT

8.1 Are there regulations pertaining to the voluntary conduct of a product repair or recall by a supplier?

The competent authority promotes voluntary actions by producers and distributors in fulfilment of their obligations under the General Product Safety Act and encourages the development of good practice in product safety.

The Act on Technical Requirements for Products and on Conformity Assessment prescribes the obligation of producers, distributors and importers to undertake, without delay, actions in order to bring products into compliance, withdraw them from the market or prevent their distribution if they believe or ought to believe that products they placed on the market are not in line with applicable provisions.

9. EMERGING ISSUES AND LAW REFORM

9.1 Are there important developing and emerging issues or trends in product liability law in your country?

Due to the accession of the Republic of Croatia to the European Union in 2013 numerous changes have been made in the Croatian legal system, including in the area of product safety and consumer protection in order to harmonise national law with the European Union legislation.

Provisions regulating product liability were significantly changed in 2005 due to the implementation of the European Union Council Directive of 25 July 1985 regulating product liability (85/374/EEC).

The same applies to consumer protection and product safety requirements. The Consumer Protection Act as the first unified act governing the protection of consumer rights was introduced in 2003 and has been amended several times afterwards for the purpose of its harmonisation with the European Union legislation.

9.2 Please describe any proposed important law reform in the area of product liability in your country.

We are not aware of any proposed law reform in the area of product liability. The Republic of Croatia as a member of the European Union will continue harmonising its legal system with the changes made on the level of the European Union.

10. REGULATORY WEBSITES/INFORMATION

10.1 Please identify any useful regulatory references relating to product liability law in your country, for example, a product safety/consumer law website maintained by the main regulator.

Regulatory references relating to product liability law are:

- The Official Gazette: *http://narodne-novine.nn.hr/default.aspx*
- The Ministry of Economy/Consumer Protection: *http://potrosac.mingo.hr/en/potrosac/*
- 'Potrošač' the Association for Protection of Consumers of the Republic of Croatia: *www.potrosac.hr/index.php*

Denmark

Kromann Reumert
Jens Rostock-Jensen & Jakob Dahl Mikkelsen

1. LIABILITY

1.1 What are the principal sources of law and regulation relating to product liability?

The principal source of law relating to product liability in Denmark is the Product Liability Act, which implements Directive 85/374 on liability for defective products.

Directive 85/374 was implemented into Danish law by Act no. 371 of 7 June 1989 concerning product liability and amended by Act no. 1041 of 28 November 2000 implementing Directive 1999/34. The Act was amended again in 2006 after the European Court of Justice overturned section 10 of the Act in case no. C-402/03 and again in 2007 in order (to a limited extent) to accommodate the new Statute of Limitations that took effect on 1 January 2008.

The Product Liability Act applies only to personal injury and damage to consumer goods.

The producer's liability for defective products was based on the principles of the Law of Tort as developed through case law until the Product Liability Directive was implemented into Danish law, and these principles still apply alongside the Product Liability Act. Due to the mandatory nature of the Product Liability Act, the principles of the Law of Tort as developed through case law only apply to damage to commercial goods caused by products, as this type of damage is not governed by the Product Liability Act.

In Denmark the Law of Tort is not set out in any Act, but has been developed over the years by the courts. The Product Liability Act thus supplements existing Danish law on product liability and does not replace the principles already in existence.

Product liability has generally been defined as a producer's liability for damage caused by a defect in his product. According to the ordinary rules of Danish law on product liability, it is a condition for liability that the defect in the product is due to negligence on the part of the producer. The burden of proving negligence is not onerous.

The Danish Sale of Goods Act of 1906 (*Købeloven*) with later amendments, governs the obligations between purchaser and vendor in sales of goods. The Sale of Goods Act does not govern the right to compensation for damage caused by the product. The Sale of Goods Act governs damage to the actual product sold, including any damage to the product caused by the product's own ingredients, as this type of damage is not governed by product liability rules.

It should be noted that Denmark has implemented the Convention on Contracts for the International Sale of Goods (CISG).

The main difference between contract law and tort in relation to product liability is the limitation period for bringing claims. According to the Sale of Goods Act the limitation period is two years from delivery of the goods.

Although product liability is not governed by the Sale of Goods Act of 1906, the existence of a contract between the parties can be of relevance. If the contract is entered into between professionals it may regulate, limit or eliminate product liability. The contract may state certain obligations of the professional purchaser to check the product. Danish courts will not accept limitation of liability for product damage in case of personal injury and, as a main rule, limitation of liability will not be accepted if the seller has shown gross negligence. Danish courts tend to be critical in their interpretation of limitation on liability using the *in dubio contra stipulatorem* rule of interpretation.

Under the Product Liability Act it is not possible to limit or eliminate product liability governed by the Act, ie, in cases of personal injury or damage to consumer goods.

1.2 What is required to establish causation under the most common causes of action available?

Under tort law it is for the claimant to prove that the product is defective, that the producer has shown negligence, that a loss has been suffered and that there is causation between the defective product and the loss suffered.

No particular rules exist as to what standard of proof must be met by a claimant or defendant in order to sustain his burden of proof. The court is free to evaluate the evidence in the particular case and on the basis of this concrete evaluation the court will determine whether the burden of proof has been sustained or not.

Under the Directive it follows from Article 4 that the injured person shall be required to prove the damage, the defect and the causal relationship between defect and damage.

The basic rule of Danish law is that the claimant must prove a causal relationship between his/her particular injury and the defect. As a matter of general principle under Danish procedural law, the courts have absolute freedom to assess the evidence provided by the parties. The standard of proof is set by the courts in each particular case from an overall assessment of the claimant's possibilities of providing evidence, the defendant's situation, the nature of the defect and the circumstances in general. Danish law does not provide specific rules on how the court is to assess the evidence.

The courts' freedom to assess evidence applies to all evidence, both direct evidence, eg, witnesses or technical equipment (cameras, measuring devices, etc.) having observed a particular event, and indirect evidence where the court from the circumstances of the case decides on what facts to base its decision. It is not impossible that a court of law on the basis of strong statistical evidence could find that it is enough for the claimant to show that the defendant wrongly exposed the claimant to an increased risk of a type of injury known to be associated with the product. Even if it cannot be proved by the claimant that the injury would not have arisen without such exposure it is, however, a prerequisite that the statistical evidence to a very high degree of certainty must exclude that the particular injury could have other causes.

If it cannot be established which of several possible producers have manufactured the defective product, the claimant has not lifted his burden of proving who the producer/responsible party is. It is for the courts to decide how onerous the burden of proof is in the particular situation. No form of market-share liability applies.

1.3 Is strict liability available and, if so, in what circumstances?

The producer's liability

Under the ordinary Danish rules on product liability as developed through case law, the producer is responsible for damage caused by a defective product if the producer has acted negligently. However, the burden of proof for establishing negligence is not onerous and if the injured party can prove that the product in question is defective, the courts will often find that negligence has been established.

Under the Product Liability Act, the producer (as defined in the Directive Article 3) is subject to a strict liability for personal injury or damage to consumer goods caused by defective products. It is still for the injured party to prove the damage caused, the defect, and causation.

The Product Liability Act provides a number of possible liability exemptions. As such, the producer will not be liable if he can establish;

(i) that he did not bring the product into commerce; or
(ii) that the product was not produced or placed into commerce for commercial purposes; or
(iii) that the defect is due to the product having to comply with mandatory statutory requirements; or
(iv) that it was impossible to uncover the defect at the time the product was brought into commerce on the basis of the scientific and technical knowledge available at the time (state of the art/development risk defence).

Further, the producer is not liable if he can establish that the defect did not exist at the time the product was placed into commerce.

A producer of part of the defective product is not liable for damage caused by the end product if he can establish that the defect is due to the design of the product that his part has been included in.

The distributor's liability

Since the 1930s it has been held that the distributor is governed by a strict liability for defects in the product supplied by the producer even though the distributor has not acted negligently himself (the distributor then has a right of recourse against the producer).

This found its way into the original section 10 of the Danish Product Liability Act according to which the distributor was immediately liable towards the claimant and any other distributors in the chain of distribution for any product liability incurred by the producer, also in case of personal injury or damage to non-commercial goods regardless of whether the distributor had acted negligently.

However, on 10 January 2006 the European Court of Justice ruled that Section 10 of the Danish Product Liability Act could not be upheld, cf. the European Court of Justice case C-402/03.

The judgment was in line with the conclusion of the French case C-52/00. A national rule according to which the distributor is liable without restriction for the producer's strict liability is therefore no longer possible.

As a consequence of the European Court of Justice case C-402/03, section 10 of the Product Liability Act was changed in 2006. According to the new section 10 of the Act, any distributor in the supply chain is strictly liable only for the producer's fault-based liability.

The change entails that a distributor in the supply chain is only immediately liable if the claimant can prove that the producer acted negligently. As mentioned above, the burden of proof for establishing negligence is not onerous and it will often be sufficient for the injured party to prove that the product in question is defective.

Outside of the scope of the Product Liability Act, ie, in cases of damage to commercial goods, the distributor will be immediately liable towards the injured party for the producer's product liability. Should the injured party claim damages from the distributor, the distributor will have a right of recourse against the producer.

1.4 Are guarantees or warranties as to quality implied by law?

The Danish Sale of Goods Act provides a two-year warranty period for consumer products from the time of sale and a one-year warranty period for commercial goods.

Should a defect occur before the end of the warranty period, the buyer will be entitled to a repair or replacement and may be entitled to damages under the circumstances.

As the Sale of Goods Act does not govern product liability, the warranty period provided has no immediate impact on a producer's (or distributor's) product liability. However, should a defect occur within the warranty period, the courts may be prone to conclude that the product was most likely defective already at the time of sale.

1.5 How is a product 'defect' defined?

Under Danish law, a product will be considered defective when it does not provide the safety which a person is reasonably entitled to expect, taking all circumstances into account (as provided by the Directive).

The assessment of whether or not a product is defective is made at the time when the damage occurred. It is for claimant to prove that the product is defective. If a product suffers from an inherent well-known and unavoidable risk (eg, cigarettes) the product will not be considered defective in terms of product liability.

1.6 Who in the supply chain has obligations or duties for defective products? What obligations or duties do they owe and to whom?

Under Danish product liability law, the producer and distributor(s) may be liable towards any injured party for damage caused by defective products. Please refer to question 1.3 for an explanation of the producer's and distributor's liability.

1.7 By what means can a supplier limit their liability for defective products?

Under the Product Liability Act it is not possible to limit or eliminate product liability towards the injured party or any party subrogating in the injured party's claim, i.e. in case of personal injury or damage to consumer goods. As such, liability cannot be limited towards the injured party or a distributor who subrogates in the injured party's claim towards a prior distributor or the producer.

However, it is possible for producers and distributors to agree on the allocation of the risk *inter partes*, for example by agreeing that the distributor or producer must compensate the other party for any damages paid to the injured party.

In relation to damage to commercial goods, Danish courts will not accept limitation of liability for product damage if the supplier has shown gross negligence. Danish courts tend to be critical in their interpretation of limitation on liability using the *in dubio contra stipulatorem* rule of interpretation.

1.8 Are there particular goods or services which have specific obligations or duties attached to them?

Patients who suffer damage from drugs may claim damages from the Government according to the Act on Complaints and Damages in the Health Service. The Act gives the Government the right of recourse against the producer according to product liability rules, cf. section 53, subsection 1.

Existing acts on liability for nuclear plants, vaccine damage and damage occurring during military service, deal with product liability in these specific areas.

2. DEFENCES

2.1 What are the possible defences to a product liability claim?

Under the Product Liability Act it is for the claimant to prove that the product is defective, the scope of the damage and that there is causation between the defect and the damage. As such, the defendant can always claim that the claimant has not lifted the burden of proof in relation to any of these circumstances.

Under the general principles of tort law which apply in relation to damage to commercial goods, the defendant can also claim that the defect and/or damage was not due to any negligence on the part of the defendant.

Further, the producer will not be liable under the Product Liability Act or the general principles of tort if he can prove that he did not place the product into commerce, that the product was not produced or marketed for commercial purposes, that the defect is due to the product having to comply with mandatory statutory requirements, or that it was impossible to uncover the defect at the time the product was brought into commerce on the basis of the scientific and technical knowledge available at the time (*state of the art/development risk defence*).

Moreover, the producer is not liable if he can establish that the defect did not exist at the time the product was brought into commerce.

If a product suffers from an inherent well-known and unavoidable risk (such as cigarettes) the product will not be considered defective in terms of product liability and this may also serve as a defence for the producer.

It is not necessarily a defence for the producer that he has complied with regulatory or statutory requirements, but it will be a strong argument when assessing whether the product is defective.

The defendants can and will usually summon a third party to the same proceedings and make a recourse claim towards that third party if the third party caused the defect and acted negligently.

If the claimant has not acted in accordance with, for example, instructions for use or has otherwise acted inexpediently, the defendant can claim that the claimant has shown contributory negligence.

2.2 Is there a limit on the time in which proceedings may be brought (limitations and repose)?

According to the new Statute of Limitations that came into retroactive effect on 1 January 2008, the general time bar in all product liability cases is three years calculated from the date the injured party knew or ought to have known of the damage, defect and the relevant producer or supplier. The requirement is that the injured party must be able to identify his claim and the producer or supplier. The time bar is interrupted by the defendant acknowledging the claim and the scope of the damages or when litigation is commenced.

There is an absolute limitation period in addition to the general three-year time limit, mentioned above. The length of that period will depend both on the nature of the claim and on whether the claim is against a producer or supplier.

Claims against a producer within the scope of the Product Liability Act (personal injury and damage to consumer goods) will be subject to an absolute 10-year limitation period – in accordance with the Product Liability Directive – calculated from the date when the producer placed the product into commerce.

Claims against a producer relating to damage to commercial goods will in most cases also be subject to an absolute 10-year limitation period, but if the claim relates to pollution (air, water, soil etc.) or disturbances (noise, tremors etc.) the absolute limitation period will be 30 years.

Claims against a supplier will be subject to an absolute 10-year limitation period, but if the claim relates to pollution (air, water, soil etc.) or disturbances (noise, tremors etc.) or personal injury the absolute limitation period will be 30 years.

Furthermore the new Statute of Limitations introduces detailed provisions regarding additional one-year minimum time limits under certain circumstances, including in relation to recourse and criminal behaviour.

As a main rule the same time limit applicable between the claimant's claim against the defendant will be applicable to the defendant's recourse claim against a third party, but in some instances additional time limits of one year will apply.

In case the claimant interrupts the time bar by commencing litigation against the defendant or the defendant fulfils the claim or gives an extension of time, the defendant's recourse claim will, according to section 12 of the Statute of Limitations, be subject to a time limit of no less than one year calculated from the interruption/fulfilment/extension.

However, with regard to a supplier's recourse claim against the producer within the scope of the Product Liability Act, the absolute time limit of 10 years calculated from the date when the producer placed the product into commerce cannot be extended in this way.

3. LITIGATION OF PRODUCT LIABILITY DISPUTES

3.1 In which courts are product liability proceedings brought?

Product liability claims must be brought before the district court with jurisdiction over the claim, usually the district court at the defendant's place of residence. If the dispute is of a principle nature, the case can subsequently be referred to one of the two Danish high courts (Eastern and Western division). Only rarely will a dispute be considered sufficiently principled to warrant a referral to the High Court.

3.2 How are proceedings commenced?

Proceedings are commenced by submitting a writ of summons to the court, which will subsequently be served upon the defendant. By sending a copy of the writ directly to the defendant or its lawyer, claimant may avoid the process of having the writ served.

In addition to the writ of summons, the claimant must fill out a standard claims form which must be submitted alongside the writ.

3.3 Are disputed issues decided by a judge or a jury?

The trial is decided by a judge, never a jury.

3.4 Who has the burden of proof and to what standard?

Please refer to question 1.2 above. Under tort law the claimant must prove that the product is defective, that the producer has shown negligence, that a loss has been suffered and that there is causation between the defective product and the loss suffered.

No particular rules exist as to what standard of proof must be met by a claimant or defendant in order to sustain his burden of proof. The court is free to evaluate the evidence in the particular case and on the basis of this concrete evaluation the court will determine whether the burden of proof has been sustained or not.

Under the Directive it follows from Article 4 that the injured person must prove the damage, the defect and the causal relationship between defect and damage.

3.5 How is evidence given in proceedings and are witnesses cross-examined?

Evidence can be submitted freely by all parties until the end of the preparatory stage as fixed by the court. The court is free to assess the evidence submitted.

Witnesses that a party wishes to examine during the oral hearing must be listed before the end of the preparatory stage. As a main rule, the party who first listed a witness will be able to examine that witness first during the oral hearing. All witnesses can be cross-examined.

Evidence submitted or witnesses listed after the expiry of the preparatory stage may still be admitted if the court so decides. In its decision, the court will take into account whether the late submission was due to excusable circumstances and the importance of the particular piece of evidence or witness. Danish judges are generally pragmatic and will often allow crucial evidence to be submitted even though the preparatory stage has expired.

3.6 Are the parties able to rely on expert opinion evidence and, if so, are there any special rules or procedures for expert opinion evidence?

The parties can ask for a court-appointed expert to answer questions formulated by the parties and accepted by the court with regard to factual or scientific issues. The expert is appointed by the court and the rules on judges' impartiality apply to these experts as well. The expert will give written answers to the questions raised prior to the oral hearing, which may give rise to supplementary questions. The expert can be heard as a witness by all parties.

An expert opinion unilaterally obtained by a party before legal proceedings have been instituted usually cannot be admitted as evidence. Instead, the parties must rely on the court appointed expert.

Under certain circumstances the court may decide that the case must be heard by one judge with a legal background and two judges with a lay background, ie, experts within a particular field, to ensure that the court has sufficient technical knowledge.

3.7 Is pre-trial discovery permitted? If so, in what circumstances? If not, what other mechanisms, if any, are available for obtaining evidence from a party or a third party?

A party can request that the court allow evidence to be obtained prior to the trial, eg, in the form of an expert investigation or by requesting a party to submit certain documents or other evidence.

The party requesting the evidence to be submitted must specify exactly what documents etc, he requests and substantiate the reason for the request including the circumstances that the party intends to prove on the basis of the requested evidence. Further, the court must find it likely that the evidence requested will in fact be relevant in relation to the party's request and claim.

A party cannot make a widespread request for the other party to submit all evidence relating to certain circumstances but must specify exactly what documents etc, the party requests and why.

3.8 Is there liability for spoliation of evidence/a remedy for destruction of or failure to preserve evidence (most relevantly, the product)?

The court is free to assess the value of the evidence submitted by the parties and the consequences of a party failing to submit certain evidence.

If a party has failed to preserve (or destroyed) relevant evidence, this will most likely have an adverse impact on the court's assessment of that evidence, ie, the court will assume that the evidence would have been in favour of the other party.

3.9 Is interlocutory or interim relief available prior to the full trial of a proceeding? If so, in what circumstances?

There are two pre-action remedies available in the Danish civil legal system, arrest of property and injunctions.

As both of these remedies are used before the justification of the claimant's claim has been determined, the claimant generally has to provide security for a potential claim for damages caused by the pre-action remedy. Furthermore, both remedies must be followed by a confirmatory suit within 14 days.

Arrest of property can only be used to secure a pecuniary claim, and only when there is a specific reason for the use of an arrest, for example a risk that the other party might otherwise try to conceal his finances.

Injunctions are used to prohibit certain actions which were unlawful already before the injunction was issued. By issuing an injunction, the act will be subject to sanctions in the future.

For an injunction to be issued, the claimant must render probable that:

(i) the action he wishes to end is unlawful;
(ii) that the defendant intends to make this action; and
(iii) that the purpose of the injunction will be wasted

if the claimant has to pursue his claim before the courts.

The authority to issue both pre-action remedies lies with the enforcement court, and the claimant must file his application to this court.

3.10 Can the winning party recover its costs?

The costs of civil court proceedings in Denmark vary considerably depending on the size of the claim and the scope and complexity of the proceedings.

The claimant pays a court fee when filing the claim form and another fee prior to the hearing of the case. The fee is calculated as a percentage of the value of the case.

As part of the final decision, the court can choose to divide the costs between the parties or decide that one of the parties, usually the losing party, must compensate the other his or her expenses for the proceedings. However, the compensation awarded hardly ever measures up to the actual legal fees incurred during the trial.

3.11 What avenues of appeal are available?

All disputes must be initiated at the district courts. If the claim is of a principle nature, the district court may as an exception upon request from one or both parties refer the dispute to one of the two Danish High Courts (Eastern and Western division).

Judgments from the district courts can be appealed to the High Courts. If the claim has a financial value of no more than DKR10,000 (approx. £900) the judgment can only be appealed with permission from the Appeals Permission Board. The appeal term is four weeks from the date the judgment was announced.

The Appeals Permission Board will give permission to appeal if the case is a matter of general interest, or if there are other specific reasons for an appeal.

First instance judgments from the High Courts or judgments from the Maritime and Commercial Court in Copenhagen can be appealed to the Supreme Court. The appeal term is eight weeks from judgment.

Judgments from the High Court in appeal cases cannot be appealed to the Supreme Court, unless permission is given by the Appeals Permission board. The criteria for giving permission are the same as listed above.

4. CLASS ACTIONS/REPRESENTATIVE PROCEEDINGS

4.1 Is there a mechanism for class actions or representative proceedings, or coordinated proceedings for product liability claims? If so, what are the basic mechanics?

A group action system took effect on 1 January 2008.

The provisions regarding group actions are laid out in chapter 23a of the Administration of Justice Act.

There is an 'opt-in' as well as an 'opt-out' procedure available.

The 'opt-out' procedure will normally only be available in case the individual claims are so small (up to approx. DKR2,000) that filing individual claims would be disproportionate. A group action procedure based on the 'opt-out' procedure can only be brought by public authorities that have been granted statutory power to do so. As of yet only the Danish Consumer Ombudsman has been granted such a power.

Group action based on the 'opt-in' procedure can be brought by either an individual member of the group, private organisations/associations or public authorities with statutory power to do so (The Danish Consumer Ombudsman).

The first group action claim procedure before a Danish court was initiated in February 2008 and since then only a few new procedures have been instigated. It is, therefore, too early to tell whether group action claims will commonly be brought in Denmark.

5. LITIGATION FUNDING

5.1 Is litigation funding by third parties permissible in your country? If so, is it common?

Yes, third party funding of litigations is permitted in Denmark and is usually provided through product liability insurance policies. Third party funding outside the scope of insurance policies is uncommon.

5.2 Are contingency fee or 'no win no fee' arrangements permissible?

The Danish Bar and Law Society's ethical Code of Conduct prohibits lawyers from charging contingency fees. However, a 'no win no fee' arrangement is allowed, so long as the amount of the fees does not otherwise depend on the outcome of the case.

6. REMEDIES

6.1 What remedies are available to a party who successfully pursues a product liability claim?

Monetary compensation as well as declaratory relief is available.

The Danish Safety Technology Authority can subject to conditions laid out in the Act on Product Safety issue interim notices, including prohibition and recall notices regarding products that are deemed to be unsafe.

If the supplier or producer objects to such a notice, the Danish Safety Technology Authority will have to obtain an injunction awarded by a court to replace the interim notice.

In case of total loss of or damage to property, the replacement cost, less a deduction for depreciation due to age, wear and tear and reduced applicability, determines the amount of damages payable.

In case of partial loss or damage to property, damages payable equal the cost of repair. If repair does not fully restore the utilisation value or commercial value of the damage to property, compensation may also be claimed for the remaining loss.

In addition to the above the claimant can recover consequential damages.

In case of personal injury the Danish Act on Liabilities and Damages applies. In general, compensation for personal injury in Denmark is low when compared with other Western European countries and the US.

The following types of damages are recognised: medical expenses; temporary loss of earnings; pain and suffering; permanent injury; permanent loss of earning capacity; and compensation for loss of support.

6.2 How are damages calculated/are there limitations on available damages?

Damages are only awarded for an actually suffered loss. Please refer to question 6.1 for details.

6.3 Are punitive or exemplary damages available and in what circumstances?

No, punitive or exemplary damages are not available.

6.4 Is liability joint and several/how does apportionment of liability work, including where a partially responsible entity is not a party to the proceeding?

The apportionment of liability is decided by the court. Defendants may be jointly and severally liable if the circumstances so warrant.

If an entity who is partially responsible is not a party to the proceedings, the court may decide to dismiss the portion of claimant's claim which that entity was liable for. However, the court may also decide that the other defendant(s) must bear the entirety of claimant's claim even though a portion of that claim could in principle be allocated to another entity not part of the proceedings. If the defendants are able to subsequently direct a recourse claim against the third party entity, the court may be reluctant to dismiss claimant's claim relating to that entity.

7. ROLE OF REGULATORS

7.1 Please explain the role, responsibilities and powers of the regulators in your country which have jurisdiction over product liability issues.

The Product Liability Act is administered by the Ministry of Justice, which is responsible for implementing amendments to the Act.

The Danish Safety Technology Authority monitors that consumer products brought into commerce in Denmark are safe and comply with applicable statutory requirements. Subject to conditions laid out in the Product Safety Act, the Authority can issue interim notices, including prohibition and recall notices regarding products that are deemed to be unsafe.

If the supplier or producer objects to such a notice, the Danish Safety Technology Authority will have to obtain an injunction awarded by a court to replace the interim notice.

7.2 Are there any mandatory reporting requirements related to product safety issues?

If a producer or distributor becomes aware that a product is unsafe, the Safety Technology Authority must be notified immediately and the producer or distributor must inform of the measures taken to prevent any incidents.

A product will be considered unsafe if it poses an unacceptable risk to consumers when used under ordinary and expected circumstances.

7.3 Do the regulators have the power to:

(i) ban certain goods or services?

The Safety Technology Authority can prohibit a manufacturer or distributor from bringing unsafe products into commerce and can require that unsafe products are destroyed. Further, if a product is suspected of being unsafe, the Authority can temporarily ban products from being placed into commerce.

(ii) require a supplier to recall a product?

Yes, the Safety Technology Authority can require a supplier to immediately and effectively withdraw unsafe products from the market and/or recall the products from consumers who have purchased the products.

(iii) prescribe standards in respect of certain goods or services and require that the goods or services meet those standards?

The Safety Technology Authority monitors whether products are safe, including whether the products comply with statutory requirements. Further, the Authority can require producers or distributors to warn consumers of the risks posed by the products and to remedy the defects causing the risks.

While not mentioned specifically in the Product Safety Act, the broad scope of possible measures that the Authority can use must be interpreted as including the possibility of prescribing standards for the unsafe products to meet.

(iv) require production of information without court process?

Yes, the Safety Technology Authority can request producers and distributors to pass on relevant information and documentation necessary for the Authority to assess whether a product is safe or not. Further, the Authority can take out and investigate products.

If the supplier or producer fails to comply with the Safety Technology Authority's requests as explained in questions 7.1-7.3, they may be punished by fine. Further, the Authority is authorised to carry out the necessary precautions by itself, including issue warnings and withdraw or recall products, if the supplier or distributor does not comply with the Authority's requests.

8. VOLUNTARY CONDUCT

8.1 Are there regulations pertaining to the voluntary conduct of a product repair or recall by a supplier?

Under the Product Safety Act, distributors or producers must take all relevant precautions to ensure that products do not pose any risk to consumers, including the initiation of a voluntary repair or recall, if necessary. The Act specifies that distributors, producers and the Safety Technology Authority must cooperate to the highest extent possible to ensure the implementation of the relevant safety measures and distributors and producers are obligated to comply with the Authority's requests in this regard.

Under the Sale of Goods Act, distributors must offer to either repair or replace defective products if the defect occurred within the warranty period (two years for consumer goods, one year for commercial goods).

9. EMERGING ISSUES AND LAW REFORM

9.1 Are there important developing and emerging issues or trends in product liability law in your country?

N/A

9.2 Please describe any proposed important law reform in the area of product liability in your country.

An amendment to the Danish Administration of Justice Act concerning the taking of evidence is under way, which will reform the procedure for carrying out expert investigations as well as expand the parties' options for submitting their own expert reports.

While not directly related to product liability, this reform will have a significant impact on trials concerning product liability, where expert reports and investigations often are of crucial importance.

The amendment is still under way but is expected to be passed sometime in 2015.

10. REGULATORY WEBSITES/INFORMATION

10.1 Please identify any useful regulatory references relating to product liability law in your country, for example, a product safety/ consumer law website maintained by the main regulator.

The Safety Technology Authority's website: *www.sik.dk/global/english*

England & Wales

Hogan Lovells International LLP
Rod Freeman & Anthea Davies

The product liability regime in place in England and Wales is multi-layered, comprising national product liability laws based on contract and tort, in addition to the product liability regime in place across the European Union (EU), by virtue of their EU membership (via the United Kingdom).[1]

1. LIABILITY

1.1 What are the principal sources of law and regulation relating to product liability?

At the centre of the product liability systems of the countries that comprise the EU, of which the United Kingdom is a member, is the Product Liability Directive.[2] The Directive is the linchpin of the product liability system for EU member states and introduced a uniform system of no-fault liability for defective products. As detailed in the European Union chapter (p125), the Directive provides for liability on producers and suppliers based on the defective condition of the product, without any need to establish fault or negligence on the part of the producer or supplier. In England and Wales, the Consumer Protection Act 1987 (CPA) implements the Product Liability Directive.

Consumers injured by a defective product in England or Wales will potentially have various causes of action available to them and can choose whichever is most advantageous to them.

Furthermore, product liability issues may give rise to criminal proceedings against entities in the supply chain (notwithstanding the success or otherwise of any civil proceedings).

Civil liability

In England and Wales, a producer of a defective product may be exposed to claims for injury to persons or property damage pursuant to:

- statute (including EU legislation);
- contract; and
- tort.

Criminal offences

It is a criminal offence under the General Product Safety Regulations 2005 (which implements in England and Wales the EU General Product Safety

1 See the European Union chapter on p125 for details on the product liability regime in place across the European Union.
2 Directive 85/374/EEC.

Directive) to put an unsafe product on the market. The offence is punishable by a fine of up to £20,000, or a maximum prison term of 12 months, or both.

Failure to comply with some of the other requirements of the Regulations, such as producers' duties to provide information about product risks to consumers and to notify authorities about unsafe products, can incur penalties of up to £5,000, or a maximum prison term of three months, or both.

It is also a criminal offence by virtue of the CPA to breach sector-specific product safety regulations.

An example of the imposition of criminal penalties for product safety offences is shown in the case of *Staffordshire County Council v Terrance Howells*, in which an owner of a sunbed rental business was sentenced to 56 days' imprisonment for supplying a sunbed that caused a customer severe burns.[3]

In the case of fatal accidents caused by products, criminal liability may also arise under the Corporate Manslaughter and Corporate Homicide Act 1987, where the accident is caused by serious failures in the management of the company responsible for manufacturing the product or placing it on the market.

Liability can also arise under the Health and Safety at Work etc Act 1974, under which it is an offence to supply a product for use at work that is not safe.[4]

1.2 What is required to establish causation under the most common causes of action available?

Claims based on statute

The CPA, (implementing the terms of the Product Liability Directive) imposes liability to pay compensation for damage caused by a defect in a product, even if there is no proof of fault on the part of responsible party.

The system of liability under the CPA (in line with the provisions of the Product Liability Directive) does not exclude other rights an injured party might have under existing national laws.[5] Effectively, the Directive adds a system of no-fault liability to the existing systems of liability under the English common law. Accordingly, actions grounded on contract and tort may be brought concurrently with claims based on the statutory product liability provisions in England and Wales.

Claims based on contract

Consumers suffering personal injury or property damage as a result of the defect of a product may seek compensation in a contractual claim. Such a claim can be made where the product purchased does not comply with the applicable contractual terms (express or implied, oral or written), and as a result of that non-compliance, loss, damage or injury results.

Claims based on tort

A tort claim is predicated on the basis that a person has failed to act with

3 Unreported, 16 June 2006.
4 Health and Safety at Work etc Act 1974, s6.
5 Product Liability Directive, Article 13.

reasonable care and that failure has caused injury or damage. In order to succeed in a negligence claim, a claimant must establish that:

- a duty of care existed;
- the duty of care was breached;
- damage was suffered by the claimant; and
- the damage was caused by the defendant's breach of duty.

As noted above, parties seeking compensation for damage caused by defective products may elect to bring a claim under the CPA, a negligence claim, a contractual claim, or all three, if the conditions for each cause of action are made out.

1.3 Is strict liability available and, if so, in what circumstances?

Under the CPA, it is not necessary for there to have been any fault on the part of the producer in order to succeed in a claim. Arguably, the conduct of the producer is not relevant to the question of whether the product was defective.[6]

1.4 Are guarantees or warranties as to quality implied by law?

In the absence of express contractual terms to the contrary, the Sale of Goods Act 1979 (SGA) implies the following terms into contracts for the sale of goods:

- goods are of satisfactory quality and reasonably fit for their purpose; and
- goods correspond with any description or sample.[7]

When determining whether goods are of satisfactory quality and reasonably fit for purpose, factors such as the state, condition and fitness for all purposes for which goods of that kind are commonly supplied, appearance/finish, freedom from minor defects, safety and durability of the product may be considered.[8]

If a product defect occurs within six months of delivery, the consumer will benefit from the presumption in section 48A(3) of the SGA, that the goods were inherently defective at the time of delivery, in order to obtain a remedy. However, if the defect occurs after the initial six months from delivery, it will fall to the consumer to prove that the goods were defective at the time of delivery in order to obtain a remedy. These provisions implement the EU Consumer Guarantees Directive 99/44/EC.

Under section 6 of the Unfair Contract Terms Act 1977 (UCTA), a seller cannot exclude or restrict liability for breach of implied terms under the Sale of Goods Act 1979.

1.5 How is a product 'defect' defined?

'Product' is defined broadly in the CPA, meaning any goods or electricity, and includes a product that is comprised in another product, whether as a component or as a raw material.[9]

6 See *A & Others v. National Blood Authority* [2001] 3 All ER 289, though cf *Sam Bogle & Others v. McDonalds Restaurants Ltd.* [2002] All ER (D) 436 (Mar), in which the court took into account steps taken by the defendant (in training its staff how to serve safely hot coffee and tea to customers) when considering whether the products were defective.
7 Sale of Goods Act 1979, s13, s14.
8 Sale of Goods Act 1979, ss14 (2).
9 Consumer Protection Act 1987, s1(2).

A product is considered to be defective if in all the circumstances 'the safety of the product is not such as persons generally are entitled to expect'. Circumstances to be taken into account include:

- the manner in which, and purposes for which, the product has been marketed, its get-up, the use of any mark in relation to the product and any instructions for, or warnings with respect to, doing or refraining from doing anything with or in relation to the product;
- what might reasonably be expected to be done with or in relation to the product; and
- the time when the product was supplied by its producer to another.[10]

A product will not be considered defective simply because a safer product is subsequently put into circulation.[11]

1.6 Who in the supply chain has obligations or duties for defective products? What obligations or duties do they owe and to whom?

Under the CPA (per the regime imposed by the Product Liability Directive), liability for defective products falls on:

- the producer;
- the first importer into the EU (in order to ensure that there will always be a defendant within the EU who can be held liable for a defective product);
- an 'own brander' (ie, someone who holds himself out as a manufacturer by including his own name or trademark on the product); and
- a 'downstream supplier' (such as the retailer, wholesaler, or supplier), but only if it fails to identify the manufacturer, the own brander, or the first importer, within a reasonable time.[12]

Under the CPA, if a defective product sold in the UK was manufactured by a producer in another EU member state, the affected consumer may sue the producer for damages suffered as a result. Where the producer is based outside the EU, the consumer may sue the importer into the EU. Where neither the producer nor the importer into the EU can be identified, each party in the supply chain may be treated by the affected consumer as the producer, and therefore liable for damage caused by defects, unless the party informs the consumer within a reasonable time of the identity of the producer or of the person who supplied the party with the product.[13]

The claimant may also elect to sue a producer based outside the EU. The producer is primarily liable for defects in a product and non-EU producers could fall within the jurisdiction of the English courts even if the product was not sold or advertised in England and Wales, provided the damage was sustained in England and Wales.

However, bringing a lawsuit against a non-EU producer would be less straightforward procedurally for a claimant. It may also be more difficult for the claimant to enforce any judgment issued by the English courts against a non-EU producer. For this reason injured parties may prefer to sue an EU-

10 Consumer Protection Act 1987, s3.
11 Consumer Protection Act 1987, s3(2).
12 Consumer Protection Act 1987, s2(2), s2(3).
13 Consumer Protection Act 1987, s2.

based importer or supplier, if they are a viable target for the claim.

1.7 By what means can a supplier limit their liability for defective products?

A supplier can avoid being held liable under the Product Liability Directive's no-fault liability regime if the supplier notifies the injured person of the identity of the producer or the upstream supplier. The European Court of Justice has held that it is unlawful for the national laws implementing the Directive to provide to the contrary.[14]

A supplier may purport to exclude liability through contractual provisions, however, whether such exclusions will be enforceable will be determined with reference to UCTA, which may render unenforceable contractual terms which purport to exclude or restrict liability for:

- personal injury or death;
- pre-contractual representations;
- loss or damage from negligence (unless the term satisfies the reasonableness test in section 11 UCTA);
- breach or non-performance of contract (unless the term satisfies the reasonableness test in section 11 UCTA).

Similarly, parties in the supply chain have contractual freedom to negotiate the terms of any indemnities and limitations of liability as between the other entities in the supply chain. However, in the event of a dispute, whether such terms are effective will be determined with reference to UCTA.

2. DEFENCES

2.1 What are the possible defences to a product liability claim?

Consistent with the Product Liability Directive, section 4 of the CPA provides a number of defences to a person against whom a product liability claim is brought:

- the defect is attributable to compliance with any requirement imposed by or under any enactment or with any (European) Community obligation;
- the product was not supplied by the person;
- the product was not supplied in the course of the person's business or the Act does not apply to them, or it only applied by virtue of things done otherwise than with a view to profit;
- the defect did not exist when the product was put into circulation;
- the state of scientific and technical knowledge at the time the product was put into circulation was not such that the producer of products of the same description as the product in question might be expected to have discovered the defect if it existed in their products while under their control (the 'development risks' defence).

In addition, a defence will be available to a manufacturer of a component, where the defect in the final product is attributable to the design of the product in which the component was fitted, and was not due to the component itself.

14 Case C-52/00 *Commission v. France European Court of Justice* [2002].

The European Court of Justice considered the scope of the development risks defence in *Commission v United Kingdom.*[15] The Court ruled that to rely on this defence a producer must prove that the objective state of scientific and technical knowledge, including the most advanced level of such knowledge, at the time when the product in question was put into circulation, was not such as to enable the existence of the defect to be discovered. However, that knowledge must have been 'accessible' at the time the product was put into circulation.

Liability may be reduced or avoided if the damage is found to be caused by both a defect in the product and by the fault of the injured party, or of any person for whom the injured party is responsible.

2.2 Is there a limit on the time in which proceedings may be brought (limitations and repose)?

The applicable limitation period depends on the cause of action upon which any claim is based.

Claims which allege breach of contact must be commenced within six years from the breach of the contract.[16] Claims under tort are in some cases also subject to limitation period of six years, however, the time runs from the date the damage is suffered.[17] The time limit for actions for damages for negligence may be extended in circumstances where facts relevant to the claim were not known by the claimant at the date the cause of action accrued, by three years from the date that the claimant had the requisite knowledge.[18]

Claims in tort which resulted in personal injury or death have a limitation period of three years from the date of accrual of the action or the date of the claimant's knowledge of damage (whichever is the latter). The court does have discretion to extend this limitation period.[19]

Actions commenced in respect of defective products under the CPA are subject to a three-year limitation period (usually from the date of injury), and are subject to a 'long-stop' 10-year limitation period. Consistent with the terms of the Product Liability Directive, the rights conferred by the CPA are extinguished 10 years from the date on which the product which caused the alleged damage was put into circulation, if proceedings are not commenced within that time.[20]

3. LITIGATION OF PRODUCT LIABILITY DISPUTES

3.1 In which courts are product liability proceedings brought?

Product liability claims are civil claims, and are therefore dealt with separately from criminal prosecutions in England and Wales.

15 [1997] All ER (EC) 481.

16 The six-year limitation period only applies to simple contracts. If the claim concerns the breach of a term in a deed, the limitation period is 12 years from the breach: Limitation Act 1980, s8(1).

17 Limitation Act 1980, s2.

18 Limitation Act 1980, s14A.

19 Limitation Act 1980, s11, s33.

20 Limitation Act 1980, s11A. A product is put into circulation when it is taken out of the manufacturing process operated by the producer and enters a marketing process in the form in which it is offered to the public: Case C-127/04 *O'Byrne v Aventis Pasteur* MSD [2005].

Product liability claims are generally heard in the Queen's Bench Division of the High Court. However, where the value of the claim is £25,000 or less (or less than £50,000 in personal injury claims), the matter can be determined in the county court. Both the High Court and the county court are first instance trial courts, but the High Court is considered more suitable for claims of high value, complexity or importance.

Criminal prosecutions for breaches of product safety regulations are heard at first instance in either a magistrate's court or the Crown Court.

3.2 How are proceedings commenced?

The Civil Procedure Rules set down the procedures for the conduct of civil litigation in England and Wales.[21]

While a claim is officially commenced in the courts by the filing and serving of the claim form on the defendant, there are a number of steps which claimants must adhere to prior to officially commencing court proceedings, in order to avoid sanctions or costs penalties.

The Pre-action Protocols require a claimant to send a detailed pre-action letter of claim specifying the allegations against the defendant and providing the defendant an opportunity to investigate those allegations. For personal injury claims, in most cases the defendant, having been given a three-month period in which to investigate the allegations, must then respond either accepting or denying liability (and outlining the basis for their denial of liability). If the claimant receives no response from the defendant, or if liability is denied, the claimant may then file and serve a notice of claim, officially commencing court proceedings. The defendant then has a period of 14 days (subject to an extension in certain circumstances) in which to file and serve their defence, responding to each of the allegations raised in the notice of claim.

3.3 Are disputed issues decided by a judge or a jury?

Civil cases in England and Wales are not generally determined by juries (exceptions are claims for defamation, fraud, malicious prosecution and false imprisonment).

Product liability claims are determined solely by a judge at trial (unless damages are sought, for instance, for fraud).

3.4 Who has the burden of proof and to what standard?

The burden of proof in product liability claims rests on the injured party. The standard of proof in civil product liability claims is the balance of probabilities, ie, 'more likely than not'. The claimant needs to establish that there was a breach of contract or of the (tortious or statutory) duty of care, that damage was suffered, and that the damage was caused by the defect.

Notwithstanding the no-fault liability regime applying to product liability claims, it is insufficient for the claimant to show merely that the product failed in an unsafe manner contrary to his or her expectations and caused

21 Available at *www.justice.gov.uk/courts/procedure-rules/civil/rules*

injury. The claimant must prove that the product was defective.[22]

3.5 How is evidence given in proceedings and are witnesses cross-examined?

Witness evidence is presented in the form of witness statements, which are filed and provided to parties prior to the hearing of the matter. This witness statement is considered the witness' evidence-in-chief.

Witnesses (both fact and expert) whose evidence is filed in proceedings may be required to attend court to give evidence. In the normal course of events, this will comprise the witness confirming the content of their witness statement for the court and then undergoing cross-examination by counsel for the party who did not file the witness statement on behalf of the witness.

3.6 Are the parties able to rely on expert opinion evidence and, if so, are there any special rules or procedures for expert opinion evidence?

In product liability cases in England and Wales, expert evidence may be submitted by the parties in accordance with Part 35 of the Civil Procedure Rules and Practice Direction 35, which each set out detailed rules concerning the appointment, conduct and objectives of experts giving evidence in civil proceedings. Permission must be sought from the court for expert evidence to be heard or put into evidence, however, the court will not itself appoint an expert to provide an opinion.

The purpose of appointing an expert is to assist the court in understanding the subject matter and issues to be considered in a case, but which lie outside the court's knowledge. An expert's primary duty is to the court and this duty overrides any obligations to the party who engaged them or by whom they are paid. Although each party may appoint an expert to provide an opinion to the court, the experts' evidence must be objective and unbiased, and their opinions must be limited to their area of expertise. Experts are required to make a declaration acknowledging that they understand their duty to give their evidence impartially.

The court has discretion to order that the experts appointed by the parties confer to narrow the issues in dispute, and the parties are encouraged to arrange for this without the court's intervention. Further, the court may, where appropriate, order that the parties' experts give their evidence concurrently to assist the court in understanding and clarifying any differences in opinion.

3.7 Is pre-trial discovery permitted? If so, in what circumstances? If not, what other mechanisms, if any, are available for obtaining evidence from a party or a third party?

All parties to civil proceedings in England and Wales must give disclosure, as means by which the parties formally state which documents or classes of documents relevant to the proceedings there are or have been. Disclosure is

22 See *Richardson v LRC Products* [2000] Lloyd's Rep. Med. 280; *Foster v Biosil* (2001) 59 B.M.L.R. 178, Central London County Court, 18 April 2000.

controlled by the court and the usual approach adopted by the court is an order for 'standard disclosure' (although judges do have discretion as to the extent of disclosure they will order in different types of cases).

Standard disclosure requires each party to disclose the documents:

- on which they rely;
- which adversely affect their case or another party's case;
- which support another party's case; and
- which they are required to disclose by a relevant practice direction.

When making a disclosure order, judges must have in mind the overriding objective of the Civil Procedure Rules to deal with cases justly and at proportionate cost. Accordingly, efforts should be made to limit disclosure to what is necessary to deal with the case justly.

Disclosure is usually effected by the parties' exchanging lists of documents in their possession, and documents not in their possession, but which they have a right to obtain, inspect, or take copies of. The parties must then produce these documents for inspection by the opposing party (which will include the exchange of copies of the documents disclosed). Parties have the right to inspect and/or take copies of all documents disclosed, subject to certain exceptions (such as privileged documents, which must be disclosed, but may not be inspected).

Parties can seek orders for specific disclosure of documents under the Civil Procedure Rules and can apply to challenge orders for disclosure. Disputes regarding disclosure are determined by the court in accordance with Part 31 of the Civil Procedure Rules and associated practice directions. Overseas parties to proceedings in England and Wales must also comply with the duty of disclosure.

The UK is a party to the Hague Convention on the Taking of Evidence Abroad in Civil or Commercial Matters. Accordingly, parties to litigation in England and Wales may obtain evidence from unwilling witnesses in other jurisdictions by seeking a letter of request from the English court, requesting the court in the other jurisdiction to take evidence and transmit that evidence to the English court.[23]

3.8 Is there liability for spoliation of evidence/a remedy for destruction of or failure to preserve evidence (most relevantly, the product)?

In the event a document, which would have been subject to disclosure, has been destroyed, the consequences, if any, will depend on the status of the proceedings when the document was destroyed.

In the normal and proper course of business, it is usual for companies to routinely destroy documents, usually in accordance with a document retention policy.

In circumstances where no litigation has been commenced or contemplated, the question to be asked is whether there was an attempt by the company to pervert the course of justice.[24]

23 If the overseas witness is willing to give evidence there are no particular procedural issues.

24 *Douglas v Hello* (No 3) [2003] EWHC 55 (Ch) (adopting *British American Tobacco Australia Services Ltd v Cowell and McCabe* [2002] VSCA 197).

However, where a claim has been commenced, all potentially relevant documents should have been preserved (and where appropriate, the disposal of documents in accordance with a document retention policy, suspended). Indeed, solicitors are required to inform clients on document preservation upon receipt of instructions.[25] In the event a document is destroyed at this stage, it is open to the Court to make adverse inferences against the party who destroyed the documents.

After an order for disclosure has been made, the parties are under an express obligation to preserve documents. In the event disclosable documents are destroyed (whether intentionally or unintentionally) after such an order is made, an application for the proceedings to be struck out may be made to the court. In a strike out application, the court will consider whether a fair trial can still take place, despite the destruction of the documents. If it is the case that a court determines the matter may proceed, it may still be possible that the party who destroyed the documents will be subject to adverse inferences and sanctions (including costs implications).

3.9 Is interlocutory or interim relief available prior to the full trial of a proceeding? If so, in what circumstances?

As for most civil matters, interlocutory or interim relief is available to parties prior to the final determination of the claim. Part 25 of the Civil Procedure Rules refers to an extensive (although non-exhaustive) list of interim remedies, including:

- interim injunctions;
- orders for the detention, custody, preservation or inspection of relevant property;
- order to deliver up goods;
- freezing injunctions.

The court may grant such relief upon consideration of the following factors:

- whether there is a serious question to be determined;
- whether the balance of convenience favours granting the interim relief claimed (including a consideration as to whether damages would be an adequate remedy to compensate for the loss alleged).

3.10 Can the winning party recover its costs?

The general rule in civil litigation in England and Wales is that the successful party may recover its reasonable costs as against the unsuccessful party/ parties. This general rule is subject to the wide discretion granted to the court, which may make alternative costs orders taking into consideration the conduct of the parties, compliance with the Civil Procedure Rules and Pre-action Protocols, and the efficiency (or more likely, the lack thereof) with which the matter was conducted.

In reality, even the most favourable costs order will usually only result in a portion of the costs actually incurred by a successful party in pursuing or defending an action being recovered.

25 See Practice Direction 31B.7

3.11 What avenues of appeal are available?

For civil causes of action, appeal from first instance decisions in the county court and the High Court is available to the Court of Appeal on points of law only. The Court of Appeal does not re-hear the evidence or, generally, admit new evidence, but may affirm, vary or reverse the lower court's decision.

The highest court in the UK is the Supreme Court (formerly the House of Lords), which hears appeals from the Court of Appeal. Again, the Supreme Court will not re-try the civil case, but will only consider appeals on points of law.

Appeals against criminal offences are to the Criminal Division of the Court of Appeal, and from the Court of Appeal to the Supreme Court.

4. CLASS ACTIONS/REPRESENTATIVE PROCEEDINGS

4.1 Is there a mechanism for class actions or representative proceedings, or coordinated proceedings for product liability claims? If so, what are the basic mechanics?

Claims concerning product liability are particularly susceptible to multi-party actions, as a defective product may cause injury or property damage in multiple instances.

Part 19 of the Civil Procedure Rules makes provision for group litigation in England and Wales in the form of a 'group litigation order' (GLO). The court has discretion to implement a GLO where there are or are likely to be a number of claims giving rise to common or related issues of fact or law.

Claims for which a GLO is in place are managed as a group by the court. The GLO itself ought to make provision for the establishment of a group register for all claims managed under the GLO and specify the related issues which will identify the claims to be managed under the GLO.

Where a judgment or order is made in respect of one of the claims under the GLO, it will be binding on all other parties in all claims under the GLO (subject to the court ordering otherwise). A party may appeal the order or judgment, on certain conditions, or apply for an order that it is not binding on them.

Disclosure of any document relating to the GLO in one claim is considered disclosure of that document to all parties to all claims subject to the GLO, unless the court orders otherwise.

5. LITIGATION FUNDING

5.1 Is litigation funding by third parties permissible in your country? If so, is it common?

Litigation funding by third party funders is available to claimants in England and Wales, however, the market is still developing. Nevertheless, there has been an increasing trend in recent years towards litigation funding, resulting in increased self-regulation in efforts to address concerns as to the appropriate conduct of such arrangements and addressing potential ethical issues (see the Code of Conduct for Litigation Funders[26]).

26 Available at *http://associationoflitigationfunders.com/wp-content/uploads/2014/02/Code-of-conduct-Jan-2014-Final-PDFv2-2.pdf*

5.2 Are contingency fee or 'no win no fee' arrangements permissible?

Arrangements allowing conditional fees whereby a client pays differing amounts for legal services, depending on the eventual success or loss of the case, are permissible, albeit highly regulated in England and Wales.[27] Such arrangements usually provide that in the event that the client succeeds in the matter, they will pay all fees and expenses, including a conditional or success fee (if provided for in the agreement). Conversely, if the client is unsuccessful, they are not liable to pay the fees and expenses, which are subject to the agreement.

In 2013, the 'Jackson reforms' came in effect by way of the Legal Aid, Sentencing and Punishment of Offenders Act 2012. The reforms are aimed at producing a fairer and less expensive costs regime in England and Wales. Relevantly to contingency fee arrangements, the reforms provide:

- contingency fee agreements should be lawful across all types of civil litigation – these will be known as 'damages based agreements' (DBAs); and
- the success/conditional fee and/or the premium for 'after the event' insurance is no longer recoverable from an unsuccessful party. The successful party is liable to bear any such fees.

6. REMEDIES

6.1 What remedies are available to a party who successfully pursues a product liability claim?

In England and Wales, a consumer can generally recover damages for personal injury or damage to property other than to the product itself, in addition to compensation for pain and suffering. An award of damages is intended to compensate the consumer for the loss or damage sustained, and not to punish the defendant.

6.2 How are damages calculated/are there limitations on available damages?

The damages recoverable in a successful product liability claim will depend on the cause of action.

Under the CPA, a producer of a defective product is liable for damage caused by death or personal injury. The producer is also liable for damage to property (other than damage to the product itself) if the defective product was a consumer product and the injured party was using the product as a consumer.

In claims arising under contract or negligence claims, the award of damages will be calculated with a view to restoring the consumer to the position they would have been in had the breach of contract or breach of duty not occurred.

Generally, 'pure economic loss' is not recoverable in claims in tort or under the CPA.

27 For example, a CFA entered into on or after 1 April 2013 must comply with section 58 and 58A of the Courts and Legal Services Act 1990 (as amended by section 44 of the Legal Aid, Sentencing and Punishment of Offenders Act 2012), the SRA Code of Conduct 2011 and the Civil Procedure Rules.

6.3 Are punitive or exemplary damages available and in what circumstances?

As damages in a product liability claim are calculated on a compensatory basis and are not intended to punish the defendant, the awarding of punitive or exemplary damages by a court is possible, but rare. Such damages will only be awarded pursuant to the court's discretion, and in limited circumstances, such as where the defendant has deliberately engaged in oppressive conduct. In practice, punitive or exemplary damages are rarely awarded in product liability cases.

6.4 Is liability joint and several/how does apportionment of liability work, including where a partially responsible entity is not a party to the proceeding?

In practice, producers bear the heaviest responsibility, however, liability is by no means restricted to producers. The producer, importer and each party in the supply chain who could potentially be held liable are jointly and severally liable under the CPA.[28]

7. ROLE OF REGULATORS

7.1 Please explain the role, responsibilities and powers of the regulators in your country which have jurisdiction over product liability issues.

There is no single institution with responsibility for enforcing product safety requirements in England and Wales. The responsibility for monitoring compliance with, and enforcing, safety laws falls to local authorities, which administer these duties through their Trading Standards departments.

Particular product sectors have their own enforcement agencies, for example, the Medicines and Healthcare products Regulatory Agency (MHRA) and the Driver and Vehicle Standards Agency.

The UK's market surveillance activities under the European product safety regime are carried out by these bodies, co-ordinated by the Department of Business Innovation and Skills (BIS). The general approach adopted is that of 'no inspection without reason': market surveillance should be targeted against deliberate non-compliance, to avoid wasting resources on routine inspections and unnecessarily burdening compliant businesses.

7.2 Are there any mandatory reporting requirements related to product safety issues?

In the case of consumer products not otherwise covered by sector-specific safety legislation, producers and suppliers must notify Trading Standards when they become aware that a consumer product that they have placed on the market, or have supplied, is, or may be unsafe.[29] Notification using the EU Rapid Alert System for Non-food Consumer Products (RAPEX) electronic business application form suffices to fulfil this requirement, although a more

28 Consumer Protection Act 1987, s2(5).

29 General Product Safety Regulations 2005, implementing Directive 2001/95/EC on general product safety (GPSD).

direct approach with the relevant Trading Standards office is usually more prudent for larger businesses.

7.3 Do the regulators have the power to:
(i) ban certain goods or services?
(ii) require a supplier to recall a product?
(iii) prescribe standards in respect of certain goods or services and require that the goods or services meet those standards?
(iv) require production of information without court process?
If so, broadly explain the circumstances in which the regulator can exercise the power and any penalties that apply if a supplier fails to comply.

Trading Standards may initiate an investigation of potentially unsafe products following complaints from the public or a referral from another agency.

The authorities will generally seek voluntary compliance from businesses in the first instance, but a range of enforcement powers are available to Trading Standards. These include requiring warnings about product risks to be published; seizing products; suspending the supply of products in the market; requiring a product recall to be conducted; and bringing criminal prosecutions. Prosecutions are rare, but can result in financial penalties, or imprisonment in the most serious cases.

8. VOLUNTARY CONDUCT

8.1 Are there regulations pertaining to the voluntary conduct of a product repair or recall by a supplier?

While there are no prescriptive regulatory requirements governing the conduct of voluntary corrective action undertaken by suppliers in England and Wales, suppliers are, of course, required to notify the relevant Trading Standards when they become aware that a consumer product that they have placed on the market, or have supplied, is, or may be unsafe (see above). Nevertheless, it is prudent for suppliers to take a collaborative approach with Trading Standards and keep them informed of the extent of corrective actions undertaken in respect of consumer goods.

9. EMERGING ISSUES AND LAW REFORM

9.1 Are there important developing and emerging issues or trends in product liability law in your country?

As regulatory authorities in England and Wales (as for the rest of Europe) take a more interventionist approach in relation to product safety, liability risks for product manufacturers are expanding beyond traditional civil liability claims. There have been a number of high-profile instances of major international brands underestimating the risks in the European regulatory regime, and suffering significant regulatory action and damaging publicity as a result.

The prevalence of claims against pharmaceutical companies and medical device manufacturers continues, with multi-jurisdictional claims being a common feature. However, product liability issues also affect other product sectors including motor vehicles, electrical and electronic products, machinery, toys, food and cosmetics. The interplay between the regulatory regime and the liability regime in England and Wales, (and the rest of Europe), should not be underestimated. It is imperative that a proper approach to defending claims is taken – one which is based on a clear understanding of the unique regulatory regime in Europe, and the additional layer of risk that it brings.

Asbestos litigation is continuing to develop as the reach of health implications of prior decades of asbestos use in the UK continues to grow.[30]

Firms specialising in representing plaintiffs have signalled that significant recent changes to litigation funding in England and Wales threaten the viability of their practices. However, the market is also witnessing the entrance of sophisticated plaintiff law firms from the United States and Australia, which are expected to have a long-term impact on liability litigation and the risks faced by companies in the UK.

Supply-chain disputes arising out of product safety and quality issues are on the rise, including disputes over who will pay for the costs of expensive product recalls, as difficult market conditions lend an incentive to companies to seek redress for quality problems from other parties.

9.2 Please describe any proposed important law reform in the area of product liability in your country.

In February 2013 the European Commission adopted proposals for a revision of EU product regulation which, when implemented, will impact all operators involved in the supply of products in the EU, including the UK. The package includes proposals for a new Regulation on consumer product safety that would replace the GPSD, and a new Regulation to strengthen market surveillance of products. The new Regulations are expected to be adopted as early as 2015. Once adopted, they will be directly applicable in England and Wales, and will impose additional obligations on manufacturers, importers and retailers.

New consumer laws were enacted in England and Wales, including the Consumer Contracts (Information, Cancellation and Additional Charges) Regulations 2013, which implements the new EU Consumer Rights Directive and amends the existing law on cancellation of consumer contracts.[31]

Against this background UK lawmakers published the Consumer Rights Bill, which will overhaul existing consumer protection legislation. The Bill seeks to consolidate the rules on supply of goods and services – currently set out in eight different pieces of legislation – into a single Act. The Bill is expected to enter into force in June 2014.

30 See Hogan Lovells' International Asbestos Newsletter, *www.hoganlovells.com/newsmedia/newspubs/List.aspx?PublicationTypes=ec280163-d558-4364-88f8-7c4c3cf6fe0a.*
31 Directive 2011/83/EU.

10. REGULATORY WEBSITES/INFORMATION

10.1 Please identify any useful regulatory references relating to product liability law in your country, for example, a product safety/ consumer law website maintained by the main regulator.

- BIS – *https://www.gov.uk/government/organisations/department-for-business-innovation-skills*
- Trading Standards – *www.tradingstandards.gov.uk/*
- Hogan Lovell's International Product Liability Review – *www.hoganlovells.com/PracticeAreas/areas_pubs.aspx?op=&firmService=385*

European Union

Hogan Lovells International LLP
Rod Freeman & Anthea Davies

INTRODUCTION TO PRODUCT LIABILITY LAW IN THE EUROPEAN UNION

The European Union is a supranational political body made up of individual nations, referred to as member states. Each member state has and creates its own national law, but is also subject to law created at a European Union level.

At the centre of the product liability systems of the countries that comprise the European Union is Directive 85/374/EEC of 25 July 1985 on the approximation of the laws, regulations and administrative provisions of the member states concerning liability for defective products[1] (Product Liability Directive or Directive). It introduced into the European Union a uniform system of 'no fault' liability for defective products.

The Product Liability Directive does not prescribe an exclusive system of product liability in the member states of the European Union. Its provisions operate alongside other systems of liability in effect in each nation, especially those based on contract and tort.

The European framework

The European Union has its origins in a series of treaties leading to the Treaty of Rome, signed in 1957, under which the European Economic Community was formed. That treaty, and others that have followed, provide the basis of the powers of the European institutions to legislate and regulate, and defines the limits of those powers.

With the accession of 10 new member states in 2004, a further two new member states in 2007 and an additional member state in 2013, the European Union now comprises 28 countries. Prior to 2004, the members were: the Republic of Ireland, the United Kingdom, Sweden, Finland, Denmark, the Netherlands, Belgium, Luxembourg, Germany, France, Spain, Portugal, Austria, Italy and Greece. The new members that joined in May 2004 were Estonia, Latvia, Lithuania, Poland, the Czech Republic, Slovakia, Hungary, Slovenia, Cyprus and Malta. The new members that joined in January 2007 were Bulgaria and Romania, with Croatia joining in 2013.

The European Union operates through three central institutions:

- the European Commission, with primary responsibility for

1 OJ L 210, 7.8.1985. Subsequently amended by Council Directive 1999/34/EC of the European Parliament and of the Council of 10 May 1999 amending Council Directive 85/374/EEC on the approximation of the laws, regulations and administrative provisions of the member states concerning liability for defective products [1999] OJ L141, 4.6.1999.

administering the Union, and promoting legislation;
- the European Parliament, the primary legislative body; and
- the Court of Justice of the European Union, with ultimate responsibility for interpreting EU legislation.

European Community legislation takes a number of forms, the most important of which, for present purposes, are directives. A directive is not binding on individuals in the European Union, but is binding on the member states, requiring them to give effect to its provisions. As a general rule, directives become binding on individuals when they are implemented by the individual member states. For example, the Product Liability Directive was adopted by the European Council in 1985, but it did not become part of the law of the United Kingdom until 1987 with the introduction of that nation's Consumer Protection Act. It did not become part of domestic law of France until 1998, many years beyond the deadline specified in the Directive for implementation.

1. LIABILITY

1.1 What are the principal sources of law and regulation relating to product liability?

In 1985, after almost a decade of controversy and debate, the European institutions adopted the Product Liability Directive, which introduced into the EU (in many countries for the first time) a system of no-fault liability for defective products. That is, it provides for liability on producers and suppliers based on the defective condition of the product without any need to establish fault or negligence on the part of the producer or supplier.

The Product Liability Directive establishes a non-exclusive system of liability. Article 13 provides that the system of liability established under the Directive does not exclude other rights an injured person might have under existing national laws, specifically under the law of 'contractual or non-contractual liability' or a 'special liability system' existing at the time the Directive was adopted. In effect, this means that the Directive adds a system of no fault liability to the existing systems of liability under national laws of contract and tort. In most EU member states, therefore, consumers injured by defective products will potentially have various causes of action available to them, and can choose whichever is most advantageous to them. Those options will differ from country to country.

In most (but not all) member states, the no fault liability regime established under the Product Liability Directive is considered to be more favourable to claimants than the regimes under established principles of contract or tort. Thus, the Directive is increasingly becoming the main system of liability for product liability claims in the EU. For these reasons, the rest of this chapter will focus on the provisions of the Directive.

The system of liability under the Directive is available to persons injured by defective products across the entire European Union. It sets a baseline for liability in the member states, guaranteeing a minimum level of protection to consumers in the EU. Thus, the Directive is the starting point for understanding the nature of the claims to which manufacturers and suppliers are exposed in the EU for product liability risks, and for understanding the defences that may be available in answer to such claims.

1.2 What is required to establish causation under the most common causes of action available?

The burden of proof rests on the claimant to establish the primary elements of liability, namely the damage, the defect, and the causal relationship between defect and damage.[2]

The national courts of member states are bound by the provisions of the Directive that make it clear that the claimant bears the burden of proof.[3]

The extent of the duty differs as between EU member states with some national courts prepared to find that the mere fact of the product failing was evidence of the product being defective. Other national courts may be more inclined to require the claimant to show the cause of the product failure.

Similarly, questions concerning the standard of proof to be applied, and the evidentiary rules that are applicable in particular cases are matters of procedure that are not covered by the Directive, but will be governed by the individual national systems in each member state.

1.3 Are guarantees or warranties as to quality implied by law?

While the Product Liability Directive itself does not imply guarantees or warranties as to the quality of a product, Directive 99/44/EC of 25 May 1999 on certain aspects of the sale of consumer goods and associated guarantees[4] (Consumer Guarantees Directive) operates to impose a minimum level of protection for consumers across the EU.

The Consumer Guarantees Directive applies to 'consumer goods', defined as any tangible moveable property (excluding electricity, goods sold by way of execution or otherwise by authority of law, and water/gas where they are not put up for sale in a limited volume or set quantity).

The meaning and effect of this Directive has been the source of much confusion for product manufacturers seeking to market their products in the EU. It is also subject to inconstant implementation, interpretation and enforcement across the member states, so care needs to be taken when developing strategies and procedures for dealing with consumer guarantee issues in Europe.

The compulsory guarantees imposed by the Consumer Guarantees Directive require that a product conforms to the contract of sale. To be in conformity with the contract of sale, the product must:

- comply with the description given by the seller and possess the qualities of the product which the seller has held out to the consumer as a sample or model;
- be fit for the purposes for which goods of the same type are normally used;
- be fit for any particular purpose for which the consumer requires them

2 Product Liability Directive, Article 4.
3 See for example Decision of the Regional Court of Madrid 26 July 2011 (non-deployment of airbag), and the English Court of appeal in *Ide v ATB Sales Ltd* [2008] EWCA Civ 424.
4 OJ L 171, 7.7.1999.

and which was made known to the seller at the time of conclusion of the contract, and accepted by the seller; and
- be of satisfactory quality and performance, given the nature of the goods and taking into account the public statements made about them by the seller, the producer or his representative.

The seller is liable to the consumer for any lack of conformity which exists when the goods are delivered to the consumer and which arises within a period of two years from delivery. Unless proven otherwise, where the lack of conformity arises within six months delivery of the goods, it is presumed to have existed at the time of delivery unless this presumption is incompatible with the nature of the goods or the nature of the lack of conformity. The seller will not be able to rely on the lack of conformity, where the consumer knew or could not reasonably have been unaware of the lack of conformity at the moment of conclusion of the contract.

A seller will not be liable in circumstances where goods are not in conformity with the public statements made by the seller, the producer or their representative, if they show that:
- they did not know and could not reasonably know the statement in question;
- they corrected the statement at the time of sale; or
- the decision to buy the goods could not have been influenced by the statement.

In the event of a product not conforming to the contract of sale, a consumer may request that the seller:
- repair or replace the product, free of charge within a reasonable time and without major inconvenience to the consumer;
- make an appropriate reduction to the price, or
- rescind the contract (if repair or replacement is impossible or disproportionate, or if the seller has not remedied the shortcoming within a reasonable period or without major inconvenience to the consumer). The contract cannot be rescinded if the lack of conformity is minor.

When the final seller is liable to the consumer because of a lack of conformity resulting from an act or omission by the producer, a previous seller in the same chain of contracts or any other intermediary, the final seller will be entitled to pursue remedies against the person responsible.

Commercial guarantees are those additional undertakings given by a seller or producer, over and above legal guarantees, to reimburse the price paid, to exchange, repair or handle a product in any way, in the event of non-conformity of a product with the contract. Any commercial guarantee offered by a seller or producer is legally binding upon them under the conditions laid down in the guarantee document and any associated advertising. The guarantee must state:
- that the consumer has statutory rights and clearly state that these rights are not affected by the guarantee;
- its content, in simple and understandable terms, and indicate the conditions for claiming under it, notably its duration and territorial scope; and

- the name and address of the guarantor.

At the consumer's request, the guarantee shall be made available in writing or in the form of another durable medium.

1.4 How is a product 'defect' defined?

The Product Liability Directive gives a wide definition to 'product'. It states that 'product' means any goods or electricity and includes a product that is comprised in another product, whether as a component or as a raw material. In its original form, primary agricultural products were excluded from the Directive, although by an amendment in 1999 such products were brought within the scope of the liability regime.

A product is considered to be defective if in all relevant circumstances 'it does not provide the safety which a person is entitled to expect'.[5] Matters to be taken into account will include:

- the presentation of the product;
- the use to which it could reasonably be expected that the product would be put; and
- the time when the product was supplied.

Pursuant to Article 6(2) of the Product Liability Directive, a product will not be considered defective simply because a better product is subsequently put into circulation.

It is not necessary that there has been any fault or neglect on the part of the producer, and arguably the conduct of the producer is not relevant at all to the question of whether the product was defective.

1.5 Who in the supply chain has obligations or duties for defective products? What obligations or duties do they owe and to whom?

The Product Liability Directive imposes liability to pay compensation for damage caused by a defect in a product, even if there is no proof of fault on the part of the party responsible. Under Article 3 of the Directive, liability extends to:

- the producer;
- the first importer into the European Union, the intention being to ensure that there will always be a defendant within the EU who can be held liable for a defective product;
- an 'own brander' (ie, someone who holds himself out as a manufacturer by including his own name or trademark on the product); and
- a 'downstream supplier' (whether the retailer, wholesaler, or distributor), but only if it fails to identify the manufacturer, the own brander, or the first importer, within a reasonable time.[6]

1.6 By what means can a supplier limit its liability for defective products?

The European Court of Justice has held that a supplier will be free from liability under the Directive's no fault liability regime if the supplier

5 Product Liability Directive, Article 6.
6 See for example Italian Supreme Court of Cassation, Judgment of 1 June 2010, no.13432 (bicycle)

complies with the provisions of Article 3(3) in notifying the injured person of the identity of the producer or the upstream supplier. The Court held that it is unlawful for the national laws implementing the Directive in a member state to provide to the contrary.[7]

2. DEFENCES

2.1 What are the possible defences to a product liability claim?

(a) Development risks

Article 7(e) of the Product Liability Directive provides a defence to a claim under the Directive if the producer proves 'that the state of scientific and technical knowledge at the time when he put the product into circulation was not such as to enable the existence of the defect to be discovered'. This is an 'optional' provision in the Directive (Article 15(1)(b)), and member states are not obliged to include it in their national laws.

The European Court of Justice considered the scope of the defence in *Commission v United Kingdom*.[8] The Court took a somewhat narrow reading of the development risks defence. It ruled that to rely on this defence a producer must prove that the objective state of scientific and technical knowledge, including the most advanced level of such knowledge, at the time when the product in question was put into circulation, was not such as to enable the existence of the defect to be discovered. However, that knowledge must have been 'accessible' at the time the product was put into circulation. On this last point, the ECJ acknowledged that difficult questions may arise on the facts of particular cases in deciding whether the requisite knowledge was actually accessible to the producer.

(b) Comparative fault/contributory negligence

Liability may be reduced or avoided if the damage is found to be caused by both a defect in the product and by the fault of the injured person, or of any person for whom the injured person is responsible.[9]

(c) Misuse of the product

The test for defect under the Product Liability Directive has been described as a 'legitimate expectations' test, based on the level of safety that a person is entitled to expect from the product.

One of the considerations to be taken into account is 'the use to which it could reasonably be expected the product would be put'. If the misuse of the product could reasonably have been anticipated, the product could be considered defective if the misuse rendered the product unsafe. If, however, the misuse could not reasonably have been anticipated, and the damage was caused by that misuse, it would appear that the product ought not to be considered defective.

7 *Commission v. France, European Court of Justice*, C-52/00 [2002].
8 [1997] All ER (EC) 481.
9 Product Liability Directive, Article 8(2). This issue was considered by the Austrian Supreme Court in its decision of 22 October 2009, decision 30b171/09g (concerning swimming pool equipment).

(d) Unavoidably dangerous products and obvious risks

The defectiveness of a product is to be considered taking 'all the circumstances' into account, including the 'presentation' of the product.[10]

It is arguable that if a product contains obvious, unavoidable risks, it should not be considered defective under the terms of the Directive.

However, if the risks are unavoidable, but not obvious, and the consumer is not adequately warned in relation to those risks, the product is likely to be considered defective.

(e) Component suppliers

Article 7(f) of the Product Liability Directive provides a defence to suppliers of component parts if they prove that the defect is attributable to the design of the product in which the component has been fitted or to the instructions given by the manufacturer of the finished product.

(f) Informed intermediary

There is no express provision in the Product Liability Directive for an informed, or learned, intermediary defence for producers, although 'all the circumstances' are to be taken into account when considering whether a product is defective.

(g) Compliance with standards/regulations

Compliance with industry standards or mandatory regulations will not necessarily provide a defence to a claim under the Product Liability Directive. Where standards or regulations relevant to the safety of the product in question exist, the question of compliance with them will be expected to be of some evidentiary importance in most cases.

It is a defence if the defect itself is caused by the need to comply with mandatory regulations.[11]

(h) Privity of contract

A producer of a defective product is liable, under the Directive, for damage caused by the defect, irrespective of whether the person who suffered the damage was in a contractual relationship with the producer.

As the Directive does not deal with matters such as proof of causation and damage, questions of remoteness of damage are to be decided in accordance with the national law of the particular member state.

(i) Exclusion clauses and disclaimers of liability

A producer may not limit or exclude liability under the Directive through exclusion clauses or disclaimers.[12] However, any instructions or warnings provided in relation to the safe use of the product will be relevant when considering whether the product is defective.[13]

10 Product Liability Directive, Article 6(1).
11 Product Liability Directive, Article 7(d).
12 Product Liability Directive, Article 12.
13 Product Liability Directive, Article 6(1)(a).

(j) Defects occurring after a product is put into circulation

A producer has a defence under the terms of the Product Liability Directive if the defect that caused the damage did not exist at the time when the product was put into circulation.

Where a product becomes unsafe over time through normal use, there will invariably be an issue as to whether the product, in its design, provides the safety that persons are entitled to expect. However, it may be that if the unsafe condition arose due to wear and tear after a long period of time, it will be possible to argue that the product did not have a defect.

In some cases, European courts have placed a high evidentiary burden on manufacturers seeking to establish that the product did not bear the defect at the time it was put into circulation.

2.2 Is there a limit on the time in which proceedings may be brought (limitations and repose)?

There is a limitation period of three years from the day on which the claimant became aware, or should reasonably have become aware, of the damage, the defect, and the identity of the producer.[14] This is subject to national laws dealing with the suspension or interruption of the running of the statutory limitations periods.[15]

The rights conferred by the Product Liability Directive are extinguished 10 years from the date on which the producer put into circulation the actual product that caused the damage if proceedings are not commenced within that time.[16] There does not appear in the Directive any scope for the extension of the time limit. A product is put into circulation when it is taken out of the manufacturing process operated by the producer and enters a marketing process in the form in which it is offered to the public.[17]

3. LITIGATION OF PRODUCT LIABILITY DISPUTES

Procedural rules have not been harmonised in the EU, nor does the Product Liability Directive deal comprehensively with the question of damages. Those matters are left to the national laws of the individual member states. There will also be differences in the way the terms of the Product Liability Directive are interpreted in each member state. Accordingly, please refer to the relevant country specific chapter of this text for details of the procedural rules and processes in each jurisdiction.

4. REMEDIES

4.1 What remedies are available to a party who successfully pursues a product liability claim?

A producer of a defective product is liable, under the terms of the Product Liability Directive, for damage caused by death or personal injury.[18] The producer is also liable for damage to property (other than damage to the

14 Product Liability Directive, Article 10(1).
15 Product Liability Directive, Article 10(2).
16 Product Liability Directive, Article 11.
17 *O'Byrne v Aventis Pasteur MSD and Another* [2005] ECJ, case C-127/04.
18 Product Liability Directive, Article 9(a).

product itself) if the defective product was a consumer product, and the injured party was using the product as a consumer.

4.2 How are damages calculated/are there limitations on available damages?

Compensation for 'non-material' damages is available in most, but not all, member states in claims pursuant to the Directive.

Liability for property damage is subject to a lower threshold of €500.[19]

The Product Liability Directive includes an optional provision allowing member states to fix a cap of not less than €70 million on a producer's liability arising out of personal injury damages caused by 'identical items with the same defect'.[20] This option has been included in the national implementing laws of some of the member states.

4.3 Are punitive or exemplary damages available and in what circumstances?

The Directive is silent on the question of what types of damages are recoverable, and how they are to be calculated. These are matters to be dealt with by the national law of each member state.[21]

4.4 Is liability joint and several/how does apportionment of liability work, including where a partially responsible entity is not a party to the proceeding?

Liability of 'producers' under the Directive is joint and several.[22] This is expressed to be without prejudice to national laws concerning rights of contribution or recourse.

Article 8(1) of the Directive provides that 'the liability of the producer shall not be reduced when the damage is caused both by a defect in the product and by the act or omission of a third party'. This is also expressed to be without prejudice to national laws concerning rights of contribution or recourse.

5. ROLE OF REGULATORS

5.1 Please explain the role, responsibilities and powers of the regulators in your country which have jurisdiction over product liability issues.

Some products in the EU are governed by sector specific Directives or other EU-based legislative measures. This includes toys, cosmetics, food, pharmaceuticals, medical devices, motor vehicles, low voltage electrical products, machinery and personal protective equipment. Where consumer products are not covered by specific measures, Decision 2001/95/EC of 3 December 2001 (the General Product Safety Directive) applies. The General Product Safety Directive requires member states to enforce the requirements of the General Product Safety Directive on producers and distributors, to

19 Product Liability Directive, Article 9(b).
20 Product Liability Directive, Article 16(1).
21 *Henning Veedfald & Arhus Amtskommune*, European Court of Justice, C-203/99.
22 Product Liability Directive, Article 5.

ensure that only safe products are placed on the EU market.[23] To that end, each member state must appoint a 'competent authority' in charge of market surveillance and enforcement.

Broadly, the General Product Safety Directive was implemented for the purposes of protecting consumer health and safety and to ensure the proper functioning of the internal market. The intention of the directive is to ensure a high level of safety for consumer products in the EU by ensuring that all products on the EU market are safe.[24]

A 'safe product' is defined as *'any product which, under normal or reasonably foreseeable conditions of use including duration and, where applicable, putting into service, installation and maintenance requirements, does not present any risk or only the minimum risks compatible with the product's use, considered to be acceptable and consistent with a high level of protection for the safety and health of persons'.*[25]

In assessing whether a product is safe, the following considerations are taken into account:

- the characteristics of the product, including its composition, packaging, instructions for assembly and, where applicable, instructions for installation and maintenance;[26]
- the effect on other products, where it is reasonably foreseeable that it will be used with other products;[27]
- the presentation of the product, the labelling, any warnings and instructions for its use and disposal and any other indication or information regarding the product;[28]
- the categories of consumers at risk when using the product, in particular children and the elderly.[29]

While no centralised EU regulatory body for product safety exists, a requirement for the national competent authorities to provide notification to the European Commission (and other member states) exists in the following instances:

- where a member state takes measures that restrict the placing on the market of products, or requires their withdrawal or recall;[30] and
- where a member state adopts, recommends, or agrees with producers or distributors, measures or actions relating to products that present a serious risk, and the effects of those actions or measures may go beyond its own territory.[31]

Where the Commission becomes aware of a product posing a serious risk to consumers in the EU it may require temporary measures to be taken, after consultation with the member states.[32]

23 General Product Safety Directive, Article 6(1).
24 General Product Safety Directive, Article 1.
25 General Product Safety Directive, Article 2(b).
26 General Product Safety Directive, Article 2(b)(i).
27 General Product Safety Directive, Article 2(b)(ii).
28 General Product Safety Directive, Article 2(b)(iii).
29 General Product Safety Directive, Article 2(b)(iv).
30 General Product Safety Directive, Article 11.
31 General Product Safety Directive, Article 12 – Immediate notification is required via the Rapid Alert System for Non-Food Products (RAPEX) system.
32 General Product Safety Directive, Article 13.

5.2 Are there any mandatory reporting requirements related to product safety issues?

Article 5(3) of the Product Safety Directive requires producers and distributors to immediately notify the competent authorities of the member states in which the product is in circulation, that a product that they have placed on the market poses risks to consumers which are incompatible with the general safety requirement.

Member states, via their competent authority, are required to immediately notify the Commission upon identifying products which pose a serious risk to consumers. The mechanism of notifying the Commission is the Rapid Alert System for Non Food Products (RAPEX), which is a system aimed at the rapid exchange of information throughout the EU in the event of a serious risk.[33] Annex II of the Product Safety Directive addresses the procedures and notification guidelines applicable to the RAPEX system.

Producers and distributors are also required to co-operate with the competent authorities in any action taken to avoid risks to consumers, including withdrawal of products from the market, or a recall from consumers.[34]

5.3 Do the regulators have the power to:

(i) ban certain goods or services?

(ii) require a supplier to recall a product?

(iii) prescribe standards in respect of certain goods or services and require that the goods or services meet those standards?

(iv) require production of information without court process?

The competent authority in each member state is granted wide ranging powers under the General Product Safety Directive, including monitoring and intervention powers, in addition to the ability to impose penalties. Under the national law implementing the General Product Safety Directive in each jurisdiction, the competent authority in each member state is responsible for surveillance of their national market and for taking enforcement action for infringements.[35] Pursuant to Article 8 of the General Product Safety Directive, the specific powers of a competent authority are to include:

- the organisation of appropriate safety checks on products, even after its being placed on the market;
- requiring all necessary information to be provided by the parties concerned;
- the taking of samples of products and subjecting them to safety checks;
- requiring suitable warnings to be affixed to products;
- ensuring that appropriate persons can be informed of risks quickly;
- prohibiting, on a temporary basis, the sale of a product or particular product batch, where there are precise and consistent indications that they are dangerous;

33 Product Safety Directive, Annex II, paragraph 2.
34 Product Safety Directive, Article 5(1).
35 Product Safety Directive, Article 6.

- placing a ban on the sale of a product if it has proved dangerous and establish the accompanying measures needed to ensure compliance with the ban; and
- ordering or organising the immediate withdrawal or recall of a dangerous product or particular product batch that is already on the market and, if necessary, organise its destruction.

If so, broadly explain the circumstances in which the regulator can exercise the power and any penalties that apply if a supplier fails to comply.

The circumstances in which a competent authority can exercise the powers conferred by Article 8 depend on the level of risk identified and the seriousness of the proposed action. Article 8(1) itself provides guidance in this respect where, for example, the power to undertake relatively uncontroversial measures such as safety checks, sampling or requiring production of information, can be exercised in respect of any product.[36] At the other end of the scale, the power to immediately withdraw or recall a product may only be exercised when a product is already on the market and is dangerous (defined in Article 2(8) as any product which is not a 'safe product').[37]

In the event of a breach of the general safety requirement, sanctions are imposed under the criminal law of the member states, and penalties vary between member states.

6. VOLUNTARY CONDUCT

6.1 Are there regulations pertaining to the voluntary conduct of a product repair or recall by a supplier?

The procedures for the conduct of voluntary corrective action or recall by a supplier or producer are governed the national law of each member state, subject to the general provisions of the General Product Safety Directive and any sector Directives mentioned above.

7. EMERGING ISSUES AND LAW REFORM

7.1 Are there important developing and emerging issues or trends in product liability law in your country?

Despite the fact that the Product Liability Directive was intended to harmonise product liability law in the European Union, there remain substantial differences in the way in which the Directive, and the product liability systems more generally, operate in the various member states.

Nevertheless, the Product Liability Directive is becoming an increasingly dominant feature in each nation, as the importance and meaning of the system of no fault liability established under it becomes better recognised by claimants and their lawyers. The influence of the Directive is also enhanced significantly by the accession of the 13 new member states in 2004, 2007 and 2013, as it is generally recognised that the EU legislation in those countries will, in most cases, raise the standards of consumer protection under each nation's law.

36 Product Safety Directive, Article 8(1)(a).
37 Product Safety Directive, Article 8(1)(f).

7.2 Please describe any proposed important law reform in the area of product liability in your country.

On 3 February 2013 the European Commission published a proposal to reform the Product Safety Directive. The Product Safety and Market Surveillance Package consists of two main proposals:

(i) Regulation on Consumer Product Safety, which would repeal the existing Product Safety Directive;

(ii) Regulation on Market Surveillance, which would separate the current market surveillance provisions in the Product Safety Directive (including the RAPEX provisions), and include them in a separate regulation.

At the time of writing, the proposal had not been finalised. However, it appears the main changes proposed are:

- streamlining the obligations of economic operators, such that any producer, importer or distributor of a consumer product (not otherwise subject to a sector-specific Directive) will be subject to identical obligations under the Regulation;[38]
- an obligation for manufacturers to draw up technical documentation for their product, including a documented risk assessment (where not otherwise subject to a sector-specific Directive);
- clarification that a product will be presumed safe under the Regulation if it conforms to the requirements of a sector-specific Directive designed to protect health and safety.
- a requirement that all consumer products must be marked with the country of origin, regardless of whether covered by a sector-specific Directive.

While the proposed Regulation will impose similar obligations on member state authorities for assessing and responding to risks on their market as are currently contained in the Product Safety Directive, the proposed Regulation will go further by covering all products (whether or not intended for consumers) and more categories of risk (workplace health and safety, environmental risks and public security, in addition to the current consideration of consumer health and safety).

The proposed Regulation on Market Surveillance will require competent authorities to ensure that a product is withdrawn or recalled, regardless of whether a safety risk exists, in circumstances where an economic operator is unable to rectify instances of formal non-compliance (such as lack of a CE mark or Declaration of Conformity and incomplete technical documentation or labelling).

8. REGULATORY WEBSITES/INFORMATION

8.1 Please identify any useful regulatory references relating to product liability law in your country, for example, a product safety/consumer law website maintained by the main regulator.

- Europa – consumer safety website
  *http://europa.eu/legislation_summaries/consumers/consumer_safety/index_*

38 Consistent with Decision 768/2008/EC on a common framework for the marketing of products in the EU.

en.htm

- Hogan Lovells' International Product Liability Review: Information about how to subscribe to this publication may be found at the following URL: *www.hoganlovells.com/PracticeAreas/areas_pubs.aspx?op=&firmService=385*

France

SCP Soulié & Coste-Floret
Emmanuèle Lutfalla, Goulwen Pennec & Edouard Dufour

1. LIABILITY

1.1 What are the principal sources of law and regulation relating to product liability?

The main sources of law governing product liability are the following, bearing in mind that this list is not exhaustive.

Liability for defective products is governed by Articles 1386-1 to 1386-18 of the Civil Code. These provisions were instituted by law n° 98-389 of 19 May 1998, transposing European Directive (EC) 85/374 dated 25 July 1985 into French law. In 2010, the French Supreme Court ruled that *'the system of product liability excludes application of other systems of common law contractual or extra-contractual liability based on a defect in a product that does not provide the safety a person is entitled to expect, to the exclusion of tort liability and the warranty against hidden defects'.* (Com. 26 May 2010, appeal n° 08-18545).

The warranty against hidden defects is governed by Articles 1641 *et seq.* of the Civil Code. The seller must provide a warranty against hidden defects in the product sold that render it unfit for its intended use, or which so impair that use that the buyer would not have acquired it or would have paid a lesser price for it, had he known about them.

Article 1384 of the Civil Code, paragraph 1 provides that a person is liable for the damage caused by a thing in his care. The liability for damage caused by a thing in one's care is related to the used that is made of the thing as well as to the power of surveillance or control over that thing, which characterises its being in one's care (Cass. Ch. *réunies*, 2 December 1941, *Franck*).

Consumer law (which applies to relationships between professionals and consumers) provides that products and services must, under normal conditions of use or under other circumstances that may be reasonably foreseen by the professional, provide the level of safety that can legitimately be expected and must not be a danger to public health (Article L 221-1 of the Consumer Code).

1.2 What is required to establish causation under the most common causes of action available?

Product liability: Article 1386-9 of the Civil Code provides that 'the claimant is required to prove the damage, the defect and the causal connection between the defect and the damage'.

Warranty against hidden defects: the plaintiff (the purchaser or sub-purchaser) must supply the proof of a causal connection between the defect and the damage.

Liability for damage caused by a thing in one's care (Article 1384, paragraph 1): the injured party must provide proof that the thing did, in some way, even partially, cause the damage. For example, the courts cannot deduce from simply observing that a branch is broken that a tree was the cause of the damage (Civ. 2ème, 29 March 1971; appeal n°70-11319). Little does it matter if the exact causes of the damage (explosion of the glass in a fireplace insert) have not been determined, once the claimant has proved that the product did not provide a normal degree of safety, the producer is required to prove the existence of a ground for exemption or the fault of the user (TGI Aix-en-Provence, 2 October 2001).

1.3 Is strict liability available and, if so, in what circumstances?

The systems of liability studied (Article 1384 paragraph 1, Article 1386-1 *et seq.* and Article 1641 *et seq.* of the Civil Code) are strict liability systems.

Liability for damage caused by a thing in one's care: the principle of liability caused by inanimate things is based on the concept of care, independent of the intrinsic nature of the thing and of any personal fault on the part of the custodian (Civ. 2ème, 20 Nov. 1968).

Liability for defective products: the producer may be liable for a defect even though the product has been manufactured in conformity with good industry practice or with existing standards, or has been the subject of an administrative authorisation (Article 1386-10 of the Civil Code). In other words, the absence of a fault on the part of the producer does not exempt him from liability.

Hidden defects: the seller, by parting with the thing, guarantees that it presents all of its usual qualities. This is a strict obligation whose non-performance is proven once it has been established that the thing is defective, without any need to prove a fault on the part of the seller.

1.4 Are guarantees or warranties as to quality implied by law?

Articles 1641 *et seq.* of the Civil Code lay down a legal warranty against hidden defects. The seller is bound by the warranty with regard to any hidden defects affecting the thing sold that render it unfit for its intended use, or so impair that use that the buyer would not have acquired it or would have paid a lesser price for it, had he known about them.

1.5 How is a product 'defect' defined?

Liability for defective products: the concept of defective product is defined in Article 1386-4 of the Civil Code as follows: '*A product is defective within the meaning of this Title where it does not provide the safety which a person is entitled to expect. In order to appraise the safety which a person is entitled to expect, account shall be taken of all the circumstances, in particular the presentation of the product, the use to which one could reasonably expect that it would be put and the time when the product was put into circulation. A product shall not be considered defective for the sole reason that a better product is subsequently put into circulation*'.

Hidden defect: a hidden defect is a defect in the thing sold that renders it unfit for its intended use, or so impairs that use that the buyer would not have acquired it or would have paid a lesser price for it, had he known about it.

1.6 Who in the supply chain has obligations or duties for defective products? What obligations or duties do they owe and to whom?

Liability for defective products: the producer is liable for damage caused by a defect in his product, whether or not he was bound by a contract with the injured person (Article 1386-1 of the Civil Code), bearing in mind that the producer is described in Article 1386-6 of the Civil Code, which stipulates that: *'Is a producer, the manufacturer of a finished product, the producer of a raw material, the manufacturer of a component part, where he acts as a professional.*

For the implementation of this Title, shall be treated in the same way as a producer any person acting as a professional:

1° Who presents himself as the producer by putting his name, trade mark or other distinguishing feature on the product;

2° Who imports a product into the European Community for sale, hire, with or without a promise of sale, or any other form of distribution.

Shall not be deemed producers, within the meaning of this Title, the persons whose liability may be sought on the basis of Articles 1792 to 1792-6 and 1646-1.'

Furthermore, Article 1386-7 of the Civil Code stipulates as follows: *'If the producer remains unknown, the seller, the hirer, with the exception of a financial lessor or a hirer similar to a financial lessor, or any other professional supplier, is liable for the lack of safety of a product under the same conditions as a producer, unless he names his own supplier or producer within a time limit of three months as from the date he was notified about the injured person's claim.*

A supplier's recourse against a producer is subject to the same rules as a claim made by the direct victim of a defect. However, he must take action within the year following the date he was served the summons.'

Hidden defects: the person who must provide the warranty is the seller of the thing. That being said, the sub-purchaser is entitled to bring an action in warranty based on hidden defects against the original seller (Civ. 3ème, 7 March 1990).

1.7 By what means can a supplier limit its liability for defective products?

Liability for defective products: Article 1386-15 of the Civil Code provides that: *'Clauses that are aimed at exempting or limiting liability for defective products are forbidden and shall be deemed to be unwritten. However, for damage caused to property not used by the injured party mainly for his own private use or consumption, clauses stipulated between professionals are valid.'*

Hidden defects: As regards hidden defects, the following distinctions must be drawn:

- Professional sellers and buyers having the same speciality: in the case of a sale between professionals having the same speciality, the seller's

- warranty may not be invoked when a warranty disclaimer for hidden defects is contained in the contract (Com. 6 November 1978). The judge ruling on the merits has full discretion when deciding when a speciality is the same (Civ. 1ère , 21 July 1987).
- Lay sellers acting in good faith: it has been held that a court ruling on the merits, having observed that the sellers' bad faith has not been established, may not, without denaturing it, refuse to apply a warranty disclaimer stipulating that the buyer would purchase the building in its present state, with all its vices or defects, patent or hidden (termites in the building sold) (Civ. 3ème, 12 November 1975).

1.8 Are there particular goods or services which have specific obligations or duties attached to them?

Real estate (building to be erected) is subject to special legislation. For example, Article 1642-1 of the Civil Code provides as follows: '*The seller of a building to be erected may not be discharged, either before acceptance of the works or before the expiry of one month after the purchaser has taken possession, for construction defects that were patent at the time.*

When the seller undertakes to remedy them, there may be no cancellation of the contract or reduction in price.'

Article 1646-1 of the Civil Code also provides that: '*The seller of a building to be erected is liable, from the date of acceptance of the works, for obligations for which the architects, contractors and other persons bound to the building owner by a service contract are themselves liable pursuant to Articles 1792, 1792-1, 1792-2 and 1792-3 of this Code.*

Those warranties benefit the successive owners of the building.

If the seller undertakes to repair the damage defined in Articles 1792, 1792-1, 1792-2 and 1792-3 of this Code and to take upon himself the warranty provided for in Article 1792-3, there shall be no cancellation of the sale or reduction in price.'

Of course, these examples are not exhaustive.

2. DEFENCES

2.1 What are the possible defences to a product liability claim?

Hidden defects: for the legal warranty against hidden defects to be applicable, the defect must not be patent, it must have existed prior to the sale and be sufficiently serious (redhibitory defect). The purchaser cannot rely on the legal warranty against hidden defects if one of these conditions is not satisfied.

Notwithstanding, even if all the conditions laid down in the provisions governing the warranty against hidden defects are satisfied, the seller still has the possibility of arguing that he should only be held partially liable, or even exempted from liability in the case of a fault on the part of the purchaser. In cases of force majeure, the seller is totally exempted from liability.

Liability for damage caused by a thing in one's care: the presumption of liability of the person who has a thing in one's care that has caused damage to another person, laid down by Article 1384 paragraph 1, may only be eliminated by proof of unforeseeable circumstances or *force majeure* or an external cause not attributable to him. It does not suffice to prove that he did not commit a fault or that the cause of the event giving rise to the damage remains unknown *(Cass.,Ch. réunies,13 Feb. 1930, Jand'heur).*

Liability for defective products: Article 1386-11 of the Civil Code lists various grounds for the producer's exemption from liability:

'A producer is liable by law unless he proves:

1° that he did not put the product into circulation;

2° that, in view of the circumstances, there is reason to believe that the defect that caused the damage did not exist at the time the product was put into circulation by him or that this defect came into being afterwards;

3° that the product was not intended for sale or for any other form of distribution;

4° that the state of scientific and technical knowledge at the time the producer put the product into circulation was not such as to enable the existence of the defect to be discovered; or

5° that the defect is due to the product's compliance with mandatory rules deriving from legislation or regulations.

The producer of a component part is not liable either where he proves that the defect is attributable to the design of the product in which the component has been fitted or to the instructions given by the producer of that product.'

There are other ways in which the producer's liability can be mitigated. In particular, Article 1386-13 of the Civil Code provides as follows: *'The liability of a producer may be reduced or removed, in light of all the circumstances, when the damage is caused both by a defect in the product and by the fault of the injured person or a person for whom the injured person is responsible.'*

2.2 Is there a limit on the time in which proceedings may be brought (limitations and repose)?

Statute of limitations under common law: the statute of limitations under common law is governed by Article 2224 of the Civil Code, which provides that: *'Personal or legal actions are time-barred five years after the day when the holder of a right knew about, or ought to have known about, the facts giving rise to that right.'*

When a person has suffered a physical injury, the limitation period is increased to 10 years as from the date of consolidation of the initial or aggravated injury, pursuant to Article 2226 of the Civil Code.

Hidden defects: actions arising out of redhibitory defects must be brought by the purchaser within a period of two years following the discovery of the defect (Article 1648 of the Civil Code).

Liability for defective products: an action for recovery of damages founded on liability for defective products is time-barred after a period of three years as from the date when the claimant knew about, or should have known about, the damage, the defect and the identity of the producer (Article 1386-17 of the Civil Code). Unless he has committed a fault, the liability of the producer, founded on liability for defective products, is extinguished 10 years after the product having caused the damage was put into circulation, unless the injured person has in the meantime initiated proceedings (Article 1386-16 of the Civil Code).

3. LITIGATION OF PRODUCT LIABILITY DISPUTES

3.1 In which courts are product liability proceedings brought?

In matters of common law, the *Tribunal de Grande Instance* has jurisdiction. For disputes in which the amounts claimed are lower than €10,000, the *Tribunal d'Instance* has jurisdiction. There are also special courts whose jurisdiction is determined by law. For example, disputes between traders come within the jurisdiction of the commercial court.

3.2 How are proceedings commenced?

Proceedings are most often initiated by having a writ of summons served by a bailiff. Nevertheless, there are other ways in which proceedings can be initiated, depending on the jurisdiction that will be hearing the dispute. For example, in the *Tribunal d'Instance*, proceedings may be instituted by making a simple declaration to the clerk of the court.

3.3 Are disputed issues decided by a judge or a jury?

There is no such thing as a jury in civil or commercial cases. Only the *Cour d'Assises*, which judges criminal cases, is made up of professional judges and a jury. The civil courts are made up of professional judges sitting as a single judge or as a chamber of several judges. The judges sitting at the *Tribunal de Commerce* are special commercial court judges, ie, non-professional judges elected by their peers.

3.4 Who has the burden of proof and to what standard?

The burden of proof is governed, in particular, by Article 1314 *et seq.* of the Civil Code, which provides that: '*A person who claims the performance of an obligation must prove it. Reciprocally, a person who claims to be released must substantiate the payment or the fact that has resulted in the extinguishment of his obligation.*'

The concept of 'proof standard' does not exist in the French system. The cogency of the evidence is left to the sole discretion of the court.

3.5 How is evidence given in proceedings and are witnesses cross-examined?

As a general rule, acts (eg, contracts for amounts greater than 1,500) are proved by a written document, whereas facts may be proved by any means. Evidence can be given through a witness statement, an establishment of fact drawn up by a bailiff, photographs, etc. As concerns traders, commercial instruments may be proven by any means, unless otherwise specified by law (Article L110-3 of the Commercial Code).

There is no cross-examination in civil or commercial cases. A witness statement may be submitted in the form of an affidavit that is required to respect a certain structure (laid down in Article 202 of the Code of Civil

Procedure) in order to be cogent. The affidavit must contain an account of the facts that the affiant has witnessed or has personally noticed. It must state the surname, first name, date and place of birth, the domicile and occupation of the affiant as well as, if necessary, his family relationship or affinity with the parties, his relation of subordination towards them, his relation of collaboration or his common interests with them. It must state that the affiant is aware that he shall face criminal penalties for any false statement on his part. The affidavit must be written, dated and signed by the affiant in his own hand. He must attach to the affidavit the original or a photocopy of any official document proving his identity and bearing his signature.

3.6 Are the parties able to rely on expert opinion evidence and, if so, are there any special rules or procedures for expert opinion evidence?

The parties may each rely on the opinion of an expert that they have instructed. They may ask the judge to appoint an impartial expert, who shall give his technical opinion about the dispute. The judge is not required to follow the opinion of the court-appointed expert. The judge may base his decision solely on the court-appointed expert's report, on condition that the adversarial principle has been respected.

3.7 Is pre-trial discovery permitted? If so, in what circumstances? If not, what other mechanisms, if any, are available for obtaining evidence from a party or a third party?

There is no discovery procedure in the French system, like there is in common law. However, any interested party may ask the judge to order an investigative measure if there are legitimate grounds for preserving or establishing, prior to any legal process, the evidence of the facts upon which the resolution of the dispute could depend (Article 145 of the Code of Civil Procedure).

A third party may be ordered to disclose all documents in his possession, unless there is a legitimate impediment preventing the third party from doing so (banking secrecy, business confidentiality, privacy, etc.) (Civ. 2ème, 26 May 2011).

3.8 Is there liability for spoliation of evidence/a remedy for destruction of or failure to preserve evidence (most relevantly, the product)?

Article 11 of the Code of Civil Procedure provides that: '*The parties are required to cooperate with the investigative measures and it is up to the judge to draw all conclusions from any failure or refusal to do so.*

If a party is in possession of evidence, the judge may, at the request of the other party, order him to disclose it, under threat of a periodic penalty payment. The judge may, upon petition by one of the parties, request or order, if need by under threat of the same penalty, the disclosure of all documents held by third parties if there is no legitimate impediment to doing so.'

Hence, if a party spoliates or destroys evidence that is relevant for discovering the truth, the judge ruling on the merits may draw all conclusions from such spoliation/destruction.

Furthermore the spoliation or destruction of evidence may lead to criminal penalties. Indeed, Article 434-4 of the Penal Code provides that: *'Where it is done in order to obstruct the discovery of the truth, a penalty of three years' imprisonment and a fine of €45,000 applies to:*

1. modifying the scene of a felony or a misdemeanour either by the alteration, falsification or obliteration of clues or evidence, or by bringing, removing or suppressing any given article;

2. destroying, purloining, concealing or altering a private or public document or an article liable to facilitate the discovery of a felony or a misdemeanour, the search for evidence or the conviction of the guilty party.

Where the acts provided for under the present article are committed by a person who, because of his position, is called to take part in the discovery of the truth, the penalty is increased to five years' imprisonment and to a fine of €75,000.'

This article could find application in the case where a defective product has caused an extremely serious physical injury, if not death.

3.9 Is interlocutory or interim relief available prior to the full trial of a proceeding? If so, in what circumstances?

In cases where the obligation is not seriously challenged, the judge ruling in matters of urgency may award an interim payment to the creditor (Article 809 paragraph 2 of the Code of Civil Procedure). This can be an interim payment to be deducted from the final damages and/or an *ad litem* payment, ie, for the purposes of the suit.

Furthermore, it is possible to request an interim payment from the pre-trial judge, during the course of the proceedings, when proceedings are pending in the *Tribunal de Grande Instance* (Article 771 of the Code of Civil Procedure).

3.10 Can the winning party recover its costs?

The winning party can claim back legal costs (Article 700 of the Code of Civil Procedure) and expenses (cost of the court-ordered investigation, bailiff's fees, etc.). As a general rule, as concerns the reimbursement of legal costs, the courts award a lump sum that is lower than the costs actually incurred.

3.11 What avenues of appeal are available?

In the civil and commercial courts, the time limit for lodging an appeal is one month as from the date when the judgment is notified to the other party.

4. CLASS ACTIONS/REPRESENTATIVE PROCEEDINGS

4.1 Is there a mechanism for class actions or representative proceedings, or coordinated proceedings for product liability claims? If so, what are the basic mechanics?

Class actions do not yet exist in France, despite several attempts to develop representative proceedings.

Apart from the fact that there has been considerable resistance from the economic players, from a legal standpoint several difficulties stand in the way of class action type proceedings.

In particular, there is no provision for a person being able to take legal action on behalf of another person (except in some rare cases): the principle whereby *'nul ne plaide par procureur'* (nobody shall plead by proxy) implies that all the parties to legal proceedings must be identified and their claims must be made in their own name.

5. LITIGATION FUNDING

5.1 Is litigation funding by third parties permissible in your country? If so, is it common?

Litigation funding by third parties is not permissible in France.

Article 11.3 of the National Regulations of the Lawyers Profession (*Règlement intérieur national des avocats*) provides that 'a lawyer may only receive fees from his client or from his client's agent', which excludes any possibility of funding by a third party.

It is important to note that the State does provide legal aid for persons having limited financial means.

Also, litigation is not as costly in France as it is in the UK or the US.

5.2 Are contingency fee or 'no win no fee' arrangements permissible?

Under French law, contingency fee or 'no win no fee' arrangements are not permissible.

Article 11.3 of the National Regulations of the lawyers profession (*Règlement intérieur national*) prohibits a lawyer from fixing his fees under an agreement made between the lawyer and his client prior to any final judgment, in which the amount of the fees charged depends exclusively on the outcome of the case (*pacte de quo litis*).

Generally speaking, the code of conduct for lawyers prohibits 'no win no fee' type arrangements.

However, it is possible to fix a success fee that will be paid in addition to a fixed fee.

6. REMEDIES

6.1 What remedies are available to a party who successfully pursues a product liability claim?

The main remedies available are monetary compensation and/or mandatory injunctions to do (or not to do) something.

6.2 How are damages calculated/are there limitations on available damages?

Compensation is not calculated based on the nature of the fault committed by the person held liable, but on the extent of the loss suffered.

The law provides for full compensation (other than the defective product itself).

There are, therefore, no specific limitations.

In addition to awarding compensation for property damage or physical injury, the court has to award compensation for intangible losses such as loss of brand image, reputation, profit or opportunity.

6.3 Are punitive or exemplary damages available and in what circumstances?

Punitive or exemplary damages do not exist under French law. Of course, the court is free to increase the amount of monetary compensation awarded to the plaintiff in order to improve his indemnification (and perhaps, although indirectly, to 'punish' the opposing party).

However, quite recently, the *Cour de Cassation* (French Supreme Court) has had the opportunity to give its opinion on whether foreign judgments awarding punitive damages could be enforced in France (*Arrêt n°1090 – 1 December 2010 (09-13.303) – Cour de cassation – Première chambre civile).*

Firstly, the Court said that punitive damages as such are not contrary to public policy.

Nevertheless, in this particular case, they were found to be disproportionate and contrary to public policy since the punitive damages (US$1.46 million) awarded to the plaintiffs were too high (and even superior) to the compensatory damages (US$1.39 million).

6.4 Is liability joint and several/how does apportionment of liability work, including where a partially responsible entity is not a party to the proceedings?

Joint and several liability is an option in the case of several defendants. Defendants may claim that the defect in the product is the fault of a third party. They may ask a partially responsible entity to contribute, either in the current proceedings or, if this is not possible, later on in subsequent proceedings. It is then important to keep a close eye on statutory limitations.

7. ROLE OF REGULATORS

7.1 Please explain the role, responsibilities and powers of the regulators in your country which have jurisdiction over product liability issues.

France has many 'regulators' involved in the area of 'product liability issues'.

- General Directorate for Competition Policy, Consumer Affairs and Fraud Control (DGCCRF)
- French Food Safety Agency (AFSSA)
- National Agency for Health Products Safety (ANSM)
- Consumer associations
- Others authorities (customs, veterinary services, gendarmerie...)

Of these regulators, probably the most important is the General Directorate for Competition Policy, Consumer Affairs and Fraud Control, which was set up in 2001.

Since 2010, the missions of the DGCCRF have been transferred to the Departmental Directorates for the Protection of the Population (DDPPs), whose task is mainly to ensure the safety of foods, products and services.

The DDPPs play a role in regulating and ensuring the safety of exchanges of products and services in three ways:

- regulation of competition on the market;
- economic protection of the consumer; and
- consumer safety.

The DDPPs therefore monitor compliance with the general duty of safety and with special regulations for certain hazardous products. The objective is to protect the physical safety and health of the consumer.

The DDPPs do this by drawing up rules, often in collaboration with other authorities (health, agriculture). For the most complex cases, they rely on the opinions of scientific or expert bodies such as the French Food Safety Agency.

Checks are carried out at all levels (production, importation and distribution) and in all sectors of activity. They are particularly stringent for food products and in risk areas such as sports and leisure activities.

In the event of a crisis or serious danger, the DDPPs have various methods available to them to prohibit the sale of dangerous products, recall products or impose manufacturing changes on professionals.

At a European level, they follow product hazard indexes that are sent to them by the member states of the European Union.

Actions are strengthened in risk areas such as residue from pesticides in vegetable-based food products, toys and childcare articles, sporting and leisure activities, everyday accidents. Most actions in the field of safety are based on the expertise of laboratories (joint laboratory service of the DGCCRF/DDPP and Customs).

7.2 Are there any mandatory reporting requirements related to product safety issues?

In many areas, there is a duty to inform that extends to the safety of the product (implying the duty to warn if a safety defect is suspected).

For example, the Public Health Code provides that persons in charge of preparing, importing or distributing medicinal products are bound by the duty to inform. This information is extensive (setting up a pharmacovigilance system for gathering information on risks related to the medicinal product, warning about any adverse effects...) and must be forwarded to the ANSM for monitoring purposes in order to ensure the safety of the product.

7.3 Do the regulators have the power to:

(i) ban certain goods or services?

Withdrawal is where the marketing of an identified product is suspended by removing it from stock and distribution circuits before it is sold. Withdrawals are usually implemented by the producer, but can also be ordered by the authorities.

The DDPPs have the power to withdraw products from sale in the case of a potential or proven safety defect.

Other bodies (to whom a public service task has been delegated) may also be involved. For instance, the ANSM may authorise the marketing of a medicinal product and also withdraw or suspend it. It can also withdraw batches and products from sale.

Following the European Commission's Directive 2004/418/CE dated 29 April 2004, the European Union set up a rapid alert system for products posing a serious risk (RAPEX) and measures to withdraw products from the market that are likely to be a danger to the health and safety of consumers.

(ii) require a supplier to recall a product?

Recall involves the unexpected interruption of the consumption or use of a product due to a potential safety risk for the end user or the health of the consumer. It requires targeted withdrawals or vigorous measures throughout the distribution network, as well as communications with the media, consumers, employees, distribution networks and the authorities in order to prevent the use of a defective product.

The DDPPs have the power to recall products that have been sold in the event of a potential or proven safety defect.

(iii) prescribe standards in respect of certain goods or services and require that the goods or services meet those standards?

To ensure that consumers are properly informed, the DGCCRF develops rules for the labelling, composition and names of all types of products. Its objective is to ensure that consumers receive the quality they are entitled to expect from a product or a service.

The DGCCRF and the DDPPs check the accuracy of the product information (name, characteristics and origin) and the commercial practices of professionals with regard to consumers.

Increasingly, this mission is carried out within a European (European directives) or global context.

(iv) require production of information without court process? If so, broadly explain the circumstances in which the regulator can exercise the power and any penalties that apply if a supplier fails to comply.

A variety of criminal and financial penalties are provided for in the case where one of the regulators fails to meet a request for information. Most of those penalties can only be imposed by a court. Nevertheless, some penalties may be imposed by the regulator itself. For example, as concerns medicinal products for human use (Article L.5421-9 of the Public Health Code), the ANSM may order anyone responsible for a breach of the provisions of Article L.5421.8 (failure to inform, to report an adverse effect…) to pay an administrative fine along with a daily penalty.

8. VOLUNTARY CONDUCT

8.1 Are there regulations pertaining to the voluntary conduct of a product repair or recall by a supplier?

The Ordinance of 9 July 2004 transposes Directive 2001/95/CE pertaining to the general safety of products and adaptation of legislation with Community law in the field of product safety and conformity.

Its purpose is to ensure that products put on the market are safe and that consumers receive a high level of protection, through provisions relating to the general obligations of producers and distributors, to the control of the application of EU statutory limitations in matters of product safety and to the rapid exchange of information as well as an action at a European level in certain cases.

In Chapter 1 of the Consumer Code, called 'prevention', Article L.221-1 provides that: '*Products and services must, under normal conditions of use or under other circumstances that may be reasonably foreseen by the professional, provide the level of safety that can legitimately be expected and must not be a danger to public health*'.

Article L 221-1-2 of the Consumer Code in fact provides that the person responsible for marketing the product must take measures that, given the characteristics of the products he is supplying, enable him to:

- keep informed about the risks that the products he markets may present;
- implement all actions necessary to control those risks, including withdrawal from the market, issuing adequate and effective warnings to consumers and recalling products sold from consumers.

Article L 221-1-3 also provides that when a professional knows that the products intended for consumers that he has put on the market do not meet the requirements of Article L 221-1, he shall immediately inform the relevant administrative authorities and state what actions he is implementing to guard against risks to consumers.

Generally speaking, the distributor of the product is best placed to ensure the success of a product recall (client lists…).

The DDPP is the relevant administration for receiving notifications that are not intended for other relevant authorities.

9. EMERGING ISSUES AND LAW REFORM

9.1 Are there important developing and emerging issues or trends in product liability law in your country?

Class actions do not exist in France. However, proposals to reform the law regularly come before the French Parliament. Currently, a draft law relating to 'group actions' is under discussion.

9.2 Please describe any proposed important law reform in the area of product liability in your country.

A draft law pertaining to group actions is currently being debated in Parliament (passed at the first reading in the *Assemblée Nationale* on 3 July 2013 and on 13 September 2013 by the *Sénat*).

However, the 'group action' draft law does not appear to concern product liability issues specifically. Its limited objective is to allow collective recourse to deal with mass consumption litigation (unfair clauses…) and the repair of financial losses arising out of a breach of competition law. It should be noted that the draft law excludes the field of health.

Therefore, this development does not appear to fundamentally change the current position of the law, which already allows approved consumer associations to take legal action to defend a collective interest under certain circumstances (Article L.421-1 of the Consumer Code).

10. REGULATORY WEBSITES/INFORMATION

10.1 Please identify any useful regulatory references relating to product liability law in your country, for example, a product safety/consumer law website maintained by the main regulator.

- General Directorate for Competition Policy, Consumer Affairs and Fraud Control (DGCCRF et DDPP): *www.dgccrf.bercy.gouv.fr*
- National Agency for Health Products Safety (ANSM): *www.ansm.sante.fr*

Germany

CMS Hasche Sigle
Dr. Anton G. Maurer & Klaus-Dieter Schick

1. LIABILITY

1.1 What are the principal sources of law and regulation relating to product liability?

Generally, there are two principal sources of law relating to product liability in Germany: general tort law, and the Product Liability Act (*Produkthaftungsgesetz*).

Pursuant to § 823 (1) of the *Buergerliches Gesetzbuch* (BGB) (German Civil Code), anyone who unlawfully injures the life, body, health, property or other right of another intentionally or negligently is liable to reimburse the other for damage incurred. Under this provision, the guilt of the manufacturer is a condition for its liability. At least a negligent breach of the duty of care must have been committed when placing the product on the market; a person acts negligently if he fails to observe the relevant accepted standards of care (§ 276 (2) BGB). The manufacturer must comply with the apparent state-of-the-art science and technology with respect to construction, production (manufacturing) and instruction. The manufacturer is also obliged to monitor its own and other products which could be used as accessories for its own products for harmful qualities or other risk situations as yet unknown which could arise from the use of the product. Thereby it must take into account the technical literature and the product development of its most important competitors. If the manufacturer breaches one of these duties and if this breach causes the damage suffered by a consumer or a third party, the manufacturer is under an obligation to pay damages. The injured party must prove the defect, damage and causation, and wilful or negligent behaviour. But in certain situations there is a shifting of the burden of proof of negligence to the manufacturer.

The Product Liability Act transposed EC Directive 85/374 into German law. The Product Liability Act is based on strict liability and is applicable if, as a result of a defect of a product, a human being is killed, is injured or affected in his health, or a privately used object is damaged, the manufacturer is obliged to compensate the person who suffered the damage for ensuing harm. The Product Liability Act is not applicable for damage caused by pharmaceutical products (§ 15 Product Liability Act).

The most important Acts regulating product safety are the Product Safety Act (see question 9), Machinery Act (Directive 2006/42 EC), Medical Equipment Act (Directive 93/42/EEC), Construction Product Act (Directive 89/106/EEC).

1.2 What is required to establish causation under the most common causes of action available?

The injured party must prove that the damage was caused by a defective product, that the person or entity it wants to make liable for damages has manufactured the product or is considered as a manufacturer or quasi manufacturer, and it needs to prove the causal link between the defect and the damages suffered.

1.3 Is strict liability available and, if so, in what circumstances?

There is strict liability applicable under the Product Liability Act. The manufacturer is liable if a defective product has caused injury to a person or damage to property. In the case of damage to property this applies only if an object other than the defective product is damaged and if this object is normally intended for private use or consumption and has been used by the damaged party primarily for this purpose. Therefore, if the damaged object was used commercially, only claims based under tort law are possible. The manufacturer is the party that manufactured the end product, a basic material or a part product. The manufacturer is also the party that by attaching its name or its trademark implies that it is the manufacturer ('quasi manufacturer'). An importer may be treated as a manufacturer if he commercially imports the product into the area covered by the Treaty for the Establishment of the European Economic Community (EU plus Iceland, Liechtenstein, and Norway) with a view to sell, to lease, or other forms of distribution.

1.4 Are guarantees or warranties as to quality implied by law?

A product must be fit for the purpose agreed upon and it must be safe with regard to the intended or foreseeable use.

1.5 How is a product 'defect' defined?

Whether products are defect-free depends primarily on whether the products are suitable for the purpose stipulated in the contract and, secondly, on whether they are suitable for the usual use for such goods and have the qualities that the buyer can expect from the nature of the goods. In this respect, a product can also be defective if it does not have the qualities that the manufacturer attributes to the product in advertising. Additionally, a product is defective if it does not provide that degree of safety which can be justifiably expected having regard to all the circumstances.

1.6 Who in the supply chain has obligations or duties for defective products? What obligations or duties do they owe and to whom?

The person who manufactured the final product, a basic substance or a component of a product is a manufacturer as well as a person who represents himself as a producer by attaching his name, trademark or other distinctive mark.

The manufacturer must design and manufacture a product free of defects and safe for the intended or foreseeable use. The manufacturer must provide understandable instructions, which put the user in a position to use the product safely. A person who is labelling and selling products with its own brand may be considered a manufacturer (quasi manufacturer) and will be liable with regard to a design or production defect as if it had produced the product by itself. The manufacturer must comply with the apparent state-of-the-art science and technology with respect to construction, production (manufacturing), and instruction. The manufacturer is also obliged to monitor its own and other products which could be used as accessories for its own products for harmful qualities or other risk situations as yet unknown which could arise from the use of the product.

A seller is generally not liable for damages caused by a defective product according to the rules of product liability. Especially, the seller is not responsible for design or production flaws if it has not manufactured the product itself. The manufacturer is not regarded as the vicarious agent of the seller. Therefore, the manufacturer's responsibility for a defect is not attributed to the seller. However, under the Product Liability Act, a seller may be treated as a manufacturer if he commercially imports the product into the area covered by the Treaty for the Establishment of the European Economic Community with a view to sale, rent or other forms of distribution.

Additionally, a seller who is aware that the product sold can, in fact, pose a risk to the safety and health of its user must instruct the customer accordingly; otherwise it could be liable pursuant to § 823 (1) BGB.

1.7 By what means can a supplier limit their liability for defective products?

The liability of the manufacturer under the Product Liability Act cannot be excluded or restricted in advance; such an agreement would be void.

Further, liability cannot be excluded in contracts for the sale of consumer goods (§ 475 (1) BGB). Moreover, the seller cannot invoke a reduction or exclusion of liability if it has concealed with malicious intent (*arglistig*) the existence of a defect or if it has assumed a guarantee for the existence of a particular characteristic (§ 444 BGB). Malicious intent is deemed to exist if the seller knows or expects that the buyer will not notice the defect and that the buyer would not proceed with the purchase in this form if he were aware of the defect.

German law is very restrictive to limit or exclude liability in general terms and conditions; if a clause is actually drafted to be used in several agreements a general term and condition is shown to exist. With respect to physical injury, damage to life and health liability for wilful acts and gross negligence cannot be excluded in the general terms and conditions of an agreement (*§*309, no. 7 BGB). An exclusion of liability in the event of a breach of material duties (cardinal duties) is invalid in the general terms and conditions; limitations in the amount of liability are conceivable but must be proportionate to the risk.

1.8 Are there particular goods or services which have specific obligations or duties attached to them?

Special provisions with regard to the safety and marketing of products include, among others, the Machinery Directive, the Building Products Act, the Medical Devices Act, the Toy Directive, and the Lift Directive.

2. DEFENCES

2.1 What are the possible defences to a product liability claim?

Under tort law, possible defences are:

- the defendant is not the manufacturer of the product;
- the product was used for purposes other than those intended;
- the injured party was experienced dealing with such products;
- the injured party is at least partially to be blamed for having caused the damage (§ 254 BGB).

Under the Product Liability Act additional defences are, among others:

- the manufacturer has not put the product into the stream of commerce;
- if the product was not defective when it was put into the stream of commerce;
- the product complied with mandatory legal provisions at the time the manufacturer put it into the stream of commerce; or
- the fault could not have been recognised having regard to the state-of-the-art science and technology at the time the manufacturer put it into the stream of commerce.

2.2 Is there a limit on the time in which proceedings may be brought (limitations and repose)?

The general limitation period of three years applies under tort law and under the Product Liability Act. The limitation period commences at the end of the year in which the injured party gains or could have gained knowledge of the circumstances that caused the damage and of the identity of the party liable to pay damages.

3. LITIGATION OF PRODUCT LIABILITY DISPUTES

3.1 In which courts are product liability proceedings brought?

The *Landgericht* (regional court) is the court of first instance if the amount in dispute exceeds €5,000. The court at the registered office of the defendant or the court in whose district in which the tortious act – the accident – was committed or damages suffered (§ 32 ZPO (*Zivilprozessordnung* – Code of Civil Procedure)) has personal jurisdiction.

3.2 How are proceedings commenced?

The plaintiff has to file a complaint at the court through a lawyer admitted to practise in Germany; the complaint has to include the subject matter and the facts on which plaintiff want to base his case and a motion. The court will serve the complaint to the defendant.

In most product liability cases legal action is aimed at obtaining a payment. An action for a declaratory judgment is possible if the loss development has not been concluded at the time the claim is raised. This is especially true, if the matter risks becoming time-barred.

3.3 Are disputed issues decided by a judge or a jury?

In Germany, litigation matters are decided by professional judges. Germany does not have a jury system.

At regional courts, proceedings usually take place before a single judge. In complex cases, proceedings can take place before a panel of three judges.

3.4 Who has the burden of proof and to what standard?

The injured party must prove the defect, damage and causation. In certain situations, a reversal in the burden of proof is possible.

The court has to decide whether it is convinced that the factual allegations are true or untrue considering the full facts presented in the trial and the results of the taking of evidence (§ 286 ZPO).

3.5 How is evidence given in proceedings and are witnesses cross-examined?

Evidence can be given by documents, visual inspection by the court, an expert report, and the hearing of witnesses. Affidavits are not permitted.

Witnesses are questioned first by the judge. The judge's questioning is usually very comprehensive and relating to all legally relevant facts for which the person is named as a witness. Thereafter, the party who presented the witness and then the other party is able to put further questions to the witnesses. There is no cross-examination in an Anglo-Saxon way.

3.6 Are the parties able to rely on expert opinion evidence and, if so, are there any special rules or procedures for expert opinion evidence?

Each party may file its own expert report. But if the expert report is disputed, the court will appoint its own (usually court certified) expert who will give his/her written expert report; usually, the expert has to explain his/her report orally. The court-appointed expert must consider the expert report filed by the parties. The parties are entitled to raise objections to the results of the report of the court appointed expert, and request an oral hearing of such expert. To such a hearing, each party may bring its own expert(s). The party appointed experts may, if the court permits, raise their questions directly; otherwise, the lawyer will raise the expert's questions.

3.7 Is pre-trial discovery permitted? If so, in what circumstances? If not, what other mechanisms, if any, are available for obtaining evidence from a party or a third party?

There is no pre-trial discovery in German legal proceedings.

However, the plaintiff has the right to review the criminal investigation report of the public prosecutor if such investigation was performed. Such an investigation is often performed in a case in which a defective product may have been the cause of the death or grave injury of a person.

Further, a party may file an application to the court demanding that one or more identified document(s) shall be presented to the court. The court can order the other party or a third party to produce such identified document (§§ 422, 428 ZPO). But the document to be produced must be described in detail; a fishing expedition is not permitted. Further the application must specify what is to be proved by the document and there must be a claim for surrender of the document under substantive law. Therefore, this possibility may be relevant in a product liability case only if the party referred to such a document either during trial or in correspondence with the other party.

3.8 Is there liability for spoliation of evidence/a remedy for destruction of or failure to preserve evidence (most relevantly, the product)?

If in the above-mentioned case the opponent was ordered to produce a document and fails to do so, the court may take an adverse inference (§ 427 ZPO). There is no litigation hold with respect to electronic or other documents. But a court may take an adverse inference if a party obstructs the obtaining evidence. Therefore, a court may assume that a product is defective if, for example, the manufacturer requests the product to be sent to the manufacturer's plant 'for inspection' and it 'disappears' there. However, there is no hard and fast rule for such a mechanism. The circumstances of the individual case must be taken into account. The court has a certain degree of latitude with regard to the evaluation of evidence.

3.9 Is interlocutory or interim relief available prior to the full trial of a proceeding? If so, in what circumstances?

Prior to filing a law suit, a court may upon application of the damaged party order a separate taking of evidence through questioning of witnesses, by a visual inspection or by asking for an expert report if either the other party agrees or evidence may get lost or it may be harder to obtain evidence in the future (§§ 485 *et seq*. ZPO).

Further, a court may upon application of a party issue a preliminary injunction. By a preliminary injunction, a product could be sequestered (by the bailiff) to avoid destruction or manipulation.

3.10 Can the winning party recover its costs?

German law acknowledges the principle that the costs reflect the result of the case. If a party is only partially successful, a quota is set up which is proportionate to the respective success or failure. However, only court fees, statutory lawyer's fees, and necessary costs are reimbursable. German law regulates litigation fees based on the amount of the claim(s) filed. A party may agree with its lawyer upon higher fees than the statutory legal fees, but an unsuccessful opponent only has to refund the statutory lawyer's fees. It is noteworthy that the court fees in Germany are substantial and also based on the amount in dispute. For example, in a case where the plaintiff demands the payment of €1 million, the court fee is €13,818. In case of a settlement the fee will be reduced to one-third of the advance payment.

3.11 What avenues of appeal are available?

The aggrieved party may appeal against a decision in the first instance. The court of appeal against decisions by the regional court is the *Oberlandesgericht* (Higher Regional Court); the decision is made by a panel of three judges. Generally, the Higher Regional Court reviews the decision only for errors in the application of substantive law and procedural law. Only in very limited circumstances does it conduct its own investigations into the facts of the case.

The highest civil court is the Federal Court of Justice (*Bundesgerichtshof*). The Federal Court of Justice reviews a decision by a Higher Regional Court if the latter permits an appeal. This happens if the Higher Regional Court itself realises that a point of law of fundamental importance has not yet been clarified by the highest instance. If the appeal is not permitted, in exceptional cases an application against the denial of leave to appeal may be made to the Federal Court of Justice.

4. CLASS ACTIONS/REPRESENTATIVE PROCEEDINGS

4.1 Is there a mechanism for class actions or representative proceedings, or coordinated proceedings for product liability claims? If so, what are the basic mechanics?

There is no class action under German law. But several plaintiffs may decide to jointly file law suits against a manufacturer. However, legally speaking, these lawsuits are treated as individual claims summarised in one proceeding. But each lawsuit will be independent from the fate of the other lawsuits.

5. LITIGATION FUNDING

5.1 Is litigation funding by third parties permissible in your country? If so, is it common?

In Germany, there are litigation financiers/insurers who fund litigation in return for participation in the results, but this is a rare exception.

However, a plaintiff who can show that he cannot afford to pay the court fees and the statutory legal fees may apply for legal aid; the court will grant such legal aid if the success of the law suit based on the draft of the complaint is seen reasonably positive.

5.2 Are contingency fees or 'no win no fee' arrangements permissible?

Generally, an attorney at law admitted to practise in Germany is not permitted to act on a contingency basis or on a 'no win no fee' arrangement. The one exception to this is if the plaintiff does not have the financial means to finance litigation. A lawyer would act illegally – he may face charges for breaching the professional code for lawyers – if he would agree to a contingency fee or a 'no win, no fee' arrangement without compliance with these strict exception requirements.

6. REMEDIES

6.1 What remedies are available to a party who successfully pursues a product liability claim?

If the legal action is successful, the party is awarded compensation for any monetary damage suffered if such damage was included in the law suit filed at the end of the hearing at the latest. In addition to actual damages, damages for pain and suffering may also be awarded if such a motion is filed. The party may, but does not have to, apply for a specific amount of damage for pain and suffering. An application can be made that the court recognises the damages for pain and suffering in the amount the court sees appropriate. This is one of the few cases in which no precise demand for relief need to be made.

6.2 How are damages calculated/are there limitations on available damages?

The damages must be precisely calculated based on the actual pecuniary losses suffered. The Product Liability Act recognises maximum limits for strict liability; if death or injury to a person has been caused by a product or by products of the same kind affected by the same defect, the liability to pay damages under the Product Liability Act is limited to €85 million. If the damages payable would exceed this amount, each of the individual claims is reduced proportionally (§ 10 Product Liability Act).

6.3 Are punitive or exemplary damages available and in what circumstances?

German law does not permit punitive or exemplary damages.

6.4 Is liability joint and several/how does apportionment of liability work, including where a partially responsible entity is not a party to the proceeding?

If several persons have caused a tortious loss scenario they are jointly and severally liable. Any internal assessment among the parties is made dependent upon the degree to which each party has contributed to the claim.

German procedural law recognises the institution of third-party notices. In the event a defendant could be in the position to take recourse from a party which is not a joint defendant, the defendant may serve notice by way of a written statement before the court. In the event of proceedings for recourse, the third party in question cannot argue that the decision reached in the first proceeding was incorrect. In view of the third-party notice, the third party may participate in the proceedings and assist one of the two parties. Thus, it must not necessarily assist the party that served the notice.

7. ROLE OF REGULATORS

7.1 Please explain the role, responsibilities and powers of the regulators in your country which have jurisdiction over product liability issues.

The enforcement authorities (generally trade supervisory offices (*Gewerbeaufsichtsämter*) of the federal states) may take the necessary measures if they have reason to suspect that a product does not satisfy health and safety requirements.

7.2 Are there any mandatory reporting requirements related to product safety issues?

Under § 6 (4) of the German Product Safety Act the manufacturer, his authorised agent, and the party which places the product on the market must inform the competent authorities without undue delay if they know or if there are indications on the basis of the information available to them or from experience that a consumer product put on the market by them constitutes a risk to the health and safety of the public; in particular they must give details about the measures they have taken to avoid this risk. Germany also participates in the RAPEX System.

7.3 Do the regulators have the power to:
(i) ban certain goods or services?
(ii) require a supplier to recall a product?
(iii) prescribe standards in respect of certain goods or services and require that the goods or services meet those standards?
(iv) require production of information without court process?
If so, broadly explain the circumstances in which the regulator can exercise the power and any penalties that apply if a supplier fails to comply.

The enforcement authorities (generally trade supervisory offices (*Gewerbeaufsichtsämter*) of the federal states) may take the necessary measures if they have reason to suspect that a product does not satisfy health and safety requirements. In particular it is authorised to:

- prohibit the exhibition of a product if the exhibitor does not clearly indicate that the product does not comply with the requirements and cannot be acquired unless compliance is reached;
- take measures ensuring that a product is not placed on the market if its intended or foreseeable use does put the health and safety of persons at risk;
- order that a product be checked by a notified body, a GS *(Approved Safety)* body or a body that is similarly suited;
- prohibit a product's being made available on the market or a product's exhibition for the period absolutely needed to carry out such checks;
- require that appropriate, clear and easy-to-understand information in German about the risks which the product represents be affixed to the product;
- prohibit that a product is placed on the market;
- order that a product that was made available on the market be withdrawn or recalled;
- seize a product, destroy that product or have it destroyed or otherwise rendered unusable;
- order that the public be warned about the risks posed by a product available on the market.

Market surveillance authorities may alert the public themselves if the economic operator fails to alert or alert in time or fails to take a similarly effective measure or fails to take it in time.

Section 37 of the Product Safety Act sets out the infringements that can entail a penalty (up to €100,000).

8. VOLUNTARY CONDUCT

8.1 Are there regulations pertaining to the voluntary conduct of a product repair or recall by a supplier?

No.

9. EMERGING ISSUES AND LAW REFORM

9.1 Are there important developing and emerging issues or trends in product liability law in your country?

No.

9.2 Please describe any proposed important law reform in the area of product liability in your country.

Not relevant.

10. REGULATORY WEBSITES/INFORMATION

10.1 Please identify any useful regulatory references relating to product liability law in your country, for example, a product safety/ consumer law website maintained by the main regulator.

- *www.baua.de/de/Produktsicherheit/Produktsicherheit.html* (Site of Federal Institute for Occupational Safety and Health (Bundesanstalt für Arbeitsschutz und Arbeitsmedizin) with various links).
- *www.produktrueckrufe.de* (shows product recalls).
- *www.bmas.de/DE/Service/Gesetze/prodsg.html;jsessionid=96C0F7E6470D8383F7D51BD9C9383E88* (link to various German acts in the field of product liability.)
- *www.bmas.de/SharedDocs/Downloads/DE/PDF-Meldungen/produktsicherheitsgesetz-prdsg-englisch.pdf;jsessionid=18C475C5CB1606D9AC70F20E70539384?__blob=publicationFile* (English translation of the Product Safety Act).

Greece

Bahas, Gramatidis & Partners LLP Dimitris Emvalomenos

1. LIABILITY

1.1 What are the principal sources of law and regulation relating to product liability?

Article 6 of Law 2251/1994 on 'Consumers' Protection' (Consumers' Law) implementing Directive 85/374/EEC 'on the approximation of the laws, regulations and administrative provisions of the member states concerning liability for defective products' (as amended by Directive 99/34/EC) sets the main product liability rules in Greece. Consumers' Law has been amended several times until today and latest by Law 4177/2013; extensive amendments were introduced by Law 3587/2007. Article 7 of Consumers' Law on product safety and Ministerial Decision Z3/2810/14.12.2004 (MD), which implemented Directive 2001/95/EC on 'General Product Safety', form the basic supplementary regulation on the topic.

Further, if in a specific case the general legal provisions afford the consumer greater protection than Consumers' Law, such general provisions apply, with the exception of provisions on prescription and exclusive periods (Article 14, paragraph 5 of Consumers' Law). On such basis it is accepted that the general legal regulation may apply parallel to Consumers' Law or independently. Specifically:

- Tortious liability (Articles 914 ff. and especially Articles 914, 925 and 932, in conjunction with Articles 281 and 288 of the Greek Civil Code – GCC).
  Under liability in tort the claimant needs to establish the defendant's fault, which consists of either negligence or wilful misconduct (apart from the latter's unlawful act and a causal link required). However, based on the 'theory of spheres', case law reverses the burden of proof against the producer, requiring him to establish his absence of fault to be released from liability (see below under section 3.4).
- Contractual liability (Articles 513-573 of the GCC on contracts of sale incorporating Directive 1999/44/EC 'on certain aspects of the sale of consumer goods and associated guarantees').
  These provisions require a direct contractual relationship between the parties while the buyer may be a consumer or not. The seller is liable for any product's defect or non-conformity with agreed qualities at the time the risk passes to the buyer. Liability is strict and the claimant does not need to prove that the seller was at fault. However, the seller is not liable where, on conclusion of the contract, the buyer was aware that the product was not in conformity with the contractual specifications or

where the lack of conformity is a result of defective materials supplied by the buyer.

- Criminal liability
  Criminal liability may be derived by the Greek Criminal Code, the Rules Regulating the Market of Products and the Provision of Services (today, Law 4177/2013) and other special provisions (Article 13a, paragraph 2 of Consumers' Law, see also below under 7.3).

1.2 What is required to establish causation under the most common causes of action available?

The claimant must establish that he would not have suffered an injury had the defendant's product not been defective and need not establish the fault or negligence of the manufacturer. The burden is then shifted to the producer who is required to establish a defence in order to be relieved from liability (see below under section 2).

1.3 Is strict liability available and, if so, in what circumstances?

Yes, Greek product liability rules establish a strict liability regime; so, no fault is needed. Article 6 paragraph 1 of Consumers' Law provides that 'the producer shall be liable for any damage caused by a defect in his product'. It derives that, in order for a producer to be held liable:

(a) the product placed on the market by the producer must be defective;
(b) damage must occur; and
(c) a causal link between the product's defect and the damage occurred must exist. Greek legal theory and case law follow the theory of *causa adequata* in accepting a causal link (indicatively, Supreme Court Nos 1261/1985 and 1200/1986, *NOMOS*). Under this theory, the unlawful act or omission at issue must be considered capable of causing the specific damage on the basis of the normal course of events and common practice.

1.4 Are guarantees or warranties as to quality implied by law?

Consumers' Law does not provide for specific guarantees or warranties as to the quality of the product. However, Articles 513 ff. of the GCC re contracts of sale provide that a seller is obliged to deliver products in conformity with their agreed qualities and without defects (Article 534 of the GCC). In particular, the products must:

- comply with any description given by the seller or the sample or model that the seller has presented to the buyer;
- be fit for the purposes of the particular contract and same for which the goods are specifically used;
- be fit for the purposes for which goods of the same type are normally used; and
- be of the quality and performance which the buyer can reasonably expect for goods of the same type, taking into account any public statements made by the seller, the producer or its representative particularly in advertising or on labeling, except where the seller was

not aware and ought not to have been aware of the relevant statement (Article 535 of the GCC).

1.5 How is a product 'defect' defined?

According to Article 6 paragraph 5 of Consumers' Law (as in force after its amendment in 2007), a product is considered defective if its expected performance does not correspond to its specifications or if it does not provide reasonably expected safety in view of all special circumstances, particularly regarding:

- its external presentation;
- its expected use thereof; and
- the time when the product was circulated in the market.

However, a product is not deemed defective solely because another better product was later circulated in the market.

The above concept of defectiveness especially related to lack of safety is supplemented and completed by Article 7 paragraph 3 of Consumers' Law and the MD (see above under 1.1 and below under 1.6).

1.6 Who in the supply chain has obligations or duties for defective products? What obligations or duties do they owe and to whom?

Article 6 paragraphs 2 to 4 of Consumers' Law provide that the 'producer', who bears responsibility for the defect, is the manufacturer of a finished product or of any raw material or of any component, and any other person who presents himself as a producer by putting his name, trade mark or other distinguishing feature on the product. Moreover, any person who imports a product for sale, lease or hire or any form of distribution, within his professional commercial activity, shall be responsible as a producer. Where the producer of the product may not be identified, each supplier of the product shall be treated as its producer unless he provides the injured person with information on the identity of the producer or of the person who supplied him with the product. The same applies to the supplier of imported products when the importer's identity is unknown, even if the producer's identity is known.

Where products are imported into Greece from another EU country, the producer of the product and /or the importer within the EU may bear responsibility as above.

Further, based on Article 7 (paragraph 3) of Consumers' Law and the MD (Article 3), suppliers (including producers) are obliged to only place safe products on the market. Based on this general obligation, producers must provide consumers with the relevant information to enable them to assess the product's risks throughout the normal or reasonably foreseeable period of the product's use. Producers must also take any action needed in order to avoid these risks, as well as take any appropriate preventive and corrective action (such as a recall of the product) depending on the specific circumstances.

Greek case law accepts that a general duty of care is imposed on the producer, meaning that he should take all necessary measures to protect any third parties that reasonably trust him/his products (the principle of trust). Thus, the producer must organise his production in such a way as to serve the general duty of care, mainly by proactively conducting the requisite checks before and during the production process and by providing adequate information to consumers. It is accepted that where that duty is violated and consumers risk sustaining damage, this conduct exceeds the limits of the producer's fair activity and destroys consumers' trust in relation to the safety expectations of the product (indicatively, Court of Thessaloniki No. 2052/1991 and Supreme Court No. 891/2013, *NOMOS*).

1.7 By what means can a supplier limit their liability for defective products?

According to Article 6 paragraph 4 of Consumers' Law, where the producer of the product may not be identified, each supplier of the product shall be treated as its producer unless he provides the injured person with information on the identity of the producer or of the person who supplied him with the product. The same applies to the supplier of imported products when the importer's identity is unknown, even if the producer's identity is known.

Thus, the supplier of a defective 'anonymous product' is only released from responsibility if he informs the victim/consumer within a reasonable time of the identity of the producer or importer or of the person who supplied him with the product.

Further, the supplier of a defective product may limit his liability by taking promptly and in a timely manner any measures required in order to eliminate possible hazards from the product's use (Article 7 of Consumers' Law and the MD). Such measures can be warning notifications, instructions to consumers, invitations for servicing or repairing the product, notification recalls, etc.

1.8 Are there particular goods or services which have specific obligations or duties attached to them?

Extensive sector legislation exists, including but not limited to the following products (the relevant regulation and the supervising authority are only mentioned below):

- Toys
  Common Ministerial Decision 3669/194/2011 (Government Gazette Bulletin – GGB 549/B/2011) implementing EU Directive 2009/48/EC on the Safety of Toys. The competent authority is the First Directorate of Industrial Policy of the General Secretariat of Industry, of the Ministry of Development and Competitiveness (Industry Secretariat).
- Childcare products
  Ministerial Decision Z3-818 (GGB 1395/B/2009). Competent authorities are the General Consumer's Secretariat of the Ministry of Development and Competitiveness (General Secretariat) and the local prefectures.
- Low-voltage products
  Ministerial Decisions 470/85 (GGB 183/B/1985), B.64671/608/88

(GGB 214/B/1988) and 16717/5052/23.12.1994 (GGB 992/B/1994). The competent authority is the Fourth Directorate of the Industry Secretariat.

- Power sockets and plugs
  Ministerial Decision 529/28-1-2000 (GGB 67/B/2000), as amended by Ministerial Decisions 4822/17.3.2000 (GGB 352/B/17-3-2000) and 8991/14-5-2003 (GGB 643/B/2003). The competent authority is the Fourth Directorate of the Industry Secretariat.
- Pressure products and systems
  Ministerial Decisions B10451/929/88 (GGB 370/B/1988), 12479/F17/414/91 (GGB 431/B/1991), 14165/F17.4/373/93 (GGB 673/B/1993), 20769/6285/94 (GGB 977/B/1994), 14132/618/01 (GGB 1626/B/2001), 16289/330/99 (GGB 987/B/1999) and 12436/706/2011 (GGB 2039/B/2011). The competent authority is the Third Directorate of the Industry Secretariat.
- Boilers
  Presidential Decree 335/93 (GGB 143/A/1993) as amended by Presidential Decree 56/95 (GGB 46/A/1995) and Royal Decree 277/63 (GGB 65/A/1963). The competent authority is the Third Directorate of the Industry Secretariat.
- Machines
  Presidential Decree 57/2010 (GGB 97/A/2010), as amended by Presidential Decree 81/2011 (GGB 197/A/2011), implementing Directive 2006/42/EC. The competent authority is the Third Directorate of the Industry Secretariat in collaboration with various other directorates.
- Means of personal protection
  Ministerial Decisions 4373/1205/93 (GGB 187/B/1993), 8881/94 (GGB 450/B/1994) and B.5261/190/97 (GGB 113/B/1997). The competent authority is the First Directorate of the Industry Secretariat.
- Equipment for explosive works
  Ministerial Decision B17081/2964/96 (GGB 157/B/1996). The competent authority is the Fourth Directorate of the Industry Secretariat.
- Plastic tubes
  Ministerial Decisions 14013/ 32/327/83 (GGB 597/B/1993) and 10347/32/176/93 (GGB 432/B/1993). The competent authority is the Second Directorate of the Industry Secretariat.
- Structural construction products
  Presidential Decree 334/94 (GGB 176/A/1994) and various Ministerial Decisions specifying the provisions of such Presidential Decree.
  The competent authority is the Second Directorate of the Industry Secretariat.
- Pleasure yachts
  Ministerial Decision 4841/F7B/52/97 (GGB 111/B/1997). Competent authorities are the Third Directorate of the Industry Secretariat and the Ministry of Marine and Aegean Sea.
- Elevators
  Ministerial Decisions 9.2/32803/1308/97 (GGB 815/B/1997) and

15085/593/03 (GGB 1186/B/03). Competent authorities are the following Directorates of the Industry Secretariat: the Third Directorate and the Supporting Directorate for Industry.

- Bio-extinguishers
  Presidential Decree 205/01 (GGB 160/A/2001). The competent authority is the National Organization for Medicines (EOF).
- Air fresheners
  Ministerial Decision Y1/1880/01 (GGB 1018/B/2001). The competent authority is EOF.
- Anti-smoking products
  Ministerial Decision Y3d/515/94 (GGB 137/B/1994). The competent authority is EOF.
- Cosmetics
  Ministerial Decision 3a/132979 (GGB 352/B/2005), which implemented Cosmetics Directive 76/768/EEC and various other Ministerial Decisions issued subsequently to specify its provisions. The competent authority is EOF.
- Chemicals
  Ministerial Decisions Y1b/7723/94 (GGB 961/B/1994), 378/94 (GGB 705/B/1994), which implemented Directive 67/548/EEC and 265/02 (GGB 1214/B/2002), which implemented Directives 1999/45/EC and 2001/60/EC. Competent authorities are EOF and State's General Chemical Laboratory of the Ministry of Finance.
- Vehicles and parts for vehicles
  Various legislative documents. The competent authority is the Ministry of Transportation and Networks.

2. DEFENCES

2.1 What are the possible defences to a product liability claim?

Under Article 6 paragraphs 8 and 9 of Consumers' Law, the producer may be relieved from liability if he proves that:

(a) he did not place the product on the market;
(b) at the time that the product was placed on the market the defect did not exist;
(c) he did not manufacture the product for the purposes of having it distributed and he did not distribute it in the course of his business;
(d) the defect is due to compliance with mandatory regulations applicable; or
(e) at the time the product was placed on the market, the applicable scientific and technical knowledge did not recognise the existence of the defect (the *state of the art* defence).

The producer of a component is relieved if he proves that the defect is attributable to the design of the product in which the component has been fitted or to the instructions given by the product manufacturer; in such a case, the product manufacturer is considered to be the producer.

With regard to the reduction of producer's liability, Consumers' Law (Article 6, paragraph 11) provides this is possible when, having regard to all the circumstances, the damage is caused by a defect in the product and by the fault of the injured person or any person for whom the injured person is responsible. So, any possible third parties' co-liability does not affect the producer's liability.

Regarding general regulation the GCC provides that sellers may reduce or repeal their liability by demonstrating that the buyer contributed, in whole or in part, to the damage or to the extent of the damage or failed to mitigate the damage (Article 300).

2.2 Is there a limit on the time in which proceedings may be brought (limitations and repose)?

Yes. There are time limits set by law, within which claims must be brought, otherwise they are considered to be time-barred.

(i) For strict liability, according to Article 6 paragraph 13 of Consumers' Law, a three-year limitation period applies, while the right to initiate proceedings against the producer is extinguished upon the expiry of a 10-year period from the date that the producer put the product into circulation.

Consumers' Law (Article 6, paragraph 13) sets as the starting point from which the three-year limitation runs the time when the plaintiff 'became aware or should have become aware of the damage, the defect and the identity of the producer'. The knowledge of the defect includes the circumstances from which it results that the use of the product does not meet the consumer's safety expectations. Furthermore the consumer needs to be in a position to know that the damage is the result of the specific defect of the product so that he may prove their causal link (see also above under 1.3).

For collective lawsuits, see below under section 4.

(ii) For a claim in tort, a general five-year prescription period applies (Article 937 of the GCC) starting from the time the injured person becomes aware of the damage and the responsible person. In any case, the claim may not be raised after 20 years have elapsed from the date of the tortious act. If the tortious act is also punishable under criminal law and a longer limitation period applies, this longer time limit is also extended to the claim for damages.

(iii) Claims based on contractual liability re defects or lack of agreed qualities of goods sold, deriving from Articles 534 to 558 of the GCC, are statute barred after the lapse of two years for movables and five years for immovable property. Such period commences from the date on which the product was delivered to the buyer even if the buyer discovered the defect or the lack of agreed quality later, unless a special guaranteed period was agreed. Further detailed regulation applies (Articles 554-558 of the GCC).

3. LITIGATION OF PRODUCT LIABILITY DISPUTES

As a general note for this section, our answers below are mainly based on the provisions of the Greek Code of Civil Procedure (GCCP), as in force. However, a major reform of the GCCP is expected later this year according to information currently available. Although a draft bill on the GCCP's changes has been recently made public for consultation purposes (consultation was concluded on 28 March 2014), its final text cannot be known at the moment.

3.1 In which courts are product liability proceedings brought?

Private law disputes, including product liability claims, are tried exclusively by civil courts and by one or three judges, depending on the amount of the dispute. As a rule, justices of the peace are competent to examine claims up to €20,000, one-member first instance courts, claims between €20,000 and €250,000, and three-member first instance courts, claims exceeding €250,000 (Articles 14 and 18 of the GCCP).

Special regulation exists on collective claims (see below under section 4).

Criminal and/or administrative proceedings may also be initiated for product liability claims (Articles 13a & 13b of Consumers' Law), however their subject matter is not the compensation of the claimant and they are not dealt with herein.

3.2 How are proceedings commenced?

Proceedings are initiated by the plaintiff consumer filing a lawsuit with the competent court. As a minimum the lawsuit must set out the names and addresses of the respective parties and the particulars of the claim (ie, the material facts and remedies requested) and determine the value and the geographical limits of the dispute (esp. Articles 216 and 221 ff. of the GCCP).

3.3 Are disputed issues decided by a judge or a jury?

All civil trials, like the ones for product liability claims, are conducted only by judges.

3.4 Who has the burden of proof and to what standard?

The plaintiff consumer has to prove the defect, the damage and their causal link; proof of the defendant's fault is not needed (see above under 1.3).

Where a plaintiff sues in tort, as a rule he must also prove the defendant's fault. However, case law holds that such burden of proof is reversed if the plaintiff would otherwise be unable to prove the defendant's culpable conduct. This is accepted when the fact to be proven lies in the exclusive sphere of the defendant's influence and the plaintiff is unable to gain access thereto in order to meet his burden of proof duty; in such a case the defendant is required to prove that he was not responsible for the occurrence of the injurious fact. The reversal is applied under the case law primarily for consumers' claims (indicatively, Supreme Court Nos 1505/2008 and 891/2013, *NOMOS*; see above under 1.1).

3.5 How is evidence given in proceedings and are witnesses cross-examined?

All evidence, ie, exhibits /documents supporting the position of each party are filed together with the pleadings. In cases where the lawsuit is brought before the justice of the peace or one-member court of first instance, the pleadings are filed on the date of the hearing. Additionally, each party may file a rebuttal denying the allegations set forth in the opponent's pleadings by 12pm of the third working day following the hearing (esp. Article 238 of the GCCP).

When the lawsuit is initiated before the three-member court of first instance the pleadings and counter-pleadings must be respectively filed at least 20 and 15 calendar days prior to the hearing date. Additional pleadings may be filed by 12pm of the eighth working day following the hearing and may only be related to allegations raised during the same (Article 237 of the GCCP).

All document exhibits filed with the court must be in Greek, either originally or translated into Greek.

At the hearing, each party may (not obligatory, but it is a common practice and it is considered very important evidence for the court) examine one witness before the court, who is then cross-examined by the opponent (Articles 270 and 393 ff. of the GCCP). Such witness should be someone actually involved with the case, knowing the facts, be firm in his/her position and not 'afraid' of facing the cross-examination.

The witnesses' court examination does not last long, as a rule, and is around 1.5 to three hours as an average, but this is only indicative time since the length of such proceedings very much depends on the complexity of the case and court's discretion to allow witnesses to elaborate on the facts. It is also related to any interpreter's involvement, if so needed where the witness does not speak Greek. Firstly, the plaintiff's witness is examined by the judge(s), then the plaintiff's counsel asks questions and then the witness is cross-examined by the defendant; the defendant's witness follows in turn. The court is not a passive recipient of information and has the discretion to question witnesses and appoint experts to provide evidence. The court may, however, only consider the claims brought before it and may not adjudicate more or other than as claimed by the parties.

Witnesses may, instead of giving oral evidence before the court, testify under oath before a notary public, a justice of the peace or a Greek consular authority outside Greece by way of an affidavit, which may then be presented to the court as evidence. The opponent must be summoned to such depositions prior to two working days or eight full days, if they are given within or outside Greece respectively (Article 270 of the GCCP) and is entitled to obtain a copy of the same after they are given. Restrictions apply to the number of sworn statements.

3.6 Are the parties able to rely on expert opinion evidence and, if so, are there any special rules or procedures for expert opinion evidence?

According to Articles 368-392 of the GCCP, a court may appoint one or more experts where specialised knowledge of scientific and technical matters is required. The experts are entitled to obtain information from the case file in order to formulate their opinion. Court-appointed experts are required to submit their report within the time frame indicated by the court and the hearing of the case is postponed by the court until the expert reports requested have been submitted. However, the expert's opinion is not binding on the court, which, based on its own assessment of the case, may issue a deviating judgment.

Parties may also use experts either as witnesses (see above under 3.5) or produce, as evidence, technical reports prepared by them. The GCCP does not place any restriction on the number of expert reports that may be submitted to the court by a party. In practice, party-appointed expert reports do not have the same evidentiary value as the evidence presented by court-appointed experts.

3.7 Is pre-trial discovery permitted? If so, in what circumstances? If not, what other mechanisms, if any, are available for obtaining evidence from a party or a third party?

Courts are not allowed to try preliminary issues in separate proceedings before the main hearing and no pre-trial discovery exists. Where the court considers that specific knowledge is required in relation to scientific and technical issues or regarding the application of foreign law under rules of private international law, it may issue an interim order to obtain an expert opinion or legal advice on the relevant foreign law provisions respectively.

With regard to obtaining evidence, each party may, through the pleadings filed within the existing litigation or by way of a separate application to the court, seek the court's order for disclosure of documents in the possession of the counterparty or a third party, which may be used as evidence, except where there is a serious reason justifying non-disclosure (Articles 450 ff. of the GCCP and 901-903 of the GCC).

3.8 Is there liability for spoliation of evidence/a remedy for destruction of or failure to preserve evidence?

Generally, yes. There are no specific provisions for product liability disputes. Litigants must follow the general principles of good faith, *bonos mores*, honest and not misleading conduct, disclosing to the other party the documents he invokes except from a serious reason (esp. Articles 116 and 450 of the GCCP). However, a litigant may only submit to the court evidence that supports his case.

Injunction proceedings are available to preserve evidence and especially the product (see below under 3.9).

3.9 Is interlocutory or interim relief available prior to the full trial of a proceeding?

Yes, it is. According to Article 682 of the GCCP, interim measures may be ordered in case of urgency or necessity to prevent imminent danger and for the purpose of securing or preserving a right or of regulating a situation.

Full proof of the facts surrounding the case is not required for a court to order interim measures. The mere belief of the court in the possibility that the above conditions are met would suffice for the interim measures to be ordered. In any case, the court is not bound by the measure requested and it may order what measure it regards as appropriate per its discretion (Articles 690 & 692 of the GCCP). Injunctive measures may vary and they can be the granting of a guarantee, the pre-notation of mortgage, the temporary regulation of a situation or award of a claim, the temporary seizure of an asset, etc.

Further, upon the filing of an injunction petition and until the hearing of the same and the issue of the court decision, which in 'busy' courts like that in Athens it may in practice even take six months or so, the temporary order of a judge may be issued, again depending on the judge's discretion (Article 691 of the GCCP).

As a rule, if an injunctive measure is ordered before the filing of the lawsuit under the ordinary proceedings, the petitioner must file the lawsuit within 30 days from the injunctions decision (Article 693 of the GCCP).

Lastly, an exceptional procedure for the preservation of evidence is provided for by Articles 348 to 351 of the GCCP. In short: during the ordinary proceedings after the filing of a lawsuit and prior to its hearing date, as long as there is a risk that specific means of evidence will be later lost or its use will become more difficult or if the determination of the present condition of an object or project is material for the purpose of the case, an early evidential procedure may be requested by the court in relation to a particular topic even prior to the opening of the trial.

3.10 Can the winning party recover its costs?

The loser-pays rule applies. Court expenses are 'only the court and out-of-court expenses that were necessary for the trial' and in particular are:

(a) stamp duties;
(b) judicial revenue stamp duty;
(c) counsels' minimum fees set by the Greek Lawyers' Code;
(d) witnesses' and experts' expenses; and
(e) the successful party's travelling expenses in order for him to attend the hearing.

However, the expenses that the successful party recovers are, as per the general practice, substantially lower than his actual expenses, whereas the court very often offsets the expenses between the litigants on the basis of complex legal issues involved in the litigation (Article 173 ff. of the GCCP).

3.11 What avenues of appeal are available?

In ordinary proceedings, every definite judgment issued by a first instance court may be contested before a designated second instance court. An appeal can be filed not only by the defeated party, but also by the successful party whose allegations were partially accepted by the court. Further, a cassation before the Supreme Court may be filed against appellate courts' decisions for questions of law only.

4. CLASS ACTIONS/REPRESENTATIVE PROCEEDINGS

4.1 Is there a mechanism for class actions or representative proceedings, or coordinated proceedings for product liability claims? If so, what are the basic mechanics?

Class action proceedings do not exist in Greece, but there are provisions regarding collective actions (Article 10, paragraphs 16 ff. of Consumers' Law). A collective action is distinguished from an action where more claimants connected to each other with a specific object of the trial are represented before the court by one or more of their co-claimants (Articles 480 ff. of the GCC and 74 ff. of the GCCP). Collective actions may only be filed by consumers' associations under special regulation. Specifically, consumer associations, which have more than 500 active members and have been registered prior to one year, may bring an action to protect the general interests of consumers. Such an action may also be brought if the unlawful conduct harmed the interests of at least 30 consumers.

By such an action, a consumer's association may claim:

(a) the cessation of the supplier's unlawful conduct;
(b) monetary compensation for moral harm;
(c) the issue of injunctive measures to secure consumers demands for cessation of the unlawful conduct or monetary satisfaction until an enforceable court decision is issued, including the temporary seizure of defective products; and
(d) an acknowledgment of the right to restore the damage sustained by consumers due to the unlawful conduct in question.

Collective actions are brought before the multi-member first instance court where the defendant resides or has its seat within six months of the last unlawful behaviour challenged, unless a declaratory judgment is sought, in which case the general five-year prescription period for torts applies.

The court's decision issued has a (very special under Greek law) *erga omnes* effect binding non-litigants as well. However, the *res judicata* effect of the decision accepting (even partially) a lawsuit for a declaratory judgment recognising the damages suffered by consumers due to the unlawful behaviour challenged, works in favour of any consumer damaged, even if he did not participate in the specific trial. As a result, any such damaged consumer may notify his claim to the producer once the decision at issue becomes irrevocable and, after the lapse of 30 days without consumer's compensation or any other settlement of the dispute, file a petition before the competent court asking for a judicial order to be issued against the producer, provided the claim is proven and liquidated and the general requirements are met. Also, other consumers' rights are not affected by the collective pursuance of a claim as above and the rejection of a collective lawsuit does not preclude individual proceedings.

It is noted that collective lawsuits are not commonly brought in relation to product liability disputes, although they are frequent in relation to abusive general terms and conditions, especially in credit financial and insurance agreements.

5. LITIGATION FUNDING

5.1 Is litigation funding by third parties permissible in your country? If so, is it common?

Third-party litigation funding has not been practised much in Greece. Private funding is not known, although not expressly prohibited by law.

Articles 194 to 204 of the GCCP regulate public litigation funding providing for legal aid to any person who is unable to fund the cost of the trial without endangering his maintenance and that of his family, under conditions and special proceedings that the petitioner must follow. In addition, Law 3226/2004 on the provision of legal aid to low income citizens, implementing Directive 2003/8/EC, enables low-income individuals to obtain legal aid in connection with civil, commercial and criminal law cases (Article 3 of Law 3226/2004).

5.2 Are contingency fee or 'no win no fee' arrangements permissible?

Yes, such agreements and other conditional arrangements on lawyers' fees are allowed between clients and lawyers per the Lawyers' Code, under the basic restrictions that:

(a) they are made in writing; and

(b) the maximum fee percentage agreed may not exceed 20% of the case's value or 30%, if more than one lawyers are involved.

Further regulation on such arrangements and the collection of the fees is provided by the law (Article 60 of the recently amended Lawyers' Code – Law 4194/2013).

6. REMEDIES

6.1 What remedies are available to a party who successfully pursues a product liability claim?

Monetary compensation is available to the victim successfully pursuing a civil claim (see below under 6.2). Criminal or administrative proceedings possibly pursued (see below under 7.3) do not have a monetary benefit to the victim.

For the remedies that may be pursued by a collective action and same related to collective proceedings, see above under 4.1.

6.2 How are damages calculated/are there limitations on available damages?

According to Article 6 paragraphs 6 and 7 of the Consumers' Law, the types of recoverable damages are:

(a) damages caused by death or by personal injury to anyone; and

(b) damage or destruction caused due to the defective product to any consumer's asset other than the defective product itself, including the right to use environmental goods, and provided that:
   (i) the damage exceeds €500; and
   (ii) the product was ordinarily intended for and actually used by the injured person for his own private use or consumption.

Furthermore, compensation for moral harm or mental distress may also be claimed (in the latter case by the family of the deceased victim).

Additionally, under tortious liability (basically, Articles 914 ff. in conjunction with Articles 297-299 of the GCC) the aggrieved party may claim full compensatory damages including lost profit as well as moral damages. In the case of personal injury, which includes bodily and health injury, compensation includes, apart from hospitalisation, expenses and damages already incurred, anything the aggrieved party will be deprived of in the future or will further sustain as a result of increased expenses.

Lastly, contractual liability provisions (Articles 534 to 558 of the GCC and especially Articles 540 and 543 of the GCC) provide that the buyer is entitled to request:

(a) at no additional charge, the repair of a defective product or its replacement with another; or
(b) a reduction in the purchase price; or
(c) rescission of the contract or/and over and above his previous rights; or
(d) compensation, under conditions.

6.3 Are punitive or exemplary damages available and in what circumstances?

In Greece the duty to compensate has no penal character. The notion of sanctions is not a feature of civil law because this is geared towards the injured party and not the tortfeasor. The damages actually suffered represent the limit of and correspond to the compensation awarded because otherwise compensation would result in an unjustified enrichment of the injured party.

However, especially in collective claims (see above under 4.1) the way the amount for moral harm awarded is calculated and invested for purposes of promoting the policies for consumers' protection as well as the effect of the relevant decision (Article 10, paragraphs 16b, 20 and 22 of the Consumers' Law) brings it closer to a pecuniary sentence, a so-called 'civil sanction' imposed on the producer.

6.4 Is liability joint and several/how does apportionment of liability work, including where a partially responsible entity is not a party to the proceeding?

If two or more persons are responsible for the same damage, these persons are jointly and severally liable as against the consumer and have a right of recourse against each other on the basis of their contribution to the damage (Article 6, paragraph 10 of Consumers' Law). Likewise, Article 926 of the GCC provides that where several persons contributed to the damage suffered or are responsible for the same damage, then their liability is joint and several.

Practically speaking, the plaintiff (consumer) may bring an action against all persons he considers that have contributed to his damage suing them jointly and severally, obtaining satisfaction from one or more responsible persons depending on the decision issued. The co-defendant which ultimately pays the plaintiff's damages awarded is entitled to subrogate against the other co-defendants, requesting their contribution to the compensation. Such claims may be brought in the same or in subsequent proceedings, provided that they are not time-barred per each particular case.

A partially responsible entity being not a party to the proceedings initiated by a plaintiff may become a litigant of the same if it is invited by any of the defendants to participate therein (Article 86 ff. of the GCCP).

7. ROLE OF REGULATORS

7.1 Please explain the role, responsibilities and powers of the regulators in your country which have jurisdiction over product liability issues.

The General Secretariat is the central regulator. It consists of three departments:

(a) Consumer's Policy;
(b) Consumer's Protection; and
(c) Technical Control.

Each has specified duties. The main responsibilities of the General Secretariat are (Presidential Decree 197/1997, as in force):

- development of consumer policy;
- harmonisation of the Greek legislation in line with the European Community Law in issues of consumer protection;
- monitoring of legislation at national level and abroad with regard to consumer protection;
- exercising the powers set out under Consumers' Law concerning the consumer organisations and the National Consumer Council;
- consumer information & education;
- constant updating of the website (*www.efpolis.gr*) which provides information to consumers on basic issues (consumer protection legislation, product safety, consumer organisations);
- handling of consumers' complaints with regard to the infringements of regulations in force aiming at consumer protection;
- imposition of administrative sanctions to those who infringe the legislation in force for consumer protection;
- offering advice and assistance to consumers;
- implementation and enforcement of the General Product Safety legislation;
- operation of RAPEX (Rapid Exchange Information System).
- surveillance on the conditions of circulation of products;
- supervision of the controls, surveillance and sampling performed by the local administration authorities and offer of guidelines and instructions required.

As mentioned above under 1.8, apart from the General Secretariat and depending on the particular product, other authorities may be competent.

7.2 Are there any mandatory reporting requirements related to product safety issues?

Should producers (considered broadly, any supplier) become aware that any of their products presents dangers to consumers, they must notify the General Secretariat, immediately and without delay, and any other competent authority depending on the type of the product at issue, for the prevention of any danger or hazard to consumers. The notification is made in a form provided by the competent authority and has to include information to identify the product, a complete description of the defect and the risk involved with the usage of the product, information to locate the product in the market, description of the actions already taken by the producer and the actions that can be taken by consumers to prevent any further risk.

The reporting as above to the competent authority does not release a producer from his obligation to take any appropriate measure in a timely manner and to properly inform consumers on a safety matter.

If the product has been marketed outside Greece as well, the procedure under the RAPEX notification system may be followed. The system allows the fast, almost simultaneous, transfer of information on dangerous products within the EU. Respective procedures apply especially to food and medicines.

The notified authorities may request additional information, the submission to them of relevant documents/data or measures to be taken by the producer and can set a deadline, within which the action requested must be implemented. Also, the authorities have to be kept informed by the producer of the results of any ongoing research in order to be updated and monitor the case.

7.3 Do the regulators have the power to:
(i) ban certain goods or services?
(ii) require a supplier to recall a product?
(iii) prescribe standards in respect of certain goods or services and require that the goods or services meet those standards?
(iv) require production of information without court process?
If so, broadly explain the circumstances in which the regulator can exercise the power and any penalties that apply if a supplier fails to comply.

Yes, the regulator has broad powers to safeguard that unsafe products do not remain in the market. Mandatory standards for certain products may be prescribed by ministerial decisions together with monitoring proceedings that such standards are met.

Also, products that present or may present serious dangers to the safety and health of consumers when used in conditions that are normal or predictable may be recalled or withdrawn, as a precaution, by the competent authority. The procedure, the terms and conditions for the recall, withdrawal or disposal under terms, destruction and any other relevant topic, are regulated by ministerial decisions. Such decisions must be challenged by the producer involved before the Minister of Development before judicial proceedings are followed (Article 7, paragraphs 6 and 12 of Consumers' Law).

Further, subject to the stipulations of the Criminal Code, the Rules Regulating the Market of Products and the Provision of Services (today, Law 4177/2013) and other special provisions, the following administrative sanctions may be imposed against a producer (and generally, any supplier) by a ministerial decision, taken either *ex officio* or after a complaint is filed:

- a recommendation for compliance within a specified deadline as well as an order to stop the infringement and refrain from it in the future;
- a fine in the range between €1,500 and €1 million; this maximum amount of the fine may be doubled if more than three fines are imposed on a producer; or/and
- if more than three fines are imposed on a producer, the temporary closure of his business may be ordered for a period ranging from three months to one year.

Other administrative fines ranging from €500 to €50,000 are provided for against a producer who fails to respond in a timely way to a consumer's complaint filed with the General Secretariat. All the above fines may be adjusted by ministerial decisions.

The competent minister has the authority, considering the nature and gravity of the violation, as well as its general repercussions on the consuming public, to publicise, through the press or any other means available, the sanctions imposed and the restraining measures taken with regard to the circulation of a product in the market (Article 13a, paragraphs 1-5 of Consumers' Law).

8. VOLUNTARY CONDUCT

8.1 Are there regulations pertaining to the voluntary conduct of a product repair or recall by a supplier?

There are no specific provisions pertaining to the voluntary conduct of a product repair or recall or other corrective action by a producer or a distributor or a supplier.

A product's supplier (generally viewed and including the producer) must take any measure and corrective action appropriate to eliminate the possible hazard from that product's use, as soon as he knows of any defect. Such defect would constitute a breach of supplier's general obligation to only place safe products on the market (Article 7 of Consumers' Law and the MD). The needed measures may vary and can include warning notifications, instructions to consumers, invitations for servicing or updating of the product in order to become safe or notifications recalling the product. Within that general frame a product's recall must regarded the last action taken in the event that no other measure would eliminate the danger. As said (above under 7.3) a product's recall may be also mandated by the competent authority.

Regarding the repair of a product, the GCC includes it within the buyer's various options for a defective product and, if exercised, the supplier is obliged to comply with the same within a reasonable time and without buyer's material inconvenience (Article 540 ff. of the GCC).

9. EMERGING ISSUES AND LAW REFORM

9.1 Are there important developing and emerging issues or trends in product liability law in your country?

- Consumers' Law continues to be amended relatively often. In 2013, changes to it regarded, among others, the sanctions that may be imposed for non-compliance with its provisions and a new categorisation of complaints filed under it (Articles 13a & 13b). Earlier, in 2012, the right to bring collective actions granted to other EU member states' entities authorised for must be noted (Article 10, paragraph 30). So, a trend towards enforcing consumers' rights and imposing increased sanctions may be noted.

- Another trend is towards increased settlement alternatives for the avoidance of litigation. Within that frame, in 2012 Consumers' Law was supplemented regarding entities that pursue alternative consumer dispute resolution (new Article 11a of Consumers' Law implementing the EU Commission's Recommendations Nos 98/257/EC and 2001/310/EC). This trend is broader in Greek law. So, recent changes to the GCCP were introduced to facilitate settlement against the litigation of disputes (Articles 214A, 214B & 233, apart from older provisions of 208-214 of the GCCP). Within the same frame, Law 3898/2010 implemented Directive 2008/52/EC 'on certain aspects of mediation in civil and commercial matters'. However thus far, application of the above 'mediation' settlement provisions remains very limited.
- Consumer awareness must be considered rather low. Although a few consumer organisations have become more active in the recent years, their activities have been rather limited – focusing on challenging abusive general terms and conditions.
- Regarding Greek authorities, they have been especially active in using the RAPEX procedure. Based on official data from the past six years, the General Secretariat made annually an average of approximately 109 notifications (2013: 61, 2012: 82, 2011: 69, 2010: 159, 2009: 153, 2008: 129).

Also, during the past few years, market controls regarding unsafe products have intensified. For example, in 2011, 211 fines of a total amount of €5,390,500 were imposed and in 2012 1,506 fines of a total amount of €1,195,600 were imposed. There are currently no available data for 2013.

9.2 Please describe any proposed important law reform in the area of product liability in your country.

Nothing is ongoing today.

10. REGULATORY WEBSITES/INFORMATION

10.1 Please identify any useful regulatory references relating to product liability law in your country, for example, a product safety/consumer law website maintained by the main regulator.

General Consumer's Secretariat of the Ministry of Development and Competitiveness: email: info@efpolis.gr; website: *www.efpolis.gr.*

The author gratefully acknowledges the assistance of Manto Charitos and Panos Koromantzos in the compilation of this chapter.

India

AZB & Partners Zia Mody & Vivek Bajaj

1. LIABILITY

1.1 What are the principal sources of law and regulation relating to product liability?

The substantive civil laws that relate to product liability in India are:

(i) The Sale of Goods Act, 1930 (SGA);
(ii) The Consumer Protection Act, 1986 (CPA); and
(iii Indian Contract Act, 1872 (Contract Act).

In cases involving public health and safety, the Indian Penal Code, 1860 (IPC) may apply wherein criminal liability is appended to acts that may pose a threat to public interest at large.

Further, since India is a common law country, in addition to civil and criminal laws, principles of tort law such as duty of care, negligence, strict liability (including absolute liability in exceptional circumstances) among others would also apply in cases dealing with product liability.

Separately, pan-industry regulations such as Bureau of Indian Standards Act, 1986 (BIS Act) and the Bureau of Indian Standards Rules, 1987 (BIS Rules) set out mandatory and voluntary standards for products covered under different sectors. Additionally, for identified sectors such as food, pharmaceuticals and the automobile industry, there are specific laws such as the Food Safety and Standards Act, 2006 (FSSA), Drugs and Cosmetics Act, 1940 (Drugs Act), and Motor Vehicles Act, 1988 (MVA) which govern and regulate standards, product safety and liability. These are discussed in responses to subsequent questions.

1.2 What is required to establish causation under the most common causes of action available?

Typically, to establish causation in cases such as product liability, every fact establishing the elements of a cause of action must be proved. These are generally: (i) the breach of duty owed by one person to another and the resulting damage or loss to the other from the breach; and/or (ii) existence of combination of facts which gives rise to a right to sue. Therefore, for civil actions, every plaint by an aggrieved person is required to set out the facts or combination of facts, which give rise to a right to sue without which the plaint is liable to be rejected.

1.3 Is strict liability available and, if so, in what circumstances?

Indian courts have applied the principles of strict liability laid down in *Rylands v Fletcher* (1868) LR 3 HL 330) ie, 'a person who uses his land to keep or accumulate a potentially dangerous thing will be liable for all the damages that result as a natural consequence of its escape' in several cases.

It must be noted here that Indian courts have significantly developed the concept of strict liability first laid down in *Rylands v Fletcher.* A more stringent rule of strict liability (ie, principle of absolute liability) was laid down by the Supreme Court of India in the case of *M.C. Mehta v Union of India* (AIR 1987 SC 965) where it held that persons carrying on hazardous or inherently dangerous activities shall be strictly and absolutely liable to compensate for damage caused by their activities to both persons and environment. Further, such liability is not subject to any of the exceptions that operate *vis-a-vis* the tortious principle of strict liability under the rule in *Ryland v Fletcher*. The Supreme Court of India emphasised that the duty imposed on the enterprise is 'absolute and non-delegable' and liability cannot be escaped by showing that all reasonable steps had been taken and that there was no negligence on the part of the enterprise. However, so far Indian courts have not applied the principles of absolute liability in cases relating to product liability and have restricted its application to cases concerning environment and public interest.

1.4 Are guarantees or warranties as to quality implied by law?

In respect of implied warranties and conditions as to quality, Indian law recognises and has codified the following principles and the corresponding rights under the SGA:

(i) In a sale of goods by description, there is an implied condition that the goods shall correspond with the description.

(ii) In the event the purchaser has: (a) expressly or by implication, made known to the seller the particular purpose for which he purchases the goods; (b) relies on the skill and judgement of the seller; and the goods are of a description which is in the ordinary course of the seller's business to supply; then there is an implied condition that the goods shall be reasonably fit for such purpose. However, this implied condition of fitness for a particular purpose does not extend to sale of goods under its patent or trade name.

(iii) In cases where goods are purchased by description from a seller who deals in goods of that description, there is an implied condition that the goods shall be of merchantable quality. The term 'merchantable quality' has not been defined in the SGA. However, Indian courts have held 'merchantable' to include the following characteristics; (a) fit/suitable for the purpose the good has been sold for; and (b) free from defects. However, such an implied condition will not extend to patent defects if the buyer had examined the goods.

Separately, while no warranties (implied or otherwise) have been prescribed, certain categories of products such as electronics, automobile and food have applicable laws, which govern standards in relation to such products and the consequences of not complying with such standards.

1.5 How is a product 'defect' defined?

There is no universally applicable definition of the term 'defect' and different statutes may construe non-compliance with provisions of the statute or standards contained therein as 'defects'. However, the CPA (legislation primarily to protect the interest of consumers) defines a 'defect' to mean any fault, imperfection or shortcoming in the quality, quantity, potency, purity or standard which is required to be (i) maintained by or under any law for the time being in force; or (ii) under any contract, express or implied; or (iii) as is claimed by the trader in any manner whatsoever in relation to any goods.

1.6 Who in the supply chain has obligations or duties for defective products? What obligations or duties do they owe and to whom?

The CPA extends liability to manufacturers and distributors/vendors for defective goods. However, under the SGA and Contract Act, typically, the seller is liable for any defects in goods. Indian law also recognises manufacturer's liability under principles of tort law. In addition to these, laws specific to certain sectors identify persons and entities that will be considered liable (either jointly or severally) for any defective products that are manufactured, distributed, or otherwise dealt with in any manner.

1.7 By what means can a supplier limit its liability for defective products?

Suppliers may limit their own liability in respect of defective products by specifically including provisions in relation to (i) limitation of liability', ie, capping the liability of the supplier in all cases of defective products; (ii) limited warranty such as only replacement of defective part or defective product; and (iii) exclusion of all implied and express warranties under law; in their agreements with the purchasers. It must be borne in mind that any contractual limitation of liability *vis-à-vis* contracting parties (such as the supplier/manufacturer and the buyer) cannot override liability imposed on the supplier/manufacturer under a statute.

1.8 Are there particular goods or services which have specific obligations or duties attached to them?

Food business operators, manufactures, packers, distributors and sellers of products such as drugs, cosmetics, food and agricultural produce have specific obligations and duties attached to them. These have been explained in detail in our responses below.

In addition to the above, services such as those for chartered accountants, medical and legal services have specific detailed regulations governing these services. These regulations have specific obligations and duties attached to medical practioners, lawyers, and chartered accountants in relation to standard of services, negligence and payment for services among others.

2. DEFENCES

2.1 What are the possible defences to a product liability claim?

Defences to product liability claims include among others:

(i) product being compliant with requisite statutory standards prescribed;
(ii) defect caused by negligence or misuse by the consumer/buyer;
(iii) consumer/buyer had examined the goods prior to purchase and accepted on being satisfied of its quality or specification;
(iv) contractually agreed disclaimers or limitations on warranties in terms of scope, period and amount; or
(v) civil action or complaint by the complainant being barred by the law of limitation.

2.2 Is there a limit on the time in which proceedings may be brought (limitations and repose)?

Limitation on filing of suits in India is governed by the Limitation Act, 1963 (Limitation Act). The period of limitation for a civil proceeding for monetary compensation on account of contractual breach as set out under the Limitation Act is three years from the date on which the breach occurs. Please note that the limitation period under the CPA is two years from the date the cause of action has arisen. However, under the CPA, a complaint may be entertained after the limitation period if the consumer court is satisfied with the reasons for the delayed filing of the complaint.

Further, the Code of Criminal Procedure (CrPC) provides for limitation periods in respect of criminal offences under the IPC.

In addition to the above general law on limitation, specific statutes regulating certain products expressly set out applicable periods of limitation. For example, the FSSA provides for a limitation period of one year, extendable up to three years at the discretion of the relevant authorities.

3. LITIGATION OF PRODUCT LIABILITY DISPUTES

3.1 In which courts are product liability proceedings brought?

Any person intending to initiate legal action in respect of a defective product may bring an action as:

(i) a consumer under the CPA before the appropriate consumer court/forum; or
(ii) an aggrieved or interested party by filing a suit before a civil court pursuant to a violation of contract or specific statute; or
(iii) an appropriate arbitration forum in accordance with the arbitration provision/agreement entered into by the relevant parties; or
(iv) a jurisdictional magistrate in the event criminal proceedings are commenced in relation to product liability claims.

In addition to the above, specific statutes such as the Drugs Act, MVA and FSSA have set out dedicated courts or tribunals to take cognizance of offences under these statutes. Therefore, aggrieved parties/relevant authorities may approach such courts/tribunals for defective goods or product liability proceedings.

3.2 How are proceedings commenced?

While there is no mandatory requirement under Indian law, parties usually send notices to the relevant parties in the event of disputes or claims with the view to settle the claims prior to commencement of formal legal proceedings.

An action may be initiated by:

(i) filing a complaint under the consumer protection law; or
(ii) filing a plaint/suit in accordance with the provisions of the Code of Civil Procedure, 1908 (CPC); or
(iii) if the parties have agreed to resolution of disputes by way of arbitration, appointing an arbitrator in accordance with the arbitration agreement between the parties; or
(iv) filing a compliant with the jurisdictional police station or magistrate.

As discussed in our responses above, commencement of proceedings including filings of complaints under specific statutes such as the FSSA, MVA and Drugs Act are statutorily driven and therefore, governed by the procedures set out in these statutes.

3.3 Are disputed issues decided by a judge or a jury?

Disputed issues are decided by the court, which is presided over by judge(s) or in case of tribunals, they are supervised by the presiding officer(s). Please note India does not follow a jury system of trial.

3.4 Who has the burden of proof and to what standard?

As a general rule of evidence, any party seeking the court's intervention as to enforcement of any legal right must prove that those facts exist. Specifically, the burden of proof to prove the breach of warranty and the resultant loss lies on the claimant (ie, the party alleging the defect). In a criminal case, the burden of proof lies on the prosecution, unless the statutes specific to certain products expressly provide otherwise. However, certain criminal offences provide for presumption of a criminal act in certain circumstances shifting the burden of proof on the accused.

3.5 How is evidence given in proceedings and are witnesses cross-examined?

Evidence may be given either orally or by producing documents including electronic records. All facts (except the contents of documents or electronic records) may be provided by oral evidence. Oral evidence is usually given by way of an affidavit or a sworn statement in the presence of a public notary or in the presence of the judge. On the other hand, the contents of documents may be produced either in original or certified copies including electronic records as per the provisions of the Indian Evidence Act, 1872 (Evidence Act) and information technology laws.

The CPC sets out the order of production and examination of witnesses including cross-examination. Failure to cross-examine a witness renders the evidence tendered in that respect unchallenged and therefore accepted.

Proceedings before the consumer courts under the CPA are summary in nature and therefore, fully-fledged trials are typically not undertaken. However, the consumer courts have the same powers as are vested in a civil court, including summoning and enforcing of attendance of any defendant, discovery and production of documents, reception of evidence and any other matter as may be prescribed.

Similarly, evidence taking in arbitral proceedings is summary in nature and the parties can contractually agree on the procedure in relation to evidence collection and examination of witnesses.

Further, the CrPC sets out procedure specific to offences under the IPC and other criminal legislations for filing of a complaint, investigation and evidence in enquiries and trials including examination of witnesses.

3.6 Are the parties able to rely on expert opinion evidence and, if so, are there any special rules or procedures for expert opinion evidence?

Expert opinion may be relied on by the parties to a suit or proceeding. The Evidence Act sets out the instances when the court can rely on experts and these include instances when the court has to form an opinion on foreign law, science, art and handwriting, among others. It must be noted that there are no special procedures for expert opinion evidence and the procedure as set out in the CPC for witnesses in general is applicable to opinions of experts.

Indian criminal courts are also vested with the power to summon, examine and receive evidence from an expert including receiving reports from certain governmental scientific experts under the provisions of the CrPC.

3.7 Is pre-trial discovery permitted? If so, in what circumstances? If not, what other mechanisms, if any, are available for obtaining evidence from an party or a third party?

The CPC contemplates discovery of evidence only on or after the institution of a civil proceeding and not prior to initiating civil proceedings.

However, once a civil proceeding has been instituted, a party to a civil suit has the option to apply to the court for an order directing the other party or a third party to make discovery of the documents, which are or have been in the possession or power of such party and relating to any matter raised in the suit. Do note that courts will not order for discovery if it is of the opinion that it is not necessary either for disposing of the matter fairly or for saving costs.

The CPC also empowers courts in India by its own motion to make such orders as may be necessary or reasonable, at any time (including pre-evidence stage but post the filing of the plaint), in all matters relating to:

(a) delivery and answering of interrogatories;
(b) admission of documents and facts; and
(c) discovery, inspection, production, impounding and return of documents or other material objects producible as evidence.

However, in arbitration proceedings, the arbitral tribunal is not bound by provisions of the CPC or the Evidence Act. The contracting parties are free to agree on the procedure to be followed by the arbitral tribunal in conducting such proceedings. However, in the absence of an agreement in this regard between the parties, the arbitral tribunal may conduct the proceedings in the manner it considers appropriate subject to the provisions of the relevant arbitration regulations. Practically, arbitral tribunals tend to follow the provisions of the CPC and Evidence Act, since contracting parties generally appoint retired judges as arbitrators.

3.8 Is there liability for spoliation of evidence/a remedy for destruction of or failure to preserve evidence (most relevantly, the product)?

Under criminal law, destruction of any document or electronic record which would have been required to be produced as evidence is an offence punishable with imprisonment which may extend to two years, or a fine, or both. However, under civil law, there are no specific remedies for destruction of evidence that may be invoked by a party as a matter of legal right unless agreed under a contract. However, failure to produce documents or such other evidence as directed by a court (for any reason including destruction of or failure to preserve evidence) could amount to contempt of court.

Certain statutes mandate maintenance of records and registers and/or furnishing of information to an officer or authority (constituted under such statute) and these statutes set out the penalty for obstructing investigations carried out by relevant officer/authority (which presumably would include destruction of information and products which may be considered as evidence).

3.9 Is interlocutory or interim relief available prior to the full trial of a proceeding?

Yes, Indian courts have the power to pass interim or interlocutory orders prior to a full trial. However, such interim orders can be passed by the court only after civil proceedings have been initiated by filing of a plaint. The courts have wide powers in this regard and interim orders can be passed at any time during suit proceedings when considered necessary and proper in light of the facts and circumstances of the case. Generally, interim relief is granted by the court if the following conditions are satisfied:

(i) where there is *prima facie* case in favour of the party seeking such an order;

(ii) irreparable injury may be caused to the party which cannot be adequately compensated for by damages; and

(iii) the balance of convenience is in favour of the plaintiff, ie, the plaintiff is likely to suffer substantial mischief if the interim relief is refused when compared with the mischief which might be caused to the defendants if the interim relief is granted.

Further, Indian courts are empowered to pass interim orders to prevent wasting, damaging, alienation, sale, removal or disposition of property, dispossession of the plaintiff or otherwise causing injury to the plaintiff in relation to any property in dispute in the suit.

In case of domestic arbitration, unless contractually excluded by the parties, a party may before the commencement of, or during arbitral proceedings or at any time after the making of an award but before it is enforced apply to a court for interim measures in accordance with provisions of the Indian Arbitration and Conciliation Act, 1996.

3.10 Can the winning party recover its costs?

Yes, courts in India have the power to award costs to the winning party (including consumers) incurred in relation to a suit or proceeding. However, it must be noted that Indian courts are generally conservative in granting substantial costs in civil cases.

3.11 What avenues of appeal are available?

The court structure in India is hierarchical in nature with the Supreme Court of India being the highest court of appeal. Each state in India has a High Court, which is the highest court of appeal in the state. It must be noted that in certain metropolitan cities (erstwhile presidency towns) High Courts have original jurisdiction in matters above a certain pecuniary threshold, in addition to being the highest courts of appeal in the state. Jurisdiction of courts may be pecuniary, territorial or specific to the subject matter of the suit. The CPC requires every suit to be instituted in the court of the lowest grade competent to try it and also sets out the original or appellate jurisdiction of courts.

On being aggrieved by any order/judgment passed by the civil court, a party may approach the higher court under the provisions of the CPC within a prescribed period of limitation. A second appeal may be preferred depending on the court of first appeal. Please note appeals from appellate decrees (a second appeal) is allowed only on certain specific grounds such as:

(i) the case involves a substantial question of law and the memorandum of appeal sets out precisely state the substantial question of law;
(ii) appellate decree passed *ex parte*;
(iii) the court is of the view that the case involves a substantial question of law, although not formulated in the memorandum of appeal.

For criminal cases, the CrPC sets out the classes of criminal courts, their territorial divisions for taking cognizance of criminal matters and the appellate structure of courts. Appeals in criminal cases may be preferred only in instances specified in the CrPC before the appellate courts depending on the order or judgment of the lower court against which the appeal is preferred.

In addition to the above, the Constitution of India provides for special powers to High Courts and the Supreme Court. In this context, it must be noted that High Courts have superintendence over all courts and tribunals throughout the territories in relation to which it exercises jurisdiction. Furthermore, the Supreme Court may, in its discretion, grant special leave to appeal from any judgment, decree, sentence or order in any cause or matter passed or made by any court or tribunal.

Finally, special tribunals set up under specific statutes have their own appeal structure including the hierarchy of courts and grounds for appeal. In relation to arbitration proceedings, Indian Arbitration and Conciliation Act, 1996 has very limited grounds for appeal, where aggrieved parties can approach jurisdictional principal civil court or the High Court (in exercise of its ordinary original civil jurisdiction) for setting aside arbitral awards.

4. CLASS ACTIONS/REPRESENTATIVE PROCEEDINGS

4.1 Is there a mechanism for class actions or representative proceedings, or coordinated proceedings for product liability claims? If so, what are the basic mechanics?

The CPC provides for ordinary civil suits to be brought as representative actions and allows for one party to sue or defend on behalf of all in same interest. In matters where there are numerous persons having interest in one suit, either: (i) with the permission of the court; or (ii) on the court's direction, one or more such persons may sue or be sued, or may defend such suit, on behalf of, or for the benefit of, all persons so interested.

The CPA also allows for a complaint to be filed by one or more consumers, where there are numerous consumers having the same interest. A complainant can be a consumer, any voluntary consumer association, the Central or State Government and in the case of death of a consumer, his legal heir or representative.

In a considerable deviation from the position relating to contractual claims, claims arising out of tort can be made by affected persons, their legal representatives or heirs or by public-spirited individuals or organisations representing the interests of affected persons. Needless to say, such claims can be made even in the absence of any contractual dealings between the parties. Indian courts have followed the proposition first laid down in *Donoghue v Stevenson* (1932 AC 562 (HL) to assign liability. The case laid down the 'neighbour principle' which relates to the duty of care owed to persons whom one reasonably ought to have known, would be affected by their act or your omission.

In addition to the above, any person (to safe guard the interest of public at large and not vested interest of specific parties) may file a public interest litigation representing a class of the public seeking enforcement or protection of fundamental/legal rights. Public interest litigation represents an effort to provide legal representation to sections of society that have traditionally not had access to justice owing to factors such as poverty, illiteracy and lack of awareness about their legal rights. Public interest litigations are typically instituted in the form of 'writ petitions' invoking an extraordinary jurisdiction of the Supreme Court of India and the High to enforce obligations and duties imposed on the state and its instrumentalities.

5. LITIGATION FUNDING

5.1 Is litigation funding by third parties permissible in your country? If so, is it common?

While there is no prohibition on litigation funding in India, litigation funding is not a common practice in India. It must also be noted that any agreement involving a third party in promoting litigation (not being a public interest litigation) either for funding or otherwise must, in any event, pass the test of 'not opposing public policy or justice, equity and good conscience'.

5.2 Are contingency fee or 'no win no fee' arrangements permissible?

Contingency or 'no win no fee' arrangements are not permissible and go against the standards of professional conduct expected of an advocate in India. The rules framed by the Bar Council of India, the governing authority for advocates in India expressly prohibits an advocate from stipulating a fee that is contingent on the results of the litigation or agree to share the proceeds of the litigation.

6. REMEDIES

6.1 What remedies are available to a party who successfully pursues a product liability claim?

Typically, the following remedies and reliefs are available to the parties/ consumers under civil cases who have successfully pursued a product liability claim:

(i) removal of defect in the product;
(ii) replacement of goods with new goods of similar description;
(iii) refund of amounts;
(iv) compensation for loss suffered by the complainant/consumer on account of negligence; and
(v) award of damages and costs.

It is not necessary that only one of the above reliefs can be claimed and awarded. The affected party can claim more than one relief and depending on the facts and circumstances of the case, the courts can award reliefs in combination.

Further, courts in India have also granted monetary damages towards mental distress, loss of business and litigation costs suffered by the affected party as relief in addition to those set out above, although such damages are usually nominal.

The provisions of Indian criminal law, in respect of product liability, are attracted when the element of cheating, fraud offences affecting public health and safety can be attributed to such defects. For criminal liability, punishment is by way of imprisonment or fine or both can be imposed by courts in accordance with provisions of IPC or specific statutes relevant to the case.

6.2 How are damages calculated/are there limitations on available damages?

The Contract Act provides for the payment of damages by the defaulting party to the aggrieved party as a result of such breach. It entitles the aggrieved party to receive compensation for any loss or damage which arose as a natural consequence of such breach; or which the parties knew, at the time of entering into the contract, to be likely to result from such a breach. Further the Contract Act expressly excludes liability for remote and indirect loss.

Damages under a contract may be either liquidated or unliquidated damages. Liquidated damages are such as have been agreed upon and fixed by the parties in anticipation of the breach whereas unliquidated damages are required to be assessed and quantified. In either case, courts have a wide discretion in the assessment of damages. Applying the reasonableness test, the court usually awards the actual loss proved to have been suffered by the aggrieved party as a direct result of the breach of the contract by the defaulting party. However, if the parties have stipulated liquidated damages in the contract, the courts subject to such stipulated amount being a genuine pre-estimate of the loss, will not grant damages in excess of the stipulated amount.

Another principle considered by Indian courts while awarding damages is the principle of mitigation. This principle imputes on the party who has suffered the loss, caused by another's breach, the obligation to act in a manner that ensures that the loss is minimised. A court may deny a plaintiff's claim to the extent that it finds that the plaintiff has failed to mitigate the loss.

6.3 Are punitive or exemplary damages available and in what circumstances?

In contractual disputes, Indian courts do not normally award punitive or exemplary damages. However, the courts may do so where elements of fraud, oppression or malice are established.

Further, exemplary damages have been awarded by the courts in cases where damages are recoverable for harm caused by ultra hazardous or dangerous industries. In such cases, the courts have held that the compensation is designed to have a deterrent effect and thus 'must be correlated to the magnitude and capacity of the enterprise' such that 'the larger and more prosperous the enterprise, the greater must be the amount of compensation payable by it.' However, these principles have been limited to public interest and environmental cases and have not yet been extended to product liability claims.

Under the CPA, courts have in the past awarded exemplary damages by way of compensation in exceptional cases where it is established that the consumer suffered harassment and agony due to the conduct of the manufacturer/supplier/distributer.

6.4 Is liability joint and several/how does apportionment of liability work, including where a partially responsible entity is not a party to the proceeding?

Liability in case of defective products under the Contract Act and SGA is ordinarily contractually driven and may be joint and/or several depending on the facts and circumstance of each case. Further, under tort law, in cases of composite negligence, courts have in the past held that liability is joint and several and jurisdiction may extend to other joint tortfeasors (not already parties to the suit). Specific statutes also set out liability of parties (joint or several) in the event of non-compliance and products not complying with the standards and requirements set out in these statutes.

Although courts have the power to direct or allow the party initiating proceedings to implead another party to the proceedings, it does not typically intervene in respect of choosing the party against whom the relief is sought unless substantial evidence is adduced and inherent powers of the courts are invoked.

7. ROLE OF REGULATORS

7.1 Please explain the role, responsibilities and powers of the regulators in your country which have jurisdiction over product liability issues.

The regulatory system in India that deals with product safety is two-fold, comprising of both uniformly applicable and sector specific regimes. With regards to pan-industry application, the BIS Act and the BIS Rules framed thereunder provide for establishment of a bureau for the development, standardisation and quality certification for goods in India. The Bureau of Indian Standards (BIS) is the agency established under the BIS Act for formulating and laying down quality standards and certification requirements for goods in India. Manufacturers and importers in India are required to comply with these quality and certification standards, some of which are mandatory standards while others are voluntary.

Separately, the drugs and cosmetics and food industries are some of the notable sectors that are governed by distinct regulators as set out below:

(i) Drugs

The Drugs Controller General of India (DCGI), who acts under the mandate of the Drugs Act and the Drugs and Cosmetics Rules, 1945 (Drugs Rules), is the designated licensing and controlling authority to grant and renew licences to manufacture, sell and distribute drugs. The DCGI has the power to suspend and cancel licences and/or order for cessation in manufacture, sale and distribution of drugs if the conditions under the licences, which include devising of a prompt and effective recall system of defective products, are not met by the licensees.

(ii) Food

The Food Safety and Standards Authority of India (Food Authority) has been established under the FSSA to regulate the manufacture, storage, distribution, sale and import of food to ensure availability of safe and wholesome food for human consumption. The Food Authority has wide powers under the FSSA including specifying standards and guidelines in relation to food articles including its enforcement, food labeling, and guidelines for accreditation of certification bodies among others.

7.2 Are there any mandatory reporting requirements related to product safety issues?

There are no standard mandatory reporting requirements in India that are applicable to all industries. However, laws governing certain sectors such as drugs/cosmetics and food have provisions containing reporting requirements in the event of product safety issues.

Under the FSSA, a food business operator must immediately initiate procedures to withdraw the food in question and inform the competent authority if it considers that a food item which it has processed, manufactured or distributed is not in compliance with the FSSA or has reasons to believe that a food which it has placed on the market may be unsafe for the consumers. In this regard, the food business operator is also under an obligation to inform the competent authorities of the action taken to prevent risks to the consumer.

The provisions of the Drugs Rules require a manufacturer/licensee to devise a prompt and effective product recall system of defective products, including a written procedure standard operating procedure. The Drug Rules also provide that the records pertaining to distribution of drugs should be available to the designated authorities. Further, the licensee is required to furnish all records maintained in accordance with the Drug Rules to the relevant authorities, provide all information requested for by these authorities and allow the authorities to take sample of the manufactured drugs. The Drug Rules also contains requirements for reporting of the recalled products.

7.3 Do the regulators have the power to:

(i) ban certain goods or services?

While regulators in India do not have the general overarching power to ban goods or services *per se*, certain statutory authorities do have powers to prohibit the manufacture and distribution of goods if they are found to be non-compliant with the relevant standards. For example, the Drug Rules empowers the DCGI to order for suspending the manufacture, sale and distribution of drugs where the licensee has not complied with the conditions of the licence and provisions of the Drug Act and Drug Rules. Additionally, the Drug Act gives broad powers to the Indian government to regulate, restrict or prohibit the manufacture, sale or distribution of any drug or cosmetic that in the opinion of the government: (i) is likely to involve risk to human beings or animals; or (ii) does not have the therapeutic value claimed or purported to be claimed; and (iii) that in the public interest it is necessary or expedient to do so.

(ii) require a supplier to recall a product?

As highlighted in our responses above, regulators under different statutes governing specific sectors have the power to order recall of products and there is no single governmental authority which has the general power to order recall of products. Some of the significant sectors which have provisions in relation to recall of products are discussed below.

Under the Drugs Rules, the licensing authority can direct a manufacturer to withdraw or recall a batch of drugs if it finds that the batch of drugs or other substances does not conform to the standards of strength, quality and purity prescribed by the Drugs Act or the Drugs Rules.

Under the FSSA, in the event a food business operator considers that a food item, which it has processed, manufactured or distributed, is not in compliance with the FSSA, it must immediately initiate procedures to withdraw the food in question and inform the competent authority.

In addition to the above mandatory provisions, please note that the following draft regulations in relation to recall of drugs and food have been issued, which are proposed to be notified and brought into force in the near future. Briefly, set out below are obligations under the drafts regulations:

- The Food Authority's Food Recall Procedures Regulations, 2009 (Food Recall Regulations) under the FSSA were issued on 4 May, 2011 for comments from all stakeholders and have not yet been brought into force. The Food Recall Regulations contain provisions and procedures pertaining to removal of marketed food which is unsafe and violate the provisions of the FSSA, the rules and regulations made thereunder for distribution, sale and consumption. One of the requirements under the Food Recall Procedures Regulations is that all food businesses engaged in the wholesale supply, manufacture or import of food regulated by the food authority must have an up-to-date recall plan. This requirement of a recall plan does not extend to food retailers and businesses within the food service sector such as restaurants, caterers and takeaways (unless they are running multi-outlet food business chains having integrated manufacturing and distribution network). The Food Recall Regulations also provide for procedures to be followed in case of food recall and classification of recalls according to the level of hazard involved. The regulations also include formats for food recall notifications and status reports, among others.
- The Central Drugs Standard Control Organization (CDSCO) released a draft version of guidelines on recall and rapid alert system for drugs including biologics and vaccines (Draft Drug Recall Guidelines) on 22 October, 2012. The Draft Drug Recall Guidelines are applicable to manufacturers, importers, stockists, distributors and retailers of drugs and have classified recalls into voluntary and statutory and by numerical designation I, II or III as per the degree of health hazard caused by defective/non-compliant drugs. They provide for the procedure to be followed for recalls and the timelines within which such recalls must be completed.

(iii) prescribe standards in respect of certain goods or services and require that the goods or services meet those standards?

Regulators in India have the power to prescribe manufacturing and distribution standards for their respective sectors and are empowered to monitor compliance with these standards. Most standards are provided for in the product-specific legislations framed by government itself. In addition to sector-specific standards, certain generic regulations such as the BIS Act and the BIS Rules set out voluntary and mandatory certification and quality standards. Certain products such as cement, infant foods and plastic feeding bottles, certain electrical goods, dry batteries, gas cylinders, pneumatic tyres etc. have to mandatorily comply with standards set out under the BIS Act and other laws governing these specific products.

For example, the Electronics and Information Technology Goods (Requirements for Compulsory Registration) Order, 2012 (Electronics Order) sets out certain mandatory compliance requirements for certain types of electronic goods including compliance with specified standards. It also prohibits the import, sale or distribution of any electronic goods which do not conform to the specified standard and do not bear the self declaration mark on such electronic goods, after obtaining registration from the BIS. Similarly, the Directorate General of Foreign Trade, Ministry of Commerce, Government of India has notified certain quality standards for toys which must be mandatorily complied with before the toys are imported into India.

Another example is the MVA and the rules framed thereunder, which stipulate certain mandatory standards and specifications which motor vehicles are required to comply with. In this regard, the rules under the MVA stipulate that the sale of every motor vehicle manufactured will be accompanied by a certificate of roadworthiness issued by the manufacturer in a prescribed form.

(iv) require production of information without court process?
If so, broadly explain the circumstances in which the regulator can exercise the power and any penalties that apply if a supplier fails to comply.

Regulators in India have the authority to call for information by requiring production of documents, records, etc. by manufacturers without court process or intervention in order to determine compliance with the applicable law. However, these powers can be exercised by concerned regulators in relation to specific regulated sectors (such as pharmaceutical and food sectors) only in accordance with relevant statutes, which empowers them to compel production of information. Some of the examples of where relevant governmental authorities can require production of information are set out below:

The Drug Act and Drugs Rules specifically require that the licensee provide all information as required by designated authorities to ascertain whether the provisions of the Drug Act and the Drug Rules have been observed by it. In the event of non-compliance with any of these provisions by the licensees, the relevant authorities under the Drug Act have the right to cancel or suspend the licence issued or direct the manufacturer to stop manufacture, sale or distribution of drugs.

The Electronics Order also specifically empowers the relevant authorities to call for any information in relation to manufacture, import, sale, distribution of the prescribed electronics goods to ascertain compliance with the Electronics Order. In this context, the relevant authority is also permitted to enter, inspect and search premises where such goods are manufactures, distributed or sold.

Under the FSSA, the food safety officer may search any place, seize any article of food or adulterant or carry out an investigation if there is a reasonable doubt about them being involved in commission of any offence relating to food. Further, the FSSA also provides for penalties including imprisonment in the event any person provides false information or obstructs/resists the relevant authorities from carrying on their functions under the FSSA.

8. VOLUNTARY CONDUCT

8.1 Are there regulations pertaining to the voluntary conduct of a product repair or recall by a supplier?

The automobile industry in India is one of the major sectors to have guidelines dealing with voluntary conduct of manufacturers and suppliers with regard to product recall. The Voluntary Code of Vehicle Recall dated July 2012 (Voluntary Code) issued by the Society of Indian Automobile Manufacturers (SIAM) contains guidelines for a voluntary recall of vehicles containing safety defects. The Voluntary Code contains provisions that define 'recall', 'safety defects' and provides examples of safety related defects and sets out the procedure for reporting defects to governmental authorities and vehicle owners and recall vehicles.

Do note that under the present Indian legal framework there is no provision where an automobile manufacturer is responsible for recall of its faulty products. Past cases of recall of automobiles for faulty/defective parts have been entirely voluntary exercises by such automobile manufacturers where they were free to devise their own procedures to best effect the product recalls. The recall exercises were usually carried out by the manufacturers in conjunction with the dealers/vendors where the potentially affected customers were directly contacted and informed of the recall exercise and consequent replacements of their defective vehicles.

9. EMERGING ISSUES AND LAW REFORM

9.1 Are there important developing and emerging issues or trends in product liability law in your country?

Following a spate of quality issues in automobiles, the government authorities are deliberating making recalls mandatory in India in the event of defects to improve the degree of compliance among automobile manufacturers.

Separately, Food Recall Regulations and Draft Recall Regulations, as discussed above, are expected to be notified as law in the near future. These regulations for the first time set out steps, in a clear and distinct manner, that are required to be followed by manufacturers and distributors in the event products are found to be defective. In addition to these, the Indian Parliament is also considering enacting/amending certain laws to better protect the rights of Indian consumers, which are discussed below.

9.2 Please describe any proposed important law reform in the area of product liability in your country.

Some of the important law reforms in relation to product liability in India are discussed below.

The Indian Government introduced Consumer Protection (Amendment) Bill, 2011, in the Parliament on 16 December, 2011, to facilitate quicker disposal of cases and to widen and amplify the scope of some of the provisions of the CPA. The proposed amendment provides for the following, among others:

(i) online filing of consumer complaints;
(ii) enforcement of orders of the consumer courts as decrees of civil courts including the power to attach the property of the defaulting person;
(iii) levy of penalty for each day of delay of non-compliance of the order of the consumer forums; and
(iv) a monitoring system for pending cases.

The Bill is still pending before the Indian Parliament.

In the pharmaceutical sector, in addition to the Draft Drug Recall Regulations, the Drugs and Cosmetics (Amendment) Bill, 2013 proposes changes in the regulation of the import, export, manufacture, distribution and sale of drugs, cosmetics and medical devices to ensure safety, efficacy, quality and conduct of clinical trials. In order to ensure standard quality of drugs, cosmetics, and medical devices, the Bill specifies conditions under which they will be considered misbranded, adulterated and spurious and specifies penalties and offences for the same. The Bill is still pending before the Indian Parliament.

10. REGULATORY WEBSITES/INFORMATION

10.1 Please identify any useful regulatory references relating to product liability law in your country, for example, a product safety/consumer law website maintained by the main regulator.

- Bureau of India Standards: *www.bis.org.in*
- Food Safety and Standards Authority of India: *www.fssai.gov.in*
- Society of Indian Automobile Manufacturers: *www.siamindia.com*
- Central Drugs Standard Control Organisation: *www.cdsco.nic.in*
- Department of Consumer Affairs: *http://consumeraffairs.nic.in/consumer/index.php*
- PRS Legislative Research: *www.prsindiaorg*

Indonesia

Hutabarat, Halim & Rekan – Lawyers Pheo M. Hutabarat

1. LIABILITY

1.1 What are the principal sources of law and regulation relating to product liability?

In 1999, Indonesia enacted products liability legislation entitled The Law on Consumer Protection (LCP) to regulate consumer warnings and information provided about products, guarantees as to the quality of goods, fulfilment of product servicing and warranties and the promotion of products.

The LCP confers rights and duties on both consumers and business undertaking of a wide variety of products and services; both tangible and intangible, movable, immovable, consumable, non-consumable, tradable, and products that can be utilised or exploited by consumers. The business undertaking means manufacturer, retailer, advertising company, importer or any other third party involving in the selling of the products and services in Indonesia.

Products liability offences can be subject to civil and criminal sanction in Indonesia. The LCP stipulates alternative criminal sanction of a maximum five years imprisonment or a fine of up to 2 billion Indonesian Rupiahs, if the business undertaking violates Article 11, Article 12, Article 13(1), Article 14, Article 16, Article 17 (1) paragraphs d and f of the LCP. The less severe violations are punishable with a maximum two years imprisonment or a fine of up to 500 million Indonesian Rupiahs, if the business undertaking violates Article 8, Article 9, Article 10, Article 13(2), Article 15, Article 17(1) paragraphs a, b, c and e, and Article 18 of the LCP.

Article 63 (3) of LCP further stipulates that any violation that causes serious injury, serious illness, permanent disability or death will also subject to the prevailing criminal provisions as contained in Indonesian Criminal Code. This means that in addition to the above criminal sanctions, the provisions of the Indonesian Criminal Code related to the distribution or provision of the products/services could also be applied accordingly. For example, Article 359 of the Indonesian Criminal Code provides that a person who is negligently caused the death of any person may face up to 5 years imprisonment.

It should be noted, however, that a successful civil action for products liability under the LCP does not preclude a criminal charge in the same circumstance.

1.2 What is required to establish causation under the most common causes of action available?

In practice, there are two important implications introduced by the LCP to development of consumer law in Indonesia. Firstly, the LCP has given certain protections to the customers in having a standard contract with the business undertakings. Therefore, the applicability of the general principle of the freedom of contract as guaranteed in the Civil Code has been restricted in the standard contract of goods/services. In concluding the contact, the business undertaking must also adhere to the restrictions to be applied in preparing the standard clauses or contract. Article 18 of the LCP among other stipulates that the business undertaking is not allowed to insert clauses which will have the following implications:

(i) the responsibility of the business undertakings will be transferred to the costumers;
(ii) the business undertaking will have the rights to reject redelivery of the products from the customers or the repayments of the purchase price to the customers;
(iii) the business undertakings will have the authorisation or power of attorney from the customers to unilaterally conduct all necessary actions in connection with the products purchased by the customers and encumber the products which are purchased based on instalments basis;
(iv) the provision on the evidence for losing of the usage or benefit of the products;
(v) the provision to give right for the business undertaking to reduce the benefit or the usage of the services; and
(vi) the provision that the customers will bind on the future regulations, attachments, revisions or amendments of the contract to be unilaterally made by the business undertaking.

Further, Article 18 (3) of the LCP stipulates that the expression, the meaning and the structure/location of standard clauses must be clear and readable, failing of which, such standard clauses shall be declared null and void.

Secondly, the LCP has also stipulated certain restricted acts and behaviours of the business undertakings for giving the protection of the customers in Indonesia.

1.3 Is strict liability available and, if so, in what circumstances?

Nowadays, the existence of a strict liability principle has been widely accepted in Indonesian law regime. Different with the common law legal system which has a long tradition on the strict liability principle, Indonesia which adopts civil law tradition basically did not recognise the strict liability, but acknowledge only the tort liability principle (liability based on negligence or fault). The introduction of the strict liability in Indonesia was adopted through the ratification the several international conventions by Indonesia which contain the provisions of the strict liability, and then the adoption of this principle in the national laws. Other than in the LCP, the Environment Law 1999, currently the principle of strict liability have been adopted in other basic laws, among others:

(i) Law No. 5 of 1983 on Exclusive Economic Zone;
(ii) Law No. 23 of 1997 on Management of Environment;
(iii) Law No. 10 of 1997 on Nuclear Technology; and
(iv) Law No. 41 of 1999 on Forestry.

The LCP in its Article 19 has introduced a strict liability against any damage, contamination or loss experienced by the customer in using the products/services, regardless whether or not there is any contract exists between the customer and the business undertaking. Different with the general principle of onus of proof under the Indonesian civil proceedings, in which the plaintiff/customer will have the burden to prove its claim, Article 28 of the LCP specifically stipulates that in a strict liability case the burden of proof has shifted from the customer/plaintiff to the defendant/business undertaking. Therefore, in any strict liability cases in which the customer experiences any damage, contamination and losses as a result of consuming the products or services, the defendant/business undertaking is the party who must prove that there is no fault or negligence conducted by the business undertaking in relation to such case.

1.4 Are guarantees or warranties as to quality implied by law?

The LCP generally prohibits certain acts or behaviour of the business undertaking that will against the consumer protections. These prohibitions contained in Article 8 up to and including 17 of the LCP. It prohibits the business undertakings, among others:

(i) from falsely representing products;
(ii) providing misleading or deceptive information to the consumer;
(iii) providing no label and indication on the lapse of time or best for consumption;
(iv) providing no information and/or guidelines in Indonesian language;
(v) distributing defect, contaminated, damaged or used products without giving a clear information to these conditions;
(vi) providing big sales, auctions, special rates, gifts or lotteries with certain misleading and prohibited actions as contemplated in Articles 11, 12, 13 and 14 of the LCP; or
(vii) making pre-contractual statements which prove to be false following the consumer entering such a contract.

As far as it is related to the advertising company, Article 17 of the LCP stipulates that an advertising company is prohibited (i) to provide false or misleading information on the products and warranty/guaranty, (ii) to provide no information on the risk to use the products/services, (iii) to exploit an event or person without having a proper authorisation to do so, and (iv) to violate advertising code of ethics. Further, Article 20 of the LCP imposes the responsibility against the advertising companies for all implications arising out of the advertisement made by them.

1.5 How is a product 'defect' defined?

The LCP does not specifically stipulate the definition of 'product defect'. However, Article 8 prohibits the business undertaking to distribute (a) products, (b) pharmaceutical supply and (c) food supply which are defective, damaged, used products or contaminated without providing complete and truthful information on the said goods.

1.6 Who in the supply chain has obligations or duties for defective products? What obligations or duties do they owe and to whom?

Under the LCP, the business undertaking shall be responsible for the defective products. The business undertaking means manufacturer, retailer, advertising company, importer or any other third party involving in the selling of the products and services in Indonesia. The LCP requires that the business undertaking must recall the distribution of the defective products, without precluding any possibility of civil claim and/or criminal charge arising out of the distribution of such defective products.

In addition to the provisions of LCP above, the Indonesian Civil Code has stipulated the following provisions on the defective products:

(a) Sellers (business undertaking) are obliged to guarantee that goods are free from hidden defects which may render them unsuitable, or only partially suitable, to be used intended, such that if buyers had known about the defects, they would not have bought the goods, or would only have bought them at a reduced price (vide Article 1504 of the Indonesian Civil Code);

(b) Sellers must guarantee against hidden defects, even if they were unaware of them, unless they have previously stipulated that they were not making any guarantees (Article 1506);

(c) If sellers are aware of defects in their goods, they are obliged, in addition to returning the purchase price, to compensate buyers for all costs and losses incurred, plus interest (Article 1509); and

(d) If sellers were not aware of the defects in the goods, they need only return the purchase price and compensate buyers for costs incurred in the purchase and delivery of the goods (Article 1509).

In line with the provisions of the LCP, the provisions contained in the Indonesian Civil Code impose liability for the business undertaking for the defective products, and the above provisions are also broad enough to encompass fault repair as the obligation of the business undertaking.

1.7 By what means can a supplier limit their liability for defective products?

Please see explanation under question 1.6 above.

1.8 Are there particular goods or services which have specific obligations or duties attached to them? If so, explain what they are.

The LCP regulates variety of goods and services in general, both tangible and intangible, movable, immovable, consumable, non-consumable, tradable, and products that can be utilised or exploited by consumers. Therefore there is no particular goods or services which have specific obligations attached to them.

2. DEFENCES

2.1 What are the possible defences to a product liability claim?

An available defence to a contractual breach in Indonesia is that the event causing the breach was unforeseeable according to Article 1244 of the Civil Code. A party cannot be held liable for unforeseeable harm, or foreseeable harm despite having taken all reasonable care. Further, Article 1245 of the Civil Code stipulates that damages and interest need not be paid to a claimant under contract if a *force majeure* or unintended event prevented the contracted party from carrying out his/her contractual obligations or forced a breach of contractual duty.

Subject to Article 18 of the LCP on the provisions of the standard clauses as discussed above, a contracting party may draft a limitation of liability clause into the agreement, however this provision must not purport to limit or transfer a seller's liability at the expense of offending public policy and good morals. This roughly operates as a test of reasonableness and little guidance is provided through case law to establish exactly what is deemed by an Indonesian court to offend public policy and good morals.

If the seller is aware of a defect in their goods, they can discharge their liability under Article 1508 of the Civil Code by refunding the purchase price and compensating the buyer for the loss incurred plus interest. If they were unaware of the defect they are only required under contract to refund the purchase price of item and for costs incurred in the purchase and delivery of the goods.

However, if the defect of the product causes damage, contamination and losses to the costumers as a result from the consumption or using of the products/services, Article 19 of the LCP stipulates that the business undertaking must provide compensation damages which may in the form of refunding the purchase price, replacement of the products, funding health care and/or other allowances as stipulated in the prevailing laws and regulations.

Article 27 of the LCP provides general defences that a business undertaking will be not be liable for losses sustained by consumers of its products, if the business undertaking as the defendant can prove:

(a) that the goods should not have been distributed or were not intended for distribution;
(b) the goods were subsequently damaged, which damage occurred after the lapse of the warranty period as agreed or given by the business undertaking, both verbally or in written;
(c) the damage to or defect of the goods occurred as a consequence of complying with provisions concerning the qualification of goods;
(d) the damage caused by the negligence of the customer; or
(e) the claim period of four years from the time the goods were purchased has lapsed and the claim is statute-barred.

2.2 Is there a limit on the time in which proceedings may be brought (limitations and repose)?

The Indonesian general limitation period for claims under tort and contract is 30 years, however shorter period will be apply in specific types of civil litigation. A claim brought under the LCP is only valid if brought four years from the date the goods were purchased.

3. LITIGATION OF PRODUCT LIABILITY DISPUTES

3.1 In which courts are product liability proceedings brought?

Indonesia's court system generally contains three parts – the District Courts, High Courts and Supreme Courts, all of which can hear civil or criminal matters, including products liability actions. The LCP also established the Consumer Dispute Settlement Board (CDSB), which is an alternate mechanism for products liability claims in Indonesia.

Under the LCP, individual consumer may alternatively submit either tortious liability or contractual liability claim to CDSB or to the district court. A join or class action or government claim may only be submitted to the district court.

CDSB, as a quasi-judicial power, has the competence to examine and decide sanction for any allegation submitted by the individual consumer in connection with:

(i) the damage, contamination and losses to the costumers as a result of consuming the products or services (Article 19 of the LCP);
(ii) the responsibility of the advertising companies from the advertisement made by them (Article 20 of the LCP);
(iii) the obligation of the manufacturer to provide after sales services and spare parts as well as guaranty for the products to be continuously used by the customers within at least one year (Article 25 of the LCP); and
(iv) the obligation to fulfill the warranty or guaranty agreed or given in a contract (Article 26 of the LCP).

CDSB has the authority to impose administrative sanction in the form of the payment of compensation damages to the business undertakings in a maximum amount of 200 million Indonesian Rupiahs. The decision is final and binding and it cannot be appealed. The relevant party may, however, submit any objection against the decision to the relevant district court. The procedures for submitting an objection on the CDSB decision to District Court is regulated under Republic of Indonesia Supreme Court Regulation Number 01 of 2006, dated 13 March 2006, regarding Procedures Objection Submission on CDSB Decision. In practice, the district court based on its examination can annul the decision made by CDSB.

The imposition of the criminal sanctions against consumer protection are not vested to CDSB, but may only be imposed by a district court based on the investigation made by the police/certain civil service official and the prosecution submitted by the public prosecutor to the district court.

3.2 How are proceedings commenced?

Generally, proceedings in an Indonesian civil court will commence with submission of the initial pleading. Subsequent hearings follow, the defendant presents a written response to the plaintiff's claim, the plaintiff's submission of a counterplea, the defendant to again present a written response to the counterplea, a hearing each for the plaintiff and defendant to present their evidences and witnesses, the plaintiff and the defendant presents their written concluding arguments. The court then reviews the submissions and sets a date for judgment. As a general rule, the defendant when submits its response may also file a counterclaim against the plaintiff. Under Article 46 of the LCP, consumers have the right to bring an individual action or join a class action. Further, consumer organisations are empowered to assist consumers to file class actions against business undertaking whose products or services are defective and/or marketing strategies are misleading or deceptive.

3.3 Are disputed issues decided by a judge or a jury?

The Indonesian general legal system and its court system adopt civil law system, in which the decision of the court shall be made by the presiding judges. Indonesian legal system does not acknowledge a jury system. The decision of CDSB will be made by panel of commissioners which consists of odds number with the minimum members of at least three (3) commissioners of CDSB.

3.4 Who has the burden of proof and to what standard?

In the general civil proceedings, both in breach of contract as well as tort actions, the pleading must be proved by the customer/plaintiff. This general principle of onus of proof is stipulated in Article 1865 of the Civil Code, which stipulates that the party/plaintiff who asserts any claim has the burden of proving its existence.

Different with the above contractual and tort liabilities, Article 19 of the LCP provides a strict liability to the business undertaking, in the sense that business undertaking must indemnify consumers for damages, contaminations or losses incurred as a result of the consumption of goods or services provided or traded by the business undertaking. As explained previously under question 1.3 above, in a strict liability case the burden of proof has shifted from the customer/plaintiff to the defendant/business undertaking, and therefore if the customer experiences any damage, contamination and losses as a result of consuming the products or services, the defendant/business undertaking is the party who must prove that there is no fault or negligence conducted by the business undertaking in relation to such case.

3.5 How is evidence given in proceedings and are witnesses cross-examined?

The Indonesian procedural laws follow the tradition of a civil law system. It does not acknowledge any procedure relating to discovery, depositions or interrogatories. There is no mechanism to enforce any order relating to above disclosure or discovery both in the Indonesian courts. As a matter of practice, if a party requests the disclosure of documents by the other party, and the other party refuses to disclose such documents, the presiding judges may draw whatever inference they deem appropriate from such non-disclosure.

The general rules on evidence of civil procedure could be found in Indonesian Civil Procedure Law (*Het Herzeine Indonesische Reglement – HIR*) and Article 1866 up to and including Article 1993 of the Indonesian Civil Code. Indonesian courts hold a strong preference for original evidence and documentation, however authenticated duplicates are acceptable. Article 1866 of the Civil Code and Article 164 of the HIR define that evidence consists of written evidence (including electronic information and/or document – based on Law No 11 of 2008 regarding Information and Electronic Transaction), testimony of witnesses, inference, acknowledgements and oath. The Indonesian law distinguishes between authentic written evidence and privately made written documents. The authentic written evidence in the form as prescribed by the laws and made before the government official is considered as the strongest evidence (prima facie evidence). Affidavits sworn outside Indonesia must be notarised and legalised by the appropriate embassy or consulate for the documents to be recognised in Indonesian court.

Indonesian judges play an active role in relation to the examination of evidence and have the discretion to call or reject for direct or expert testimony/opinion. Their wide discretionary powers also provide for refusal of evidence as they see appropriate and individual interpretation of evidence and arguments presented. Therefore, the ability to require expert opinion, the production of documents and to examine the witnesses is entirely within the court's discretion. There is no procedure for compelling the opposite side to present facts, or documents reflecting examination outside the court hearings.

The court retains no verbatim transcript. The clerk takes notes of the testimony and of any cross-examination that takes place. Frequently, these notes are incomplete and inaccurate, particularly if the subject matter is technical and new to the appointed clerk. This record forms the basis of the court's decision on factual matters. Copies are not made available to counsel whether during the trial or at the appellate stage. Although counsel may review and has access to such records at the clerk's office, neither counsel nor the party to the action may officially take copies.

New evidence may be presented on appeal to a High Court; however this practice is not generally permitted in the Supreme Court, although the court has the discretion to admit new evidence in the interests of justice.

3.6 Are the parties able to rely on expert opinion evidence and, if so, are there any special rules or procedures for expert opinion evidence?

Please see explanation under question 3.5 above.

3.7 Is pre-trial discovery permitted? If so, in what circumstances? If not, what other mechanisms, if any, are available for obtaining evidence from a party or a third party?

Please see explanation under question 3.5 above.

3.8 Is there liability for spoliation of evidence/a remedy for destruction of or failure to preserve evidence (most relevantly, the product)?

Please see explanation under question 3.5 above.

3.9 Is interlocutory or interim relief available prior to the full trial of a proceeding?

Indonesian court procedure also allows for a court attachment (pre-judgment attachment – '*sita jaminan*') to be granted in claim for damages. This is available in situations where the plaintiff can prove that a significant danger exists that the defendant will attempt to dispose of assets so as to make them unavailable to meet potential judgment.

This motion may be submitted together with the claim or submitted before the judgment made by the court of the first instance. Based on Circular Letter of Indonesian Supreme Court No. 5 of 1975 and based on legal practice, the pre-judgment attachment may only be granted by the court of the first instance after the presiding judges have examined all evidences in relation to the case.

The plaintiff also may seek the possibility of obtaining an interim court injunction ('*putusan sela*') to prevent the defendant to conduct any action that may hamper or jeopardise the interest of the plaintiff in submitting its claim in the court. To enable the interim court injunction be considered by the presiding judges, there are some requirements to be fulfilled by the plaintiff, which among other that the submission of this application must be based on a *prima facie* evidence or the written valid evidence to support the necessity of requesting of this motion. In practice, the presiding judges will also reject the motion if the substance of the matters is similar or the duplicate of the claims on the merit of the case submitted by the plaintiff in the lawsuit. If this interim court injunction be granted by the court, this judgment will be as a specific relief decision in nature, ie, a court order to direct or prohibit certain conducts of the defendants or the co-defendants. Based on Circular Letter of Indonesian Supreme Court No. 3 of 2000 and based on legal practice, the interim court injunction can only be granted by the court after the presiding judges have examined all evidences in relation to the case.

3.10 Can the winning party recover its costs?

Theoretically, the winning party can recover its costs through a civil lawsuit through court. However, it should be noted that litigation in Indonesia is a relatively expensive and time-consuming process, and much of the cost which the disputed party will incur may not be automatically recoverable from the other party, especially when the final court judgment will be executed against the defendant(s).

3.11 What avenues of appeal are available?

If the matter submitted to the court, the High Courts are the courts of first appeal in civil matters, reviewing lower court decisions on questions of law and fact. The Supreme Court is the highest judicial body in Indonesia. A decision of a High Court may be appealed by way of removal to the Supreme Court but generally only on the basis of a question of law. Under certain limited conditions, following the binding decision of the Supreme Court has been given, the losing party may request the so-called *'Peninjauan Kembali'* (Request Civil – Review) in order to nullify the final and binding court decisions that have been made in the case. One of the popular legal bases for a party to make a request civil is the condition that a new fact (*novum*) has been found after the court decisions have been made, which is important and may affect to the case. Such request civil must be submitted to the Court of First Instance which first decided the case. The presiding judges in this Request Civil's level will make decision by having a closed hearing among them in deciding the case, and there is no public hearing to be made by the presiding judges in level. The legal process of the Request Civil can generally take anything from two to five years.

4. CLASS ACTIONS/REPRESENTATIVE PROCEEDINGS

4.1 Is there a mechanism for class actions or representative proceedings, or coordinated proceedings for product liability claims? If so, what are the basic mechanics?

Class action cases are common in Indonesia. Several laws in Indonesia, including the LCP, have also specifically endorsed the possibility of submitting the class action petitions to the general civil court of the first instance.

The basic requirements and general procedures for submitting class action petitions are regulated in Indonesian Supreme Court Regulation No. 1 of 2002, dated 26 April 2002 regarding the Procedures for Class Action (SC Regulation No.1/2002). The following are some important general requirements and procedures in submitting the class action petition in Indonesia:

(i) Any class action petition may be filed if: (a) the number of class members is so large that it is ineffective and inefficient to make individual claim, (b) there are common questions of fact or situation and common questions of law that are substantial, as well as there are same claims among class representatives and their class members, and (c) a class representative must have the fairness and seriousness in protecting the interest of the represented members (adequacy of representation).

(ii) In a preliminary hearing, a judge must hear and consider whether the above criteria of the class action petition has been fulfilled or not. If the petition has complied with the above criteria, through a court order the judge will certify the validity of the class action and order the plaintiff to submit a draft of the proposed model of a notice for the judge's approval. If the judges determine that the petition is not valid or complied with the above criteria, the judges will discontinue the proceedings by issuing a court judgment.

(iii) To represent the legal interests of class members, class representatives shall not be required to have a special power of attorney from the class members.

(iv) The general civil procedural laws will generally be applicable in the class action court proceedings, with some lex specialist or specific requirements need to be attended, as these set forth in the SC Regulation No. 1/2002. For example, a class action petition must at least contain: (a) complete and clear identity of the class representatives, (b) detailed and specific class definition even if no names of class members are enumerated, (c) descriptions of class members that are necessary in connection with an obligation to serve notice, (d) a cause of action of all classes, whether class representatives or class members, whether or not identified, that is set out expressly and thoroughly, (e) in one class action, division into several classes or subclasses may be made if the claims are different due to differences in nature and damage, and (f) a claim or request for damages must be set forth expressly and thoroughly which contains a proposal on mechanisms or methods for the distribution of damages to all class members, including a proposal on the creation of a team or panel for expediting the distribution of damages. It is common that in the preliminary hearing, a judge may give advice to the parties, so that a class action petition will comply with the above requirements.

(v) The presiding judges may recommend a class representative to replace a lawyer if the lawyer has performed acts against an obligation to defend and protect the interests of the class members.

(vi) The procedures for serving notice to class members may be made through media, government officers or directly served to the class members, and this notice must be served (i) promptly after the judges have declared that the class action petition is valid and (ii) at the stage of the settlement and distribution of damages when the claim is granted by the court.

(vii) The notice must also provide the mechanism of opt-outs, i.e. the right of a class member within period of time to have the chance to opt out from the class membership by submitting a specific form as provided in the attachment of the SC Regulation No. 1/2002. A class member who has stated to opt out shall not be legally bound by any judgment of the class action case concerned.

5. LITIGATION FUNDING

5.1 Is litigation funding by third parties permissible in your country? If so, is it common?

No specific stipulation under the laws of Indonesia on this particular matter. Based on the Advocate Law No. 18 of 2003 and the Indonesian Lawyers Code of Ethics 2002, the parties are freely to agree on the legal fee to be paid by client to its lawyers (freedom of contract). This agreement for the provision of the legal fees can be made either verbally or in writing.

It is not uncommon in practice that the litigation funding be facilitated by a disinterested third party. However, no specific circumstances or prohibitions in concluding this funding litigation case.

5.2 Are contingency fee or 'no win no fee' arrangements permissible?

The Advocate Law of 2003 only requires that the amount of the legal fee must be agreed based on the fairness principle, which means that the determination of the legal fees should consider the risk, time, capability and interest of the client. Indonesian Lawyers Code of Ethics 2002, in its article 4 only stipulates that in determining the legal fee, lawyers must consider the ability of the client, and lawyers cannot impose its clients with unnecessary expenses. It is not uncommon in practice that the contigency fee is implemented in Indonesian legal practice.

6. REMEDIES

6.1 What remedies are available to a party who successfully pursues a product liability claim?

Under Indonesian law there are four principle remedies for breach of contract:

(a) compensation for costs, damages and lost profits;
(b) cancellation of the contract and restitution of purchase price to the buyer; and
(c) payment of court costs (generally excluding counsel fees) in the event of court proceedings.

A breach of the agreement must also be established and proof of the damage caused as a direct result of the breach.

6.2 How are damages calculated/are there limitations on available damages?

The common ground for a civil claim requesting compensation damages on the consumer could be submitted before the court based on (i) a breach of contract or (ii) an unlawful act/tort. Under general contract or tort, the damage caused by the product and the subsequent compensation must be proved by the plaintiff. Generally damages in contract will not available to a plaintiff for losses which were not foreseeable at the time the contract was entered into. Article 1247 of the Civil Code sets out this obligation and provides an exception where non-performance was caused by some deception on the part of the other party.

Liability for manufacturers, retailers and advertising companies under the LCP is both civil and criminal. Breaching provisions concerning the warranty or guaranty may result in a fine of up to 200 million Indonesian Rupiahs. Violations concerning unfair competition resulting in serious injury, permanent disability or death attract criminal liability and potential imprisonment. The less severe violations are punishable with up to two years imprisonment or a fine of up to 500 million Indonesian Rupiahs, whereas offences considered more serious are punishable with up to five years imprisonment or a fine of up to 2 billion Indonesian Rupiahs.

Article 19 of the LCP provides that business undertaking must indemnify consumers for damage incurred as a result of the consumption of goods or services provided or traded by the business undertaking. Such compensation is in the form of a refund or replacement of the good or service of the same type or equivalent value, funding health care and or providing an allowance to the claimant for the damage or injury incurred.

6.3 Are punitive or exemplary damages available and in what circumstances?

In addition to damages as explained under b. above, under the LCP, the Indonesian courts have the power to confiscate goods, provide injunctive relief, recall the circulation of the goods from the market and revoke business licenses.

6.4 Is liability joint and several/how does apportionment of liability work, including where a partially responsible entity is not a party to the proceeding?

Theoretically a consumer who purchased a defective product can sue the retailer, and subsequently the retailer could bring a contractual claim for indemnity against its wholesaler or manufacturer of the product. However, in practice this is rife with difficulty. For example, if the retailer cannot be located, the consumer is left to rely on an action in tort for negligence against the producer. Where claims against manufacturers of defective products have been brought successfully under tort, comparatively small amounts are awarded in damages.

7. ROLE OF REGULATORS

7.1 Please explain the role, responsibilities and powers of the regulators in your country who have jurisdiction over product liability issues.

The monitoring and supervision of the consumer protection under the LCP will be implemented by the government which is represented by the Ministry of Trade ('MITI'), society and the non-governmental organisations (NGOs). The MITI has established National Agency for Consumer Protection (*Badan Perlindungan Konsumen Nasional* – BPKN). The members of BPKN are appointed by the President of Indonesia, as recommended by the MITI and this body serves and coordinates with the international consumer organisation and provide suggestions, recommendations, as well as supervision on the implementation of the LCP.

7.2 Are there any mandatory reporting requirements related to product safety issues?

Other than the MITI and BPKN as explained above, there exists a National Agency of Drug and Food Control (*Badan Pengawas Obat dan Makanan* – BPOM), as a regulator for the mandatory registration of drug and food control in order to protect the consumers security and health in Indonesia.

7.3 Do the regulators have the power to:

(i) ban certain goods or services?

(ii) require a supplier to recall a product?

(iii) prescribe standards in respect of certain goods or services and require that the goods or services meet those standards?
(iv) require production of information without court process?
Under the Indonesian law, BPOM has obligation to implement technical procedures for the registration of drugs and foods to be distributed in the territory of Indonesia, including the submission of the registration with the disclosure on detail ingredients and composition of the products to be in accordance with the technical regulations issued by BPOM. As the regulator, BPOM has the authority to ban and recall the circulation of a product, if it is found out that the circulation of the products is not in accordance with the regulations issued by BPOM.

8. VOLUNTARY CONDUCT

8.1 Are there regulations pertaining to the voluntary conduct of a product repair or recall by a supplier?

The regulations of BPOM are specifically deal with the recall of the drugs circulation. A drug recall could be done in the form of a mandatory recall or a voluntary recall. These product recalls are stipulated in the Regulation of the Head of BPOM No. HK.04.1.33.12.11.09938 regarding Criteria and Procedure of the Standard-Inappropriate Drug Withdrawal (Drug Withdrawal Regulation).

The Drug Withdrawal Regulation stipulates that a voluntary recall is possible, and could be done based on the initiative conducted by the holder of circulation/distribution permit (*izin edar*) if it is found out that the product is not met with standards and/or requirements as required under the BPOM. The mandatory recall is initiated by BPOM. All drugs that have been recalled must be destroyed and this activities must be reported to the BPOM. Any failures to comply with this regulation will subject to penalties in a form of warning, temporary suspension of the business activity of the business undertaking, the suspension of the circulation permit (*izin edar*), and/or the revocation of the circulation permit.

9. EMERGING ISSUES AND LAW REFORM

9.1 Are there important developing and emerging issues or trends in product liability law in your country?

9.2 Please describe any proposed important law reform in the area of product liability in your country.

A proposal for revision and/or amendment to the LCP has already been submitted by BPKN to the MITI. Some of the basic provisions of the LCP which are proposed to be amended are relating to the issues on:

(i) the separation of the responsibilities of the provider of the goods and services;
(ii) liability of the business undertaking shall be divided into two types, ie, (a) contractual liability and (b) product liability (strict liability);
(iii) improvement on the consumer dispute procedures for litigation and non-litigation settlement; and
(iv) the empowerment of the customer protection government authorities.

The proposed amendment has been submitted since 2007, however, to date the amendment of the LCP has not yet enacted.

Products liability-related jurisprudence is not highly developed in Indonesia. This is mostly due to (i) relatively new introduction of the LCP in Indonesia (1999), which is different with other jurisdictions that have a long tradition on consumer law, and (ii) cultural characteristics of Indonesian society (litigious solutions to product liability issues are generally discouraged). In serious cases where a product defect has led to death, especially before the enactment of the LCP, the Indonesian Government generally seeks criminal convictions against the manufacturer/retailer of the product, rather than the deceased's family seeking civil remedy. However, it should be anticipated in the future that there will be more product liability cases, both in the form of individual as well as class action claims, to be brought in front of the CDSB and/or the court, as the result of the advocacy movements conducted by the NGOs and the consumer education developed by the National Agency for Consumers Protection. The important role of these two institutions to protect consumers is acknowledged and endorsed by the LCP.

10. REGULATORY WEBSITES/INFORMATION

10.1 Please identify any useful regulatory references relating to product liability law in your country, for example, a product safety/consumer law website maintained by the main regulator.

The site references maintained by the government authorities relating to the product liability issues in Indonesia can be accessed in (i) *www.kemendag.go.id*, the website of the Directorate General of Standardization and Consumer Protection and (ii) *www.pom.go.id*, the website of BPOM.

Italy

Studio Legale Giorgetti
Alessandro P. Giorgetti & Prof. Giovanni Iorio

1. LIABILITY

1.1 What are the principal sources of law and regulation relating to product liability?

Product liability is currently regulated by Articles 114-127 of Legislative Decree no. 206 of 6 September 2005 (the 'Consumer Code'), which implemented Directive 85/374/EEC. Articles 114 *et seq*. do not apply to damage caused by nuclear accidents as set forth in Law no. 1860 of 31 December 1962 and subsequent modifications (Article 127[2] of Legislative Decree no. 206 of 2005). Articles 114 *et seq*. also do not apply to products put into circulation prior to 30 July 1988 (Article 127[3] of Legislative Decree no. 206 of 2005). The provisions of Articles 114 *et seq*. of the Consumer Code do not exclude nor limit the rights to which the injured person is entitled by other laws (Article 127[1] of Legislative Decree no. 206/2005).

1.2 What is required to establish causation under the most common causes of action available?

In order to obtain damages, the injured person has the burden of proving the defect, the damage, and the causal relationship between the defect and the product (Article 120[1] of the Consumer Code). The manufacturer must instead prove any facts that could exclude liability in accordance with the provisions of Article 118 (Article 120[2] of the Consumer Code; see the response to question 1.3 on Article 118 of the Consumer Code).

1.3 Is strict liability available and, if so, in what circumstances?

Articles 114 *et seq*. of the Consumer Code provide for strict liability: liability without fault, dependant on the objective fact of damage deriving from a defective product put into circulation. Pursuant to Article 118 of the Consumer Code, in fact, the manufacturer can be relieved of liability only by proving one of the following circumstances:

(a) that it did not put the product into circulation;
(b) that the defect that caused the damage did not exist when the product was put into circulation;
(c) that it did not manufacture the product for sale or for any other form of distribution for valuable consideration, nor manufacture or distribute it in the course of its commercial activity;
(d) that the defect is attributable to the product's compliance with mandatory regulations or a binding measure;

(e) that the state of technical and scientific knowledge at the time the product was put into circulation was not such as to enable the existence of the defect to be discovered;
(f) that, in the case of the manufacturer of a component or raw material, the defect is entirely attributable to the design of the product in which the component or raw material was incorporated, or to compliance with the manufacturer's instructions by whoever used it.

1.4 Are guarantees or warranties as to quality implied by law?

Articles 114 *et seq*. of the Consumer Code allow product liability even if no specific clause was provided by the contracting parties. It is noted that any agreement that preventively excludes or limits the liability provided by Articles 114 *et seq*. of the Consumer Code (Article 124 of the Consumer Code) with respect to the injured person is null.

1.5 How is a product 'defect' defined?

'Product' means all movables, even if incorporated in another movable or immovable, including electricity (Article 115[2] of the Consumer Code), as long as it has been put into circulation (Article 118[1] of the Consumer Code), ie, delivered to the buyer, user, or to someone associated with them, even if under approval or while being tested (Article 119[1] of the Consumer Code). A product is 'defective' if it does 'not provide the safety which can legitimately be expected, taking all circumstances into account' (Article 117[1] of the Consumer Code). In particular, the following circumstances must be considered:
(a) the manner in which the product was put into circulation;
(b) the use for which the product is reasonably intended;
(c) the time when the product was put into circulation (Article 117[2] of the Consumer Code).

Further, a product is defective if it does not provide the safety normally offered by other products of the same series (Article 117[3] of the Consumer Code). Instead, a product is not considered to be defective if the state of technical and scientific knowledge at the time the manufacturer put the product into circulation was not such as to enable the existence of the defect to be discovered (Article 118[1][e] of the Consumer Code). This is the case of a pharmaceutical product whose collateral effects are only determined after scientific knowledge has been developed.

1.6 Who in the supply chain has obligations or duties for defective products? What obligations or duties do they owe and to whom?

It is necessary to distinguish the 'manufacturer' from the 'supplier'. The 'manufacturer' (Article 114 of the Consumer Code) is the manufacturer of the finished product or of one of its parts, ie, the producer of the raw material, as well as farmers, breeders, fishermen and hunters (for agricultural products deriving from the soil as well as from stock-farming, fisheries and hunting) (Article 115[2]*bis*: such law was introduced by Article 14.2 of Legislative Decree no. 221 of 23 October 2007). The manufacturer must indemnify a person injured by the defective product.

If the manufacturer cannot be identified, liability rests with the 'supplier' that distributed the product in the course of a commercial activity, without prejudice to Article 116 of the Consumer Code, which will be discussed below (see the response to question 1.7 below). When the manufacturer operates outside of the member states of the European Union, liability rests with the importer that introduced the product into the European Union, even if the manufacturer is known (Article 116[6] of the Consumer Code).

1.7 By what means can a supplier limit their liability for defective products?

When the manufacturer has not been identified, the supplier which distributed the product in the course of a commercial activity is subject to such liability if it fails to inform the injured person, within the term of three months from a request, of the identity and domicile of the manufacturer or party which supplied it with the product (Article 116[1] of the Consumer Code). The request must be made in writing, with an indication of the product that caused the injury, the place, and, with reasonable approximation, the purchase date; it must also contain the offer under approval of the product, if it still exists (Article 116[2] of the Consumer Code). If service of the summons and complaint is not preceded by the request set forth in Article 116[2] of the Consumer Code, the defendant can provide such notice within the following three months (Article 116[3] of the Consumer Code). In any case, upon the motion of the supplier made at the first hearing of the proceedings on the merits, the court can allow an additional term not to exceed three months for the notice provided by Article 116[1] of the Consumer Code (Article 116[4] of the Consumer Code), if justified by the circumstances. The third party indicated as the manufacturer or previous supplier can be joined in the trial pursuant to Article 106 of the Italian Code of Civil Procedure, and the defendant supplier can be exonerated, if the indicated party appears and does not contest such indication. In the case provided by Article 116[3] of the Consumer Code, the defendant can request that the plaintiff be ordered to reimburse the expenses that it incurred (Article 116[5] of the Consumer Code).

See, instead, the response to question 1.3 above on the exclusion of the manufacturer's liability.

1.8 Are there particular goods or services which have specific obligations or duties attached to them? If so, explain what they are.

The Italian product liability regime (Articles 114-127 of the Consumer Code) does not refer to particular goods or services.

2. DEFENCES

2.1 What are the possible defences to a product liability claim?

The 'manufacturer' has the following possible defences:

- it can demonstrate that there is a reason for the exclusion of liability,

based on the cited Article 118 of the Consumer Code (see the response to question 1.3, above);
- an objection can be raised that the injured person did not provide evidence of the defect, the damage and causation between the defect and damage (Article 120[1] of the Consumer Code);
- an objection can be raised that the prerequisites are lacking for damages (based on the cited Article 123 of the Consumer Code; see the response to question 3.4, below);
- an objection can be raised that the injured person is responsible for contributory negligence, requesting that Article 1227 of the Italian Civil Code be applied, which limits the creditor's right to be indemnified (Article 122[1] of the Consumer Code); it can also be argued that damages are not due because the injured person was aware of the product defect and the danger deriving from it and nevertheless voluntarily exposed himself to such danger (Article 122[2] of the Consumer Code):
- an argument can be made that the claim has lapsed and that the right to receive damages has been extinguished (Articles 125 and 126 of the Consumer Code; see the response to question 2.2, below).

The 'supplier' can instead inform the injured person of the identity and domicile of the manufacturer or party which supplied the product to it and, in such manner, be relieved of liability; if there is a pending trial, it can be removed as a defendant if the named party appears and does not contest the indication (Article 116[5] of the Consumer Code).

2.2 Is there a limit on the time in which proceedings may be brought (limitations and repose)?

There are statutes of limitations and repose. The statute of limitations for the right to compensation is three years from the date on which the injured person was or should have been aware of the damage, the defect and the identity of the responsible party. In cases of aggravation of damages, the statute of limitations does not begin to run until the date on which the injured person was or should have been aware of damage of sufficient gravity to justify a legal action (Article 125 of the Consumer Code).

Further, the right to compensation shall be extinguished upon the expiry of 10 years from the date on which the manufacturer or importer of the European Union put the product that caused the damage into circulation. Such forfeiture is impeded only by a judicial claim, unless the trial is dismissed due to a request for admission of the credit in a bankruptcy procedure or recognition of the right by the liable party. The act that impedes forfeiture with respect to one of the liable parties has no effect with respect to the others (Article 126 of the Consumer Code).

3. LITIGATION OF PRODUCT LIABILITY DISPUTES

3.1 In which courts are product liability proceedings brought?

Proceedings seeking damages for product liability take place in front of the ordinary courts: a 'justice of the peace' (competent for proceedings related to personal property for a value that does not exceed €5,000: Article 7[1] of the Italian Code of Civil Procedure) or the 'Tribunal'. The judgment of the justice of the peace or court can be appealed. The judgment of the Court of Appeals can also be appealed, on grounds of misinterpretation or wrong application of the law in front of the Court of Cassation in Rome or, on grounds of constitutionality, at the Constitutional Court.

3.2 How are proceedings commenced?

Usually the proceedings are initiated by a 'summons and complaint' (provided by Article 163 of the Italian Code of Civil Procedure), which is served on the defendant (manufacturer or supplier). The proceedings can be considered to be pending in front of the justice of the peace or the Tribunal upon service of the summons and the complaint upon the defendant/s.

3.3 Are disputed issues decided by a judge or a jury?

The issues are decided by a professional judge (see the response to question 3.1, above).

3.4 Who has the burden of proof and to what standard?

In order to obtain damages, the injured person has the burden of proving:
(a) the damages suffered;
(b) the product defect (see the response to question 1.5, above); and
(c) the damages suffered (Article 120 of the Consumer Code).

With respect to the damages suffered, the injured person or the injured person's heirs must demonstrate, specifically:
(a) the damage caused by death or personal injuries;
(b) the destruction or deterioration of something other than the defective product, as long as of a type normally intended for private use or consumption, and primarily used by the injured person.

Damage to things is paid only to the extent that it exceeds the amount of 387 (Article 123(e) of the Consumer Code). The manufacturer can provide exonerating evidence pursuant to Article 118 of the Consumer Code (see the response to question 1.3, above).

3.5 How is evidence given in proceedings and are witnesses cross-examined?

During the evidentiary phase of the proceedings, both the plaintiff (injured person) and the defendant (manufacturer or supplier) can produce evidence to the court, such as documents or reports prepared by their experts. Further, they can request the court that some witnesses be summonsed to respond to questions prepared by the parties: it is the court, however, that admits witness testimony, as long as it is considered 'admissible' and 'relevant' according to the Italian legal system. The court can therefore decide not to hear the witnesses who are indicated (which occurs, for example, when the testimony is not deemed to be useful or admissible under Italian law); or it can decide to hear only some of the witnesses (and not everyone indicated by the parties); further, the court can decide whether the witnesses are heard only on some and not all of the questions prepared by the parties.

The parties to the proceedings can also request the court that the counterpart be heard directly (the hearing of one of the parties to the proceedings is considered a 'formal examination').

3.6 Are the parties able to rely on expert opinion evidence and, if so, are there any special rules or procedures for expert opinion evidence?

In accordance with the Italian Code of Civil Procedure, both the plaintiff and the defendant can produce a written expert opinion in the proceedings: this is documentary evidence. In addition, the parties to the proceedings can request that the court appoint an expert consultant (court-appointed expert – CTU), entrusted with preparing an expert opinion to be used for the decision. The court-appointed expert's opinion is prepared on the basis of the documents acquired in the proceedings. The court can also reject the request of the parties to appoint an expert. Further, the opinion of the court-appointed expert is not binding on the court: usually it will base its decision on the report filed by the court-appointed expert, but it can also deviate from it.

There are no specific rules on experts in the Italian legal regime on product liability.

3.7 Is pre-trial discovery permitted? If so, in what circumstances? If not, what other mechanisms, if any, are available for obtaining evidence from a party or a third party?

There are no specific rules on pre-trial discovery in the Italian regime on product liability. Nevertheless, the Italian Code of Civil Procedure provides for a 'preliminary expert investigation and report' (Article 696 of the Italian Code of Civil Procedure), which can be used even before the initiation of the proceedings to determine the liability of one of the parties. The preliminary expert witness investigation and report can be requested in cases of urgency: for example, if there is a need to act to resolve the harmful situation, danger or unavailability caused by the event giving rise to the damage. The court, upon a motion, appoints an expert who describes the situation that is the object of contestation: the expert's opinion will also be used during the subsequent proceedings.

Further, anyone who has a justified reason for believing that one or more witnesses might not be available whose depositions might be required in a future trial can request that they be heard for use in future proceedings (Article 692 of the Code of Civil Procedure).

The 'judicial attachment' of an asset can also be requested prior to the proceedings on the merits (Article 670[1] of the Italian Code of Civil Procedure): this is a precautionary measure that ensures the preservation of the asset through its custody or even its temporary management. The asset can be the object of the controversy, but it can also be an object that is instrumentally required to resolve the controversy.

3.8 Is there liability for spoliation of evidence/a remedy for destruction of or failure to preserve?

No liability or specific remedies are provided by the Italian regime on product liability. However, as noted above (see the response to question 3.7, above), prior to the initiation of the proceedings a request can be made for a preliminary expert witness investigation and report (Article 696 of the Code of Civil Procedure), witnesses can be heard for future use (Article 692 of the Code of Civil Procedure), and assets can be subjected to judicial attachment (Article 670[1] of the Code of Civil Procedure).

Further, on the basis of a general rule of civil procedure (Article 116 of the Italian Code of Civil Procedure), the court can infer elements of proof from the behaviour of the parties to the proceedings: therefore, the concealment or destruction of an asset by the party to whom it was available (the inspection of which was important) can be evidence against the party that concealed or destroyed the asset.

3.9 Is interlocutory or interim relief available prior to the full trial of a proceeding? If so, in what circumstances?

There are no specific interlocutory measures provided by the Italian legal regime on product liability. However, some provisions of the Italian Code of Civil Procedure make it possible to obtain some interlocutory relief prior to judgment, (Articles 186 *bis et seq.* of the Italian Code of Civil Procedure). The Code provides, for example, that upon the motion of one of the parties the court can order, starting from the specification of the final requests (ie, starting from the final phase of the proceedings) the payment of amounts that are uncontested by the parties who appeared (Article 186-*bis* of the Italian Code of Civil Procedure). Further, once the evidentiary phase has concluded, upon motion by the party claiming payment, the court can issue an order of payment to the extent it determines that sufficient evidence has been provided (Article 186-*quater* of the Italian Code of Civil Procedure).

Other interlocutory measures, which primarily regard the preservation of evidence, are noted above (see the response to question 3.7, above.

3.10 Can the winning party recover its costs?

According to a general rule (Article 91[1) of the Italian Code of Civil Procedure) the court, by means of a judgment that concludes the proceedings, can order the losing party to reimburse costs to the other party and to pay such amount together with the legal fees for the defence. Such general rule can be subject to some derogations (compare Articles 92-97 of the Italian Code of Civil Procedure). For example, in its decision the court can exclude the reimbursement of the expenses sustained by the winning party if it deems them to be excessive or superfluous; it can also, regardless of which party loses, order one of the parties to pay the expenses, even if not reimbursable, that it caused the other party to incur due to breach of the duty of loyalty and probity (Article 92[1] of the Italian Code of Civil Procedure).

3.11 What avenues of appeal are available?

The judgment of the court of merit (justice of the peace or court) can be appealed to a higher court (respectively, court or Court of Appeals). The judgment of the higher court (Court or Court of Appeals) can be appealed, but only due to violation of law ('constitutionality'), in front of the Court of Cassation of Rome.

4. CLASS ACTIONS/REPRESENTATIVE PROCEEDINGS

4.1 Is there a mechanism for class actions or representative proceedings, or coordinated proceedings for product liability claims? If so, what are the basic mechanics?

The Consumer Code provides that individual homogeneous rights of consumers and users, as well as societal interests, can also be protected by means of a class action, in accordance with Article 140-*bis*. Among others, the class action protects the homogeneous rights of the final consumers of a specific product or service with respect to the relative manufacturer, regardless of whether or not there is a direct contractual relationship (Article 140-bis[2][b] of the Consumer Code).

Consumers and users who intend to use this form of protection can join, without the assistance of legal counsel, even by means of certified email and by fax. Joining a class action results in a waiver of any individual proceeding for restitution or damages based on the same claim (Article 140-*bis*[3] of the Consumer Code).

The claim is made by means of a summons and complaint filed with the court of merit (Article 140-*bis*[4] of the Consumer Code). At the conclusion of the first hearing, the court decides by means of an order whether or not the claim is admissible (Article 140-*bis*[6] of the Consumer Code). In the order in which it allows the action to proceed, the court establishes the terms and procedures for the most opportune public notice, so that anyone belonging to the class can join in a timely manner. Public notice is a condition for the admissibility of the claim (Article 140-*bis*[9] of the Consumer Code).

If the claim is accepted, the court issues a judgment in which it orders the final sums due to anyone who joined the class action, or it establishes homogeneous criteria so that the amounts to be paid can be calculated. In the latter case, the court assigns the parties a term, not to exceed 90 days, in which to reach an agreement on the payment of compensation. The report of findings of the agreement, signed by the parties and by the court, is an enforceable instrument. Once the term has expired without an agreement having been reached, the court, upon motion of at least one of the parties, orders the payment of the amounts due to the individuals who joined the class action (Article 140-*bis*[12] of the Consumer Code).

5. LITIGATION FUNDING

5.1 Is litigation funding by third parties permissible in your country? If so, is it common?

In Italy there are no provisions for litigation funding by third parties.

5.2 Are contingency fee or 'no win no fee' arrangements permissible?

Contingency fees *strictu sensu* are prohibited; but a fee calculated in proportion with the success obtained can be negotiated in writing in accordance with Article 45 of the Lawyer Professional Rules. There are no provisions for 'no win no fee' arrangements.

6. REMEDIES

6.1 What remedies are available to a party who successfully pursues a product liability claim?

An injured person who obtains a favourable judgment has the right to receive compensation (Article 123 of the Consumer Code). The judgment is immediately enforceable: therefore the injured person, if he or she does not receive the payment of what is provided, can proceed with an enforcement procedure against the party that has been held liable. See also the response to question 6.2, below.

6.2 How are damages calculated/are there limitations on available damages?

Available damages can consist of the following in accordance with Article 123 of the Consumer Code:

(a) the damage caused by death or personal injuries;

(b) the destruction or deterioration of something other than the defective product, as long as it is of a type normally intended for private use and consumption and was primarily used by the injured person.

Damage to things is paid only to the extent that it exceeds the amount of €387.

6.3 Are punitive or exemplary damages available and in what circumstances?

Damages are available to the extent that they injure a person or cause the destruction or deterioration of something other than the defective product (Article 123 of the Consumer Code). They therefore cannot be classified as punitive or exemplary damages.

6.4 Is liability joint and several/how does apportionment of liability work, including where a partially responsible entity is not a party to the proceeding?

The regime on product liability deals specifically with the case in which more than one person is responsible for the same damage (Article 121 of the Consumer Code). It provides that they are jointly liable for damages. Whoever has paid damages has a right of recourse against the others to the extent determined by the scope of the risk referable to each of them, the gravity of any fault, and the extent of the consequences deriving from it. When in doubt, damages are divided in equal shares.

If one of the jointly liable parties was not a party to the proceedings, the general rule prevails provided by the Italian Civil Code (Article 1306[1] of the Italian Civil Code): a judgment issued regarding the creditor and one of the joint debtors, or between the debtor and one of the joint creditors, has no effect with respect to the other debtors or creditors.

7. ROLE OF REGULATORS

7.1 Please explain the role, responsibilities and powers of the regulators in your country which have jurisdiction over product liability issues.

In Italy, the Ministries of Productive Activities, Health, Labour and Social Policies, the Interior, Economy and Finance, Infrastructures and Transportation, as well as the other public administrations provided from time to time by law, have power with respect to consumer product safety. Such administrations create a rapid system for the exchange of information by means of adequate electronic informational support (Article 106[1] of the Consumer Code).

The criteria for the coordination of the controls are provided by a special Conference of Services among the component offices of the Ministries and competent administrations, which is convened at least twice each year by the Minister of Productive Activities; the Minister of Justice and other administrations competent from time to time also participate at the Conference (Article 106[2] of the Consumer Code).

The Ministries and other competent administrations have control power (Article 107 of the Consumer Code: see the response to question 7.3, below), as well as 'market review':

(a) through the creation, periodic update and implementation of sector programs to review categories of products or risks, as well as monitoring the reviews, comments and results;
(b) to update scientific and technical knowledge related to product safety;
(c) through the examination and periodic assessment of the control activities and their effectiveness (Article 109 of the Consumer Code).

The Ministry of Productive Activities notifies the European Commission of the measures taken pursuant to Article 107 of the Consumer Code, specifying the grounds therefore (Article 110 of the Consumer Code).

The Ministries and competent authorities can adopt sanctions within the limits indicated by the law (Article 112 of the Consumer Code: see the response to question 7.3, below). The provisions set forth in Articles 114 *et seq.* remain unchanged, however, on product liability (Article 111 of the Consumer Code).

7.2 Are there any mandatory reporting requirements related to product safety issues?

Yes, various obligations are provided, above all for products that might present risks in specific conditions and for any product that might be or which is dangerous (Article 107 of the Consumer Code: see, in detail, the response to question 7.3, below).

In general, it is provided that the manufacturer can only put safe products into circulation (Article 104[1] of the Consumer Code). The manufacturer, in particular, must provide the consumer with all information that is useful to assess and prevent risks deriving from the normal use or reasonably foreseeable use of the product, if not immediately perceptible without sufficient warnings, as well as for the prevention of such risks (Article 104[2] of the Consumer Code). Further, the manufacturer must adopt proportional measures based on the characteristics of the product supplied, so that the consumer is informed of the risks related to its use, and it must take the necessary initiatives to avoid such risks, including product recall and appropriate and effective information to consumers (Article 104[3] of the Consumer Code; on the sanction deriving from the violation of such obligations, see the response to question 7.3, below).

7.3 Do the regulators have the power to:
(i) ban certain goods or services?
(ii) require a supplier to recall a product?
(iii) prescribe standards in respect of certain goods or services and require that the goods or services meet those standards?
(iv) require production of information without court process?
If so, broadly explain the circumstances in which the regulator can exercise the power and any penalties that apply if a supplier fails to comply.

The Ministries and competent public authorities have various powers.

(a) They can, for any product (Article 107[2][a] of the Consumer Code):
   (i) conduct, even after a product has been put into circulation as a safe product, adequate controls of its safety characteristics through the state of use or consumption, including by means of inspections at the manufacturing and packaging facilities, warehouses and storerooms;
   (ii) demand all necessary information from the interested parties;
   (iii) take samples of products to submit to testing and analysis intended to verify their safety and prepare a report of findings, a copy of which must be given to the interested parties.
(b) With respect to any product that might present risks in specific conditions (Article 107[2][b] of the Consumer Code):
   (i) require that adequate warnings of potential risks be placed on the product, in Italian, that are prepared in a clear and easily understandable manner;
   (ii) subject putting a product into circulation to prior conditions, in order to render the product safe.
(c) With respect to any product that might present risks for specific parties (Article 107[2][c] of the Consumer Code):
   (i) provide that such parties be timely and adequately warned of such risk, including by means of the publication of specific warnings.
(d) With respect to any product that might be dangerous (Article 107[2][d] of the Consumer Code):
   (i) prohibit the supply of the product, proposals to supply it or its display for the time required to conduct controls, assessments or verifications of product safety;

   (ii) order, within a mandatory term, that the product or lot of products already distributed be adjusted to comply with the safety requirements provided by this Article, if there is no imminent risk to health and public safety.

(e) With respect to any dangerous product (Article 107[2][e] of the Consumer Code):
   (i) prohibit that they be put into circulation and adopt any necessary measures to guarantee compliance with the prohibition.

(f) With respect to any dangerous product already put into circulation with respect to which the action already taken by the manufacturers and distributors is unsatisfactory or insufficient (Article 107[2][f] of the Consumer Code):
   (i) order and organise its effective and immediate recall and provide information to consumers regarding the risks it presents. The relative costs are borne by the manufacturer or, if this is not possible in all or in part, by the distributor;
   (ii) order or coordinate or, if such is the case, organise with the manufacturers and distributors its recall also by consumers and its destruction in opportune conditions. The relative costs are borne by the manufacturers and distributors.

The above measures can regard (Article 107[7] of the Consumer Code):

(a) the manufacturer;
(b) the distributor and, in particular, the party responsible for putting the product into circulation the first time;
(c) any other party holding the product, if this is necessary in view of coordination with acts taken to avoid the risks deriving from the product.

With respect to sanctions (which can be imposed regardless of whether or not the injured person of a defective product initiates legal proceedings), it is necessary to refer to Article 112 of the Consumer Code. Unless the fact constitutes a more serious crime, a manufacturer or distributor who puts dangerous products into circulation in violation of the prohibition set forth in Article 107[2][e] is punished by detention from six months to one year and with a fine ranging from €10,000 to €50,000 (Article 112[1] of the Consumer Code).

A manufacturer who puts dangerous products into circulation is punished by detention up to one year and a fine ranging from €10,000 to €50,000 (Article 112[2] of the Consumer Code), unless a more serious offence has been committed.

A manufacturer or distributor who is noncompliant with the measures issued pursuant to Article 107[2][b][1] and [2][c] and [d][1] and [2] is punished by a fine ranging from €10,000 to €25,000 (Article 112[3] of the Consumer Code), unless a more serious offence has been committed.

A manufacturer or distributor who does not provide the necessary collaboration required to carry out the activities set forth in Article 107[2][a] is subject to an administrative fine ranging from €2,500 to €40,000 (Article 112[4] of the Consumer Code).

Finally, unless the act constitutes a criminal offence, a manufacturer or distributor who violates any provision set forth in Article 104 is subject to an administrative fine ranging from €1,500 to €30,000 (Article 112[5] of the Consumer Code).

It is specified that the above is without prejudice to specific sector standards that require special safety standards with reference to particular categories of goods. It is also without prejudice to regional provisions that regulate the controls that are within their powers (Article 113[2] of the Consumer Code).

8. VOLUNTARY CONDUCT

8.1 Are there regulations pertaining to the voluntary conduct of a product repair or recall by a supplier?

In the specific product liability regime there are no regulations that reward voluntary conduct by the manufacturer or supplier. However, in the relationship between manufacturers/distributors and regulators (see the response to question 7.3, above on this issue), there are regulations intended to encourage voluntary conduct by manufacturers and distributors, as well as their participation in decision-making processes of the competent authorities.

In fact, it is provided that the competent administrations, in the context of measures taken based on the principle of precaution, should encourage and enhance voluntary acts of manufacturers and distributors to adjust to the obligations imposed on them, including through Codes of Conduct and agreements with industrial categories (Article 107[5] of the Consumer Code).

Further, in compliance with the principle of the right of participation, except for cases of grave or immediate danger to health or to the public or private safety, prior to adopting the measures set forth in Article 107[2][3] of the Consumer Code, the interested parties must be allowed to participate during the phase of the administrative proceedings and controls regarding their products (Article 108[2] of the Consumer Code). The interested parties can present written comments, including subsequent to the issue of the measure, even if, due to the urgency of the measure to be taken, they were unable to participate in the proceedings (Article 108[3] of the Consumer Code).

9. EMERGING ISSUES AND LAW REFORM

9.1 Are there important developing and emerging issues or trends in product liability law in your country?

The following are some issues that have recently been debated in Italy, including by the organisation of conferences and written texts: pharmaceutical product liability (an issue discussed during the conference on 'The Responsibility of Healthcare Workers', organised by the University of Camerino on 9-10 May 2013); information to consumers on defective products (see the conference organised by the Chamber of Commerce of Pistoia entitled 'The Consumer Code and product safety' held on 18 July 2013).

Case law has, at times, discussed the issue of the burden of proof (see, for example, judgment no. 13432 of the Court of Cassation of 1 June 2010, according to which 'the fact that the injured person did not ask the storeowner in writing for the manufacturer's details does not impede the client from obtaining damages').

9.2 Please describe any proposed important law reform in the area of product liability in your country.

At present there are no proposed laws in the area of product liability.

10. REGULATORY WEBSITES/INFORMATION

10.1 Please identify any useful regulatory references relating to product liability law in your country, for example, a product safety/consumer law website maintained by the main regulator.

www.sviluppoeconomico.gov.it

Japan

Anderson Mori & Tomotsune Shinji Kusakabe & Aoi Inoue

1. LIABILITY

1.1 What are the principal sources of law and regulation relating to product liability?

In product liability cases, in which a person who incurs damage due to a product defect (the 'victim' or 'plaintiff') seeks compensation from the manufacturer, etc. of the defective product (the 'defendant'), the main legislation is the Product Liability Act (Act No. 85 of 1994) (PLA). PLA Article 3 specifically provides that a manufacturer, etc. (see question 1.6 below) of a defective product will be liable for damages arising from the infringement of life, body or property of others which is caused by the product defect.

Since the PLA was enacted to serve as special tort provisions in addition to the general tort provisions of the Civil Code (Act No. 89 of 1896), the applicability of the PLA does not prevent a claim from being brought under the Civil Code. Under the Civil Code Article 709, the general tort law provision, a manufacturer, importer, retailer and others who have intentionally or negligently infringed any right of consumers through defective products shall be liable to compensate for damages.

In addition to the PLA and the Civil Code, if there is a direct contractual relationship between the victim and the defendant, such as purchase agreement, there are two provisions under the Civil Code that may also provide for the liability of the defendant under contract law:

- Under the Civil Code Article 570, if a product contains a latent defect, and such defect causes harm to the purchaser, the purchaser may seek damages against the vendor of the product.
- Under the Civil Code Article 415, if the vendor provides a defective product, and it can be said that the vendor failed to provide an appropriate product in a manner that is consistent with the purpose of its obligations, the purchaser shall be entitled to demand damages arising from such failure.

Thus, in short, the main laws governing product liability cases are the PLA and the Civil Code. However, often a victim may want to seek damages from a defendant with which it has no direct contractual relationship (eg, the manufacturer or importer). In such cases, the victim usually relies on the PLA.

1.2 What is required to establish causation under the most common causes of action available?

Under PLA Article 3, a plaintiff can only claim damages which have proximate causation with the product defect. This can be established by proving the existence of a product defect, the damage incurred, and proximate causation between the defect and the damage. The plaintiff does not need to prove that the defendant was negligent.

In contrast, in a general tort case for negligence under the Civil Code Article 709, a plaintiff must establish the negligence of the defendant, the damage incurred, and proximate causation between the negligence and the damage.

1.3 Is strict liability available and, if so, in what circumstances?

Prior to the enactment of the PLA, the plaintiff had to prove as a substantive requirement that the defendant was negligent under the Civil Code Article 709 (see question 1.2 above).

However, now under the PLA the plaintiff only needs to prove the existence of a product defect as an objective requirement, and does not need to prove the existence of the defendant's negligence. In this sense, product liability under PLA Article 3 could be said to be a form of strict liability as the defendant will be liable if the plaintiff can simply prove the existence of a product defect and that such defect caused the damages being claimed.

1.4 Are guarantees or warranties as to quality implied by law?

Under the PLA, a manufacturer, etc. (see question 1.6, below for definition of 'manufacturer, etc') will be liable to compensate a victim for damages arising from a product defect, with 'defect' meaning a lack of safety that a product ordinarily should provide (PLA Article 2(2), see also question 1.5 below). Accordingly, the product liability under the PLA does not apply to product defects which are not related to product safety, such as defects merely relating to the quality, specifications and performance of a product.

On the other hand, the Civil Code Article 570 provides that the vendor's liability to the purchaser will arise if there is a latent defect in the product. A latent defect means that the quality, specifications or performance of the product being sold does not meet the purpose for which the product was sold, and is not limited to defects that threaten safety.

1.5 How is a product 'defect' defined?

The PLA defines 'defect' as a lack of safety that a product ordinarily should provide, taking into account the nature of the product, its ordinarily foreseeable manner of use, the time the manufacturer, etc, delivered the product, and other circumstances concerning the product (PLA Article 2(2)). Generally speaking, such defects may be divided into three categories:

- manufacturing defects (product is unsafe due to not being made in accordance with its design or specifications);
- design defects (product is unsafe because of insufficient consideration being given to safety at the design stage); and
- defect in instructions or warnings (product is unsafe because the manufacturers, etc, fail to provide appropriate information so as to help users avoid accidents from occurring as a result of inherently dangerous aspects of the product).

1.6 Who in the supply chain has obligations or duties for defective products? What obligations or duties do they owe and to whom?

Under PLA Article 3, a 'manufacturer, etc' can be liable to compensate a victim for damages arising from the infringement of life, body or property of others, which is caused by a product defect. 'Manufacturer, etc' is defined in PLA Article 2(3) as:

- any person who manufactured, processed, or imported the product in the course of its business (the 'manufacturer');
- any person who provides his/her name, trade name, trademark or other indication ('representation of name, etc') on the product as the manufacturer or provides representation of name, etc, which misleads others into believing that he/she is the manufacturer;
- any other person who provides any representation of name etc, on the product which holds himself/herself out as the substantial manufacturer in light of the manner in which the product was manufactured, processed, imported, sold and other circumstances.

Thus under the PLA, not only a manufacturer but also a processor and an importer of a product can be liable for certain damages caused by a product defect. In addition, as an example, an entity that is not the real importer of a product, but nevertheless places its trade name on the packaging of the product and holds itself out as the importer, or an entity which provides its brand name to an OEM product, can be liable under the PLA.

On the other hand, the mere retailer of a product will not be liable to consumer purchasers under the PLA. Nevertheless, retailers that directly sell the products to consumers would have a contractual relationship with such consumers, and thus may be liable for defective products under the Civil Code Articles 570 and 415 (contractual liability, see question 1.1 above).

1.7 By what means can a supplier limit their liability for defective products?

PLA Article 4 provides certain exemptions of liability to a manufacturer, etc, with respect to liability based on PLA Article 3 (see question 2.1 below).

In addition, if a supplier sells products directly to purchasers, generally speaking it is possible for the supplier and purchaser to agree on contractual exemptions of liability. However, such exemptions will only be effective between the parties to the agreement. Furthermore, the mere displaying of a notice of limitation or exemption of liability on the packaging of a product or in an instruction manual etc, will in many cases be insufficient to constitute an agreement exempting or limiting a supplier's liability.

1.8 Are there particular goods or services which have specific obligations or duties attached to them?

Special laws and regulations provide administrative product safety standards that should be met when manufacturing or selling certain types of goods and services for which ensuring safety is of particular necessity. Examples of such laws and regulations include the Pharmaceutical Affairs Act (Act No. 145 of 1960), the Food Sanitation Act (Act No. 233 of 1947), and the

Electrical Appliances and Materials Safety Act (Act No. 234 of 1961) (see also question 7.1 below).

In principle, whether or not a product satisfies such administrative product safety standards will not necessarily correspond to whether or not a product is defective under the PLA, although in practice a failure to conform to such product safety standards makes it highly likely that the product will be found to be defective.

2. DEFENCES

2.1 What are the possible defences to a product liability claim?

PLA Article 4(1) provides that a manufacturer, etc. shall not be liable under PLA Article 3 if it can prove that the state of scientific or technical knowledge at the time the product was delivered was insufficient to allow the discovery of the product defect. Generally speaking, this defence is very difficult to establish as the burden of proof is on the manufacturer, etc. and the state of knowledge is judged based on the highest standard of scientific and technical information that could possibly be obtained.

PLA Article 4(2) provides that a manufacturer, etc, shall not be liable under PLA Article 3 if its product is used as a component or raw material of another product and the defect in the product is primarily attributable to compliance with instructions concerning the specifications given by the manufacturer of the said another product, and the manufacturer, etc. is not negligent on occurrence of the defect. The burden of proof is also on the defendant.

In addition, the defences applicable to tort liability under the Civil Code are also applicable to a product liability claim under PLA Article 3 (see PLA Article 6). Accordingly, the defence of comparative negligence may apply to reduce the liability of the manufacturer, etc. if the plaintiff was negligent in relation to the product accident (Civil Code Article 722(2)). However, if the misuse of the product by the plaintiff was reasonably foreseeable by the manufacturer, etc., such reasonably foreseeable misuse by the plaintiff will be taken into account in a judgement as to whether or not a product is defective under the PLA. This significantly limits the cases in which the comparative negligence defence is applicable due to such reasonably foreseeable misuse.

2.2 Is there a limit on the time in which proceedings may be brought (limitations and repose)?

Yes. The PLA provides a specific limitation period that extinguishes the right to seek damages and compensation under PLA Article 3. It should be noted that under Japanese law, a limitation period only extinguishes the right to seek damages and compensation as a substantive law, and does not prevent a party from exercising its right under procedural law to file an action.

Under PLA Article 5(1), the right to demand compensation for damages under PLA Article 3 extinguishes if three years has passed since the victim came to know of the damage and the identity of the perpetrator (PLA Article 5(1), first sentence ('extinctive prescription')). This is the same as the extinctive prescription for the right to seek damages and compensation under the tort provisions of the Civil Code (Civil Code Article 724, first sentence).

Further, the right to seek damages and compensation under PLA Article 3 also extinguishes if 10 years has passed since the time the manufacturer, etc. delivered the product (PLA Article 5(1), second sentence ('period of exclusion')). In contrast, the right to demand compensation for damages in tort under the Civil Code extinguishes if 20 years has passed from the time of the tortious act (Civil Code Article 724, second sentence). Thus the PLA has shortened the period of exclusion from 20 years to 10 years. However, if the damages are caused by substances which become harmful to human health after accumulating in the body, or where the symptoms which represent such damages appear after a certain latent period, this 10-year period of exclusion under the PLA will be calculated from the time such damages occurred (PLA Article 5(2)). This exemption was made in recognition of the fact that a 10-year limitation period from the delivery of the product is not sufficient to ensure the rights of victims in such special circumstances.

As stated in 1.1 above, since the PLA was enacted to serve as special rules in addition to the tort provisions of the Civil Code, the PLA does not prevent the applicability of the Civil Code. Therefore, the extinguishment of a claim under the PLA does not prevent a claim from being brought under the Civil Code, provided the claim under the Civil Code has not extinguished as well.

3. LITIGATION OF PRODUCT LIABILITY DISPUTES

3.1 In which courts are product liability proceedings brought?

The rules for determining the courts to which ordinary civil lawsuits should be brought also apply to litigation of product liability disputes.

As for the type of court that has jurisdiction, such will be determined by the value of the dispute. The court of first instance will be a Summary Court if the value of the dispute is equal to or less than ¥1.4 million (the Court Act (Act No. 59 of 1947) Article 33(1)(i)); or the District Court if it exceeds ¥1.4 million (Court Act Article 24(i)).

As for territorial jurisdiction, if the defendant is a legal entity, the court with jurisdiction over the location of the defendant's main office will have jurisdiction over the case (the Code of Civil Procedure (Act No. 109 of 1996) (CCP) Article 4(4)). In addition, it is common for there to be more than one court that has territorial jurisdiction. For instance, in tort cases, the court that has jurisdiction over the place at which the tort was committed will also have jurisdiction over the case. The plaintiff may file a lawsuit at any of those courts at its discretion.

3.2 How are proceedings commenced?

The procedures applicable to commence ordinary civil lawsuits also apply to litigation of product liability disputes.

In order to bring an action before a District Court, the plaintiff must submit a written complaint to the competent court (CCP Article 113(1)). The court will then conduct a formality review of the written complaint, and if it does not contain any errors in formalities, the court will serve a duplicate copy of the written complaint to the defendant. In Japan, the plaintiff is not permitted to directly serve the complaint to the defendant on behalf of the court.

3.3 Are disputed issues decided by a judge or a jury?

Disputed issues in product liability cases are always decided by judges, because Japan does not have a system of juries deciding disputed issues in civil cases.

3.4 Who has the burden of proof and to what standard?

When a plaintiff claims damages under PLA Article 3, the plaintiff has the burden of proving the existence of the product defect, the damages incurred and proximate causation between such defect and damages. As to the existence of a product defect, in practice, the plaintiff (victim) is only required to specify the defective nature of the product. It is not necessary to scientifically specify the exact sites or parts of the product that cause the product to be defective.

The standard of proof for product liability cases is the same as that for ordinary civil lawsuits, whereby there must be a high probability such that an ordinary person would not doubt the truth of the allegations being made.

3.5 How is evidence given in proceedings and are witnesses cross-examined?

Evidence can be divided into two groups: physical evidence (such as documentary evidence and objects to be inspected) and witness evidence (such as the examination of witnesses, experts and the parties themselves). In principle, evidence is examined at court hearing sessions upon the application of either party.

For physical evidence, each party may submit the physical evidence, which will then be examined by court at a court hearing session.

For witness evidence, each party may apply to the court to conduct a witness examination, and if the court accepts such a request, the witness examination will be conducted at a court hearing. In general, witnesses will first be examined by the party that requested the examination, followed by a cross-examination by the other party (CCP Articles 202 and 210).

As for examination of the parties themselves, such can be conducted by the court at its discretion without an application from the parties, although ordinarily the court will only do so upon receiving an application from either or both parties.

In relation to expert witnesses, please see question 3.6 below.

3.6 Are the parties able to rely on expert opinion evidence and, if so, are there any special rules or procedures for expert opinion evidence?

Yes. A party can privately request an expert to provide a written expert opinion, which may then be submitted as documentary evidence. The CCP does not provide any special rules for written expert opinions and thus they are usually treated the same as ordinary documentary evidence.

In practice, a court may require, upon an application by either party, the author of the written expert opinion to be examined as a witness so as to allow that party to cross examine the author, if it is deemed necessary in light of the contents of the opinion or the qualifications and suitability of the author to provide such an expert opinion.

In addition, the parties may apply to have an expert witness appointed by the court state his/her opinions (CCP Article 215) and to have the court commission a private or public institution to provide an expert opinion (CCP Article 218).

3.7 Is pre-trial discovery permitted? If so, in what circumstances? If not, what other mechanisms, if any, are available for obtaining evidence from a party or a third party?

In Japanese court procedures, there is no distinction between trial and discovery stages, which exists in other jurisdictions such as in the US.

In Japan, the court will hold regular periodic hearings soon after a plaintiff files a lawsuit. During such hearings, the parties may submit briefs and physical evidence, and the court will examine such evidence. Usually, after the points in dispute are organised, witness examinations are conducted. Thus there is no concept of pre-trial discovery. However, there are the following procedures that can be used to obtain evidence before and after a lawsuit is filed:

- **Preservation of evidence (CCP Article 234)**

If there is a risk that evidence may be difficult or impossible to examine unless a prior examination of evidence is conducted (such as if there is a risk that the evidence will be altered or discarded, or the witness will die), the court may permit an examination of evidence at early stage upon petition.

- **Request for information (the Attorney Act (Act No. 205 of 1949) Article 23-2)**

An attorney qualified under the Attorney Act may request the bar association to which he or she belongs to make enquiries with public offices or private organisations regarding information that is necessary for a case which the attorney is retained. The bar association will make such inquiries unless the request is inappropriate.

- **Enquiries prior to or after filing an action (CCP Articles 163, 132-2 and 132-3)**

A party that has filed a legal action may make inquiries to the other party about matters necessary for preparing allegations and evidence. A party intending to commence legal action and who has given advanced notice of such to the potential defendant may also make enquiries to the potential defendant about matters necessary for preparing allegations or evidence. The potential defendant that has been given such advanced notice may also make enquiries to the potential plaintiff for the same purposes.

- **Document/object production order (CCP Articles 220 to 225 and 232)**

A party can request the court to order a document holder to submit a document and the court may grant such order if it determines that the holder has an obligation to produce the document under CCP Article 220 and it is necessary for the document to be examined. Provided these requirements are met, a document production order can be made against any document holder, including non-parties to the litigation. A failure to comply with such a court order may result in a court ruling that the requesting party's assertions regarding the document are true. Legal sanctions may also apply to a failure to produce a document subject to a court order. A similar production order is also available for objects to be inspected.

- **Commission of document/object submission prior to or after filing an action (CCP Articles 226, 132-4 and 232)**

A party may request the court to commission a document holder to submit a document notwithstanding whether the holder has an obligation to produce the document. A party intending to commence legal action and who has given advanced notice of such to the potential defendant may also request the court to commission a document holder to submit a document. A similar commission is also available for objects to be inspected.

- **Commission of examination prior to or after filing an action (CCP Article 186 and 132-4)**

Government agencies, public offices, foreign government agencies and public offices, schools, chambers of commerce, stock exchange and other organisations such as hospitals and places of employment may be commissioned by a court to conduct a necessary examination and report the results to the court. In practice, the matters to be commissioned are limited to objective matters for which there will be no dispute between the parties. Further, a party intending to commence legal action and who has given advanced notice of such to the potential defendant may request the court to commission such necessary examination to be conducted.

3.8 Is there liability for spoliation of evidence/a remedy for destruction of or failure to preserve evidence (most relevantly, the product)?

There are no specific rules imposing liability for the concealment, spoliation or destruction of evidence. However, if the court makes an order for document/object production against one party (see question 3.7 above), and that party violates the order by intentionally spoiling, altering or destroying, failing to provide, or otherwise taking any action in relation to the relevant documents/objects in order to make them unavailable to the other party, the court may make a ruling that the other party's assertions regarding the document/object are true (CCP Articles 224 and 232).

In addition, if the court finds that a party intentionally concealed, spoiled, altered or destroyed evidence which is unfavourable to that party, the court may, as a matter of practice, make unfavourable findings against that party. If it is foreseeable by one party that the other party will tamper with evidence, they can use the procedures in 3.7 above to secure the preservation of evidence.

3.9 Is interlocutory or interim relief available prior to the full trial of a proceeding? If so, in what circumstances?

Yes, the Civil Provisional Remedies Act (Act No. 91 of 1989) (CPRA) provides interlocutory or interim relief that can be used before or after a lawsuit has commenced.

If there is a risk that the defendant or a potential defendant may conceal or dispose of its assets, an order for provisional seizure may be made so as to freeze such assets and preserve them for the enforcement of any future monetary judgement (CPRA Article 20(1)).

In addition, a temporary injunction for the purpose of preserving the non-monetary rights of the parties and other rights arising from legal relationships may be possible (CPRA Article 23).

A petition for an order for these provisional remedies must *prima facie* establish the rights that must be preserved and the necessity of protecting such rights (CPRA Article 13).

3.10 Can the winning party recover its costs?

In cases with a clear losing party, the losing party will bear the costs of the litigation (CCP Article 61). In cases with a partial loss, each party's burden for the costs of the litigation will be decided by the court at its discretion (CCP Article 64).

The Act on Civil Litigation Costs (Act No. 40 of 1971) Article 2 stipulates the costs of litigation that may be claimable from other party including filing fees, travel expenses, daily allowances and accommodation expenses necessary for witnesses attending court hearing sessions, and expenses for preparing and producing documents, all of which are costs handled by the court. Each party's attorney fees are not included in the litigation costs that are ordinarily recoverable. However, in tort litigation, including claims for damages made under PLA Article 3, a plaintiff may claim attorney fees as part of the damage incurred as a result of the product defect or other tortious act. Generally, the amount of damages awarded to a successful plaintiff for attorney fees will not exceed 10% of the total amount of other damages awarded.

3.11 What avenues of appeal are available?

Where the court of first instance is the District Court, the losing party may first appeal to the High Court, and further appeal to the Supreme Court of Japan. However, the grounds for appeal to the Supreme Court do not include errors in findings of fact. There must be an error of law by the previous court. Accordingly, opportunities for appeals to the Supreme Court in product liability cases are quite limited.

4. CLASS ACTIONS/REPRESENTATIVE PROCEEDINGS

4.1 Is there a mechanism for class actions or representative proceedings, or coordinated proceedings for product liability claims? If so, what are the basic mechanics?

Under the Japanese laws currently in force, there is no system in Japan which is similar to a 'class action' in US civil litigation. Further, there are no special proceedings, such as coordinated proceedings, particularly designed for product liability claims.

If a lot of victims have suffered from accidents arising from the same type of product, an attorney would sometimes contact the victims and invite them to form a group of plaintiffs and file a lawsuit. In general, such attorney will represent all the plaintiffs in the group. However, the claims of each plaintiff in the group are theoretically separate from those of other members, even though in the lawsuit their claims are consolidated into one joint proceeding. Further, victims that do not join plaintiff groups are not affected by the outcome of such related joint proceedings.

There is also a system of 'appointed party proceedings' where numerous persons with a common interest may appoint a representative party from among them to file a lawsuit on their behalf (CCP Article 30(1)), but this is not commonly used in practice.

In 2013 the Cabinet submitted a bill to the Diet for introducing a so-called Japanese class action system with the main aim of facilitating the simple and efficient recovery of wide-spread damages incurred by consumers. On 4 December 2013, the bill for the new class action system was finally enacted (the Act on Special Provisions of Civil Court Procedures for Collective Recovery of Property Damage of Consumers (Act No. 96 of 2013)). This Act was promulgated on 11 December 2013, and will take effect within three years from the date of promulgation and on a date which will be separately designated by a cabinet order. However, based on the Act it appears that the situations in which the new class action system can be used in product liability cases will be significantly limited (see question 9.2 below).

5. LITIGATION FUNDING

5.1 Is litigation funding by third parties permissible in your country? If so, is it common?

Litigation funding by third parties is generally not prohibited in Japan, although it is not common either. However, except in special circumstances, attorneys cannot lend or borrow money to or from clients, or ask clients to provide a guarantee or security for the attorney's obligations to third parties, or provide clients with a guarantee or security to enable them to secure financing from a third party (Basic Regulations on Attorney Duties Article 25).

5.2 Are contingency fee or 'no win no fee' arrangements permissible?

While 'no win no fee' arrangements are generally not prohibited, attorneys must only charge appropriate and reasonable fees to clients in light of the economic benefits of the litigation, the difficulty of the case, the time and work spent and other relevant circumstances (Basic Regulations on Attorney Duties Article 24). If the attorney fees are quite expensive when compared with the benefits which the clients receive from the litigation, such attorney fees may not be regarded as appropriate and reasonable.

6. REMEDIES

6.1 What remedies are available to a party who successfully pursues a product liability claim?

Under the PLA, the liability of a manufacturer, etc. to compensate for damages arising from a product defect shall be subject to the provisions of the Civil Code (PLA Article 6).

Accordingly, monetary damages are the principle form of compensation ordered (Civil Code Articles 417 and 722(1)). Public apologies and orders for the provision of replacement products are generally not given under the PLA.

6.2 How are damages calculated/are there limitations on available damages?

As to a claim based on PLA Article 3, the methods for determining the scope of damages to be awarded are similar to those for claims based on the general tort provisions of the Civil Code, whereby a successful plaintiff will generally receive compensation for damage for which proximate causation with the defect in the product is established. Such damage theoretically includes:

- damage which would ordinarily occur as a result of the product defect; and
- damage which occurred as a result of the product defect under special circumstances that are reasonably foreseeable.

This would apply to damage to life, body and property, as well as damages for pain and suffering and other special kinds of damage such as loss of profits, as long as there is proximate causation between the defect and the damage.

However, the manufacturer, etc, will not be liable under the PLA when damage only occurs to the defective product itself (PLA Article 3). In relation to such cases, damages can be claimed based on the general tort law and contract law provisions of the Civil Code.

6.3 Are punitive or exemplary damages available and in what circumstances?

No, punitive and exemplary damages are not available in Japan. Even if a case which is governed by the laws of a foreign jurisdiction that recognises punitive or exemplary damages is heard by a Japanese court, punitive and exemplary damages would still not be awarded.

6.4 Is liability joint and several/how does apportionment of liability work, including where a partially responsible entity is not a party to the proceeding?

The PLA does not have any special provisions governing cases where multiple entities are partially responsible for the defect(s) in a product. Therefore, general principles of the Civil Code will apply to such cases.

According to such general principles of the Civil Code, all partially responsible entities are jointly and severally liable, and therefore each has an obligation to initially compensate the victim for the full amount of damage incurred.

However, if one entity is required to pay an amount of damages that is greater than its contribution to the damage suffered by the victim, it may then seek reimbursement from each of the other partially responsible entities for an amount that reflects those entities' respective contribution to the damage.

Therefore in a product liability lawsuit, if a defendant made a full or partial payment to the plaintiff which exceeds its contribution to the plaintiff's damages, that defendant may later seek reimbursements from other partially responsible entities (regardless of whether they were parties to the lawsuit) which reflect their respective contributions to the damage.

7. ROLE OF REGULATORS

7.1 Please explain the role, responsibilities and powers of the regulators in your country which have jurisdiction over product liability issues.

As for the laws and regulations on product safety and liability issues, in addition to the PLA (see question 1.1 above), there is the broad Consumer Product Safety Act (Act No. 31 of 1973) (CPSA) which regulates 'consumer products' meaning any product to be supplied mainly for use by general consumers for their general activities and which is not otherwise excluded from the scope of the CPSA, such as foods, medicines and automobiles that are regulated by special legislation (CPSA Article 2(1)).

Other legislation which specifically regulates certain kinds of products includes:

- the Road Tracking Vehicle Act (Act No. 185 of 1951) (RTVA);
- the Pharmaceutical Affairs Act (Act No. 145 of 1960) (PAA);
- the Food Sanitation Act (Act No. 233 of 1947) (FSA);
- the Electrical Appliances and Materials Safety Act (Act No. 234 of 1961) (EAMSA);
- the Gas Business Act (Act No. 51 of 1954); and
- the Act on the Security and Transaction of Liquefied Petroleum Gas (Act No. 149 of 1967).

Each of the laws and regulations above has empowered a governmental authority to be responsible for implementing and enforcing their provisions. For example:

- the Ministry of Health, Labour and Welfare (MHLW) is the relevant authority for the PAA;
- the Ministry of Land, Infrastructure and Transport (MLIT) is the relevant authority for the RTVA;
- the Ministry of Economy, Trade and Infrastructure (METI) is responsible for regulating the EAMSA; and

- the METI and the Consumer Affairs Agency (CAA) are both responsible for regulating the CPSA.

7.2 Are there any mandatory reporting requirements related to product safety issues?

Yes. If a problem arises in relation to product safety, the respective legislation which regulates the product may impose a reporting obligation on the manufacturer, importer and vendor.

For example, CPSA Article 35(1) provides that any person engaging in the manufacture or import of consumer products who comes to know that serious product accidents have originated with the consumer products that he/she manufactured or imported, shall report to the CAA the name and type of the consumer products, a detailed account of the accidents, and the quantity of said consumer products manufactured/imported and sold.

Further, RTVA Article 63-3 provides that if there is a defect in the design or manufacturing process of a vehicle, or a vehicle may or does not comply with the relevant safety requirements, and if the automobile manufacturer or importer decides to take any necessary remedial measures, such manufacturer or importer must notify the MLIT of the problem, the cause of the problem and the remedial measures to be taken, in advance of actually taking such remedial measures.

Similarly, PAA Article 77-4-2 provides that a manufacturer must report if it is aware of any adverse effects of a medical product or device, and PAA Article 77-4-3 provides that a manufacturer must report if it has commenced carrying out a recall of products from the market.

7.3 Do the regulators have the power to:

(i) ban certain goods or services?

This depends on the type of product and the relevant laws. In some cases, the manufacturing or selling of certain products is prohibited unless authorisation is obtained from the relevant authority. In other cases, the manufacture or sale of certain products is completely prohibited.

For example, FSA Article 8 stipulates that the regulators may prohibit the sale of specific foods and additives manufactured by specific persons or in specific countries or areas in order to prevent harm from arising as a result of foods being prepared in unsanitary conditions.

Further, PAA Article 72 provides that the regulators have the power to issue an order to the manufacturers and suppliers that they should improve their methods of quality control or post-marketing safety control or suspend all or part of their business until such improvements have been made in order not to jeopardise public health and hygiene.

(ii) require a supplier to recall a product?

There is no general legislative provision imposing a legal obligation to conduct product recalls. However, each relevant law governing the safety of specific products (such as the RTVA, PAA, FSA and CPSA) provides governmental authorities with the authority to order that necessary measures be taken, including a product recall, in order to avoid the occurrence or spreading of danger arising from a defect in a product. If such manufacturers are ordered by the relevant authority to make a recall, such recall will be mandatory.

For example, CPSA Article 39 provides that upon the occurrence of serious product accidents, or actual or imminent danger to the lives or bodies of general consumers, the competent minister may, to the extent necessary to prevent such danger, order the person engaging in the manufacture or import of the products to recall them and take measures necessary to prevent such danger.

(iii) prescribe standards in respect of certain goods or services and require that the goods or services meet those standards?

Depending on the type of product, some laws stipulate safety standards for certain types of products, and manufacturers will be prohibited from manufacturing or selling such products if they fail to meet such standards. Even in those cases where the law does not require a manufacturer to obtain approval that its products meet the relevant safety standards, in practice if the products do not meet such standards, it is highly likely that such products will be judged to be defective under the PLA in the event of a lawsuit for product liability.

For example, RTVA Articles 40-46 provide safety standards which road tracking vehicles must meet. Moreover, the Safety Standards for Road Tracking Vehicles (MLIT Order No. 67 of 1951) stipulates even more detailed safety standards for road tracking vehicles.

Further, FSA Article 11 provides that the MHLW can establish criteria for methods of preparing, processing, using and storing food and additives, and their ingredients, which are to be served for marketing purposes. In accordance with this provision, the MHLW has in fact established such criteria.

(iv) require production of information without court process?

This varies depending on the laws and regulations which regulate the specific product in question. In some cases, a government authority can require that information be reported, without using court processes.

For example, CPSA Article 40(1) provides that the relevant authority may, if deemed necessary to enforce the CPSA, direct a manufacturer, importer or seller of consumer products to report on the status of its business.

CPSA Article 41(1) also provides that the relevant authority may, if deemed necessary to enforce the CPSA, order an on-site inspection and cause officials to enter the offices, factories, workplaces, stores or warehouses of a person engaging in the manufacture, import or sale of consumer products and to conduct an inspection of the consumer products, books, documents and other items. CPSA Article 42(1) further states that if consumer products are found in an on-site inspection conducted under Article 41(1), and inspecting such products on-site is extremely difficult, the relevant authority may order that such products be submitted within a designated period.

If so, broadly explain the circumstances in which the regulator can exercise the power and any penalties that apply if a supplier fails to comply.
It depends on the specific laws and regulations, but generally the relevant governmental authority will stipulate safety standards necessary to ensure the safety of product users, etc. The relevant authorities usually require suppliers to report violations of the safety standards and product accidents. Generally, the authorities will not impose a mandatory order on a supplier to take specific measures, such as the recall of a product, unless it determines that the voluntary measures taken by the supplier are insufficient. The suppliers have an obligation to observe such mandatory orders if issued by the relevant authorities.

If an entity fails to observe such mandatory order or otherwise violates critical provisions, the relevant laws and regulations generally stipulate administrative penalties, such as the revocation of necessary authorisation to manufacture or sell the products. Criminal penalties are also common.

For example, PAA Article 75 provides that the MHLW may cancel a manufacturer's licence or order the suspension of all or part of its business for a specified period if it has violated the PAA or any other laws and ordinances related to pharmaceutical affairs.

In addition, if a manufacturer breaches CPSA Article 39 by failing to take necessary measures ordered by the relevant authorities (see 7.3 (iii) above), it may be sanctioned with up to one year imprisonment and/or a fine of up to ¥1 million (CPSA Article 58(iv)).

8. VOLUNTARY CONDUCT

8.1 Are there regulations pertaining to the voluntary conduct of a product repair or recall by a supplier?

Yes. Some laws have provisions pertaining to voluntary product repairs or recalls by suppliers. For example, CPSA Article 38(1) stipulates that a manufacturer or importer of consumer products should investigate the cause of accidents originating from its products, and if necessary to prevent the occurrence and increase of danger, the manufacturer or importer must endeavour to recall said consumer products or otherwise take preventive measures. Thus this imposes an obligation on manufacturers and importers to endeavour to take preventive measures, such as voluntarily conducting a product recall.

In some cases, the relevant governmental authority stipulates guidelines for voluntarily repairs or recalls. Although such guidelines are not legally binding, in practice the government authorities recommend and request that suppliers and other relevant entities comply and take measures in accordance with such guidelines.

In addition some industry bodies create rules for voluntary repairs and recalls, which suppliers are requested, and sometimes required, to observe.

When suppliers are considering whether to conduct voluntary repairs or recalls, they can consult relevant governmental authorities (such as METI) and professional third party organisations (such as the National Institute of Technology and Evaluation (NITE)) for their advice.

9. EMERGING ISSUES AND LAW REFORM

9.1 Are there important developing and emerging issues or trends in product liability law in your country?

Regarding product safety laws, from time to time the relevant government authorities will take action in response to new societal problems and issues that arise. For example, after the accident at the Fukushima nuclear power plant, which occurred as a result of the 2011 Great East Japan Earthquake, food safety became a big issue among consumers. In response to this, the CAA established a system of testing food products for radioactive materials, provided easy-to-understand information for consumers, and strengthened its education of consumers about relevant risks, with the goal of ensuring the safety and security of food supplies and preventing unnecessary damage to the reputation of suppliers.

One example of such efforts is the below website, which contains a Q&A in relation to food safety and radiation, released by the CAA. *www.kantei.go.jp/foreign/policy/documents/2011/__icsFiles/afieldfile/2012/01/27/FoodandRadiation_QA.pdf*

9.2 Please describe any proposed important law reform in the area of product liability in your country.

As stated in section 4 above, the Japanese Government has been working on legislation to introduce a bill submitted by the Cabinet for the purpose of introducing a new Japanese class action system ('new system'). This new system proposes to enable consumers to recover damages collectively in a simple and prompt manner. On 4 December 2013, the bill for the new system was finally enacted (the Act on Special Provisions of Civil Court Procedures for Collective Recovery of Property Damage of Consumers (Act No. 96 of 2013) ('new Act')). The new Act was promulgated on 11 December 2013, and will take effect within three years from the date of promulgation and on a date which will be separately designated by a cabinet order.
The new system is being developed solely for the purpose of protecting consumers in relation to a contract concluded between a consumer and a business operator ('consumer contract'). It should be noted that the new system will not apply, in principle, to claims in connection with consumer contracts concluded before the new Act takes effect.

Under the new system, class action litigation in Japan will consist of two stages. In the first stage, the court will decide whether a business operator (defendant) has obligations arising from factual or legal causes that are common among a considerable number of aggrieved consumers. Only a 'specified qualified consumer organisation' (SQCO) can file to commence first stage proceedings.

If the SQCO is successful at the first stage, whereby the defendant is found to be liable, the second stage will commence where the amount to be paid to each aggrieved consumer will be determined in brief proceedings.

Based on the new Act, the new system has many limitations in terms of product liability cases, as follows.

Firstly, the new Act lists five types of claims that can be brought under the

new system:
(i) performance of contractual obligation;
(ii) restitution of unjust enrichment;
(iii) compensation arising from breach of contract;
(iv) compensation based on liability for defect warranty; and
(v) tort under general tort provision of the Civil Code.

Accordingly, claims based on the PLA are not covered by the new system.

Secondly, claims must be for monetary compensation or other payments relating to a consumer contract. Accordingly, this limits victims to pursuing only entities with which it has a contractual relationship. If the victim wishes to pursue a third party such as the manufacturer, it would have to rely on ordinary lawsuit procedures.

Thirdly, in the new system, recoverable damages are limited so as to expressly exclude so-called extended damage, bodily injury and loss of profits etc. (Article 3(2) of the new Act.)

As for product accident cases, the CAA has also made public comments, stating that the new system anticipates that defendants will only return the amount that is paid by consumers for the products, and compensation will not extend to other forms of damage. The rationale is to avoid creating excessive risks for business entities. The CAA has also stated that if a manufacturer voluntarily conducts a wide-spread product recall which compensates a large number of consumers for the damages that they incurred, the remaining number of consumers who are not compensated and may take legal action will decrease significantly, and as a result it is considered that such manufacturer will not be sued in the form of a class action because the requirement under the new system for a considerable number of aggrieved consumers will not be satisfied.

Thus under the new Act, the new system may not necessarily be greatly used by victims in product liability disputes. However, it is necessary to watch the ongoing developments with respect to the new system, since certain product accident cases may be covered by the new system in future.

10. REGULATORY WEBSITES/INFORMATION

10.1 Please identify any useful regulatory references relating to product liability law in your country, for example, a product safety/ consumer law website maintained by the main regulator.

- The CAA website (includes a summary of the PLA and CPSA, and the Serious Accident Reporting and Notification System):
  www.caa.go.jp/ (Japanese)
  www.caa.go.jp/en/index.html (English)
- Outline of the CPSA on the website of the METI:
  www.meti.go.jp/policy/consumer/seian/shouan/contents/outline_psc_act090331e.pdf (English)
- Website of NITE (see question 8 above)
  www.nite.go.jp/jiko/e/index.html (English)

New Zealand

Simpson Grierson Robert Gapes

1. LIABILITY

1.1 What are the principal sources of law and regulation relating to product liability?

The law relating to product liability in New Zealand is principally derived from four main sources, namely statute, contract law, the law of torts and the criminal law. One important aspect, New Zealand's unique accident compensation scheme, sets New Zealand's product liability regime apart from other jurisdictions.

As explained below, where the statutory accident compensation scheme applies, the right to sue for compensatory damages for personal injury is removed and replaced by an entitlement to compensation through a statutory administrative body with limited recourse to the judicial system.

For the aspects of the New Zealand system not covered by the accident compensation regime, a broadly similar approach is taken to the approaches in other common law jurisdictions such as England, Australia and Canada.

Statute law

Accident compensation

The accident compensation legislation, initially passed in 1972 and in effect in various forms since 1974, effectively abolishes the right to sue for compensatory damages for most types of personal injury suffered after 31 March 1974 and some earlier injuries. Where the legislation applies, 'no fault' compensation is provided by the Accident Compensation Corporation and claims for compensatory damages are barred. In the product liability context, while the accident compensation regime does not bar all damages claims for personal injury, it certainly prevents a large proportion.

Personal injury claims that are not covered by the regime, and are therefore not barred, include claims for exemplary or punitive damages, compensatory damages claims for some breaches of the New Zealand Bill of Rights Act 1990, most claims for purely mental injury (not associated with physical injury, work or certain criminal offences), damages claims for property damage and business losses, and some claims resulting from personal injuries arising under approved clinical trials. The circumstances in which exemplary or punitive damages will be awarded in New Zealand are limited, and the level of exemplary or punitive damages available is small by international standards.

Statutory liability

Apart from the accident compensation legislation, the most important statutes in New Zealand with regard to product liability are the Sale of Goods Act 1908, the Consumer Guarantees Act 1993, and the Fair Trading Act 1986.

The Sale of Goods Act 1908 was enacted to codify elements of the common law relating to the sale of goods within New Zealand. Subject to certain conditions, the 1908 Act implies certain terms into contracts for the sale of goods, for example, implied conditions that goods are reasonably fit for purpose and that goods are of a merchantable quality.

New Zealand has also enacted legislation bringing into effect the Vienna Convention on the International Sale of Goods. Different implied terms may arise as a consequence in international sale transactions.

The Consumer Guarantees Act 1993 applies where there is a 'supply' of 'goods' or 'services' in 'trade' to a 'consumer'. A 'consumer' is a person who acquires from a supplier goods or services of a kind ordinarily acquired for personal, domestic or household use or consumption, and not for the purpose of resupplying them in trade or consuming them in the course of a process of production or manufacture.

The Fair Trading Act 1986 contains an array of provisions imposing liability for various types of misleading and deceptive conduct.

The Fair Trading Act also contains special provisions which empower the Government to make regulations prescribing product safety standards and to declare goods 'unsafe'. There are currently six product safety standards in New Zealand issued under the 1986 Act, relating to baby-walkers, children's nightwear, children's toys for the under-three age group, cigarette lighters, household cots and pedal bicycles. It is a criminal offence to supply, or offer to supply or advertise to supply goods which do not comply with a prescribed standard or which have been declared unsafe.

Section 32 of the Fair Trading Act enables the Government to require a supplier to recall goods which do not comply with a product safety standard.

The Fair Trading Act has recently been the subject of reforms (discussed in more detail later) which have amended consumer product safety requirements.

Contract

New Zealand contract law has its origins in the common law of England. In more recent years, statutory reforms (particularly, the Contractual Remedies Act 1979 and the Contracts (Privity) Act 1982) have had a significant impact on the evolution of the common law in New Zealand as regards the law of contract.

The Contractual Remedies Act 1979 abolishes the common law rules regarding misrepresentation and the remedies available for breach of contract and wrongful cancellation. Statutory rules have been enacted instead.

The Contracts (Privity) Act 1982 allows, in some cases, a beneficiary of a promise conferred by a contract to enforce the promise even though the beneficiary is not a party to the contract. The 1982 Act does not, however, allow parties to a contract to impose contractual obligations on beneficiaries who are not parties to the contract.

Tort

As with contract law, New Zealand tort law has its origins in the common law of England.

The tort of negligence is particularly important to product liability. As in many other common law jurisdictions, liability in negligence generally arises where a duty of care is owed by one party to another, the duty is breached, and this results in loss which is not too remote.

Liability in negligence may arise both in respect of a defect in a product and also for a failure to warn or a misleading statement in respect of the product. Negligent statements of both fact and opinion may result in liability where they have induced reliance by another person and resulted in financial loss. The most obvious applications of this form of negligence are in relation to product instructions, warning labels and advertisements.

Where responsibility for tortious negligence may be attributed to both the plaintiff and the defendant, the Contributory Negligence Act 1947 provides for the apportionment of damage.

Criminal liability

Criminal liability in relation to defective products may arise under a number of statutes, including some general statutes such as the Crimes Act 1961 and the Fair Trading Act 1986, and other statutes of more limited application such as the Food Act 1981 and the Health and Safety in Employment Act 1992.

Contravention of Part 3 of the Fair Trading Act (which deals with product safety standards, 'unsafe goods' and product recalls) is an offence. Currently, fines of up to NZ$60,000 may be imposed for a breach in the case of a person and NZ$200,000 in the case of a body corporate. From 18 June 2014 onwards the maximum fines will increase to NZ$200,000 in the case of an individual person and NZ$600,000 in the case of a body corporate.

The Crimes Act 1961 contains wide-ranging provisions which include provisions in relation to criminal nuisance and breaches of various duties, for example, owed by persons in charge of dangerous things and persons required to avoid omissions dangerous to life.

Criminal nuisance is committed where a person does an unlawful act or omits to discharge a legal duty, and the act or omission was known by the person to be one which would endanger the life, safety or health of one or more individuals. The offence is punishable by imprisonment for up to one year.

Where a product fault or defect results in death, then this may constitute murder or manslaughter.

Criminal proceedings in relation to defective products in New Zealand have been relatively rare.

1.2 What is required to establish causation under the most common causes of action available?

In New Zealand, the courts have often applied a 'but for' test of causation. That is, whether the plaintiff would have suffered the particular loss 'but for' the defendant's actions (or inaction). A positive response to this test would result in the defendant being liable for that loss. No matter how the relevant test is framed, however, the ultimate issue is whether the plaintiff's loss is sufficiently linked to the defendant's actions or omissions to merit recovery in the circumstances.

1.3 Is strict liability available and, if so, in what circumstances?

Contractual liability for defective products is strict. Both parties are entitled to the benefit of their respective bargains. The supplier cannot escape liability in contract merely by asserting the exercise of all reasonable care or the absence of fault on the supplier's part. 'Supplier' in this context can mean the actual manufacturer, distributor, wholesaler or retailer.

Sections 10 and 11 of the Fair Trading Act 1986 prohibit conduct that is liable to mislead the public as to the nature, characteristics, suitability for purpose, or quantity of goods and services. With regard to goods, the prohibition also extends to misleading or deceptive conduct in respect of manufacturing processes. Contravention of these provisions may be a criminal offence under the 1986 Act, and for these offences the Act imposes strict liability subject to certain limited defences.

In any prosecution under the Food Act 1981 involving the sale of food, strict liability rules apply and the prosecution need not prove any element of knowledge.

1.4 Are guarantees or warranties as to quality implied by law?

As discussed earlier, subject to certain conditions, the Sale of Goods Act 1908 implies terms into contracts for the sale of goods, that the goods sold are reasonably fit for purpose and are of a merchantable quality. In particular, where a buyer, expressly or by implication, makes known to a seller the particular purpose for which goods are required, so as to show that the buyer relies on the seller's skill or judgment, and the goods are of a description which it is in the course of the seller's business to supply (whether the seller is the manufacturer or not), there is an implied condition that the goods must be reasonably fit for this purpose. Where goods are bought by description from a seller who deals in goods of that description (whether that seller is the manufacturer or not), there is an implied condition that the goods will be of merchantable quality.

It is important to note, however, that these implied terms may be negated or varied by express agreement of the parties to the contract, or by the course of dealing between the parties. There is nothing to stop contracting out of the provisions of the 1908 Act.

The Consumer Guarantees Act 1993 implies similar guarantees into contracts for the sale of goods to consumers. In particular, there are guarantees that the goods are of acceptable quality, and that the goods are reasonably fit for any purpose that the consumer makes known, expressly or impliedly, to the supplier. In contrast to the 1908 Act, the provisions of the 1993 Act are usually upheld notwithstanding any provision to the contrary in any agreement between the parties.

1.5 How is a product 'defect' defined?

The key consideration under the Consumer Guarantees Act 1993 is not whether the goods are defective, but whether they breach the guarantee of acceptable quality. Under the Act, the term 'defect' is generally accepted as meaning any failure of the goods to comply with the guarantee of acceptable quality.

It is possible for products to breach the guarantee of acceptable quality without themselves being inherently defective (eg, they may simply fail to align with the manufacturer's or supplier's representations). Likewise, products will not automatically fail to comply with the guarantee of acceptable quality simply by reason of any defect.

It will be a matter of interpretation (taking into account the intended purpose, use, safety, durability, appearance, nature, price, manufacturer's or supplier's representations, and any other relevant considerations) as to whether goods will be considered defective and/or in breach of the guarantee of acceptable quality under the Act.

1.6 Who in the supply chain has obligations or duties for defective products? What obligations or duties do they owe to whom?

The manufacturer, the importer, the distributor, the wholesaler and the retailer are all potentially liable where loss is suffered by the purchaser because of a defect in the products.

A purchaser (whether it be the ultimate purchaser, a wholesaler, distributor or importer) may be able to sue a vendor for breach of contract, depending on the express terms of the contract. The vendor in turn may sue the next person in the supply chain, depending on the contractual arrangements, and this may continue so that ultimate liability falls on the manufacturer. The Contracts (Privity) Act 1982 may also allow a third party beneficiary of the defective products to sue the vendor for breach of contract.

A purchaser may also sue a vendor for breach of certain implied terms under the provisions of the Sale of Goods Act 1908 or the Consumer Guarantees Act 1993.

Liability for negligence requires the existence of a duty of care. Following the landmark decision in *Donoghue v Stevenson* [1932] AC 562 (HL), the New Zealand courts have recognised that manufacturers will usually owe a duty of care to anyone who ought reasonably to have been foreseen as likely to be affected by a defect in their products.

Under the Fair Trading Act 1986, any party in the chain who engages in misleading or deceptive conduct in trade may be liable under the 1986 Act and face criminal liability. Criminal liability under other legislation may also apply in a wide range of circumstances.

1.7 By what means can a supplier limit its liability for defective products?

As discussed, it is possible for a supplier to contract out of the terms of the Sale of Goods Act 1908 which would otherwise be implied into the contract of sale. Statutory amendments regarding contracting out of the provisions of the Consumer Guarantees Act and the Fair Trading Act come into force on 18 June 2014.

1.8 Are there particular goods or services which have specific obligations or duties attached to them?

Parts 2, 3 and 4 of the Fair Trading Act 1986 empower the Government to enact consumer information standards, product safety standards and service safety standards. There are currently four consumer information standards and six product safety standards.

Consumer information standards specify the information that must be provided to consumers about a product. The existing consumer information standards relate to country of origin labelling for most clothing and footwear, care labelling for clothing and textiles, fibre content labelling for clothing and textiles, and supplier information for motor vehicle traders. Consumer information requirements are addressed in other legislation as well, including for example the Motor Vehicle Sales Act 2003, the Food Act 1981, the Animal Products Act 1999, and the Weights and Measures Act 1987.

A breach of an information standard may not only amount to an offence under the Fair Trading Act 1986. It may also give rise to liability under the Contractual Remedies Act 1979, the Consumer Guarantees Act 1993 and other legislation.

Product safety standards address the quality of products as opposed to information about the products. As discussed, there are currently product safety standards in place for baby-walkers, children's toys for the under-three age group, children's nightwear, cigarette lighters, household cots and pedal bicycles.

Under section 32 of the Fair Trading Act 1986, the Government may order a supplier to recall products which fail to comply with a product safety standard. A failure to comply with a compulsory recall amounts to an offence.

As discussed above, general quality standards for products are imposed by the Sale of Goods Act 1908 and the Consumer Guarantees Act 1993. Additional product safety requirements can be found in legislation such as the Electricity Regulations 1997 (electrical appliances) and the Land Transport Act 1998 (vehicles and their component parts).

There are a number of legislative instruments relating to food safety, including for example the Food Hygiene Regulations 1974, the Health Act 1956, the Food (Safety) Regulations 2002, the Food Act 1981, the Animal Products Act 1999 and the Wine Act 2003.

2. DEFENCES

2.1 What are the possible defences to a product liability claim?

A range of different defences are available depending on the type of claim being made.

In contract claims, it may be possible to raise the following defences:
(i) the express terms of the contract exclude liability;
(ii) the relevant product did not cause the plaintiff's claimed loss;
(iii) the nature of damage is not one which is recoverable in law;
(iv) the defendant is not a party to the contract, nor is the defendant entitled to recover under the terms of the Contracts (Privity) Act 1982; and
(v) there has been no actionable breach of the contract.

Where the claim is in negligence, defences may include:
(i) there is no duty of care;
(ii) the duty of care has not been breached;
(iii) the defective product was not the cause of the loss claimed; and
(iv) the damage is too remote.

The defence of *volenti non fit injuria* may also apply where there has been a voluntary assumption of risk by the plaintiff.

While they may not strictly constitute defences, the limitations set out in the Limitation Act 1950 and the Limitation Act 2010 (time bars), and the accident compensation legislation (barring many claims for compensatory damages for personal injury) may also provide an effective 'defence' to a claim.

2.2 Is there a limit on the time in which proceedings may be brought (limitations and repose)?

There are a number of different rules which apply to the commencement of proceedings, depending on the nature of the claim.

Limitation Act 1950

Limitation periods for contract and tort claims involving acts or omissions which occurred on or before 31 December 2010 are governed by the Limitation Act 1950. (The relevant time limits for contract and tort claims involving acts or omissions which occurred on or after 1 January 2011 are governed by the Limitation Act 2010.)

The general rule under the Limitation Act 1950 is that claims in contract or tort must be brought within six years from the date on which the cause of action accrues. For contract claims, time usually runs from the date of the breach of contract. For tort claims, time will usually run from the date when the relevant damage occurred.

Where the action is for bodily injury, proceedings must be commenced within two years of the date on which the cause of action accrued, although a court may extend the time up to a maximum of six years.

Under the 1950 Act, the ordinary time limits are extended for people under disabilities when the cause of action arose and in cases of concealment or fraud.

In relation to representative actions, in *Credit Suisse v Houghton* [2014] NZSC 37 the Supreme Court held that time ceased to run for all members of the identified class on the date when the proceedings were filed and the representative order was made.

Limitation Act 2010

The Limitation Act 2010 introduced an umbrella provision for 'money claims', which are claims for monetary relief, whether at common law, under an enactment or in equity. Money claims generally have a limitation period of six years from the date of the act or omission on which the claim is based. Limitation periods for other types of claims (ie, not 'money claims') vary between six and 60 years depending on the type of claim.

The six-year period for a money claim may be extended under the 'late knowledge' provisions of the Limitation Act 2010. Where a plaintiff does not discover their claim before the end of the relevant limitation period, they will be entitled to a further three years from the 'late knowledge date' within which to file their claim. A claim's 'late knowledge date' is the date on which the plaintiff gained or ought reasonably to have gained knowledge of the key facts/essential elements of the claim. These provisions are, however, tempered with a 15-year long stop (after the date of the act or omission) so as to avoid indefinite liability for money claims.

Fair Trading Act 1986

The time limit for claims under the Fair Trading Act 1986 is generally three years after the date on which the loss or damage, or the likelihood of loss or damage, was discovered or ought reasonably to have been discovered.

In relation to representative actions, the Supreme Court decision in *Credit Suisse v Houghton* referred to above applies to time limits under the Fair Trading Act as well as to the limits under the Limitation Act 1950.

Accident compensation claims

For accident compensation claims for personal injury, a claimant is required under the accident compensation legislation to lodge any claim with the Accident Compensation Corporation within 12 months, although the Corporation cannot refuse a claim lodged after this time unless the delay prejudices the Corporation's ability to make decisions.

3. LITIGATION OF PRODUCT LIABILITY DISPUTES

3.1 In which courts are product liability proceedings brought?

There is no specialist court with sole jurisdiction to hear product liability proceedings. Claims may be brought in the Disputes Tribunal, the District Court, or the High Court, depending on the value of the claim.

Most significant product liability claims are commenced in the High Court.

The District Courts have jurisdiction to hear and determine civil proceedings where the value of the damages claimed is not more than NZ$200,000. However, the Judicature Modernisation Bill would, if passed in its original form, increase the District Court's civil jurisdiction from NZ$200,000 to NZ$350,000.

The Disputes Tribunal can determine claims for less than NZ$15,000 (or NZ$20,000 if each of the parties agree). There are proposals to increase the maximum monetary threshold to NZ$30,000 and a Bill addressing this is due to be introduced in Parliament in 2014.

3.2 How are proceedings commenced?

Civil proceedings are usually commenced in the High Court by filing a statement of claim in the High Court registry closest to the defendant's residence or principal place of business. General requirements as to content of the statement of claim are prescribed by the New Zealand High Court Rules.

A civil claim is commenced in the District Court by filing a notice of claim in the District Court nearest to where the defendant resides and serving the notice of claim on the defendant. The notice of claim is a standard form document, which may also be downloaded from the New Zealand Ministry of Justice website. The form and procedure for claims in the District Court are governed by the District Courts Rules 2009. However, there is currently a Bill before Parliament seeking to abolish the notice of claim procedure in the District Court and amend many District Court processes and procedures so that they resemble those of the High Court.

In order to have a claim heard by the Disputes Tribunal, it is necessary to complete a claim form, which may be downloaded from the New Zealand Ministry of Justice website (*www.justice.govt.nz/forms*). The forms must be submitted to the District Court located closest to the claimant's physical address and served on the defendant.

3.3 Are disputed issues decided by a judge or jury?

Judges in the High Court regularly sit with juries in criminal trials. Civil jury trials are seldom used in New Zealand except for defamation proceedings.

Jury trials are available for some District Court criminal hearings, but are not available for civil hearings in the District Court.

Disputes Tribunal hearings are not presided over by judges or juries, rather, a specially trained 'referee'. Any ruling made by the referee is binding, and if necessary, can be enforced by the courts.

3.4 Who has the burden of proof and to what standard?

In civil proceedings, the plaintiff will generally have the burden of proving his or her case and will be required to do so on the balance of probabilities. Where, however, the defendant advances a counterclaim or affirmative defence, the burden of proving this will revert to that defendant.

The prosecution will usually have the burden of proving a criminal offence beyond a reasonable doubt.

3.5 How is evidence given in proceedings and are witnesses cross-examined?

The general rule is that evidence in civil trials is to be given orally by witnesses. However, witness statements and expert reports are normally exchanged prior to trial. Cross-examination of witnesses is permitted in civil trials. In some cases cross-examination is necessary in order to comply with section 92 of the Evidence Act 2006 which effectively requires parties to cross-examine opposing parties' witnesses on significant contradictory evidence in order to give these witnesses the opportunity to respond to that evidence. The witness may also be re-examined by or on behalf of the party for whom they are giving evidence, on matters arising during cross-examination.

In criminal trials before a judge sitting with a jury, evidence is also given orally by factual and expert witnesses, and they may be required to provide a statement or reports to the defence prior to trial.

3.6 Are the parties able to rely on expert opinion evidence and, if so, are there any special rules or procedures for expert opinion evidence?

In both civil and criminal trials, oral evidence is put before the court by witnesses with relevant knowledge or expertise. A party may be able to call expert evidence to support its case. However, an expert witness is not an advocate for the party who has engaged the expert. The expert must be qualified, in the sense that they must satisfy the court that they have sufficient expert knowledge or experience to comment on the particular matters in issue.

In civil proceedings, experts must prepare and give expert evidence in accordance with the rules set out in the Evidence Act 2006 and the High Court Rules which relate to the conduct of experts. An expert witness must state in any witness brief that he or she has read the relevant part of the High Court Rules and that he or she agrees to comply with them. If an expert does not comply with this requirement, then his or her evidence may only be given with the permission of the court.

The court may direct an expert to confer with another expert witness and try to reach agreement with the other expert witness on matters within the field of expertise of the witnesses. The expert witnesses must exercise independent and professional judgment and must not act on the instructions or directions of any person to withhold or avoid agreement.

3.7 Is pre-trial discovery permitted? If so, in what circumstances? If not, what other mechanisms, if any, are available for obtaining evidence from a party or a third party?

The New Zealand discovery regime (as prescribed by the High Court Rules and the District Courts Rules) has recently undergone major reform, with a view to reducing costs (by introducing a more flexible and co-operative discovery process) and enabling discovery and inspection to occur at an early stage.

The Rules generally require parties in civil proceedings to disclose documents that are or have been in that party's control, and that are relied on by that party or adversely affect that party's case or that support or adversely affect another party's case. This pre-trial disclosure relates to all High Court claims (depending on the nature of the claim) and occurs in two parts. After filing a pleading (ie, a statement of claim or a statement of defence) a party must serve their pleading on the other party, together with a bundle containing all documents referred to in that pleading and any additional principal documents in that filing party's control that have been used in preparing the pleading, or on which the filing party intends to rely. This is known as 'initial disclosure'.

Later in the proceedings, once the parties (with the court's assistance) have discussed and refined the scope of discovery necessary, the parties must file and serve an affidavit of documents, listing the documents and confirming that the party understands its discovery obligations, gives particulars of the steps taken to fulfil those obligations, and states the categories or classes of documents that have not been searched and the reasons for not searching them.

Upon application, a court may order a third party to file an affidavit of documents if it appears that the third party may be in control of documents relevant to the proceeding.

There are few grounds on which a party is able to resist discovery. The main types of privilege which may assist are: privilege against self-incrimination, non-litigious legal professional privilege, litigation privilege and professional/indemnity insurers' privilege. In some circumstances disclosure of confidential documents may not be required or may be subject to conditions limiting access.

In criminal proceedings, the prosecution is ordinarily required to provide copies of its non-privileged documents to the defence.

3.8 Is there liability for spoliation of evidence/a remedy for destruction of or failure to preserve evidence?

The new disclosure regime now requires parties to, as soon as a proceeding is reasonably contemplated, take all reasonable steps to preserve documents that are, or are reasonably likely to be, discoverable in the proceeding.

Where a party fails to make discovery of documents or to produce documents for inspection, the court may make any order it thinks just, including an order that the action be dismissed or an order that any pleading of the party in default be struck out and judgment entered accordingly. In the event of deliberate destruction of evidence, the person responsible may also be liable to committal for contempt.

3.9 Is interlocutory or interim relief available prior to the full trial of a proceeding?

An application for an interim or interlocutory injunction may be made by a party prior to trial. The court will usually consider whether there is a serious question to be tried in the proceeding and where the balance of convenience lies, with the final question being where the overall justice of the case lies. An undertaking as to damages must normally be provided by the applicant.

Applications for summary judgment can also be made in civil cases in the High Court and the District Court. In the High Court the application is usually made at the time of filing the statement of claim or statement of defence. In the District Court, the application is usually made after the time for filing the notice of response has passed. A plaintiff applicant is required to show why the defendant has no defence to the allegations set out in the statement of claim. A defendant applicant must show why none of the causes of action in the plaintiff's statement of claim can succeed.

3.10 Can the winning party recover its costs?

In civil proceedings the general rule is that a party who fails with respect to a proceeding or an interlocutory application should pay the legal costs of the party who succeeds. All matters relating to costs are at the discretion of the court, although the courts usually make orders for costs according to the High Court or District Court scale.

Disbursements, which include court fees, service fees, photocopying and witness expenses and fees, are generally recoverable by the successful party from the unsuccessful party.

In criminal proceedings, a successful defendant will normally recover little, if any, of his or her legal costs.

3.11 What avenues of appeal are available?

Final decisions of the District Court can generally be appealed to the High Court. In exceptional cases, including some criminal decisions, appeals from the District Court are heard in the Court of Appeal.

Appeals of final decisions in the High Court are usually heard in the Court of Appeal. The Supreme Court is the final court of appeal, and appeals there can only proceed with leave of the Supreme Court.

4. CLASS ACTIONS/REPRESENTATIVE PROCEEDINGS

4.1 Is there a mechanism for class actions or representative proceedings, or coordinated proceedings for product liability claims? If so, what are the basic mechanics?

New Zealand does not have detailed class action rules akin to those used in England, the United States and Australia. The New Zealand High Court Rules allow for one or more persons to sue or be sued on behalf of, or for the benefit of, all persons with the same interest in the subject matter of a proceeding.

The Court of Appeal in *Saunders v Houghton* [2010] 3 NZLR 331 held that a representative action can be brought where each member of the class is alleged to have a separate cause of action, provided:

(i) the representative action may not confer a right of action on the member of the class represented who could not have asserted such a right in separate proceedings, nor may it bar a defence which might have been available to the defendant in such separate proceeding;

(ii) there must be an interest shared in common by all members of the group; and

(iii) it must be for the benefit of other members of the class that the plaintiff is permitted to sue in a representative capacity.

5. LITIGATION FUNDING

5.1 Is litigation funding by third parties permissible in your country? If so, is it common?

Third-party agreements are not common in New Zealand but are increasingly being used. The tort of champerty has not been abolished, but judicial attitudes to litigation funding in New Zealand have changed in recent years and the courts have more readily accepted that litigation funding is a reality of commercial life. The recent Supreme Court decision in *Waterhouse v Contractors Bonding Ltd* [2014] 1 NZLR 91 suggests that in individual actions (rather than representative or class actions) the New Zealand courts have no general role in regulating litigation funding agreements and there is no automatic requirement on a plaintiff receiving third party funding to provide a costs indemnity or security.

5.2 Are contingency fee or 'no win no fee' arrangements permissible?

Conditional fee arrangements were traditionally regarded as being contrary to the torts of maintenance and champerty. However, they now have statutory backing under sections 333 and 334 of the Lawyers and Conveyancers Act 2006 in some circumstances. A conditional fee agreement is permissible under those provisions if the resulting fee is:

(i) the normal fee which would have been charged for the service provided; or

(ii) the normal fee accompanied by a premium, expressly provided for in the agreement, which is payable only if the outcome of the matter to which the agreement relates is successful and which:
- compensates counsel for the risk of not being paid at all;
- compensates counsel for waiting to be paid until proceedings have been concluded; and
- is not calculated as a proportion of the amount recovered by the proceedings.

Where a lawyer enters into a conditional fee arrangement with a client, the lawyer must ensure that the client has been informed of any other appropriate arrangements that may be available, including, where relevant, the possibility of legal aid. The total fee charged must be fair and reasonable in accordance with Rule 9 of the Lawyers and Conveyancers Act (Lawyers: Conduct and Client Care) Rules 2008.

A conditional fee arrangement must be in writing and must specify the method by which the fee is to be determined, the condition(s) that will amount to success and upon the occurrence of which the fees or any part will become payable, the method by which the fee is to be determined in the event that an offer of settlement or compromise is made which the client declines to accept against the advice of the lawyer, and that the client may give notice cancelling the conditional fee arrangement within five working days after it has been entered into.

Conditional fee arrangements are prohibited for criminal proceedings.

6. REMEDIES

6.1 What remedies are available to a party who successfully pursues a product liability claim?

A number of different remedies may be available for a civil product liability claim. The ordinary remedy in contract and tort claims is damages. Other remedies which may be claimed for common law causes of action include injunctions, declarations, payment of interest, taking of accounts, inquiries and costs.

For statutory causes of action, the statute itself will usually provide a range of remedies for breach, eg, for damages or compensation.

6.2 How are damages calculated? Are there limitations on available damages?

Damages for breach of contract are generally assessed as at the date of breach and the measure of damages is determined with reference to the position the person claiming the loss would have been in had the contract been performed. Damages in tort are usually aimed at restoring the plaintiff to the position he or she would have been in if the tort had not been committed.

There is no maximum limit on damages prescribed by New Zealand law, but the amounts awarded in New Zealand by way of exemplary or punitive damages are generally modest by international standards.

6.3 Are punitive or exemplary damages available and in what circumstances?

Exemplary damages are not barred by the accident compensation legislation. Exemplary damages can be awarded in tort claims, but cannot be awarded in contract claims unless the conduct complained of also amounts to a tort or there is a breach of fiduciary duty.

Exemplary damages are generally awarded when compensatory damages are inadequate punishment for the defendant. For exemplary damages to be awarded, the defendant must have acted with outrageous, flagrant, high-handed or contumelious disregard for the plaintiff's rights. Accordingly, exemplary damages will not be awarded unless the defendant had a conscious appreciation of the risk of causing harm and had run that known risk.

6.4 Is liability joint and several? How does apportionment of liability work, including where a partially responsible entity is not a party to the proceeding?

Joint tortfeasors (those who commit the same tort) and several or concurrent tortfeasors (those who commit different torts, producing the same damage) are each liable in full for the entire loss caused.

The usual procedure, where there is more than more tortfeasor, is for the plaintiff to sue them all in one action, in which case contribution may be sought by one of the parties on application at the close of the plaintiff's action. Alternatively, a defendant who is sued may apply to join another potential defendant as a third party.

Section 17(1) of the Law Reform Act 1936 allows a tortfeasor liable in respect of damage suffered by a person as a result of a tort, to recover a contribution from another tortfeasor, who is, or would if sued in time, have been liable in respect of the same damage, whether as a joint tortfeasor or otherwise. This statutory right to contribution does not affect any express or implied contractual right to contribution.

Notwithstanding the above, a plaintiff is free to bring successive actions against different defendants. However, if more than one action is brought in respect of the same damage, the sums recoverable under the judgments given in those actions may not in the aggregate exceed the amount awarded in the first. Moreover, in any action other than the first, the plaintiff is not entitled to costs unless the court is of the opinion that there were reasonable grounds for bringing the action.

The issue as to whether liability under a contract is joint, or several, or joint and several will depend on the terms of the contract.

7. ROLE OF REGULATORS

7.1 Please explain the role, responsibilities and powers of the regulators in your country which have jurisdiction over product liability issues.

The Minister of Consumer Affairs has powers under the Fair Trading Act 1986 to implement mandatory recalls, ban products from the market and to set Product Safety Standards. These measures are enforceable by the Commerce Commission.

The Ministry of Consumer Affairs and the Ministry of Business, Innovation and Employment (MBIE) assist with the regulating of product liability matters generally.

Other government departments such as the Ministry of Health, the Environmental Protection Authority and the Ministry for Primary Industries act as regulators in their relevant industries.

7.2 Are there any mandatory reporting requirements related to product safety issues?

Under the Fair Trading Act 1986 (as amended in 2013), a supplier who voluntarily recalls products for any of a range of safety-related reasons must report the recall to the appropriate regulatory agency. If no other agency is specified by legislation, then the notification must be made within two working days to the chief executive of the Government Ministry responsible for the administration of the Fair Trading Act.

7.3 Do the regulators have the power to:

(i) ban certain goods or services?

The Minister of Consumer Affairs has the power to stop the sale of goods by declaring them to be 'unsafe goods'. This action can be taken 'where it appears to the Minister that goods of any description or any class or classes of goods will or may cause injury'. A ban stays in force for 18 months, unless withdrawn earlier by the Minister. At this point it can be imposed indefinitely or for a further specified time. These powers are enforceable by the Commerce Commission.

Under the recent reforms to the Fair Trading Act, the chief executive of the relevant Government Ministry is now able to appoint officers who have powers to inspect goods and business premises where the officer believes on reasonable grounds that there are unsafe goods at the premises. Product safety officers may issue 'suspension of supply notices' to persons in possession of unsafe goods, prohibiting supply of the goods before the expiry of the notice.

(ii) require a supplier to recall a product?

The Minister of Consumer Affairs can order a compulsory product recall where goods being sold do not comply with a product safety standard, or are of a kind which will or may cause injury and the supplier has not recalled the goods or taken appropriate action to recall the goods.

(iii) prescribe standards in respect of certain goods or services and require that the goods or services meet those standards?

As discussed, section 29 of the Fair Trading Act 1986 empowers the Government to promulgate product safety standards in relation to product performance, composition, contents, manufacture, processing, design, construction, finish or packaging, required tests during or after manufacture, and the form and content of any markings, warnings or instructions accompanying the goods.

The Trading Standards unit of the Ministry of Business, Innovation and Employment administers product safety standards. The Commerce Commission investigates complaints about products that have a product safety standard, and may proceed to prosecute the matter.

(iv) require production of information without court process?

Where products do not comply with a product safety standard, the Minister of Consumer Affairs may require the supplier to disclose, by notice, information to the public relating to:

- the characteristics of the goods which render them unsafe;
- the circumstances in which use of the goods is unsafe; and
- any other matters relating to the goods or the use of the goods as may be specified.

As mentioned above, the chief executive of the relevant Government Ministry may now appoint product safety officers who have the power to enter and inspect premises without a warrant if the officer believes on reasonable grounds that there are unsafe goods at the premises. The product safety officer may also require a person who appears to be in charge of the goods to identify:

- where the goods were acquired from; and
- who the goods have been supplied to.

If so, broadly explain the circumstances in which the regulator can exercise the power and any penalties that apply if a supplier fails to comply.

The relevant circumstances have been briefly outlined above. Failure to comply with the requirements amounts to an offence, and the manufacturer or supplier may be liable on conviction to a fine of up to NZ$200,000 (in the case of a body corporate) or NZ$60,000 (in the case of an individual). The maximum fines are due to increase from 18 June 2014 to NZ$600,000 (in the case of a body corporate) and NZ$200,000 (in the case of an individual).

8. VOLUNTARY CONDUCT

8.1 Are there regulations pertaining to the voluntary conduct of a product repair or recall by a supplier?

As a result of recent reforms to the Fair Trading Act, where a company voluntarily recalls a product because the goods will or may cause injury to a person, or because the goods do not comply with a product safety standard, the company must notify the chief executive of the relevant Government Ministry within two working days of doing so. The chief executive must ensure that public notice is given of such a recall.

9. EMERGING ISSUES AND LAW REFORM

9.1 Are there important developing and emerging issues or trends in product liability law in your country?

(i) There has been an increased focus on making consumer law more accessible and understandable for both consumers and businesses, and a desire to strengthen consumers' rights, which have resulted in the recent reforms to the Fair Trading Act and Consumer Guarantees Act. The most significant reforms in the area of product liability are outlined below.

(ii) Litigation funding agreements, which have been little used in the past, are becoming more common in New Zealand. In *Waterhouse v Contractors Bonding Ltd* [2014] 1 NZLR 91 the New Zealand Supreme Court recently issued a definitive ruling on disclosure of such agreements in the context of individual claims (as distinct from representative and class actions). In particular, the Supreme Court held that in the ordinary course, only the existence of such an agreement and location of the funder, but not the agreement itself, must be disclosed when proceedings are issued. This ruling does not address representative or class actions.

(iii) A draft Class Actions Bill regarding proposed class action rules in the High Court, is currently with the Ministry of Justice. The Court of Appeal indicated (in *Saunders v Houghton* [2010] 3 NZLR 331) that when draft class action legislation and rules are available, they are likely to provide a framework that will be useful to the judiciary. It is not yet clear whether, and if so when, the proposed legislation will be progressed.

9.2 Please describe any proposed important law reform in the area of product liability in your country.

The Fair Trading Amendment Act 2013 and the Consumer Guarantees Amendment Act 2013 brought about some important changes to the law regarding product liability in New Zealand. The following resulting changes are now in effect:

(i) where a supplier voluntarily recalls an unsafe product, that supplier now must, within two working days of recalling the product, notify the MBIE of the recall. Certain requirements for the contents of the notice are now prescribed in section 31A of the Fair Trading Act 1986;

(ii) the Minister of Consumer Affairs may now also declare goods unsafe (prohibiting sale of those goods) if it appears to the Minister that a reasonably foreseeable use (including misuse) of the goods would, or may cause injury to a person; and

(iii) the chief executive of the relevant Government Ministry now has the power to appoint product safety officers who can enter and inspect business premises without a warrant, if the officer believes on reasonable grounds that unsafe goods are being supplied at or dispatched from that place.

On 18 June 2014, further amendments to the Fair Trading Act and Consumer Guarantees Act will come into force. The amendments include an increase in the maximum fines payable for contravening the Act (as discussed above) and new criteria for contracting out of the provisions of that legislation. In particular, the Fair Trading Act will expressly permit contracting out where this is agreed in writing by parties who are in trade and it is fair and reasonable to uphold the contracting out. The contracting out provisions in the Consumer Guarantees Act will be amended at the same time so as to align its contracting-out provisions with the changes to the Fair Trading Act.

The Food Bill, introduced into Parliament in 2010, is expected to be passed in 2014.

10. REGULATORY WEBSITES/INFORMATION

10.1 Please identify any useful regulatory references relating to product liability law in your country, for example, a product safety/consumer law website maintained by the main regulator.

(i) There is useful information regarding product safety laws, unsafe product and product recalls on the Consumer Affairs website: *www.consumeraffairs.govt.nz*

(ii) Other consumer product safety legislation and the organisation to which complaints regarding certain products should be referred are:

Product	Relevant organisation	Contact details
Products subject to a product safety standards or unsafe goods notice	Commerce Commission	*www.comcom.govt.nz*
Food	Ministry for Primary Industries (MPI)	*www.foodsafety.govt.nz*
Medicines and therapeutic goods	Ministry of Health	*www.moh.govt.nz*
Motor vehicles	Ministry of Transport New Zealand Transport agency	*www.transport.govt.nz* *www.nzta.govt.nz*
Gas and electrical products	Energy Safety (MBIE)	*www.energysafety.govt.nz*

Hazardous products and products used in the workplace	Occupational Safety and Health (MBIE)	*www.osh.govt.nz*
Hazardous substances and organisms	Environmental Protection Agency (EPA)	*www.epa.govt.nz*
Products used in building and construction	MBIE's Building and Housing branch	*www.dbh.govt.nz*

Portugal

PLMJ, Sociedade de Advogados, RL
Daniel Reis & Juliana Marcondes

1. LIABILITY

1.1 What are the principal sources of law and regulation relating to product liability?

Product liability is specifically governed in Portugal by Decree-Law 383/89 of 6 November (the Product Liability Law), which implemented Directive 85/374/EEC of the Council of 25 July 1985 in Portugal. Decree-Law 383/89 was subsequently amended by Decree-Law 131/2001 of 24 April implementing Directive 1999/34/EC of the European Parliament and Council of 10 May 1999 in Portugal.

Portugal also has some general regulations that affect product liability: Law 83/95 of 31 August 1983, which deals with class action claims, Law 24/96 of 31 July, the general consumer law, as amended; Decree-Law 67/2003 of 8 April, as amended, which implemented Directive 1999/44/EC of the European Parliament and Council of 25 May 1999 in Portugal, and Decree-Law 69/2005, concerning general safety of products and producer's liability, which implemented Directive 2001/95/ EEC of the Council of 17 March 2001 in Portugal.

The Product Liability Law only deals with damages caused by products.

Decree-Law 67/2003 grants consumers certain rights, such as the right to obtain repair or substitution of defective products.

1.2 What is required to establish causation under the most common causes of action available?

The Portuguese Civil Code, in Article 483, contains the basic provisions on non-contractual liability (tort), according to which anyone who, with fault (with intent or mere negligence) and in an unlawful way, violates the right of another or any legal provision aimed at protecting third parties' interests, is liable for the damages caused as a result of the violation.

Thus, according to the Portuguese tort model, anyone who suffers damages may claim compensation alleging and proving the five abovementioned prerequisites:

(i) the fact;
(ii) the unlawfulness;
(iii) the attribution of the fact to the injuring party;
(iv) the damages; and
(v) the existence of adequate causation between the fact and the damages.

1.3 Is strict liability available, and if so, in what circumstances?

Yes, strict liability is available under Portuguese law. Liability on the part of a producer in Portugal based on the Product Liability Law arises directly from the law, regardless of the existence of fault on the part of the manufacturer.

As per the Product Liability Law the producer may only be held liable for certain types of damages. The producer will be liable for damages for death or personal injuries and for damage to any product other than the defective product itself, provided that the same is ordinarily intended for private use or consumption and the injured party mainly used it for that purpose – damages to products are only recoverable to the extent they exceed the value of €500.

Please note that damages arising from nuclear accidents and covered by international conventions in force in Portugal are not subject to the Product Liability Law.

The Product Liability Law also does not apply to products put into circulation before the date on which it entered into force, ie, on 11 November 1989.

This type of liability may not be contractually excluded or limited in relation to the injured party and any written provisions to the contrary are deemed null and void.

1.4 Are guarantees or warranties as to quality implied by law?

Yes, according to Article 913 of the Civil Code, the sale of products includes implied warranties, namely fitness for purpose. Exclusion of implied warranties are null and void.

1.5 How is a product 'defect' defined?

Article 913 of the Civil Codes defines 'defect' as a problem that affects the value of the product, prevents the product from being used for its intended purpose, or does not have the qualities described by the seller.

In sales to consumers (natural persons purchasing for non-professional use) Decree-Law 67/2003 uses the concept of 'conformity with the sales contract'. The seller is under the obligation to deliver to the consumer a product that complies with the contract of sale and purchase.

Products are deemed not to be in compliance if they:

- do not comply with the description given by the seller or do not possess the characteristics of the product that the seller has held out to the consumer as a sample or model;
- are not fit for any particular purpose for which the consumer requires them and which he made known to the seller at the time of conclusion of the contract and which the seller has accepted;
- are not fit for the purposes for which products of the same type are normally used;
- do not have the quality and performance which are normal in products of the same type and which the consumer can reasonably expect, given the nature of the products and, if applicable, the public statements on the specific characteristics of the products made by the seller, the

producer or his representative, particularly in advertising or labelling.

Any lack of compliance resulting from incorrect installation of the consumer product is deemed to be equivalent to a lack of compliance of the said product if installation forms part of the contract of sale and purchase of the product and the product was installed by the seller or under his responsibility. This will also apply if the product is intended to be installed by the consumer and the incorrect installation is due to a shortcoming in the installation instructions.

1.6 Who in the supply chain has obligations or duties for defective products? What obligations or duties do they owe and to whom?

The retailer is principally responsible to the consumer for liability arising from Decree-Law 67/2003.

Nevertheless, and without prejudice to that, in accordance with Article 6 of Decree-Law 67/2003, the consumer may also claim the repair or replacement of the defective product directly from the producer, or from its representative in the area of residence of the consumer.

The producer for this purpose is deemed to be the producer of a consumer product, the importer of the consumer product into the European Union or any person purporting to be a producer by placing its name, trade mark or other distinctive sign on the consumer product.

The party responsible for satisfying the claim of the purchaser – the consumer or an intermediary in the distribution chain – has a right of redress against the previous seller of the defective consumer product.

If several entities are liable for the damages, they will be jointly and severally liable. Liability will be assigned to them in the basis of the circumstances of the case, especially the risk created by each of them, the level of fault in their conduct and their contribution to the damage. In the case of doubt, liability will be assigned to them equally.

1.7 By what means can a supplier limit their liability for defective products?

The liability for defective products cannot be excluded or limited. Any provisions to this effect are deemed null and void. Article 10 of Decree-Law 67/2003 determines the absolute nullity of clauses limiting the liability of producers.

1.8 Are there particular goods or services which have specific obligations or duties attached to them?

No.

2. DEFENCES

2.1 What are the possible defences to a product liability claim?

The Product Liability Law determines that any producer alleging exclusion or reduction of liability and/or limitation of reparable damages may present a defence against claims made if it is able to demonstrate that:

- it did not put the product into circulation;

- having regard to the circumstances, it is reasonable to hold that the defect did not exist at the time when the product was put into circulation;
- the product was neither manufactured by it for sale or any form of distribution for economic purposes nor manufactured or distributed by it in the course of its business;
- the defect is due to compliance of the product with mandatory regulations issued by the public authorities;
- the state of scientific and technical knowledge at the time when it put the product into circulation was not such as to enable the existence of the defect to be discovered;
- in the case of a component, the defect is attributable to the design of the product in which the component has been fitted or to the instructions given by the manufacturer of the product.

Without prejudice to the above, in cases where a fault in the injured party's conduct contributes to causing the damage, the court may, having regard to all the circumstances, reduce or exclude the liability of the producer.

2.2 Is there a limit on the time in which proceedings may be brought (limitations and repose)?

The right to recover damages is subject to a limitation period of three years from the date on which the injured party became aware, or should have become aware, of the damage, the defect and the identity of the producer.

As regards direct liability of the producers pursuant to Article 6 of Decree-Law 67/2003, 10 years after the date on which the producer put the product that caused the damage into circulation, the right to obtain redress (repair or substitution of the product) is extinguished, unless the injured party has instituted proceedings to claim damages in the meantime.

3. LITIGATION OF PRODUCT LIABILITY DISPUTES

3.1 In which courts are product liability proceedings brought?

Portugal has a civil law system. The main division established is between judicial jurisdiction and administrative jurisdiction (including tax).

The organisation of the courts is complex and the competence of each type of court is defined considering the nature of the dispute to be settled. Product liability actions are generally heard in the court of the place where the damage occurred.

Portugal is divided into judicial districts and normally each municipality has its own judicial court. Judicial courts have generic competence. However, in several municipalities (and always in the main cities) there are sub-types of judicial courts with specific jurisdiction to deal with matters such as civil, criminal, family, commerce, labour, etc.

Taking into account the economic value of the claim, the type of proceedings and other circumstances, there may be sub-types of courts within the civil and criminal courts.

3.2 How are proceedings commenced?

A civil case to be decided in a Portuguese court passes through two different phases: a written phase (pleadings), where almost all procedural activity is conducted by the parties with very little intervention from the judge, and a subsequent oral phase (hearings).

Procedural law imposes an obligation on the claimant to describe all the factual grounds of the case and the relief sought in the first written pleading (petition). The claimant must also indicate all the evidence he wishes to produce (lists of witnesses, requests for the production of documents, etc), although it is possible to file additional documents and to amend the witnesses list at a later point in the proceedings (additional documents are only admitted until 20 days prior to preliminary hearing to trial and as long as the party pays a penalty, or under special circumstances). It is advisable to present the outlines of the legal arguments during the written (pleadings) phase.

In turn, the defendant's defence must contain all the factual or legal arguments as the defendant will not have another opportunity to do so. The defendant must also indicate all the evidence he wishes to produce at this point. If in the defence the defendant only challenges the truth of the facts alleged in the claimant's petition or alleges legal arguments that may lead to the dismissal of the case (for example time-bar, lack of jurisdiction, forfeiture of the right to claim), the written pleadings stage will be closed.

However, if the defendant alleges new facts that may imply a solution to the case different from the one claimed by the claimant, the latter will have the right to file a reply devoted to answering such new facts. The claimant may change the relief sought at any time, provided the defendant accepts the change required (otherwise, the relief sought can only be amended under specific circumstances). The facts not expressly challenged by the defendant in the pleading are deemed to have been admitted (except if the admission of those facts is not legally permitted or if the defendant declares that it does not know whether the fact is true and is not under an obligation to know it, ie, provided that is not a personal fact).

Together with the defence, the defendant may file a counterclaim (which must be connected with the initial claim of the claimant). This counterclaim is deemed to be an autonomous case (although decided and judged together with the claimant's claim).

The court will be bound by the essential facts and claims presented by the parties, except in respect of particular legal issues.

Once the exchange of pleadings is complete, the terms of the dispute are defined and, save for exceptional situations, cannot be altered.

The court will then schedule a preliminary hearing at which the legal obstacles to the claims (and any possible counterclaims) will be discussed (although no evidence is presented yet). This preliminary hearing may lead to the dismissal of the case. If the judge considers that all the relevant facts are already evidenced in the file (by documents), he may also decide to rule on the merits of the case.

If the court decides that the case should proceed to trial (and this is the normal outcome of the preliminary hearing) it will issue an order, after a debate between the parties, determining the precise subject of the proceedings and the themes of evidence. Parties may also amend the evidence they have indicated before at this stage, since only the list of witnesses may be amended afterwards.

3.3 Are disputed issues decided by a judge or a jury?

The issues are decided by a judge. Juries do not exist in civil courts.

In some criminal cases, the possibility of requesting a jury is possible, although not frequent and, when constituted, the role of the jury is merely to advise the judges.

In Portugal judges must be law graduates and, after obtaining their degree in law, they have to go through two additional years of legal training in a State institute. After graduating from the said institute, the new judges are placed in different courts.

At the beginning of their careers, judges tend to be placed either in very small municipalities or, when placed in large cities, in courts with restricted jurisdiction. The evolution to more important courts (eg, with wider jurisdiction) will depend on the outcome of evaluations performed on a regular basis. There are several sub-types of first instance courts and, thereafter, a judge may be promoted to one of the courts of appeal and, subsequently, to the Supreme Court.

3.4 Who has the burden of proof and to what standard?

Under Portuguese law, there are two standards of proof:

Civil cases

Claimant of a right has the burden of proving the relevant facts substantiating the alleged right.

In turn, the party against whom the claim is made has the burden of proving facts that hinder, modify or extinguish the rights of the claimant.

Although no specific provision exists in this context on the burden of proof, under the general rule of Portuguese law, the injured party must produce evidence of the facts grounding his claim.

However, it should be noted that there are several legal presumptions (as described in section 2.1 above) regarding the product's failure to comply. Nevertheless, they do not cause the reversal of the burden of proof of the facts required to be shown in order to sustain the existence of a lack of compliance of the product.

Finally, in case of doubt, facts will have to be proved by the party invoking the right. If doubts remain after the production of evidence, the issue will be resolved against the party who would benefit from the proof of the fact.

The Portuguese system also admits the relevance of legal presumptions – the most relevant example is the presumption applying to contractual liability, according to which, in case of breach of contract, the law presumes that the same is due to fault of the breaching party, although the latter will be entitled to prove that it was not his fault (of the burden of proof of fault by the breaching party).

Criminal cases
All relevant facts composing the criminal conduct must be proved by the prosecution at trial.

3.5 How is evidence given in proceedings and are witnesses cross-examined?

As the law does not allow written statements – except for cases in which it is not possible or it is difficult to have the witness appear in court – all the evidence is produced orally.

The trial starts with the examination of the claimant's witness, conducted by the claimant's lawyer. At the end of each deposition, the lawyer of the other party may cross-examine the witness, but is restricted to the explanations provided by the witness during the direct examination.

Witness may be challenged and documents may be filed in order to discredit a statement or a witness. If the court so agrees, a witness can be called back and it is possible to hold a direct confrontation between witnesses. Witnesses are obliged to swear to tell the truth.

Witness may be confronted with documents in the file and may use their own documents, even if they are not in the file (but the documents may not be accepted if they could have been filed earlier by the party bringing the witness). However, they cannot bring written statements or any notes summarising their evidence.

In a normal civil case each party may list up to 10 witnesses. If a counterclaim has been filed, an additional group of 10 witnesses may be listed by each party. Whenever the proceedings' value corresponds to less than €5,000 the number of witnesses is reduced by half.

Witnesses have to give evidence under oath and have to explain their connection with the parties and the reason why they are aware of the facts.

Anyone may be a witness except the parties, or the parties' representatives. If a company wishes its representatives (such as directors, managers, etc, provided that they have powers to bind/represent the company) to be heard in proceedings involving the relevant company as party, whether as claimant or defendant, it may require their testimony (not as witness, but as party) until the end of the presentation of evidence on trial.

An expert retained by one party who was not involved in the preparation of the expert report ordered by the court may testify as a witness.

It is entirely up to the court to evaluate and establish the relevance of each testimony.

3.6 Are the parties able to rely on expert opinion evidence and, if so, are there any special rules or procedures for expert opinion evidence?

The parties may also request an expert report, usually to be prepared by three experts – typically, each party nominates one expert and the court nominates the third. Medical expert reports are prepared by state authorities.

The experts receive a list of technical questions to which they should provide answers. The parties are under an obligation to cooperate with the experts, providing all information they request. In view of the outcome of the expert report the parties or the court are allowed to request a second expert report. In any case, the court will not be bound the answers given by the experts.

Expert reports produced outside of the scope of an expert report ordered by the court, whether legal or technical, may be filed at any stage of the court proceedings. The experts who prepared the said reports are not required to go to court to defend their reports, but they may appear as witnesses.

3.7 Is pre-trial discovery permitted? If so, in what circumstances? If not, what other mechanisms, if any, are available for obtaining evidence from a party or a third party?

No, pre-trial discovery is not available in Portugal. In case there is reasonable concern, evidence will become unavailable the testimony, examination or inspection may be carried out in advance and before the lawsuit begins.

The party applying for this type of evidence has to briefly justify to the court the need for anticipation, must give precisely the facts about how evidence may become unavailable and identify the people who are to be heard in case of testimony of a party or witnesses.

3.8 Is there liability for spoliation of evidence/a remedy for destruction of or failure to preserve evidence (most relevantly, the product)?

If one of the parties makes it impossible for the other to have access to evidence, the burden of proof will be reversed, without prejudice to any sanctions for disobedience or making false statements (most of the time characterised by procedural fines).

3.9 Is interlocutory or interim relief available prior to the full trial of a proceeding? If so, in what circumstances?

Yes. Before the main action begins or at any time during the main action, if one of the parties demonstrates a well-founded fear that somebody may cause serious damage to their right, that party may apply to the court for an injunction to protect the threatened right.

This application may be based on an existing right or a right that emerges as a result of a decision made in the main action.

Injunction applications are urgent in character and take precedence over any other non-urgent court business.

3.10 Can the winning party recover its costs?

During the proceedings both parties will be called on to make payments on account of court fees and, upon rendering the decision, the court determines the total amount of fees payable. The losing party is responsible for all court fees.

However, Portuguese law does not establish an effective rule regarding the possibility of a party to recover its own legal costs. Except for court fees, which can be recovered, the winning party is not entitled to claim the costs of the litigation from the defeated party and will be awarded 'compensation' that may not exceed 50% of the value of the court fees (which is a small amount and will represent a small fraction of the total legal costs).

3.11 What avenues of appeal are available?

A decision rendered by a judicial court may be challenged in an appeal court and, in most cases, the decision of the latter may be appealed to the Supreme Court.

Portugal has no binding precedent rule, although the Supreme Court may be called to standardise a legal question that has been decided in different ways in different cases (in any case, even such a standardisation may be disputed in future cases).

4. CLASS ACTIONS/REPRESENTATIVE PROCEEDINGS

4.1 Is there a mechanism for class actions or representative proceedings, or coordinated proceedings for product liability claims? If so, what are the basic mechanics?

In Portugal, the procedural instrument for the protection of collective rights is a class action (called *acção popular*) and is regulated by Law 83/95.

This mechanism is aimed at safeguarding diffuse interests (as opposed to the individual interests) in the areas of public health, quality of life, environmental protection, cultural heritage and consumers' rights, which include product liability claims.

Any individual; associations and foundations that defend the interests listed above; local authorities; the Public Prosecutor´s Office representing minors, absent persons or persons lacking legal capacity and public entities when authorised by law, have legal standing to bring a class action.

However, it should be noted that the Portuguese class action has some significant differences from the Anglo-American equivalent. It is an 'opt-out' system in which the claimant represents, with waiver of representation by a lawyer, all other holders of rights and interests and the final decision covers all them, unless they have exercised the right to opt out of the action.

The General Consumer Law (Law 24/96) and Standard Terms and Conditions Law (DL 446/85) also provide for types of injunctions (called *acção inibitória*) to protect collective interests. These are used on order to make the (potential) producers act or abstain from action, to prevent significant damage or avoid further damage to the consumer.

Those mechanisms are frequently used by the Portuguese consumers' association, which means that the class action under Law 83/95 it not a very popular procedure. Other reasons contribute to this situation:

- the existence of alternative dispute resolution mechanisms;
- the payment of individual compensation to a specific injured person in place of payment of compensation into a public fund;
- the existence of obstacles to actually putting the judgment into effect:

after calculating the amount of damages payable, the high number of injured persons and the lack of criteria for dividing the amount between them make it difficult to ensure payment of compensation to all the injured persons.

5. LITIGATION FUNDING

5.1 Is litigation funding by third parties permissible in your country? If so, is it common?

Litigation funding by private third parties (eg, companies specialising in financing litigation) is not available in Portugal.

5.2 Are contingency fee or 'no win no fee' arrangements permissible?

The rules of Portuguese Bar Association forbid contingency fees (*quota litis*). This means it is impossible to make an agreement that fees will amount to a certain percentage of the damages awarded or that they will depend entirely on the outcome of the case.

The said rules also provide that lawyers' fees should be charged according to pre-defined criteria, principally the time spent working on the case. Other relevant criteria would be the complexity of the issue, the importance of the service provided, the wealth of the client and the results achieved.

In practical terms these provisions allow a margin of flexibility in the calculation of fees and it is widely accepted that a success fee can be agreed, provided that it is established within reasonable limits.

6. REMEDIES

6.1 What remedies are available to a party who successfully pursues a product liability claim?

The most common remedy is payment of monetary damages. However, depending on the claim made by the injured party, the judge may also order measures consisting of an obligation to, for example, replace the product or repeat the service.

Due to a sentence imposed by a court of law, the party can execute it directly and enforce – through some procedural mechanisms like fines or pledge of properties – the compliance of the decision.

6.2 How are damages calculated/are there limitations on available damages?

According to Portuguese law, a party is entitled to recover the damages that it would not probably suffer if the damaging fact had not occurred (adequate causation).

The compensation is intended to put the injured party in the position it would have been in if the damage had not occurred, ie, there is an obligation to replace whatever was lost by the injured party. Only when such specific replacement is not possible will the obligation to compensate be converted into an obligation to pay monetary compensation.

The compensation will cover both the damages suffered and the benefits (lost profit) the injured party did not obtain as a consequence of the damage.

6.3 Are punitive or exemplary damages available and in what circumstances?

Punitive damages are not available. Moral damages (pain, suffering, death) are recoverable, but compensation granted for such damages is normally relatively low, although some evolution (increasing the amount of moral damages) has been noted in recent years.

6.4 Is liability joint and several/how does apportionment of liability work, including where a partially responsible entity is not a party to the proceeding?

If several entities are liable for the damages, they are jointly and severally liable. Liability will be apportioned between them according to the circumstances of the case, in particular, the risk created by each of them, the level of fault in their conduct and their contribution to the damage. In case of doubt, liability is apportioned equally.

If a liable entity is not a party at the proceeding, the parties that are held liable may pursue this entity to recover the damages that they have to pay.

7. ROLE OF REGULATORS

7.1 Please explain the role, responsibilities and powers of the regulators in your country which have jurisdiction over product liability issues.

The regulatory authorities are independent bodies of the Public Administration whose members are appointed by the Government or the Parliament and may not be dismissed, except in situations explicitly provided for by law.

Their main role is to ensure a proper functioning of the internal market. In summary, they aim to:

- enforce the applicable law existing for each sector;
- establish rules that the companies and other entities present in the market must observe;
- decide on conflicting interests between businesses and consumers when the law imposes.

There are authorities that focus on particular sectors and they act together with the Safety Commission for Consumer Products and Services. This Commission is a collegiate organ composed of representative members from the Government, industry, commerce and civil society and has an important role regarding any product and service that could endanger the consumer.

7.2 Are there any mandatory reporting requirements related to product safety issues?

Among other powers, the Safety Commission for Consumers Products and Services has the power to issue studies and set mandatory reporting requirements.

There are documents on different sectors, all of which are available on the Safety Commission for Consumers Products and Services' website: *www.consumidor.pt/*.

7.3 Do the regulators have the power to:

(i) ban certain products or services?

Yes, in relation to any dangerous or potentially dangerous product the Safety Commission for Consumers Products and Services can:

- ban the product from being placed on the market, defining the necessary accompanying measures to ensure the ban is complied with;
- ban the supply, offer to supply or product exposure during the period necessary to carry out the various checks, verifications or safety assessments.

(ii) require a supplier to recall a product?

Yes, for any dangerous product already placed on market the Commission can order:

- its effective and immediate withdrawal and/or alert consumers about the risks of the said product;
- if necessary, recall the product and order its destruction in suitable conditions.

(iii) prescribe standards in respect of certain products or services and require that the products or services meet those standards?

Yes, the Commission has power to impose conditions on the sale of a product designed to ensure product safety and requiring that suitable warnings be affixed regarding the risks the product may present.

(iv) require production of information without court process?

Yes, the producer and the distributor, within the limits arising from the exercise of their activities, are obliged to cooperate with the competent authorities upon request, to prevent risks to products placed on the market.

All relevant information has to be provided within five days, including any information covered by professional secrecy, which for the purposes of the Commission are considered confidential.

If so, broadly explain the circumstances in which the regulator can exercise the power and any penalties that apply if a supplier fails to comply.

The failure or refusal to provide information requested by the competent authorities is punishable with a fine of €2490-€3490 or €24,940-€44,890 according to whether the offender is an individual or a legal entity. Trying to refuse to provide information and failure to provide information caused by negligence are also punishable.

8. VOLUNTARY CONDUCT

8.1 Are there regulations pertaining to the voluntary conduct of a product repair or recall by a supplier?

The voluntary conduct of product repair or recall by a supplier is triggered when other alternatives are not sufficient to prevent the risk or in any cases in which the producer deems this to be necessary.

9. EMERGING ISSUES AND LAW REFORM

9.1 Are there important developing and emerging issues or trends in product liability law in your country?

There have been very few class action lawsuits in Portugal, in part because of the limitations contained in Law 83/95. Following the publication of the Commission Recommendation of 11 June 2013 on common principles for injunctive and compensatory collective redress mechanisms in the member states concerning violations of rights granted under Union Law (2013/396/EU) there has been some debate on the possible need of amending Law 83/95.

9.2 Please describe any proposed important law reform in the area of product liability in your country.

There are no current proposed reforms in the area of product liability in Portugal.

10. REGULATORY WEBSITES/INFORMATION

10.1 Please identify any useful regulatory references relating to product liability law in your country, for example, a product safety/consumer law website maintained by the main regulator.

Portugal has an explanatory website (in Portuguese) with relevant information about consumer issues: *www.consumidor.pt*

On this site it is possible to find about all Portuguese/European Union rules, technical regulations and news concerning consumers, producers and suppliers.

Republic of Ireland

Arthur Cox Isabel Foley, Orla Clayton & Domhnall Breatnach

1. LIABILITY

1.1 What are the principal sources of law and regulation relating to product liability?

Contract

Liability can arise under the Sale of Goods Act 1893, as amended by the Sale of Goods and Supply of Services Act 1980 (SGA).

Tort

The general common law principle of negligence applies in Ireland. Therefore, product manufacturers owe a duty of care to all those who may be foreseeably injured or damaged by their products.

Statutory liability

The Liability for Defective Products Act 1991 (LDPA) implements Directive 85/374/EEC on liability for defective products (Product Liability Directive) into Irish law.

Criminal

The principal criminal sanctions arise under the European Communities (General Product Safety) Regulations 2004 (GPSR) which implement Directive 2001/95/EC on general product safety (the Revised General Product Safety Directive) into Irish law. Once the new proposal for a regulation on consumer product safety (which was adopted by the European Commission in February 2013) is finalised and comes into force, Directive 2001/95/EC will be repealed.

1.2 What is required to establish causation under the most common causes of action available?

In a negligence claim, factual and legal causation must be established by the injured person. An objective standard applies when assessing whether there has been a breach of duty. An act is held to be the cause of an event if the event would not have occurred without it (commonly known as the 'but for' test).

If the circumstances of an accident speak for themselves, they give rise to a presumption of negligence (the doctrine of *res ipsa loquitur*). In such circumstances, the burden is on the defendant or defendants to prove that they were not negligent. This doctrine rarely applies in practice.

Under the LDPA, the onus is on the injured person to prove the damage, the defect, and the causal relationship between the defect and damage (section 4, LDPA).

1.3 Is strict liability available and, if so, in what circumstances?

Yes. The LDPA provides a strict liability regime, under which a producer is liable for damages in tort for injury resulting wholly or partly by a defect in his product (section 2, LDPA). The liability of a producer to an injured person, arising by virtue of the LDPA, cannot be limited or excluded by any term of a contract, notice or any other provision (section 10, LDPA).

1.4 Are guarantees or warranties as to quality implied by law?

Yes. Under section 14 of the SGA, where a seller sells goods in the course of a business, there is an implied condition that the goods supplied under the contract are of merchantable quality. Goods are of merchantable quality if they are fit for the purpose or purposes for which goods of that kind are commonly bought, and are as durable as it is reasonable to expect, having regard to any description applied to the goods, the price (if relevant), and all the other relevant circumstances. No implied condition as to merchantable quality is implied as regards defects that are specifically drawn to the buyer's attention before the contract is made or, if the buyer examines the goods before the contract is made, as regards defects which that examination ought to have revealed. Where a seller sells goods in the course of a business and the buyer, expressly or by implication, makes known to the seller any particular purpose for which the goods are being bought, there is an implied condition that the goods supplied under the contract are reasonably fit for that purpose, whether or not that is a purpose for which such goods are commonly supplied, except where the circumstances show that the buyer did not rely, or that it is unreasonable for him to rely, on the seller's skill or judgement.

1.5 How is a product 'defect' defined?

For the purposes of the LDPA, a product is defective if it fails to provide the safety which a person is entitled to expect, taking all circumstances into account, including the presentation of the product, the use to which it could reasonably be expected that the product would be put, and the time when the product was put into circulation (section 5(1), LDPA). However, a product is not considered defective for the sole reason that a better product is subsequently put into circulation (section 5(2), LDPA).

1.6 Who in the supply chain has obligations or duties for defective products? What obligations or duties do they owe and to whom?

Under tort law, product manufacturers owe a duty of care to all those who may be foreseeably injured or damaged by their products.

Under Section 2(2) of the LDPA, a producer of a product is liable in damages in tort for damage caused wholly or partly by a defect in his product. Under the LDPA, a 'producer' can be:

- the manufacturer or producer of a finished product;

- the manufacturer or producer of any raw material or the manufacturer or producer of a component part of a product;
- in the case of the products of the soil, of stock-farming and of fisheries and game, which have undergone initial processing, the person who carried out such processing;
- any person who, by putting his name, trade mark or other distinguishing feature on the product, or using his name or any such mark or feature in relation to the product, has held himself out to be the producer of the product;
- any person who has imported the product into an EU member state from a place outside the EU in order, in the course of any business of that person, to supply it to another; or
- any person who is liable as producer of the product pursuant to Section 2(3) of the LDPA.

Section 2(3) of the LDPA provides that, where the producer of a product cannot, by taking reasonable steps, be identified, then where damage is caused wholly or partly by a defect in a product, any person who supplied the product (whether to the person who suffered the damage, to the producer of any product in which the product is comprised, or to any other person) shall be liable as the producer for the damage if:

- the injured person requests the supplier to identify any person (whether still in existence or not) to whom section 2(2) of the LDPA applies in relation to the product;
- that request is made within a reasonable time after the damage occurs, and at a time when it is not reasonably practicable for the injured person to identify all those persons; and
- the supplier fails, within a reasonable time after receiving the request, either to comply with the request, or to identify the person who supplied the product to him.

1.7 By what means can a supplier limit their liability for defective products?

Under the LDPA, a supplier can limit their liability for defective products by ensuring that they can identify the producer of a product, and that they promptly identify the producer of a defective product after receiving a request to do so in accordance with the LDPA.

A supplier could also seek to limit their exposure generally under contract law by seeking certain indemnities or warranties from the producer of a product, or from others in the supply chain, if appropriate, although this will not affect a supplier's primary legal liability to an injured party.

1.8 Are there particular goods or services which have specific obligations or duties attached to them?

A number of different types of goods and services are the subject of specific detailed statutory regimes, which impose particular obligations and duties in relation to those goods and services. Such goods include food and feed stuffs, medicinal products, medical devices, machinery, chemicals, electronic equipment, cosmetics and tobacco products. The provision of certain types of services, for example, financial services, and package holidays, are also the subject of specific statutory regimes, which again impose particular obligations or duties on the providers of the services. These particular statutory regimes, and the specific obligations and duties they impose, are outside the scope of this chapter.

2. DEFENCES

2.1 What are the possible defences to a product liability claim?

Statutory defences

A producer is free from liability under the LDPA if he proves any of the following (section 6, LDPA):

- he did not put the product into circulation;
- it is probable that the defect causing the damage came into being after the product was put into circulation by him;
- the product was not manufactured for profit-making sale;
- the product was not manufactured or distributed in the course of business;
- the defect was due to compliance of the product with mandatory regulations issued by the public authorities;
- the state of the scientific and technical knowledge at the time when the product was put into circulation was not such as to enable the defect to be discovered (development risks defence); or
- in the case of a manufacturer of a component of the final product, the defect was attributable to the design of the product or to the instructions given by the product manufacturer.

Common law defences

A defendant essentially seeks to establish that:

- he was not negligent;
- he did not owe a duty of care;
- there was no causal link between the action/inaction and the injury.

Contributory negligence

Under the Civil Liability Act 1961 (CLA), damages are reduced if there has been contributory negligence on the part of the claimant.

Voluntary assumption of risk

Although not often relied on, the defence of voluntary assumption of risk arises where it can be established that a claimant, fully knowing and appreciating the risks of a particular activity, voluntarily accepted and exposed themselves to that risk.

2.2 Is there a limit on the time in which proceedings may be brought (limitations and repose)?

There is a limitation period of three years from the date on which a claimant became aware (or should reasonably have become aware) of the damage, the defect and the identity of the producer (section 7(1), LDPA). Rights conferred on an injured party are extinguished after 10 years from the date on which the producer puts the actual product which caused the damage into circulation (section 7(2), LDPA).

The Civil Liability and Courts Act 2004 (CLCA) reduced the limitation period for personal injury cases from three years to two years, with effect from 31 March 2005. However, the Irish courts have considered this point and held that the limitation provisions of the LDPA remain unaffected by the enactment of the CLCA. It follows that in an action for personal injuries this longer limitation period could apply for any element of the claim in relation to statutory liability for defective products, in which the provisions of the LDPA are relied upon.

3. LITIGATION OF PRODUCT LIABILITY DISPUTES

3.1 In which courts are product liability proceedings brought?

Product liability proceedings are generally brought in the High Court, which has unlimited jurisdiction. Personal injuries claims that do not exceed €60,000, and other claims that do not exceed €75,000, are brought in the Circuit Court, while claims that do not exceed €15,000 are brought in the District Court.

Save for certain very limited exceptions, all claims for personal injuries must first be the subject of an application to InjuriesBoard.ie, which is a statutory body that is designed to assess claims, and to decrease unnecessary litigation. Product liability claims are generally considered to be too complex to be assessed by this body and so, usually, parties simply decline to agree to an assessment. An 'authorisation' is then issued by InjuriesBoard.ie, and court proceedings can then be issued by the claimant.

3.2 How are proceedings commenced?

Product liability proceedings that involve claims for personal injuries are commenced in the High Court, Circuit Court or District Court by way of a personal injuries summons. A plaintiff must also swear an affidavit verifying the assertions or allegations contained in the personal injuries summons.

A personal injuries summons must specify:

- the plaintiff's name, the address at which he or she ordinarily resides, and his or her occupation;
- the plaintiff's personal public service number;
- the defendant's name and, if known to the plaintiff, the address at which he or she ordinarily resides, and his or her occupation;
- the injuries to the plaintiff alleged to have been occasioned by the wrong of the defendant;
- full particulars of all items of special damage in respect of which the plaintiff is making a claim;
- full particulars of the acts of the defendant constituting the said wrong and the circumstances relating to the commission of the said wrong;
- full particulars of each instance of negligence by the defendant.

Product liability proceedings that do not involve personal injuries claims are generally commenced in the High Court by way of plenary summons, with such proceedings being commenced in the Circuit Court by way of Civil Bill, and in the District Court by way of Civil Summons.

3.3 Are disputed issues decided by a judge or a jury?

Disputed issues are decided by a judge, sitting alone. There is no right to a jury in product liability proceedings in Ireland.

3.4 Who has the burden of proof and to what standard?

The plaintiff generally carries the burden of proof in product liability proceedings. However, where the doctrine of *res ipsa loquitur* applies, there is a presumption of negligence and the burden of proof is reversed. However, this doctrine is rarely held to apply. The general standard of proof in civil proceedings in Ireland is the balance of probabilities.

3.5 How is evidence given in proceedings and are witnesses cross-examined?

Both factual and expert witness evidence in product liability proceedings is generally given orally in court, with the opposing party or parties having a right to cross-examine witnesses. In certain circumstances, a court can direct that evidence be given by way of affidavit. In such instances, the opposing party or parties retain the right to cross-examine witnesses.

3.6 Are the parties able to rely on expert opinion evidence and, if so, are there any special rules or procedures for expert opinion evidence?

Yes. Parties can adduce and rely on expert opinion evidence. In personal injuries actions, the plaintiff must furnish a schedule to the other party or parties, within a month of service of the notice of trial, which lists all reports from expert witnesses they intend to call at the trial of the proceedings. The opposing party or parties must then, within seven days of receipt of the plaintiff's schedule, furnish to the plaintiff a similar schedule, listing all reports from expert witnesses that they intend to call at the trial of the proceedings. The parties must then exchange copies of their expert reports within a month of the service of the notice of trial. For the purposes of these rules, an expert 'report' is very broadly defined, and includes any report or statement, in any form, from any expert, intended to be called to give evidence in relation to an issue in an action, which contains the substance of the evidence to be adduced at the trial. Any report obtained from an expert after the exchange of expert schedules and reports must also be given to the other party or parties. A party can withdraw reliance on an expert report by providing written confirmation that they do not intend to call the expert to give evidence at the trial of the proceedings. In this instance, the party withdrawing the report is entitled to the same privilege, if any, that would have applied to the report notwithstanding the exchange of the report with other party or parties to the proceedings.

In personal injuries actions, there is provision under the CLCA for a court to appoint certain approved persons to carry out investigations and give expert evidence in relation to such matters as the court directs. However, this is rarely done.

3.7 Is pre-trial discovery permitted? If so, in what circumstances? If not, what other mechanisms, if any, are available for obtaining evidence from a party or a third party?

Yes. Pre-trial discovery is available in Ireland. A party is obliged to discover only documents which it has, or has had, in its 'possession, power or procurement', and which are relevant to the issues in the proceedings, and are necessary for disposing fairly of the matter or saving costs.

Any party or parties seeking discovery must firstly do so on a voluntary basis, by writing to the other party or parties requesting the category or categories of documents it considers are relevant and necessary to the matters at issue between the parties in the proceedings. If agreement to make discovery on a voluntary basis is reached, then this has the same effect, in terms of the obligations to be met in making the discovery, as if the discovery was being made pursuant to a court order.

If the parties do not agree on what categories of discovery should be made, an application can be made to court to have the issue determined. The relevance of any particular category of documents is tested by relevance to issues in dispute in the pleadings. If an allegation is admitted, and is therefore no longer in dispute between the parties, then documents relating to the issue are generally not discoverable.

The test as to what is a relevant and necessary document is relatively wide. The meaning of a 'document' has also been liberally interpreted by the Irish courts, and essentially means anything which imparts information, or is capable of being produced in written form, including electronically stored information and data.

A document is deemed to be in a party's possession if that party physically holds or has custody of the document, while a document is within a party's 'power or procurement' if the party has a legal entitlement to inspect, or to obtain possession or control of, a document from the person who ordinarily has it, for example, any documents in the possession of a party's advisors (lawyers, accountants, corporate advisers etc.).

A party is also obliged to discover, by listing in its Affidavit of Discovery, documents which were formerly in its possession, power or procurement, but which it no longer has, and to explain why it no longer has those documents (for example, that the documents were destroyed as a result of a retention of documents policy, lost in a move or fire, overwritten or deleted etc).

The party making discovery must also disclose the existence of documents over which it asserts privilege in the Affidavit of Discovery, and set out the basis on which the party claims privilege. Where the claim of privilege made in respect of a document is not challenged by the other side, or is subsequently upheld by the court, the document is immune from production. There are several types of privilege which can attach to documents, but the most common type of privilege asserted is legal professional privilege, which includes two distinct categories of documents:

- confidential documents created in apprehension or contemplation of litigation or for the purpose of prosecuting or defending litigation (known as litigation privilege); and
- confidential documents created for the purpose of giving or obtaining legal advice (known as legal advice privilege).

Under Irish law, there is a distinction between 'legal advice', which can be covered by privilege, and 'legal assistance', which cannot.

3.8 Is there liability for spoliation of evidence/a remedy for destruction of or failure to preserve evidence (most relevantly, the product)?

Generally, the spoliation or destruction of evidence, or the failure to preserve it, could result in a court drawing adverse inferences, or making adverse findings, against the responsible party. Furthermore, depending on the nature and timing of the interference with, or destruction of, the evidence, and whether or not any order had been made by the court in that regard, it could also potentially amount to contempt of court.

There is a duty on parties, when litigation is either contemplated or commenced, to preserve any evidence that may be the subject of a discovery request, and to ensure that any documents that may be potentially relevant to the issues in the proceedings are not deliberately or accidentally destroyed or lost. It is always good practice, at the outset of proceedings, to request that all items of potential relevance (documentation relating to the product, medical records etc.), including the product itself, be preserved. If an inspection is deemed necessary, this should be flagged at an early stage. An application can be made to the court for any necessary order in terms of non-destruction or inspection, if it is deemed necessary.

The Irish courts can also grant Anton Piller orders, which permit a party to enter premises in order to inspect or retrieve evidence, with a view to preventing the removal or destruction of that evidence pending the hearing of an action.

3.9 Is interlocutory or interim relief available prior to the full trial of a proceeding? If so, in what circumstances?

Both interim and interlocutory relief are available prior to the full trial of proceedings. In determining whether to grant interlocutory injunctive relief, a court must consider whether:

- there is a fair and *bona fide* question to be tried;
- damages would be an adequate remedy in the event an injunction is not granted;
- the balance of convenience lies in favour or against granting the injunction.

A party seeking an interlocutory injunction must give an undertaking as to damages in the event that they are ultimately unsuccessful in the proceedings.

3.10 Can the winning party recover its costs?

The general rule in Ireland is that costs 'follow the event', meaning that the winning party can recover the costs of, and incidental to, civil proceedings. However, the court retains a discretion as to the award of costs. In the High Court, a party can have the costs of proceedings taxed by a Taxing Master, who assesses what legal costs should be recovered. In the Circuit Court, costs are taxed by the County Registrar.

3.11 What avenues of appeal are available?

Decisions of the High Court can generally be appealed to the Supreme Court, with appeals being confined to matters of law (which can include inferences drawn by the High Court from findings of fact) only. The Supreme Court will only interfere with findings of fact made by the High Court in exceptional circumstances, for example, where there was an absence of underlying evidence or incoherence.

Decisions of the Circuit Court can generally be appealed to the High Court, where a party is entitled to a full *de novo* hearing of the proceedings. District Court proceedings can generally be appealed to the Circuit Court, again with a full *de novo* hearing in the Circuit Court.

A new Court of Appeal is currently being set up in Ireland, which will hear almost all appeals from the High Court. There will continue to be a direct right of appeal to the Supreme Court from the High Court if the Supreme Court is satisfied that there are exceptional circumstances warranting a direct appeal to it, and provided that the decision involves a matter of general public importance and/or the interests of justice require a direct appeal. It is expected that the new Court of Appeal will being hearing cases in October 2014.

4. CLASS ACTIONS/REPRESENTATIVE PROCEEDINGS

4.1 Is there a mechanism for class actions or representative proceedings, or coordinated proceedings for product liability claims? If so, what are the basic mechanics?

There is no mechanism for class actions in Ireland. While no class action mechanism exists, multiple product liability claims are frequently brought in Ireland following international class actions or multi-party litigation.

Irish law provides for representative actions, whereby one or more persons can sue on behalf of all persons with the 'same interest'. However, the 'same interest' requirement is very strictly construed by the Irish courts, and remedies in representative actions are limited to injunctive and declaratory relief. No damages are available in representative actions.

As a result of these limitations on representative actions, multi-party litigation in Ireland has historically been managed through test cases or 'path finders'. This usually involves numerous individual cases being run at the same time, generally by the same lawyers for the claimants. There are no express rules governing the running of test cases in Ireland. Which action becomes the test case is often expressly agreed between the claimants and defendants. Alternatively, the test case may simply arise as a result of timing, with the first action that is ready to be heard by the court becoming the test case. The outcome of a test case does not automatically bind parties in other cases, however, a test case creates precedent, and the findings of a test case are frequently applied by analogy to subsequent cases.

In a 2005 report, the Irish Law Reform Commission recommended, among other things, that a formal procedural structure be introduced to deal with instances of multi-party litigation. However, so far, these recommendations have not been implemented into law.

5. LITIGATION FUNDING

5.1 Is litigation funding by third parties permissible in your country? If so, is it common?

The funding of litigation by third parties who have no *bona fide* interest in the litigation, independent of the actual arrangement with a party or parties to fund the litigation, is not permissible under Irish law.

It is permissible for a third party who has a *bona fide* interest in the litigation (independent of the funding arrangement itself) to fund litigation. Such third parties can, in certain circumstances, be made liable for the costs of the proceedings they funded. In considering whether to make a third party funder liable for the costs of proceedings, the court will consider the extent to which the actual party or parties to the proceedings could meet any costs order made against them, the degree of possible benefit of the proceedings to the third party funder, and the manner in which the litigation was conducted.

5.2 Are contingency fees or 'no win no fee' arrangements permissible?

'No win no fee' arrangements are permissible under Irish law, and are often referred to in Ireland as 'no foal no fee' arrangements. However, fees that are based on a percentage of the proceeds of litigation are not permissible under Irish law.

6. REMEDIES

6.1 What remedies are available to a party who successfully pursues a product liability claim?

The primary remedy available to a claimant in product liability cases is damages. Compensatory damages, aggravated damages, and punitive or exemplary damages are available in the Irish courts.

Under the GPSR, a non-compliant producer is guilty of a criminal offence and liable to a fine of up to €3,000, or up to three months' imprisonment, or both.

6.2 How are damages calculated/are there limitations on available damages?

When assessing damages in personal injuries cases, the Irish courts must have regard to InjuriesBoard.ie's Book of Quantum (which provides guidelines for the assessment of compensation to which an injured person may be entitled, in the context of certain specific injuries). However, not all types of injuries are covered by the Book of Quantum. There is no generally prescribed method of calculation of damages in product liability cases, and the assessment of damages varies from case to case.

Compensatory damages are generally sub-divided into:

- general damages (which generally are damages for pain and suffering and which cannot easily be quantified in monetary terms; and
- special damages (which are the specifically quantifiable expenses that the claimant has incurred as a result of the defendant's tortious act).

Aggravated damages are only awarded where the claimant suffers further injury due to some or all of the following:

- the manner in which the wrong was committed;
- the conduct of the defendant after the commission of the wrong;
- the defendant's conduct in the defence of his action, including the trial.

Punitive and exemplary damages are only awarded in exceptional circumstances, as set out in further detail below. Again, there is no prescribed method for the assessment of aggravated, or punitive or exemplary damages.

There are no limits on the level of damages that can be awarded by the High Court. Damages in the Circuit Court are limited to €75,000 generally, and €60,000 in the case of personal injuries actions. Damages in the District Court are limited to €15,000.

6.3 Are punitive or exemplary damages available and in what circumstances?

Punitive and exemplary damages are available. However, they are only awarded in exceptional circumstances. These types of damages, which are not compensatory in nature, and are generally awarded at low levels, have generally been awarded where, given the nature of the wrong in question, and the manner of its commission, a court wishes to mark its disapproval of a defendant's conduct, and for its decision to publicly be seen to punish a defendant for its conduct. Punitive or exemplary damages have been awarded, for example, where there has been an infringement of a claimant's constitutional rights, but even then such damages are generally awarded at a relatively low level. There has only been one example of significant punitive or exemplary damages in Ireland (that is, exceeding €1 million), but this was very much because of the specific and extreme circumstances of that case. There have been no cases to date where material punitive or exemplary damages have been awarded for a product liability claim.

6.4 Is liability joint and several/how does apportionment of liability work, including where a partially responsible entity is not a party to the proceeding?

If two or more persons are liable under the CLA for the same damage as concurrent wrongdoers, they are jointly and severally liable to the injured person under the general law of negligence and the LDPA. Where a concurrent wrongdoer is not a party to proceedings, it is open to any concurrent wrongdoer that is a party to seek to join the non-party concurrent wrongdoer to the proceedings as a third party. The court will ultimately determine the apportionment of liability as between defendants or third parties which are before it. The court will not apportion liability as between a defendant and a party that is not before the court.

Without prejudice to the right to seek contribution from other parties under the CLA, the LDPA provides that the liability of the producer shall not be reduced when damage is caused both by a defect in a product and by the act or omission of a third party (section 9, LPDA). Under the CLA, damages are reduced if there has been contributory negligence. The LDPA provides that, where any damage is caused partly by a defect in a product, and partly by the fault of the injured person or of any person for whom the injured person is responsible, the provisions of the CLA concerning contributory negligence, shall have effect as if the defect was due to the fault of every person liable by virtue of the LDPA for the damage caused by the defect (section 9, LPDA).

7. ROLE OF REGULATORS

7.1 Please explain the role, responsibilities and powers of the regulators in your country which have jurisdiction over product liability issues.

The National Consumer Agency (NCA) has general responsibility for ensuring that consumer products placed on the market are safe, and that producers and distributors of products comply with their obligations under the GPSR and the Revised General Product Safety Directive. The powers of the NCA are set out in further details below. The Irish Government recently published the Competition and Consumer Protection Bill 2014 (which has yet to be enacted), which proposes to dissolve the NCA and the Competition Authority, and to transfer their functions to a newly-established Competition and Consumer Protection Commission.

Certain products are regulated by specific specialist regulators. For example, food products are regulated by the Food Safety Authority of Ireland, the Department of Agriculture, Food and the Marine is responsible for feedstuffs, while the Irish Medicines Board is the competent authority responsible for regulating medicinal products, medical devices and cosmetics. Each of these specialist regulators has specific statutory roles, responsibilities and powers particular to them, which are outside the scope of this chapter.

7.2 Are there any mandatory reporting requirements related to product safety issues?

Yes. Under the GPSR (section 8(1), GPSR), where a producer or distributor of a product knows or, on the basis of information in their possession and as a professional, ought to know, that a product which they have placed on the market poses a risk to the consumer that is incompatible with the safety requirements of the GPSR or the Revised General Product Safety Directive, the producer or distributor must immediately inform the NCA of the risk in a specified form, giving details, in particular, of action to prevent risk to consumers. In the event of serious risks, the information must include the following:

- information enabling a precise identification of the product or batch of products in question;
- a full description of the risk that the products in question present;
- all available information relevant for tracing the product; and
- a description of the action undertaken to prevent risks to consumers.

A producer or distributor of a product must, on a request being made by the NCA, provide every reasonable assistance to the NCA to avoid the risks posed by any product which the producer or distributor supplies or has supplied. It is an offence for a producer or distributor, without reasonable cause, to fail to comply with the notification and assistance requirements set out under the GPSR.

7.3 Do the regulators have the power to:
(i) ban certain goods or services?
(ii) require a supplier to recall a product?
(iii) prescribe standards in respect of certain goods or services and require that the goods or services meet those standards?
(iv) require production of information without court process?
If so, broadly explain the circumstances in which the regulator can exercise the power and any penalties that apply if a supplier fails to comply.

Yes. The powers of the NCA include the ability:

- to organise appropriate checks on the safety properties of a product (even after it has been placed on the market as being safe) up to the final stage of use or consumption;
- to request all necessary information in relation to a product from any person who, in the opinion of the NCA, may be in a position to provide such information;
- to take samples of products and subject them to safety checks;
- for any product that could pose risks in certain conditions, to issue a direction requiring that it be marked with suitable, clearly worded and easily comprehensible warnings, in English, on the risks it may present, or that, prior to placing the product on the market, such specified steps are taken as are necessary to ensure its safety;
- for any product that could pose risks for certain persons (for example, children or the elderly), to issue a direction requiring that persons at risk be given warning of the risk in good time, and in an appropriate form, including the publication of special warnings;
- for any product that could be dangerous, issue a direction prohibiting the supply, offer to supply, or display, of the product pending the carrying out of safety evaluations, checks and controls necessary to establish the safety of the product;
- for any dangerous product, issue a direction prohibiting the placing of the product on the market;
- for any dangerous product already on the market, take all appropriate

steps, including if necessary issuing a direction to ensure the immediate withdrawal of the product from the marketplace, its recall from consumers, and its destruction in suitable conditions, and that consumers are alerted to the risks presented to the product.

Failure to comply with a direction by, or a request from, the NCA under the GPSR constitutes an offence.

Where the NCA decides to take, whether with the agreement of a producer or distributor or otherwise, any measure or any action which is designed to prevent, restrict, or impose specific conditions on, the placing on the market or use of a product because it poses a serious risk, the NCA must immediately notify the European Commission of the decision through RAPEX.

The NCA can appoint authorised officers to ensure compliance with the GPSR and the Revised General Product Safety Directive. Authorised officers can, subject to certain limitations set out in the GPSR:

- enter, search, inspect, or secure for later inspection, any premises where a product is, or has been, manufactured, distributed, supplied or placed on the market, or where records relating to the product are kept. Private dwellings cannot be entered without a court warrant;
- require any person in charge of, or employed in, such premises to produce records or give information, and inspect and take copies of such records and information;
- remove and detain a product or records for further examination, or until the conclusion of any legal proceedings;
- require any person in charge of a premises, or any person who appears to be in possession of a product, or any article or substance used in the manufacture of a product, to supply sufficient samples for testing, examination or analysis;
- cause any product or any article or substance used in the manufacture of a product found at a premises, which appears to the officer to have caused or to be likely to cause danger to safety or health, to be dismantled or subjected to any process or test;
- in relation to any product or any article or substance used in the manufacture of a product found at a premises, take possession of it and detain it for so long as is necessary to examine it, to ensure that it is not tampered with before any examination, or to ensure that it is available for use as evidence in any proceedings;
- require any person to afford such facilities and assistance within their control or responsibilities as are reasonably necessary to enable the authorised officer to exercise any of their powers under the GPSR; and
- examine any procedure connected with the manufacture of a product.

It is an offence for a person to obstruct or interfere with an authorised officer in the exercise of their powers, or to fail to comply with a request from an authorised officer, or to make a false or misleading statement to an authorised officer.

The NCA can also apply to the District Court under the GPSR for an order for the forfeiture of any product (to which the GPSR apply) on the grounds that the product is a dangerous product. Any product that is the subject of a forfeiture order may be seized by an authorised officer.

8. VOLUNTARY CONDUCT

8.1 Are there regulations pertaining to the voluntary conduct of a product repair or recall by a supplier?

No. However, if the product has been the subject of a notification to the NCA, it is advisable to agree any voluntary repair action with the NCA.

9. EMERGING ISSUES AND LAW REFORM

9.1 Are there important developing and emerging issues or trends in product liability law in your country?

We do not perceive there to be any major developing or emerging issues or trends in product liability law in Ireland, however, the monetary jurisdictions of the Irish courts were revised on 3 February 2014. The Circuit Court's jurisdiction has been raised from just over €38,000 to €75,000 generally, and €60,000 for personal injuries claims. Claims are generally progressed faster in the Circuit Court than in the High Court. It remains to be seen whether these revised monetary jurisdictions will lead to an increase in the number of product liability cases (that would have traditionally been brought in the High Court) being brought in the Circuit Court.

9.2 Please describe any proposed important law reform in the area of product liability in your country.

We are not aware of any proposed important law reforms in the area of product liability which are specific to Ireland. However, at EU level, on 13 February 2013, the European Commission adopted a product safety and market surveillance package of measures, including a proposal for a regulation on consumer products safety. Once finalised, this regulation will be directly binding on all EU member states, including Ireland. This new regulation will repeal the Revised General Product Safety Directive. The proposed measures are currently under consideration by the European Parliament and the Council, and the new legislation is expected to come into effect in 2015.

The proposals adopted by the European Commission for a regulation on medical devices, and a regulation on *in vitro* diagnostic medical devices, continue to be considered, with the next step in the legislative process being negotiation with the European Council and EU member states. Once adopted, these regulations are intended to replace Directive 90/385/EEC regarding active implantable medical devices, Directive 93/42/EEC regarding general medical devices, and Directive 98/79 EC regarding *in vitro* diagnostic medical devices. The reforms envisaged by these regulations are likely to be wide ranging, and will overhaul certification by notified bodies, as well as traceability, monitoring and inspection. While overall reform is underway, the European Commission has, in the meantime, published Regulation 920/2013/EU on the designation and supervision of notified bodies, and a Recommendation (2013/473/EU) on audits and assessments performed by notified bodies in the field of medical devices, as part of its overall objective to improve patient safety in this area.

10. REGULATORY WEBSITES/INFORMATION

10.1 Please identify any useful regulatory references relating to product liability law in your country, for example, a product safety/consumer law website maintained by the main regulator.

- National Consumer Agency – *www.consumerhelp.ie/product-safety*
- Food Safety Authority of Ireland – *www.fsai.ie*
- Department of Agriculture, Food and the Marine – *www.agriculture.gov.ie*
- Irish Medicines Board – *www.imb.ie*

South Korea

Kim & Chang Sung Jin Kim, Jay J. Kim & Brian C. Oh

1. LIABILITY

1.1 What are the principal sources of law and regulation relating to product liability?

This is the Product Liability Act (PLA) in Korea, effective as of 1 July 2002.

Prior to the PLA, general tort principles under the Korea Civil Code (KCC) governed claims caused by defective products, based on a negligence theory. Thus, claimants had to prove the existence of a defect, causation, damages and negligence (or rarely, intent) by the manufacturer. This was a very high burden of proof for most, and the PLA was enacted to establish strict liability for defective consumer products causing injury, removing negligence as a legal requirement.

1.2 What is required to establish causation under the most common causes of action available?

The PLA does not define how causation should be established. The recent trend at Korean courts has leaned towards easing the burden of proof for causation.

For instance, the Korean Supreme Court has held that for certain mass-produced products, if the injured party can prove that the harm occurred during normal use of the product and the injury would not typically occur without negligence, a court may infer that a defect exists in the product (and that this defect caused the harm) (Decisions 2003 Da 16771 & 98 Da 15934). The manufacturer may defend itself by proving that the injury had a different cause.

1.3 Is strict liability available and, if so, in what circumstances?

Yes, under the PLA. Thus, this applies to all product liability claims in Korea.

1.4 Are guarantees or warranties as to quality implied by law?

Yes. The KCC provides a statutory warranty that a sold product is not defective, unless the buyer was or should have been aware of the defect. It is generally agreed that the above 'defect' refers to a fault reducing the product's quality or efficiency below generally expected standards (different from the PLA defect denoting risk of injury).

The above liability is strict and the seller's negligence or intent is not necessary.

As for remedies, if the defect frustrates the purpose of the contract, the buyer can rescind or terminate the contract and/or claim damages. If the defect does not rise to the above level, the buyer can seek damages or a replacement.

1.5 How is a product 'defect' defined?

The PLA defines a 'defect' as any defect in the manufacturing process, design, or indication meeting the below criteria *or* lacking the level of safety reasonably expected for the product.

(i) Defect in manufacturing: This refers to a product manufactured differently from the intended design, resulting in reduced safety. Whether the manufacturer exercised due care in the manufacturing process is irrelevant, for as long as the manufacturing was not in accordance with the design, it will be deemed a manufacturing defect.

(ii) Defect in design: This refers to a product that is unsafe because the manufacturer failed to adopt a feasible alternative design that could have avoided or reduced the harm or risk.

(iii) Defect in warning: This refers to a failure by the manufacturer to properly explain, instruct, warn, or otherwise reasonably indicate the risk posed by the product which could have avoided or reduced the harm or risk.

1.6 Who in the supply chain has obligations or duties for defective products? What obligations or duties do they owe and to whom?

Under the PLA, the manufacturer bears the responsibility for defective products. Manufacturers are defined as those engaged in the business of manufacturing (including processing, formulating, or assembling) or importing a product.

If the manufacturer's identity is unknown, the supplier (eg, by sale or lease) is liable under the PLA, unless the supplier reveals to the injured party the identity of the manufacturer or its own supplier within a reasonable time frame. The liabilities for a defective product include damages for death, personal injury, or property damage (other than the defective product itself) suffered by any consumer (including corporations).

1.7 By what means can a supplier limit their liability for defective products?

In general, any agreement limiting the liability for defective products is void under the PLA. However, an exception applies for products supplied exclusively to one consumer for use in business, in which case the parties may agree to limit the recoverable damages.

1.8 Are there particular goods or services which have specific obligations or duties attached to them?

No.

2. DEFENCES

2.1 What are the possible defences to a product liability claim?

Improper use of the product deviating from 'normal usage' is a defence, and can remove the causation between the defect and claimed injury.

The PLA also provides the below exemptions for manufacturers:

(i) if the alleged defect could not have been discovered by the available scientific or technological standards at the time of supply (ie, the 'state of the art' defence);
(ii) if the manufacturer did not supply the product;
(iii) if the alleged defect was caused by the manufacturer's compliance with the mandatory standards set forth by laws at the time of supply; or
(iv) for suppliers of raw materials, parts, or components, if the alleged defect was due to the customer's specifications/instructions.

Any of the above would serve as an affirmative defence. However, exemptions (i), (iii), and (iv) would not apply if the manufacturer knew or should have known about the existence of the alleged defect after supplying the product, but still failed to take proper action to prevent damages.

2.2 Is there a limit on the time in which proceedings may be brought (limitations and repose)?

The statute of limitations bars any claim not filed within three years of the claimant's awareness of both the harm and the identity of the responsible party, or within 10 years of the product delivery date, whichever is earlier. However, if the harm is a latent disease whose symptoms do not appear immediately, the 10-year period applies, starting as of the discovery of the damage.

3. LITIGATION OF PRODUCT LIABILITY DISPUTES

3.1 In which courts are product liability proceedings brought?

District Courts having competent jurisdiction (eg, according to the defendant's location or place of the tortious act).

3.2 How are proceedings commenced?

Litigation commences with the filing of a complaint and payment of a stamp tax. The complaint should specify the defendant, claim, grounds for the claim and, optionally, a statement of jurisdiction. Evidence supporting the claim is not required at the time of filing, but usual practice is to submit at least the basic evidence. The court then serves a copy to the defendant, who then has 30 days to submit a response.

3.3 Are disputed issues decided by a judge or a jury?

Judges.

3.4 Who has the burden of proof and to what standard?

The plaintiff bears the burden of proving the existence of a defect, causation and resulting damages. Although the standard of proof is not codified, the general principle is preponderance of the evidence. Korean courts, however, tend to be lenient when it comes to proving the existence of a defect, recognising that the technical and complex nature of a defect makes it inherently difficult to prove for most individual plaintiffs.

3.5 How is evidence given in proceedings and are witnesses cross-examined?

The parties may present and examine witnesses and submit their statements during the court hearings. Following direct examination of a party's witness, opposing counsel will be given an opportunity to cross-examine. The cross-examination questions must be prepared in writing, and submitted to the court at the time of cross-examination.

Documentary evidence may be submitted at or between hearings, and an opposing party may respond through written rebuttal submissions. When the admissibility of certain documentary evidence is contested, the presenting party may request witness testimony to prove its admissibility.

3.6 Are the parties able to rely on expert opinion evidence and, if so, are there any special rules or procedures for expert opinion evidence?

The court, on its own initiative or at a party's request, may appoint experts to assist with technical issues. After an expert report or affidavit has been submitted, the court may order the expert to testify to clarify or supplement the written submission. There are no restrictions on the nature or extent of the proffered expert evidence and judges decide on its admissibility at their discretion.

The parties may also present evidence from their own experts in the form of an expert report or testimony, but the party-appointed expert may then be subjected to cross-examination in court by the opposing party.

3.7 Is pre-trial discovery permitted? If so, in what circumstances? If not, what other mechanisms, if any, are available for obtaining evidence from an party or a third party?

No, unless a risk exists of evidence being destroyed (or otherwise unavailable later). During litigation, a common discovery option is document production, whereby the petitioner asks the court to order the production of specified documents from the opposing or third parties. Witness testimony is another tool available for obtaining evidence from a third party.

3.8 Is there liability for spoliation of evidence/a remedy for destruction of or failure to preserve evidence (most relevantly, the product)?

No liability, aside from the court accepting the requesting party's arguments as true regarding the contents of the documents.

3.9 Is interlocutory or interim relief available prior to the full trial of a proceeding?

Not in most cases. They are allowed as exceptions only where absolutely necessary to preserve legal status, prevent immediate destruction of property, etc.

3.10 Can the winning party recover its costs?

Not meaningfully. The winning party can fully recover the stamp tax, service costs and witness costs, but the attorney fees are limited to minimal amounts.

3.11 What avenues of appeal are available?

As a matter of right, District Court decisions can be appealed to the High Court within two weeks of receiving the opinion. High Court decisions can be similarly appealed to the Supreme Court, but these can be summarily rejected if not raising genuine or novel issues of law.

4. CLASS ACTIONS/REPRESENTATIVE PROCEEDINGS

4.1 Is there a mechanism for class actions or representative proceedings, or coordinated proceedings for product liability claims? If so, what are the basic mechanics?

There is currently no such mechanism for multiple product liability claims in Korea.

5. LITIGATION FUNDING

5.1 Is litigation funding by third parties permissible in your country? If so, is it common?

There are no laws or regulations that specifically prohibit the funding of a lawsuit by a third party, and a Korean insurance company has recently started offering insurance to cover the costs of a general civil litigation.

5.2 Are contingency fee or 'no win no fee' arrangements permissible?

They are permissible, but a court may reduce the amount if deemed to be excessive and/or violate good faith or equity.

6. REMEDIES

6.1 What remedies are available to a party who successfully pursues a product liability claim?

Normally, only monetary compensation is available to consumers in product liability suits. However, under the Consumer Basic Act, consumer groups or public interest organisations may file a suit on behalf of consumers to seek injunctive relief against unlawful business activities. Further, the consumer may seek the replacement of the defective product as an alternative to damages under the KCC.

6.2 How are damages calculated/are there limitations on available damages?

Damages under the PLA include harm to human life, health and/or physical property (damages to the product itself are excluded). Further, the PLA itself does not define how damages are to be calculated, but only provides that the KCC will apply for any matters that are not specifically covered by the PLA.

In this regard, the KCC has two categories of damages for tortious acts: 'ordinary damages' and 'extraordinary damages.' Ordinary damages are those that would normally be expected as a result of the tortious act.

Extraordinary damages, which encompass all other damages that may arise from the tortious act, are available only to the extent that the parties could have reasonably foreseen them under the particular circumstances.

There are no caps on recoverable damages. Thus, significant awards are possible for claims involving serious bodily harm or death.

6.3 Are punitive or exemplary damages available and in what circumstances?

Punitive or exemplary damages are not available in Korea.

6.4 Is liability joint and several/how does apportionment of liability work, including where a partially responsible entity is not a party to the proceeding?

The PLA contains a joint and several liability provision. Specifically, the PLA imposes liability on any and all parties in the manufacturing chain of a product, to ensure compensation for injuries caused by a defective product. For example, the component parts manufacturer, the assembling manufacturer and the importer of the product would be jointly and severally liable to the injured.

Further, each joint tortfeasor is wholly liable to the injured and a ratio of liability exists only among the joint tortfeasors. According to established court precedents, the court is not required to state the ratio of negligence (liability) among the tortfeasors in a suit by the injured. The relative faults of each joint tortfeasor are to be determined in a separate indemnification or contribution suit among the joint tortfeasors.

7. ROLE OF REGULATORS

7.1 Please explain the role, responsibilities and powers of the regulators in your country which have jurisdiction over product liability issues.

The Korea Consumer Agency under the Fair Trade Commission conducts the following activities under the Framework Act on Consumers:

- testing and inspecting goods for quality, safety, environment-friendliness, etc, and surveying prices and other transaction terms to promote consumer rights and interests;
- collecting and furnishing information on international cooperation to promote consumer rights, safety and interests; and
- overseeing the settlement of complaints and remedies for damages suffered by consumers.

The Korean Agency for Technology & Standards under the Ministry of Trade, Industry & Energy conducts the following activities under the Quality Management & Safety Control of Industrial Products Act:

- providing public notifications of safety standards for product inspections;
- providing public notifications of labelling standards for safety or quality of industrial products, etc;
- demanding the submission of relevant data and related reports; and

- imposing/collecting administrative fines.

In addition, the Minister of Food & Drug Safety or other competent government officials (eg, city mayors or provincial governors) may remove dangerous drug or food products from the market.

7.2 Are there any mandatory reporting requirements related to product safety issues?

If a manufacturer learns of a 'serious defect' in the manufacture, design or labelling of a product that has injured or is likely to injure consumers or their property, the manufacturer must report the defect to the mayor or governor of the region where its headquarters are located. This duty to report applies downstream and is imposed on manufacturers, importers, suppliers, operators of 'large-scale stores' and, in some cases, manufacturers of product labels.

For foods, pharmaceuticals, and medical devices, the relevant regulations require the manufacturer to notify the MFDS or local government authorities (or both) of any defects, contaminations, etc, that may pose a public health risk.

7.3 Do the regulators have the power to:
(i) ban certain goods or services?
(ii) require a supplier to recall a product?
(iii) prescribe standards in respect of certain goods or services and require that the goods or services meet those standards?
(iv) require production of information without court process?
If so, broadly explain the circumstances in which the regulator can exercise the power and any penalties that apply if a supplier fails to comply.

The Consumer Basic Act

When goods supplied by a business pose risk to consumers, the Fair Trade Commission can seek the below measures from the heads of the appropriate central administrative agencies:

- where the business fails to take safety measures stipulated in other laws, the measures stipulated in such laws; and
- where the other laws do not prescribe safety criteria or standards, removal/destruction orders or administrative fines.

A mayor/regional governor can also issue an administrative fine and order a recall where a defect is likely to place consumers at risk.

The Framework Act on Product Safety

For industrial products subject to safety certification, a mayor/regional governor may order a sales ban, improvement, collection, or destruction of such products upon any violation of the safety certification.

The Korean Agency for Technology & Standards can also order recalls when a product has a defect or fails to meet safety standards.

Failure to comply with a corrective order, the sale, import, display, or storage of industrial products without the requisite safety certification mark, failure to report, etc., are all punishable by an administrative fine or could be subject to criminal penalty.

In addition to the above, there are several other laws covering specific products.

8. VOLUNTARY CONDUCT

8.1 Are there regulations pertaining to the voluntary conduct of a product repair or recall by a supplier?

The first steps in a voluntary recall are to determine whether the defect is safety-related and to identify the controlling law. Where there is no controlling law or provision, the Consumer Basic Act will apply as the default regulation. Next, the supplier must submit a defect report, if necessary, to the proper authorities. The laws generally impose a duty to submit a notification prior to a recall for serious defects, accidents, etc, and to file a corrective action plan. The government authority may accept the corrective action plan or request changes. Finally, a follow-up report must be submitted at a designated time, eg, six months later. Most voluntary recall requirements are similar to those of a non-voluntary recall.

9. EMERGING ISSUES AND LAW REFORM

9.1 Are there important developing and emerging issues or trends in product liability law in your country?

There has been a discernible movement towards an overhaul of the current Korean civil litigation system to allow the courts to render more effective remedies for collectives or classes of plaintiffs, ostensibly by benchmarking the US civil litigation system. For example, there have been legislative proposals to implement a class action system and a representative action system (discussed below), and to allow recovery of punitive (treble) damages.

A recent notable product liability decision is the Supreme Court's ruling in the Agent Orange litigation, rendered in July 2013. The Court found that Agent Orange (a defoliant used by US armed forces during the Vietnam war in 1960s) had a design defect and affirmed the lower court's ruling in favour of some of the Korean Vietnam War veterans allegedly having chloracne. This was the first court decision in the world that found liability against Agent Orange manufacturers and causation between Agent Orange and the veterans' diseases. However, the court also remanded the claims of some of the plaintiffs who had prevailed in the lower court, as well as affirming the lower court's dismissal of other plaintiffs, on the grounds that causation between the plaintiffs' purported exposure to Agent Orange and their diseases was not sufficiently proven.

9.2 Please describe any proposed important law reform in the area of product liability in your country.

Proposed Amendment to the Framework Act on Consumers – Introduction of Representative Action

According to the proposed amendment, if 50 or more consumers are harmed by a defective product, one or more such persons may file a representative action with the approval of the court. In addition, the court may conduct an *ex officio* investigation to collect more evidence if necessary, and where damages are difficult to calculate, tools such as sampling, averaging and statistical methodology may be utilised. In addition, the court's decision may be binding on other consumers who did not take part in the litigation (excluding those who opted out). This proposed amendment is designed to introduce a class action type suit similar to that of the US and, if passed, the liabilities of business entities may significantly increase.

Proposed Amendment to the Product Liability Act – Stipulation of Reduced Burden of Proof by Presumption of a Causal Relationship

This proposed amendment would stipulate the presumption of a causal relationship between the defect and damages. Meanwhile, the courts have already rendered decisions alleviating the claimant's burden of proof in product liability claims. Thus, the passage of the proposed amendment could mean further alleviation of the claimant's burden of proof in product liability claims, exposing manufacturers to an expanded scope of liability for their products.

Bill to Allow Class Action Litigation

Under this proposed Bill, a class action is described as a lawsuit filed by representative(s) in order to recover damages sustained by a large group of persons who share a common interest. The preamble of the bill specifies that the bill intends to expand the scope of class actions from securities cases to consumer disputes, environment pollution cases, disputes between small/medium-sized suppliers and large company buyers (ie, conglomerates), etc.

10. REGULATORY WEBSITES/INFORMATION

10.1 Please identify any useful regulatory references relating to product liability law in your country, for example, a product safety/consumer law website maintained by the main regulator.

- Institutions under Fair Trade Commission (Framework Act on Consumers)
  Korea Consumer Agency: *https://www.kca.go.kr/index_frame.jsp*
  Consumer Safety Center of Korea Consumer Agency: *https://www.ciss.or.kr/index_frame.jsp*
  1372 Consumer Safety Center: *http://ccn.go.kr/index.ccn*

- Institutions under the Ministry of Trade, Industry and Energy (Framework Act on Product Safety)
  Korean Agency for Technology and Standards: *www.kats.go.kr/*
  Product Safety Information Portal of Korean Agency for Technology and Standards: *www.safetykorea.kr/*
  Korea Products Safety Association: *www.ksafety.kr/*

- Automobile Performance Research Institute under Korea Transportation

Safety Authority under Ministry of Land, Infrastructure and Transport
(Automobile Management Act)
Auto Recall Center: *www.car.go.kr/*

Sweden

Advokatfirman NorelidHolm
Susanna Norelid, Christer A. Holm & Fredrik Seemann

1. LIABILITY

1.1 What are the principal sources of law and regulation relating to product liability?

The primary source of law relating to product liability in Sweden is the Product Liability Act (SFS 1992:18). A common feature of the Nordic legal systems is the relative importance of governmental preparatory works serving as interpretational extensions of statutory legislation. Thus, the government's proposal (1990/91:197) on product liability is an important source of legal reference for the Product Liability Act.

Given that the Product Liability Act is an implementation the EG Directives 85/374/EEG and 1999/34/EEG, these directives are also of importance for court interpretation of the Product Liability Act.

Swedish Supreme Court judgments, as well as Court of Appeal judgments and general legal writing (depending of their level of authoritativeness), are also relevant sources of law for product liability.

For damages and injuries caused by products under circumstances which fall outside the scope of the Product Liability Act, claims may be brought on general grounds of contractual or non-contractual liability. For claims based on non-contractual liability, the Tort Liability Act (SFS 1972:207) applies. Claims within the scope of the Product Liability Act may also be brought on general grounds of contractual or non-contractual liability, although this is rare given that strict liability applies for claims under the Product Liability Act.

1.2 What is required to establish causation under the most common causes of action available?

Section 1 of the Product Liability Act stipulates that damages are due for:

(a) bodily injury caused by a safety deficiency in a product; and

(b) damage on consumer property, if used for consumer purposes at the time when the damage occurs, caused by a safety deficiency in a product.

It follows from the provisions outlined above, that the causes of action under the Product Liability Act are rooted in product defects, and that the necessary causation is that between the safety deficiency and the suffered loss and/or injury, ie, that the safety deficiency in question has caused the damage. The main rule for establishing causation in Swedish tort law is that the claimant must *prove* the causation. This standard of proof also applies to product liability actions.

For claims brought under the Tort Liability Act, the necessary causation is that between the intention or negligence on part of the tortfeasor and the suffered loss and/or injury.

1.3 Is strict liability available and, if so, in what circumstances?

The Product Liability Act is based on the notion of strict liability. This means that a claimant does not need to establish negligence of any kind in order to successfully claim for damages under the Product Liability Act, and conversely that the absence of negligence cannot be relied upon as defence for the liable party.

1.4 Are guarantees or warranties as to quality implied by law?

Statutory provisions on implicit guarantees and warranty as to quality exists as part of Swedish consumer legislation, most notably the Consumer Sales Act (SFS 1990:932), and as to the general safety of supplied products as part of Swedish public law in the shape of the Product Safety Act (SFS 2004:451). However, neither of these statutes provisions apply within the realm of product liability as set out by the Product Liability Act.

Given that the concept of strict liability for damages and injuries caused by products arises from product defects, it may of course be argued that entities capable of being found liable under the Product Liability Act have to guarantee that their products are free from such defects.

1.5 How is a product 'defect' defined?

According to section 3 of the Product Liability Act, a product defect which causes liability is deemed present if the product in question is not as safe as can reasonably be expected. The safety of a product shall be assessed in accordance with its expected use and how it has been marketed, as well as the operating instructions, the time it was put into circulation and other relevant circumstances.

As is apparent by the statutory provision referenced above, the definition of the product defect is rather loose. The starting point for application of the definition emanates from the properties of the particular product, and its user's legitimate expectations on a product of that particular kind. The assessment of the degree of safety required for any product shall be carried out *objectively*, based on the safety that any user in general may reasonably expect – not on the claimant's expectations or the expectations of the consumer collective as a whole. Rather, all relevant circumstances in the case must be assessed in order to determine whether or not a product is as safe as can reasonably be expected.

Although it is not required by law, products defects are often characterised as either being design defects, manufacturing defects or instruction defects.

Design defects encompass defects arising out of the design or assembly of a particular product type. The defect is a consequence of the product not being designed and assembled in accordance with the prevailing technical and scientific standards for the product type. Consequently, design defects are usually found in each product of a manufacturing series.

Manufacturing defects, on the other hand, are defects on one-off products or one-off manufacturing series of a product type, meaning that the defect in question is usually explained by some temporary mishap such as faulty raw materials, mistakes in the manufacturing process or negligence at the control stage of the manufacturing process.

Instruction defects entail defects arising out of the fact that a product is sold or delivered unaccompanied by necessary instructions or accompanied by wrongful instructions. A product is also deemed as having an instruction defect if it has dangerous or hazardous properties while not being supplied with any warning about the potential hazards or without any instructions as to how to avoid potential hazards.

1.6 Who in the supply chain has obligations or duties for defective products? What obligations do they owe, and to whom?

The Product Liability Act does not set out any express duties or obligations for defective products. It does, however, expressly outline which entities may be held liable for losses or injuries suffered by individuals as a result of product defects.

Section 6 ss1 of the Product Liability Act stipulates that anyone who manufactures, grows or gathers a damaging product may be held liable for damages. An entity potentially liable for manufacturing is one which industrially or by means of craftsmanship produces a product or a component of a product. This may be done by processing materials and/or raw materials, as well as by further processing others' products. Anyone who assembles others' ready-made components may also be held liable as a manufacturer. The starting point for the assessment of liability of a particular manufacturer is whether or not that entity has taken any measures which affect the safety of the product.

An entity potentially liable for growing a product is anyone who grows plants, breeds animals, extracts minerals, etc.

Liability arising out of gathering refers to such activities as hunting, fishing and picking. As such, every 'manufacturer' in the supply chain may be held liable for damages.

According to section 6 ss2-3 of the Product Liability Act, liability is also imposed on anyone who has imported the damaging product to the European Economic Area in order to put it into circulation, as well as to anyone who imports a damaging product from a member state of the European Free Trade Association into the European Community.

The term 'importer' is not defined by the Product Liability Act. It is, however, accepted that the term 'importer' encompasses any Swedish reseller who purchases a product in its own name and has it brought into Sweden.

According to section 6 ss4 of the Product Liability Act, anyone who markets a damaging product under its own name, brand or other identifying characteristic, may also be held liable. For instance, this applies to any retailer who sells a product manufactured by someone else under its own name or brand. The deciding factor is whether the selling party affixes the product with its own identifying characteristic. Liability under this provision applies even if a liable manufacturer or importer can be identified as well.

The Product Liability Act section 7 states that a claim for damages may be lodged against *any* entity which has supplied or provided the defective product, if a liable entity according to section 6 cannot be identified. When applying section 7 as basis for liability, however, the presumably liable entity may free itself from liability if it can identify an entity liable under section 6 within one month from receipt of the claim.

It is important to note that claimants are entitled to turn to any of the potentially liable entities in order to claim for damages.

1.7 By what means can a supplier limit its liability for defective products?

Section 5 of the Product Liability Act expressly states that any contractual provisions which limit the liability set out by the act are null and void against claimants. However, potentially liable entities throughout the supply chain may contractually divide the final divisions of liability between themselves (see answer to question 6.4 below).

Outside the scope of the Product Liability Act, however, corporations are free to limit their liability for defective products between themselves so long as the limitation does not exclude liability for gross negligence or intentional acts.

1.8 Are there particular goods or services which have specific obligations or duties attached to them?

There are a number of legislative acts which regulate the provision of specific products and services, and which contain specific duties, obligations and rules on liability. Some notable examples are:

- The Railway Traffic Act (SFS 1985:193), which stipulates liability for the proprietor of a railway for any damage to goods or injury to individuals caused by the operation of the railway. This also applies if the damage or injury is caused by an employee or subcontractor of the railway proprietor.
- The Food Act (SFS 1971:511) which stipulates duties on, *inter alia*, food and beverage safety and labelling.
- The Medicinal Products Act (SFS 1992:85) which stipulates duties as to the safety and testing of medicinal drugs.
- The Chemical Products and Biotechnical Organisms Regulation (SFS 2008:245) stipulates duties regarding the labelling, handling and information about dangerous chemical products.
- The Aviation Act (SFS 2010:500) imposes strict liability upon the carrier for personal injury caused aboard and aircraft. The same applies with respect to damage to checked luggage (although not hand baggage), and with a few exceptions, also to transported goods.
- The Electricity Act (SFS 1997:857) imposes strict liability on the proprietor of a heavy current electricity installation for injuries and damage caused by the electric installation.
- The Toys Safety Act (SFS 2011:579) imposes duties as to, *inter alia*,

general safety and mandatory CE-labelling of all toys marketed in Sweden.

2. DEFENCES

2.1 What are the possible defences to a product liability claim?

There are three main lines of defence which can be raised when facing a product liability claim. The first is, of course, to counter-claim that some prerequisite circumstance in accordance to section 1-3 of the Product Liability Act is not fulfilled. This could, for instance, be that the product should be deemed to have a safety deficiency because it was used contrary to clear instructions. For claims brought under the Tort Liability Act, an additional defence would be to deny negligence on part of the respondent.

Secondly, section 8 of the Product Liability Act stipulates four expressly defined defences. As such, a potentially liable entity cannot be held liable if it proves that it did not put the product in question into circulation, or even if it did, that the entity did not put the product into circulation within the scope of its business activities. Furthermore, an entity cannot be held liable if it proves that the alleged product defect was not present at the time when the entity put the product into circulation. Neither can an entity be held liable if the alleged product defect is caused by compliance with mandatory requirements issued by public authorities. A respondent entity can also not be held liable if it proves that the alleged product defect could not be discovered by the scientific and technological knowledge available at the time when the product was put into circulation (so-called state-of-the-art defence).

Finally, section 10 of the Product Liability Act states that the amount of damages may be reduced or forfeited if the claimant has negligently or knowingly contributed to the suffered injury or damage.

2.2 Is there a time limit on the time in which proceedings may be brought (limitations and repose)?

Section 12 of the Product Liability Act states that an action for damages must be lodged at a court of law within three years from the date on which the claimant became aware or should have become aware that he or she had a valid claim. However, an action for damages must always be lodged at a court of law within 10 years from the date on which the liable entity put the product in question into circulation. It the claimant fails to adhere to these provisions, he or she loses the right to the claim at hand.

For actions based on non-contractual grounds, the Statute of Limitations Act (SFS 1981:130) sets out a time bar which applies when 10 years have passed after the valid claim for damages arose. However, the time bar can be discontinued by means of a written notification at any point within the 10-year period. If this is done, a new 10-year period begins.

3. LITIGATION OF PRODUCT LIABILITY DISPUTES

3.1 In which courts are product liability proceedings brought?

Product liability proceedings are handled by the civil courts. The first instance of such proceedings is the district court. The main rule according to the Swedish Code of Judicial Procedure (SFS 1942:740) is that the claim shall be lodged at the competent district court in the city or county where the respondent is domiciled. If the claimed amount does not surpass SEK22,200, a consumer claimant may lodge the action at the competent district court in the city or county where the claimant is domiciled.

3.2 How are proceedings commenced?

Proceedings are commenced when the claimant lodges an action at the competent district court.

3.3 Are disputed issues decided by a judge or jury?

Product liability disputes are decided by judges. Normally, a case will be decided by three judges in the district court, by three or four judges in the Court of Appeal, and by five judges in the Supreme Court. If the parties agree thereto, or if the claimed amount is less than SEK22,400, a case may be decided by a sole judge in the district court.

3.4 Who has the burden of proof and to what standard?

The main rule is that the claimant has the burden of proof for all factual circumstances which are required to establish liability on part of the respondent. The standard of proof is that the claimant must be able to *prove* all essential elements of his or her claim. This standard of proof cannot be precisely ascertained, but it is generally accepted that proving requires less than proving beyond reasonable doubt (ie, standard for proof in criminal law), but that proving requires more than establishing mere likeliness or probability.

However, there are exceptions to the main rule in cases where a claimant may be faced with considerable difficulties in proving causation. In an authoritative judgment (NJA 1982 s. 421) issued before the entry into force of the Product Liability Act, the Supreme Court stated that the standard of proof is to be lowered when establishing causation in complex product liability claims where there is more than one possible explanation for the occurred damage and where proving causation is not possible or practical. The applicable standard of proof for the claimant in such cases is that the claimed causation must be: (a) considerably more likely than the causation claimed by the respondent; and (b) likely in and of itself.

The lowered standard of proof for establishing causation in product liability claims is generally accepted as applicable law to this day. It is important to note, however, that the court will decide if the lowered standard of proof is to be applied or not based on the facts and circumstances of the individual case.

3.5 How is evidence given in proceedings and are witnesses cross-examined?

A party wishing to rely on certain documentary or oral evidence must invoke the evidence, as well as to specify what specific circumstances the invoked evidence is supposed to prove. This is first done prior to the main hearing of the case. During the main hearing before the court, the party must invoke the evidence once more. In the case of documentary evidence, it is common that relevant excerpts are read out loud before the court. Witnesses are cross-examined.

3.6 Are the parties able to rely on expert opinion evidence and, if so, are there any special rules or procedures for expert opinion evidence?

The parties are allowed to invoke expert opinion evidence. The procedure for relying on expert evidence essentially corresponds to invoking other witnesses, with the notable exception that experts' opinions may not only be presented by means or examination at the main hearing, but also that such opinions may be presented in the shape of a written statement by the expert.

3.7 Is pre-trial discovery permitted? If so, in what circumstances? If not, what other mechanisms, if any, are available for obtaining evidence from a party or third party?

The Swedish Code of Judicial Procedure does not recognise a discovery procedure. According to chapter 38, section 2 of the Swedish Code of Judicial Procedure, however, a party can request a motion for the court to order the other party, or a third party, to present certain documentation. In order to successfully present such a motion, the requesting party must be able to clearly identify what piece of evidence it seeks to obtain. The seeking party must also be able to specify what it wishes to prove by the sought-after evidence, as well as to present convincing reasons as to why the sought-after evidence is of importance to the party's plea.

3.8 Is there liability for spoliation of evidence/a remedy for destruction of or failure to preserve evidence (most relevantly, the product)?

There is no liability or remedy for spoliation, destruction or failure to preserve evidence in Swedish law.

3.9 Is interlocutory or interim relief available prior to the full trial of a proceeding?

Interim relief within the Swedish Code of Judicial Procedure takes shape as a provisional safeguard for the execution of a final judgment. In the context of a product liability claim, the claimant may lodge an action for interim relief in accordance with chapter 15, section 1 of the Swedish Code of Judicial Procedure. In order for the court to grant such relief, the claimant must present probable cause for a monetary claim, which is or may become subject to proceedings, as well as that it can be expected that the other party will abscond, withdraw assets or otherwise avoid paying the debt. Such an action may be lodged before or during a trial. According to chapter 15, section 6 of the Swedish Code of Judicial Procedure, the claimant will normally be required to furnish collateral for any damage which the claim for interim relief may cause the respondent. If the court grants interim relief, the claimant must lodge his action within one month of the court's decision if he or she has not already done so.

According to chapter 17, section 5 of the Swedish Code of Judicial Procedure, the court may also give an interlocutory judgment regarding a substantive but isolated issue during a judicial proceeding. The purpose of interlocutory judgments is to limit legal costs in complex cases. A typical example of a situation where an interlocutory judgment may be issued within the realm of product liability procedures would be a case relying heavily on complex technical considerations, but where the respondent makes it probable that the claimant's action is time barred. In this circumstance, the court may decide to try the time bar-defence in isolation before the rest of the case, since the claimant will likely drop the action if the court indeed finds the claim to be time barred.

3.10 Can the winning party recover its costs?

Swedish judicial procedure applies 'the English rule', meaning that the losing party is normally ordered to pay the winning party's legal fees and expenses. However, the court may examine the winning party's claimed costs and fees if the losing party does not accept the claimed amount when presented with the bill of costs at the end of the main hearing.

If the claimed amount does not exceed SEK22,200, compensation for legal costs may not exceed one hour of legal counselling, the court application fee, travel and subsistence for the winning party and its legal representative for appearing in court, as well as costs for witness testimonies and translation of documents.

3.11 What avenues of appeal are available?

The district court judgment may be appealed to the competent Court of Appeal, and the Court of Appeal's judgment may in turn be appealed to the Supreme Court. To bring a case before the Court of Appeal or the Supreme Court, the appellant needs to apply for a review permit. The Court of Appeal will normally grant a review permit if there is reason to believe that the district court's judgment requires review or scrutiny, if there is reason to believe that the Court of Appeal would arrive at a different conclusion than that of the district court, or if there is a need of precedent.

Review permits in the Supreme Court are only granted if a Supreme Court judgment could provide guidance as to how other similar cases are to be adjudicated.

4. CLASS ACTIONS/REPRESENTATIVE PROCEEDINGS

4.1 Is there a mechanism for class actions or representative proceedings, or coordinated proceedings for product liability claims? If so, what are the basic mechanics?

Swedish law has introduced the possibility of bringing class actions under the Class Action Act (2002:599). Such actions may be brought by representative bodies such as trade unions, consumer organisations, government authorities and non-governmental organisations.

Such actions are open to any self-defined class of consumers or corporations which share a common claim. The Class Action Act is based upon an 'opt-in' mechanism: to enter as a member into a class, an individual must register with the class within a certain time.

Only the group representative is deemed as the claimant party. The class members in a class action suit are not deemed as parties in the proceedings, although the judgment does carry legal force for all members of the class.

5. LITIGATION FUNDING

5.1 Is litigation funding by third parties permissible in your country? If so, is it common?

Third party funding is permissible in Sweden. It is also very common since insurance companies will often fund the parties' legal costs and expenses throughout the proceedings, as normal home insurance policies and business insurance policies contain coverage for legal fees for certain types of litigation.

5.2 Are contingency fee or 'no win no fee' arrangements permissible?

There are no legal restrictions towards applying contingency fees or 'no win no fee' arrangements in Sweden. However, members of the Swedish Bar Association are generally prohibited from entering into such fee arrangements in accordance with the Code of Professional Conduct for Members of the Swedish Bar Association. The reason for this is that such fee arrangements are considered to intrude on the rule that an attorney's fee should be reasonable, as well as that such arrangements evade the principle of an attorney refraining from all financial involvements with their clients.

An important exception to this main rule applies to class actions. In such cases, the attorney may share the risk of litigation by means of risk agreements with the group representative. According to section 38 of the Class Action Act, the attorney and the group representative may enter into an agreement whereby the claimed fees are reduced or voided, and conversely that the fee is increased if the case is won. However, percentage based commissions for any successfully claimed monies are not allowed. Furthermore, the agreement has to be made out in writing, and it may only be enforced against the group members with the prior consent of the court which handles the case. According to section 39 of the Class Action Act, the court shall assess the risk agreement with basis in a 'normal fee' of the attorney, and then take into account how the risk agreement deviates from the normal fee if the case is won or lost in full. The court must also assess the validity of the agreement with basis in the complexity of the case and the financial risk assumed by the attorney. As such, it may be fully permitted in some cases to agree on doubled or tripled fees compared with the normal fee, while agreements in less complex or risky cases may be assessed more conservatively by the courts.

6. REMEDIES

6.1 What remedies are available to a party who successfully pursues a claim?

The remedy for a successful product liability claim will be compensatory damages for bodily injury, psychological injury, pain and suffering, loss of income and damage to property (other than to the defective product itself). This applies both to claims lodged in accordance with the Product Liability Act, as well to claims lodged on general non-contractual grounds. According to section 9 of the Product Liability Act, a deductible of SEK3,500 applies to all awards for damages under the Act.

6.2 How are damages calculated/are there limitations on available damages?

The general principle for calculating damages under Swedish law is that the damages shall put the claimant in the same financial situation as before the damaging event occurred. If the suffered injury and/or damage cannot be sufficiently ascertained by bringing forth evidence, the courts may appreciate the damages to a reasonable amount in accordance with chapter 35, section 5 of the Swedish Code of Judicial Procedure.

There is no legal limitation on the amount of damages which may be adjudicated, although it should be mentioned that Swedish courts have traditionally been rather conservative with respect to awarding large amounts as damages.

6.3 Are punitive or exemplary damages available and in what circumstances?

Swedish law does not recognise the awarding of punitive or exemplary damages.

6.4 Is liability joint and several/how does appointment of liability work, including where a partially responsible entity is not a party to the proceeding?

As outlined in the answer to question 1.6 above, several parties may be held liable for the same injury and/or damage caused by a defective product. In such cases, it follows from the general principle set out by chapter 6, section 4 of the Tort Liability Act that the responsible parties are jointly and severally liable. The claimant may therefore claim for full payment against any and all liable parties.

There is no express regulation on how to finally divide and settle liability for damages between several liable entities. In practice, however, entities which are jointly and severally liable for a product liability claim will often be intertwined in contractual relationships between each other. If a contract contains provisions on how to settle such situations, the contract will apply. If this is not the case, or if there is no contractual relationship between the liable entities, the general principle is that the damages shall be divided between them in accordance to what is reasonable. The decisive factors for assessing what is reasonable within the scope of a product liability claim will likely be which party had the greatest possibility to control the manufacturing of the product and which party could best assess the risks associated with the product.

The principle applies regardless of whether a partially responsible entity is party to the main proceedings or not. If the partially responsible entity is not party to the main proceedings, however, the party which is held liable in the proceedings against the claimant will have to seek relief against the other party by way of recourse.

7. ROLE OF REGULATORS

7.1 Please explain the role, responsibilities and powers of the regulators in your country which have jurisdiction over product liability issues.

The main governmental body exercising authority over product liability issues is the Swedish Consumer Ombudsman. The role of the Swedish Consumer Ombudsman with respect to product liability issues is to supervise compliance with the Product Safety Act.

If an entity which has sold a dangerous product does not voluntarily comply with the Product Safety Act, the Swedish Consumer Ombudsman may order that entity to do so under penalty. The Swedish Consumer Ombudsman may also order the liable entity to furnish its products with warning labels. The Ombudsman is also entitled to obtain access to areas, premises and other spaces where products are dealt with.

If it is found that a liable entity has breached the Product Safety Act intentionally or negligently, the Swedish Consumer Ombudsman may also lodge an action for payment of administrative fines at the administrative courts. Such fines may range from SEK5,000 to SEK5 million.

7.2 Are there any mandatory reporting requirements related to product safety issues?

According to the section 22 of the Product Safety Act, entities are required to supply the competent governmental authority (most often the Swedish Consumer Ombudsman) with information immediately in order to eliminate discovered risks related to provided products.

7.3 Do the regulators have the power to:

(i) ban certain goods or services?

Yes, according to sections 27-28 of the Product Safety Act, the competent governmental authority may issue interim or permanent bans on specific products supplied by one or more specific entities if the governmental authority finds the product in question to be dangerous or otherwise deems it necessary to issue the ban in order to achieve compliance with the Product Safety Act. Such bans will normally be issued under penalty. However, the entity subjected to an interim or permanent ban may appeal the governmental authority's decision in the administrative courts.

(ii) require a supplier to recall a product?

Yes, according to section 27 of the Product Safety Act, the competent governmental authority may require a supplier (meaning any entity which has in some way handled or concerned itself with the product) to recall products, if it is found that the product in question is dangerous or if it is deemed otherwise necessary in order to achieve compliance with the Product Safety Act. Such orders will normally be issued under penalty. However, the entity subjected to an interim or permanent ban may appeal the governmental authority's decision to the administrative courts.

(iii) prescribe standards in respect of certain goods or services and require that the goods or services meet those standards?

Applicable product safety standards are usually issued on an international level, either by means of European standards as published in the Official Journal of the European Union, as well as through the International Organization for Standardization. There are a few Swedish organs which issue national standards. The most notable of these is the Swedish Standards Institute. Standards are not binding, and entities providing products may use whatever technical specifications they want in order to show that their products are safe. However, since sections 11-12 of the Product Safety Act set out a presumption that products which comply with European or Swedish standards are safe, such standards will, in practice, be influential upon the competent governmental authorities' assessments as to any given product's compliance with the Product Safety Act.

(iv) require production of information without court process?

Section 13 of the Product Safety Act requires suppliers of products and services to provide necessary information for consumers to be able to assess and protect themselves against risks associated with any given product or service. If suppliers do not voluntarily comply with this provision, the Swedish Consumer's Ombudsman may order it to do so under penalty in accordance with section 27 and 31 of the Product Safety Act. Court proceedings are not prerequisite for such orders.

8. VOLUNTARY CONDUCT

8.1 Are there regulations pertaining to the voluntary conduct of a product repair or recall by a supplier?

There are no regulations pertaining to the *voluntary* conduct of a product repair or recall by a supplier. Sections 15-19 of the Product Safety Act do, however, contain provisions as to *mandatory* actions to be taken by an entity which has supplied dangerous products. In such situations, the supplier is required to immediately recall the affected products from distributors and consumers. The recall or repair must be offered on terms which the owners of the affected products can reasonably be expected to accept.

9. EMERGING ISSUES AND LAW REFORM

9.1 Are there important developing and emerging issues or trends in product liability law in your country?

Swedish product liability law is at a very mature stage. Since the adoption of the Product Liability Act in 1992, there has been little legal development within the scope of the legislation. Outside of the consumer area, no legislative intent has been shown. If, and to the extent that new issues within the realm of product liability arise, it can be expected that such developments will come from Supreme Court precedent.

9.2 Please describe any proposed important law reform in the area of product liability in your country.

At the moment, there is no proposed product liability law reform in Sweden.

10. REGULATORY WEBSITES/INFORMATION

10.1 Please identify any useful regulatory references relating to product liability law in your country, for example, a product safety/ consumer law website maintained by the main regulator.

As stated above, the main regulator for product safety and consumer issues is the Swedish Consumer Ombudsman. Its website is available in English at: *www.konsumentverket.se/otherlanguages/English/Product-safety/.*

An unofficial government translation of the Product Safety Act can be found at: *www.government.se/content/1/c6/03/34/49/3baa13c6.pdf.*

Switzerland

Walder Wyss Stefano Codoni & Dieter Hofmann

1. LIABILITY

1.1 What are the principal sources of law and regulation relating to product liability?

In Switzerland there are three main sources of private law relating to product liability, ie, the Product Liability Act (PLA), general tort law and contract law.

Furthermore special statutes regulating specific kinds of products, industry or activities may contain explicit product liability provisions that can serve as an additional basis for a claim in damages.

In the following we will briefly describe the main features of the three principal causes of action for product liability. Specific aspects of the three causes of action will then be referred to in the next sections 1.2 to 1.7.

According to Article 1 PLA the producer is liable if a defective product causes either death or injury to a person or damage to, or destruction of, goods which are usually intended for private use or mainly used privately by the person who suffers the damage. In contrast the damage caused to the defective product itself is not caught by the PLA liability. As it will be explained in the next sections the definition of 'producer' is very broad and the liability is strict, ie, not fault-based. Generally the PLA, which came into force on 1 January, 1994, follows the provisions of the EEC Directive 85/374 on product liability.

General tort law provides for a fault-based liability of any person who unlawfully causes damages to another (Articles 41 *et seq.* of the Swiss Code of Obligations (CO)). Particularly relevant in the product liability cases is Article 55 CO, which provides for the liability for employees and other auxiliary persons. According to this provision, a principal, eg, a company, is liable for damages caused by its employees or other auxiliary persons in the course of their employment or business. Only a limited number of defences are available to the principal (see answer 2.1 below on this).

Under contract law damages may be recovered based on the provisions on general contractual liability (Article 97 *et seq.* CO) or on special contractual provisions, in particular warranty provisions relating to the sale and purchase contract (Article 197 *et seq.* CO). One of the main requirements for a contractual liability is the existence of a contractual relationship between the damaged person and the defendant. Because of this requirement the party claiming damages generally has therefore only a claim against the last person in the supply chain, ie, the person who sold him the defective goods.

If the requirements of more than one cause of action are met, the claim in damages under one of them runs concurrently with the claim under the others. The claimant can therefore rely on one or more of them at the same time.

1.2 What is required to establish causation under the most common causes of action available?

As a general principle under Swiss law, in order to establish liability, the claimant seeking relief has to prove the existence of a so-called 'adequate causation link' between the defect of the product and the injury or damage. According to case law, a defect is deemed an adequate causation for an injury or damage if it, in accordance with every day experience and the usual course of events, is suitable to cause such injury or damage. Therefore the causation link must be a qualified one and not merely the natural link between cause and effect.

The same concept of causation link applies in all three main causes of action set out above, including the PLA.

1.3 Is strict liability available and, if so, in what circumstances?

The PLA provides for a strict liability regime and therefore the producer is liable even if he did not act negligently or with intent.

In contrast, in principle, liability under tort law is fault-based and the claimant has to prove that the defendant acted negligently or with intent. As an exception Article 55 CO (ie, the provision on which liability for auxiliary persons is based and that was referred to above) provides for a (partially) strict liability. The principal can avoid his liability if he proves that he has taken all precautions appropriate under the circumstances in order to prevent damage or that the damage would have occurred in any case despite the taking of such measures. Generally, careful selecting, instructing and supervising of the auxiliary persons are regarded as the required measures.

Liability under contract law is fault-based, too. In this respect it is worthwhile noting that, contrary to the general position under tort law, contract law provides for a reversal of the burden of proof. As a consequence fault is presumed and it is for the defendant to prove that he did not act negligently or intentionally. Further as an exception, Article 208 (2) CO (a provision governing the sale and purchase contract) provides explicitly for strict liability of the seller for 'direct damages' whereas only in the case of negligence or wilful intent of the seller, the purchaser is also entitled to 'further damages'. The law does not provide for a definition of the terms 'direct damages' and 'further damages' and the opinions of commentators partially differ on this. Generally the remoteness of the damage from the cause (length of the causation link) is regarded as one of the decisive criteria. It is often argued that the damage caused by third parties claims against the purchaser or loss of profit are to be regarded as 'further damages' and must therefore be refunded only in the case of fault of the seller.

1.4 Are guarantees or warranties as to quality implied by law?

With respect to strict liability under the PLA, as mentioned, the manufacturer, importer or supplier is liable if the product is defective. For a definition of defective see the next answer. These parties therefore impliedly 'warrant' that the products they put into circulation are not defective.

As far as the purchase contract is concerned, there is an implied sellers' warranty that the goods sold are free from physical or legal defects which eliminate or substantially impair their value or the use for which such goods were intended (Article 197 CO). Further the seller warrants that the goods sold contain the features promised by him. In this latter case it is not necessary that the defect substantially reduces the value of the goods or fitness for their intended use and it is sufficient that the purchaser relied on such features when he decided to enter into the contract.

1.5 How is a product 'defect' defined?

According to Article 4 (1) PLA a product is defective if it does not provide the safety that a person is entitled to expect taking into consideration all circumstances. The law mentions as examples of such circumstances: how the product is presented to the public; the use that one reasonably may expect from such product; and the date on which the product was put into circulation.

Beside manufacturing defects, a product defect within the meaning of the law may also result from the lack of sufficient and appropriate information on how to use it.

The PLA specifies that a product cannot *per se* be regarded as defective simply because a better and safer product has been later put on the market.

1.6 Who in the supply chain has obligations or duties for defective products? What obligations or duties do they owe and to whom?

Article 2 PLA provides a definition of the 'producer' that may be liable under the Act. The definition is broad and includes the following:

- the manufacturer of the finished product;
- the manufacturer of a component part as well as the producer of any raw material;
- any person who, by putting his name, trademark or other distinguishing sign on the product presents himself as its producer;
- any person importing the product for sale, hire, leasing or any form of distribution in the course of his business into Switzerland.

If the producer as defined above cannot be identified, each supplier is deemed a producer and is subsidiarily liable unless he discloses the identity of the producer or the person who supplied him with the product and, if applicable, the importer upon request of the injured person within a reasonable period of time.

All parties that fall within the scope of the definition of 'producer' are jointly and severally liable towards the injured person.

With respect to an action in tort or based on contract it is irrelevant if the defendant is or is not a producer. Whether a person or a company is liable will only depend on whether the relevant requirements under the respective cause of action are met. One of these requirements under contractual liability law is the existence of a contractual relationship between the injured or damaged party and the defendant. Therefore, in principle, only the last party in the supply chain, ie, the one who sold the goods to the injured or damaged person, could be liable under contract law.

1.7 By what means can suppliers limit their liability for defective products?

Pursuant to Article 8 PLA any contractual provision limiting or excluding the liability based on the PLA to the detriment of the damaged or injured party is null and void. Since no limitation is available the supplier will have to identify other ways to reduce the exposure to the liability risks, such as insurance coverage or special indemnities from its own suppliers.

With respect to other causes of action (contract, general tort law) a contractual provision which excludes liability for unlawful intent or gross negligence would also be null and void. Therefore liability can be excluded on the basis of an agreement only in the cases of simple negligence. Furthermore, the general limits set forth in Article 20 CO apply. According to this provision a contract is null and void if it provides for an impossibility, has an illegal content or is immoral. An exclusion or limitation of liability would fall under this provision, for example, in the case of a violation of the personality right of the purchaser. This is particularly relevant since according to case law any limitation of liability for personal injuries would infringe the personality right and therefore would be void. The limitation of liability would therefore be valid only to the extent that it covers damages to goods and not the health or life.

1.8 Are there particular goods or services which have specific obligations or duties attached to them?

As mentioned above, product liability related damages can be recovered based on liability provisions of public law regulating specific kind of products, industries or activities. Some examples are explosives and low voltage electronic products. The requirements do not differ substantially from those of the PLA or general tort law.

2. DEFENCES

2.1 What are the possible defences to a product liability claim?

Pursuant to Article 5 (1) PLA the producer is not liable if he proves one of the following:

- that he did not put the product into circulation;
- that, in regard to the circumstances it is probable that the defect which caused the damage did not exist at the time when the product was put into circulation by him;
- that the defective product was neither manufactured for sale or any other form of distribution for economic purposes nor manufactured or distributed in the producer's course of business;
- in the case of a producer of raw material or of a component, that the defect resulted from the design of the product in which the raw material or component was incorporated or that the defect resulted from the

instructions given by the manufacturer of the final product;
- that based on the state of the scientific and technical knowledge at the time when the product was put into circulation, one was not in a position to discover the defect; in this respect it is to note that the producer bears the burden of proof that the defect was not discoverable at the time the product was put into circulation;
- that the defect occurred due to compliance with mandatory regulations issued by public authorities (but not necessarily with existing voluntary standards if they do not reflect the state of the scientific and technical knowledge).

With respect to liability based on tort and contract law one of the main defences is the lack of negligence or wilful intent of the party potentially liable. In this respect it is important to note that the position is different depending on the cause of action. Under tort law it will be for the damaged party to prove that the damaging party acted with fault (ie, negligently or intentionally), whereas under contract law the burden of proof rests with the defendant, who has to prove that he did not act with fault. This defence is not available under the PLA since, as mentioned above, the PLA provides for a strict liability.

As already mentioned in the case of exception Article 55 CO (ie, the provision on which liability for auxiliary persons is based) the proof by the principal that he has taken all precautions appropriate under the circumstances in order to prevent damage or that the damage would have occurred in any case despite the taking of such measures, is a defence available for the principal.

2.2 Is there a limit on the time in which proceedings may be brought (limitations and repose)?

The limitation periods differ depending on the cause of action on which the liability is based.

Claims for the recovery of damages brought under the PLA are subject to a relative statute of limitation of three years starting from the day the claimant became aware or reasonably should have become aware of the damage, the defect and the identity of the producer. Additionally Article 10 PLA provides for an absolute statute of limitation barring any claims that are brought later than 10 years after the defective product that caused the damage was put into circulation. Because of this absolute statute of limitation it may occur that the claim is time barred even before the damage is caused, ie, if the defective product causes a damage only after 10 years from its being put into circulation.

Claims based on tort law are subject to a relative statute of limitation of one year after the day the claimant was aware of the damage and the liable person and to an absolute statute of limitation of 10 years after the tortious act.

It is to be noted that if the tortious act constitutes concurrently a criminal offence, the longer limitation period provided for in the penal code (that will depend on the type of crime) would also be applicable to civil claims based on the PLA or tort law.

The general statute of limitation for a contractual claim is 10 years. However a claim based on a breach of warranty in a sale and purchase contract is barred after two years after the delivery of the purchased product unless the seller has intentionally deceived the purchaser, in which case the general 10-year limitation period applies. Further such a claim is only allowed if the purchaser gives immediate notice of the defect to the seller after having discovered it (again, this is not applicable in the case of intentional deception).

3. LITIGATION OF PRODUCT LIABILITY DISPUTES

3.1 In which courts are product liability proceedings brought?

Generally speaking, in civil litigation in Switzerland, the court system consists of two instances at the cantonal level (eg, in the Canton of Zurich: district court (*Bezirksgericht*) and Superior Court (*Obergericht*). The third instance, on the federal level, is the Swiss Federal Supreme Court, the highest court in Switzerland.

Civil proceedings are governed by the Federal Civil Procedure Code (CPC). The CPC entered into force on 1 January 2011 and replaced the previous civil procedure codes of each of the 26 cantons (member states). However, the organisation of the judiciary is still regulated by cantonal law, subject to certain requirements set by the CPC.

There is one exception to the two cantonal instances rule: the cantons may determine a specialised court that hears commercial disputes. In other words, the cantons may set up commercial courts, which is the case in the cantons of Aargau, Berne, St Gall and Zurich.

Normally, product liability proceedings would be brought in a cantonal court of first instance (eg, in Zurich: in the district court).

In the cantons that have a commercial court, a product liability matter may also be brought in this court, if certain conditions are met: if both parties (claimant and respondent) are registered with the commercial register, the amount at stake is at least CHF 30,000 and if the dispute relates to the commercial activities of at least one of the parties, the matter has to be brought in the commercial court. If only the defendant is registered with the commercial register, but not the claimant (in other words, the claimant is a private individual) but all other conditions for the competence of the commercial court are met, the claimant may choose between bringing the dispute in the district court or in the commercial court (in practice, a private individual claimant would normally bring a case in the district court. This is because in the commercial court, a case is heard by five judges, two of which are professional judges, while three judges are part-time judges and business people normally from the industry to which the dispute has a connection, and a potential claimant in a product liability case would normally prefer professional judges over representatives of the industry he is bringing an action against as sitting judges in his or her matter.

3.2 How are proceedings commenced?

Before an action may be filed with a court, an attempt at conciliation before a conciliation authority must be made. There are certain exceptions to this, eg, in cases a commercial court is competent to hear a matter.

Conciliation proceedings basically consist of a hearing before the conciliation authority (also referred to as justice of peace) who tries to facilitate an amicable settlement between the parties. If no settlement can be reached, the conciliation authority grants authorisation to proceed to the claimant.

To commence proceedings in the court of first instance, the claimant needs to file a statement of claim together with the above mentioned authority to proceed (where required).

3.3 Are disputed issues decided by a judge or a jury?

There are no juries in the Swiss legal system.

3.4 Who has the burden of proof and to what standard?

Generally speaking, it is for the claimant to prove his or her case. In principle, full (or strict) proof has to be brought. This is, in principle, the case if the judge is based on objective assessment convinced that a certain fact is given. Absolute certainty is not required. It is sufficient if the judge has no serious doubts any longer or if he considers a possibly remaining doubt as small.

3.5 How is evidence given in proceedings and are witnesses cross-examined?

Swiss civil proceedings are to a large extent conducted in writing. Normally, there is an exchange of two full written briefs. The parties file the documents they rely on along with their written briefs. In essence, Swiss civil proceedings consist of two parts: first, the pleadings phase (normally exchange of written briefs) and secondly the taking of evidence phase of the proceedings. Witnesses may be heard, but here is no extensive trial as, for example, in the United States. Court hearings that last longer than a few hours or a day are rather rare. Witnesses are examined by the judge and the parties or rather their representatives may, subject to the judge's approval and control ask additional questions.

There are no cross-examinations in civil litigation in Switzerland.

3.6 Are the parties able to rely on expert opinion evidence and, if so, are there any special rules or procedures for expert opinion evidence?

Parties may rely on expert opinion evidence. However, in the Swiss civil litigation system, there is a distinction to be made between party-appointed experts and court-appointed experts. The parties may well engage their own expert and file his or her expert opinion along with their briefs. However, technically, such party appointed expert's opinion does not qualify as a means of evidence. In essence, such opinion only has the same standing as the pleadings of the respective party itself. Of course, if the expert opinion is, in substance, convincing, it will have an impact on the judge. Court-appointed expert's opinions, however, are means of evidence. In this case, it is the court that appoints the expert, after having given an opportunity to the parties to comment on both the expert as well as on the issues to be put to the expert. Given that Swiss civil litigation proceedings are overall mainly conducted in writing, written expert opinions prevail.

3.7 Is pre-trial discovery permitted? If so, in what circumstances? If not, what other mechanisms, if any, are available for obtaining evidence from a party or a third party?

In the Swiss civil litigation system, there is no discovery and no pre-trial discovery as in the United States.

In the Swiss system, each party basically files (only) those documents that support its case. In the taking of evidence phase of the proceedings (see above, question 3)) it is possible to bring a request for an order by the court to compel the other party to disclose certain specific documents . However, this is only possible with regard to specific documents that must be described in a clear manner and must be relevant in order to prove the factual allegations. In practice, it is only possible to get access to a very limited number of documents, if at all.

Under the CPC, it is also possible to request a court to take evidence before instituting ordinary proceedings (Article 158 CPC – 'precautionary taking of evidence'). Under the Code, this possibility is given where the law specifically provides for this right or where the applicant shows *prima facie* that the evidence is at risk or that he or she has a legitimate interest. Case law of the Swiss Federal Supreme Court has already narrowed the rather open and wide wording of the CPC down. In essence, an applicant needs to show that he or she has a case, and the threshold is rather high. In other words, while there is now, under the relatively new CPC, a possibility to take evidence before instituting full ordinary proceedings, the test is tough.

Depending on the circumstances, there is a further possibility to get access to documents before instituting ordinary court proceedings, namely by filing a disclosure request based on the Swiss data protection act. This possibility has mainly been explored by bank clients against their banks, but it could also be applied in other cases.

3.8 Is there liability for spoliation of evidence/a remedy for destruction of or failure to preserve evidence?

Given that in the Swiss civil litigation system, there is no such thing as discovery or pre-trial discovery, there was no need to develop rules such as to a litigation hold etc. There were therefore no specific rules developed in connection with spoliation of evidence or for failure to preserve evidence. In essence, it is rather an issue of overall credibility if a party, and in particular a commercial entity, is unable to produce certain evidence it obviously has had at an earlier time.

3.9 Is interlocutory or interim relief available prior to the full trial of a proceeding?

It is possible to obtain interim relief before or in connection with instituting ordinary proceedings. In order to obtain interim measures, an applicant needs to show *prima facie* that a right to which he or she is entitled has been violated or a violation of such right is anticipated and that the violation threatens to cause harm that would not be easily reparable.

3.10 Can the winning party recover its costs?

Yes, at least to some extent. In the Swiss civil litigation system, the 'loser pays' principle applies. The losing party therefore has to pay the court costs and compensation to the winning party for the winning party's legal costs (in addition, the losing party has, of course, to bear its own legal costs). The court costs as well as the compensation for legal fees are determined by a tariff that mainly depends on the amount at stake. It may therefore be that the actual legal fees are higher than the amount that the court will grant depending on the tariff. In this context, it should also be noted that a claimant must advance the likely court costs and, if certain specific conditions are met, also provide security for the compensation for legal fees.

3.11 What avenues of appeal are available?

As set out above (question 3.1), there is essentially a system of three levels of court instances. A judgment of a court first instance may be appealed to the cantonal Superior Court and from there to the Swiss Federal Supreme Court. A judgment of a commercial court may be appealed to Swiss Federal Supreme Court.

In the appeal proceedings before a cantonal Superior Court, the matter is, in essence, open to review in all aspects, ie, both with regard to factual and to legal issues. In appeal proceedings before the Swiss Federal Supreme Court, the scope is narrowed to essentially a legal review, with only some very limited factual review.

4. CLASS ACTIONS/REPRESENTATIVE PROCEEDINGS

4.1 Is there a mechanism for class actions or representative proceedings, or coordinated proceedings for product liability claims? If so, what are the basic mechanics?

In the Swiss civil litigation system, there is no mechanism for class actions or representative proceedings proper. In its message to parliament with regard to the new civil procedure code which then came into force on 1 January 2011, the Government had stated that there was no need to introduce class action or collective redress mechanisms since these mechanisms were 'alien' to Swiss law. There is currently some discussion going on and the Government has taken a more open position, but there is no specific amendment imminent in this regard. The discussion also seems to focus more on banking consumer issues than on product liability.

In practice, it would be possible to bring a specific case in the sense of a pilot case, or to bring claims of a number of creditors in single proceedings by way of assignment of the claims. Moreover, two or more people may file suit together if their rights and claims are based on similar factual circumstances or legal grounds. However, these possibilities are not really attractive to potential claimants.

5. LITIGATION FUNDING

5.1 Is litigation funding by third parties permissible in your country? If so, is it common?

It is now well established in Switzerland that litigation funding for civil litigation is permissible. However, by and large, it would not seem that litigation funding is already a truly common feature in Switzerland. This is perhaps also because this possibility is not yet well known among many potential claimants and perhaps also since there are only very few professional litigation funding providers active in Switzerland.

5.2 Are contingency fee or 'no win no fee' arrangements permissible?

No, contingency fee or 'no win no fee' arrangements are not permissible in Switzerland. The rules of professional conduct prevent Swiss lawyers from entering into such arrangements.

6. REMEDIES

6.1 What remedies are available to a party who successfully pursues a product liability claim?

The standard remedy is compensation for damages. In this context, it should be noted that there are no punitive damages or similar in the Swiss civil litigation system.

6.2 How are damages calculated/are there limitations on available damages?

Under the Product Liability Act (PLA), compensatory damages are available for personal injury and death and with regard to damage to property in private use. However, under the PLA there is no compensation for damage to the defective product itself.

Other damages may be compensated on the basis of contractual or tort liability. In any case, only real (specific) damages may qualify for compensation.

6.3 Are punitive or exemplary damages available and in what circumstances?

No, punitive or exemplary damages are not available.

6.4 Is liability joint and several/how does apportionment of liability work, including where a partially responsible entity is not a party to the proceeding?

Depending on the factual circumstances, there may be joint and several liability. Normally, a judgment would only take legal effect between the parties to the suit, not with regard to a third party. If a party is held liable by a claimant, and this party subsequently is held liable and wishes to take recourse against a third party, it would in essence have to bring a new suit. Under the new CPC, there is now a possibility to involve a third party to the proceedings. However, this route is often avoided for tactical reasons.

7. ROLE OF REGULATORS

7.1 Please explain the role, responsibilities and powers of regulators in your country which have jurisdiction over product liability issues.

On 1 July, 2010 the new Swiss Product Safety Act (PSA) entered into force. The PSA largely harmonises Swiss legislation on product safety to the Directive 2001/95/EC on general product safety.

The PSA provides for a set of rules in relation to product safety, which are applicable to all products to the extent that the relevant issues are not regulated by special product safety legislation. The latter concerns for example the safety of food stuff and utility products, pharmaceutical products and medical devices and low voltage electronic products. There are also specific provisions for construction products, chemical products, electrical installations, motor vehicles, telecommunication installations and other technical installations. In this contribution we will focus on the PSA rules, however, one has to bear in mind that the product concerned belongs to one of the above categories or other regulated categories, also the provisions of the relevant special pieces of legislation may have to be taken into account.

The PSA is a purely public law piece of legislation. As a consequence it does not contain nor regulate product liability aspects, which remain governed by the laws referred to in section 1 above (ie, mainly the PLA, tort and contract law).

Which regulator is in charge of the enforcement the PSA (or special legislation) provisions, will depend on the kind of product concerned. A number of laws and ordinances specify which federal or cantonal agency is acting as supervisory and enforcement authority for a specific product. According to the related Ordinance on Product Safety, the Secretariat of State of Economy (SECO) coordinates the implementation of the PSA in consultation with the relevant agencies. SECO also operates a product safety reporting and information office together with the Federal Consumer Affairs Bureau. If there are any doubts as to the agency in charge, it is recommended to contact SECO in order to ensure that the correct agency is informed in a timely way.

The relevant regulators/agency immediately informs SECO and the Federal Consumer Affairs Bureau of product safety cases arising in the field it supervises to coordinate enforcement and possibly publication of warnings etc.

With respect to the specific powers of the regulators under the PSA, we refer to section 7.3 below.

7.2 Are there any mandatory reporting requirements related to product safety issues?

According to Article 8 (5) PSA, with respect to products that are destined for use by consumers or for which a use by consumers cannot be reasonably excluded, the manufacturer or other person responsible for putting such product on to the market, that knows or has reason to believe that its product endangers the safety or health of the user or any other person, must notify this immediately to the relevant regulator/agency.

The notification must contain:

- all information to identify the products at issue;
- a complete and detailed description of the risks;
- all information about the persons from whom it received the product and the persons to whom it delivered it (in cases other than direct delivery to the final users);
- the actions taken to prevent the realising of the danger, such as warnings, discontinuation of sales, withdrawal from the market and product recalls.

7.3 Do the regulators have the power to:
(i) ban certain goods or services?
(ii) require a supplier to recall a product?
(iii) prescribe standards in respect of certain goods or services and require that the goods or services meet those standards?
(iv) require production of information without court process?

According to Article 10 PSA, the relevant regulator may:

- ban the further distribution of a product;
- issue product warnings;
- order and if it deems it necessary even organise the product recall;
- prohibit the export of a product;
- seize and destroy the products from which a serious and immediate danger arises;
- publish warnings to the population if the person responsible for putting the product on the market does not do it.

This is not an exhaustive list of the possible measures that can be taken by the regulators and they can therefore order additional measures if they deem that these are necessary to ensure public safety.

Further whoever has put the product on the market is also obliged to cooperate with the supervisory authority and provide all information it may request.

Pursuant to Article 17 PSA whoever intentionally does not comply with the obligation to cooperate with, and to provide the requested information to the supervisory authority or does not carry out the notification in accordance with Article 8 PSA, can be sanctioned with a fine of up to CHF 40,000 (CHF 20,000 in the case he acts negligently as opposed to intentionally).

8. VOLUNTARY CONDUCT

8.1 Are there regulations pertaining to the voluntary conduct of a product repair or recall by a supplier?

The PSA does not *per se* provide an obligation to notify a voluntary product recall. Whether the product recall is to be notified depends on the reason the measure was taken, ie, whether the general requirements for a notification under Article 8 (5) PSA are met or not. See in this respect section 7.2 above.

9. EMERGING ISSUES AND LAW REFORM

9.1 Are there important developing and emerging issues or trends in product liability law in your country?

After the coming into force of the PSA it remains to be seen if this new Act which also imposes post-sale obligations on the manufacturers, importers and persons responsible for putting the products into circulation will also have an impact on product liability-related litigation based on PLA and tort law. Product liability litigation is still not utilised much in Switzerland.

An interesting decision which may have an impact on product liability was rendered on 11 March, 2014, by the European Court of Human Rights in the case of *Howald Moor et al. v Switzerland* (nos. 52067/10 et 41072/11). In a liability case relating to the death of a worker connected with the exposure to asbestos several years before the damage to health became apparent, the Swiss Federal Court had ruled that the claim was time barred because the 10-year term explained in section 2.2 above had expired, and this in spite of the fact that the effects of the exposure to asbestos could not be detected during such period. The European Court of Human Rights held that under such circumstances the 10-year limitation period amounted to a violation of fair trial within the meaning of Article 6 (1) of the European Convention on Human Rights. If this decision becomes definitive (the decision can still be referred to the Grand Chamber), it may have an impact on future litigation, reopening cases that have not been pursued in view of the fact that it had been regarded as time barred. It also remains to be seen how the Federal Court will change its interpretation of the law in order to comply with the principles of the Convention. The case was based on a contractual claim. One could also wonder whether the 10-year absolute limitation period starting from the date in which a defective product has been put on the market and provided for by Article 10 PLA is also contrary to the Convention.

9.2 Please describe any proposed important law reform in the area of product liability in your country.

On 11 November 2013, the Federal Council (the Swiss Government) presented a Bill for the change of the rules on statute of limitation in the Code of Obligations. If the Bill becomes law, the absolute statute of limitation will be increased from 10 to 30 years in the case of personal injuries. This would to a large extent solve the issue also raised in the case recently decided by the European Court of Human Rights referred to in section 9.1 above, ie, the fact that a claim in damages can be time barred even before the injured person is aware of the existence of the damage to his or her health. The current Bill extends the 10-year limitation period only for claims based on general tort law and contract law. In contrast it does not provide for an extension of the limitation period for claims based on the PLA, which will remain in line with the one provided for in the EEC Directive 85/374 on product liability.

10. REGULATORY WEBSITES/INFORMATION

10.1 Please identify any useful regulatory references relating to product liability law in your country, for example, a product safety/ consumer law website maintained by the main regulator.

- The State Secretariat for Economic Affairs (SECO) coordinates the implementation of the PSA and acts as regulator for several products and for all products for which other laws do not provide that another agency is responsible for the supervision.
  The SECO website can be accessed at: *www.seco.admin.ch/index.html?lang=de*
  Its section dedicated to product safety can be accessed at: *www.seco.admin.ch/themen/00385/00440/index.html?lang=de*
  The contact details of SECO are as follows:
  State Secretariat for Economic Affairs SECO
  Holzikofenweg 36C
  CH-3003 Bern
  Tel. +41 (0) 31 322 56 56
  Fax +41 (0) 31 322 27 49
- The Federal Consumer Affairs Bureau (FCAB) is responsible together with SECO for the product safety reporting and information office and publishes the information on product recalls.
  The FCAB website can be accessed at: *https://www.konsum.admin.ch/de/*
  The section with product recall announcements can be accessed at: *https://www.konsum.admin.ch/de/dienstleistungen/rueckrufe-und-sicherheitsinformationen/*
  The contact details of FCAB are as follows:
  Federal Consumer Affairs Bureau
  Effingerstrasse 27
  3003 Bern
  Hotline: +41 31 322 20 00
  Fax: +41 31 322 43 70

Taiwan

Lee and Li Jill Niu & Katherine Juang

1. LIABILITY

1.1 What are the principal sources of law and regulation relating to product liability?

The dominating legislation addressing product liability in Taiwan would be the Consumer Protection Act (CPA) enacted in 1994, last amended in 2005, which provides the basis standards of the quality of products and services. Most specifically, it is required that the business operators engaging in the design, production, manufacture or import of goods or in the provisions of services have the following obligations:

(i) prior to selling goods into the market or at the time of rendering services, to ensure that goods and services provided meet safety standards that can be reasonably expected based on contemporary technical and professional standards; and

(ii) where goods or services may endanger the lives, bodies, health and/or properties of consumers, to label at a conspicuous place a warning and the urgent handling method.

Business operators failing to comply with the above obligations thereby endangering consumers and/or a third party will be jointly and severally liable therefor; the court may reduce their liability for damages if the business operators can prove that they have not conducted any intentional or negligent acts.

The business operators engaging in the distributing, retrofitting and repackaging of goods should be jointly and severally liable for such damages unless they can prove that they have exercised the level of due care necessary to prevent such damages from occurring, regardless of the outcome.

Under the Tort section of the Civil Code, Article 191-1 was added in 1999 to provide a shift of burden of proof to manufacturers to show due care, which is commonly referred to as one of the foundations of product liability legislation. Please note that the consumers may claim damages based on both the Civil Code and the CPA if the requirements under these two statutes are all met. Specific requirements related to product liability of different industries are provided in their respective laws and regulations, such as the Food Sanitation Act (FSA) and the Financial Consumer Protection Act.

1.2 What is required to establish causation under the most common causes of action available?

To establish causation between the defected product and the damages sustained by the product user, the standard of adequate causation theory should apply. An explanation of such theory that is commonly quoted in written judgments as the basis of the courts' determination of the establishment of causation is provided as follows:

'Causation is established if such damages would not have occurred if a specific act does not exist, while the existence of such act usually would result in such damages. Causation is not established, however, if such damages would not have occurred whether such act exists or not.'

Given the vague nature of such standard, it is commonly perceived that the burden of proving causation placed upon consumer is quite high and that the determination of causation establishment is at the judge's sole discretion.

1.3 Is strict liability available and, if so, in what circumstances?

While the CPA imposes strict liability, the Civil Code does not. As mentioned in section (1)(a) of this report, according to the CPA, as long as business operators engaging in the design, production, manufacture or import of goods fail to provide goods or services of contemporary safety standards or fail to provide necessary warning labels, they should be liable for damages sustained by consumers regardless of existence of intention and negligence. Even if the business operators can prove that they did not conduct any intentional or negligent acts, their liability for damages can only be reduced, not exempted, by the court. On the other hand, the liability of business operators engaging in the distributing, retrofitting and repackaging of goods can be exempted if they can prove that they have exercised the level of due care necessary to prevent such damages from occurring, regardless of the outcome.

However, according to the Civil Code, although the manufacturer and importer are liable for damages to another arising from the common use or consumption of their merchandise, such liability can be exempted if the manufacturer and importer can prove that there is no defective in the production, manufacture or design of the merchandise, that the damages is not caused by the existence of the defective if there is defective, and that the manufacturer has exercised reasonable care to prevent such damages from occurring.

1.4 Are guarantees or warranties as to quality implied by law?

The business operators should ensure that goods and services provided by them meet safety standard that can be reasonably expected based on contemporary technical and professional standards. Moreover, it is specifically required that under the CPA, if the business operators additionally warrant to consumers concerning the quality of goods or services, they should voluntarily provide written warranties, specifying, among others, the quantity of goods or services, the contents and period of such warranties, and the contact information of the manufacturer or the distributor. Even if the business operators do not provide such written warranties, it would still be deemed that they must honour the quality warranty that they had previously offered.

1.5 How is a product 'defect' defined?

A product is deemed defective as long as it does not meet safety standards that can be reasonably expected based on contemporary technical and professional standards. Local precedents further indicated that when determining whether a product meets the above standards, whether damages would occur even if use instructions and warning notes on label are drafted in a way that consumers can easily understand and the consumers had reasonably followed such instructions to use the product, should be considered. If the answer to the above is affirmative, then it would be deemed that the product does not meet contemporary standards and is defective. In light of the above, a defective product should be defined based on the common and reasonable anticipation of goods quality of average consumers rather than an actual malfunction. Please note that it is the business operators who bear the burden to prove that their products meet safety standards. However, goods and services cannot be presumed defective simply because better goods and services are subsequently provided.

1.6 Who in the supply chain has obligations or duties for defective products? What obligations or duties do they owe and to whom?

Almost all business operators in the supply chain have some level of duties for defective products. As mentioned in section 1.3 above, those involved in the designing, producing, manufacturing importing, distributing, retrofitting and repackaging of goods should jointly and severally compensate the consumers for the damages caused by defective products. In addition, as required under the CPA, if any business operator, based on the facts available, believes that certain goods or services are likely to endanger the safety and health of consumers, or if any business operator fails to label necessary warning notes in a conspicuous place, such business operator should immediately recall such goods or discontinue such services, unless other necessary treatments taken by the business operators are sufficient to remove such danger.

1.7 By what means can a supplier limit its liability for defective products?

It is specifically provided in the CPA that the business operators' liability for compensating damages sustained by customers cannot be limited or exempted in advance through mutual agreement. A supplier, however, may shift some of the ultimate liabilities to other business operators in the supply chain through contractual arrangements.

1.8 Are there particular goods or services which have specific obligations or duties attached to them?

Obligations imposed on food and pharmaceutical products are stricter. The FSA requires that entities engaging in food supply chain and exceeding certain business scale should have product liability insurance. Recall requirements and procedures for defective food products are detailed in such act and its relevant regulations. As for drug products, drug importers and/or local manufacturers are required to pay an imposition, a ratio of its revenue of drug sales of the preceding year, to the Drug Injury Relief Fund, which will be used to compensate patients for damages caused by necessary and legitimate drug use as defined in the Drug Injury Relief Act.

2. DEFENCES

2.1 What are the possible defences to a product liability claim?

It can be summarised from the legal framework outlined in section 1 above that when consumers claim for product liability against business operators, the business operators would bear the burden of proving that their products meet safety standards that can be reasonably expected based on contemporary technical and professional standards, while consumers should bear the burden of proving that their use of the product is common and reasonable and that the damages occurred during their reasonable use of such products. In addition, business operators engaging in the design, production, manufacture and import of goods can further prove that they did not conduct any intentional or negligent acts to reduce their liabilities, while business operators engaging in the distributing, retrofitting and repackaging of goods can prove that they have exercised with the level of due care necessary to prevent such damages from occurring regardless of the outcome so as to remove their liabilities.

Therefore, business operators may use the following defences to counter a product liability claim:

- their products meet safety standards that can be reasonably expected based on contemporary technical and professional standards;
- the consumers did not follow the use instructions to correctly use the product;
- there is no causation between the defective product and the damages;
- they did not conduct any intentional or negligent acts; and
- they have exercised due care to prevent such damages from occurring.

2.2 Is there a limit on the time in which proceedings may be brought (limitations and repose)?

The CPA is silent on statutory limitation regarding product liability claim. Local courts tend to hold that product liability is a special type of tort and most precedents indicate that statutory limitation of torts should apply to product liability claim. In this regard, the claim for damages in tort must be extinguished by prescription, if not exercised within two years from the date on which the injured person becomes aware of damages and the person liable for compensating or within 10 years from the date of the wrongful act. However, certain scholars hold the view that in order to better protect the rights and interests of consumers, statutory limitation should be the general rule given in the Civil Code, 15 years from the date of the wrongful act.

Moreover, it should be noted that under consumer class action, the statutory limitation period for consumers to seek damages should be separately determined for each consumer. In addition, the Ministry of Justice has issued an interpretation clarifying that, in addition to filing civil complaint, the filing for mediation can also *estop* the statutory limitation.

3. LITIGATION OF PRODUCT LIABILITY DISPUTES

3.1 In which courts are product liability proceedings brought?

Litigation of product liability may be brought to the district court of the place where the defendant business operator is registered in accordance with the Taiwan Code of Civil Procedure (TCCP) or to the district court of the place where the transaction of the goods/services at issue takes place in accordance with the CPA. The High Court, its lower courts and branches thereof may establish a consumer affair tribunal or designate a magistrate dedicated to the hearing of litigation of product liability cases as well as other consumer litigations.

3.2 How are proceedings commenced?

The litigation proceedings may be commenced upon the plaintiff consumer's filing of a complaint against the defendant business operator(s). A claim for product liability under NT$500,000 is required to be submitted to mediation before a litigation can be commenced.

3.3 Are disputed issues decided by a judge or a jury?

The disputed issues concerning product liability litigation will be decided by a judge at the first instance of trial and a panel of three judges at the second and the third instances of trial. The concept of jury trial is not adopted under the TCCP.

3.4 Who has the burden of proof and to what standard?

The defendant business operator shall bear the burden of proof to the following standards:

(i) the goods or services at issue were in compliance with the contemporary technical and professional standards of reasonably expected safety at the time when such goods were launched into the market or when the services at issue were rendered, they were in compliance with the contemporary technical and professional standards of reasonably expected safety;
(ii) where goods or services may likely cause personal injury or damage to property, a warning and the urgent handling measures shall be labelled at a conspicuous place;
(iii) in case of personal injury or damage to property caused by the goods or services at issue, it has exercised due care for the prevention of such injury or damage, or even if it had exercised due care, injury or damage would still have occurred;
(iv) in case of personal injury or damage to property caused by the goods or services at issue, it is not guilty of negligence, in which circumstances the court may reduce its liability for damages compensation.

3.5 How is evidence given in proceedings and are witnesses cross-examined?

Evidence may be submitted to the court by the parties to the litigation. For evidence kept by the other party or a third party, either party may request the court to subpoena for such evidence kept by the other party or the third party to be produced. Either party may also request that the court subpoena witnesses to testify in front of the presiding judge. The request for evidence investigation should detail the scope of the evidence to be produced by the other party or the third party and/or the issues or facts which need to be clarified by a competent witness. Cross-examination is not mandatory under the TCCP; however, the presiding judge may cross-examine witnesses, *ex officio* or at the request of the parties, if he/she deems it necessary.

3.6 Are the parties able to rely on expert opinion evidence and, if so, are there any special rules or procedures for expert opinion evidence?

Yes. The court may, upon the request of either party, instruct a competent individual expert or an institutional expert witness to conduct an assessment. The expert, and the number thereof, will be decided by the court; however, the court should, before making the decision, ask both parties to provide their respective opinions concerning expert witnesses. The court in principle should appoint an expert witness mutually agreed to by the parties unless the court considers the expert witness incompetent to perform the assessment at issue. The court also has the discretion to discharge and replace the appointed expert witness.

An expert witness shall be disqualified in any of the following circumstances:

(i) when the expert witness, or his/her spouse, former spouse, or fiance is a party to the proceedings;

(ii) when the expert witness is or was either a blood relative (within the eighth degree) or a relative by marriage (within the fifth degree), to a party to the proceedings;

(iii) when the expert witness, or his/her spouse, former spouse, or fiance is a co-obligee, co-obligor with, or an indemnitor to, a party to the proceedings;

(iv) when the expert witness is or was the statutory agent of a party to the proceedings, or the head or member of the party's household;

(v) when the expert witness is acting or acted as the advocate or assistant of a party to the proceedings.

An expert witness may decline the court's appointment on either of the following grounds:

(i) where the expert witness is the spouse, former spouse, or the betrothed, or the expert witness is or was a relative by blood (within the fourth degree) or a relative by marriage (within the third degree) to a party;

(ii) where the testimony of the expert witness will result in a direct loss of property to himself/herself or anyone who has such relationship with him/her as provided in the preceding subparagraph;

(iii) where the testimony of the expert witness will sufficiently expose himself/herself, or anyone who has such relationship with him/her as provided in the first subparagraph or a person who relates to him/her by guardianship, to criminal prosecution or embarrassment;

(iv) where the expert witness is to be examined with regard to a matter which he/she is obliged to keep confidential in the course of performing his/her official duties or conducting business;

(v) where the expert witness cannot testify without divulging his/her technical or professional secrets.

The court may ask the expert to provide a written assessment report certified by him/her. If further explanation or clarification is required, the court may also ask the expert to appear at a hearing to explain/clarify in front of the court.

3.7 Is pre-trial discovery permitted? If so, in what circumstances? If not, what other mechanisms, if any, are available for obtaining evidence from an party or a third party?

Pre-trial discovery is not adopted under the TCCP. However, either party may, prior to the commencement of the litigation or during the proceedings, request the court to conduct an evidence preservation procedure against the other party or a third party if: (i) the evidence at issue is likely to be destroyed or concealed or otherwise become difficult to use; or (ii) the other party agrees to the request. If the court approves the request for evidence preservation, it usually will keep the evidence (eg, documents or objects) under the custody of the court or a court-appointed third-party custodian.

3.8 Is there liability for spoliation of evidence/a remedy for destruction of or failure to preserve evidence (most relevantly, the product)?

There is no penalty under the TCCP if a party or a third party which is bound by a court order to preserve evidence fails to comply with such court order to produce the evidence or otherwise destroys the evidence. In the above circumstances, however, the court may *ex officio* deem the other party's contentions in respect of such evidence to be proven as true/correct.

3.9 Is interlocutory or interim relief available prior to the full trial of a proceeding?

A court order for preliminary attachment and/or preliminary injunction may be available under the following circumstances:

- Preliminary attachment: For monetary claims, It would be impossible or extremely difficult to enforce a favourable final judgment by compulsory execution in the future without freezing the defendant's attachable assets in advance.
- Preliminary injunction: For non-monetary claims, it would be impossible or extremely difficult to satisfy the claim by compulsory execution in the future should there arise a change in the status quo of the claimed object.

In addition, if a court renders a judgment unfavourable to the business operator(s), the court may, *ex officio*, declare provisional execution of the judgment without a security bond, or with reduced security bond, to be lodged by the plaintiff.

3.10 Can the winning party recover its costs?

Yes. The prevailing party in the action (the party that eventually wins the litigation) is usually awarded recovery for court costs against the losing party. The costs payable by one party to the other are imposed by the court pursuant to a tariff in the TCCP. The rules for calculating the court fees under the tariff are based on the value of the claim. The concept of the value of a claim is similar to that of the amount in dispute. For a lawyer's fees, only when the lawyer is appointed by the court or retained to appear at the court of third instance can the lawyer's fees be recovered. The maximum amount recoverable for lawyers' fees in the court of third instance is NT$500,000.

3.11 What avenues of appeal are available?

If the claim amount is less than NT$100,000 and is heard via summary proceedings, the losing party can appeal against the decision made by the judge at the summary tribunal to the civil tribunal of the district court, whose decision shall be final and irrevocable. If the claim amount exceeds NT$100,000 but is less than NT$1,650,000, the losing party may appeal to the High Court, whose decision shall be final. If the claim amount exceeds NT$1,650,000, the losing party can appeal to the High Court and then to the Supreme Court if the appeal is dismissed by the High Court.

4. CLASS ACTIONS/REPRESENTATIVE PROCEEDINGS

4.1 Is there a mechanism for class actions or representative proceedings, or coordinated proceedings for product liability claims? If so, what are the basic mechanics?

Under the CPA, a consumer protection group which has been established for more than three years after its registration has obtained upon application a rating of excellence by the Consumer Protection Commission (CPC), maintains a special staff dealing with consumer protection and meets any of the following requirements may, with the approval of the consumer ombudsman, bring in its own name a class action for damages compensation on behalf of the consumers or a class action for injunction on account of omission in accordance with the CPA.

(i) An association registered with the competent authority and having more than 500 members; or

(ii) a foundation registered with the competent authority and having total registered assets of NT$10 million or more.

To initiate a class action, a consumer protection group will have to assign the rights of claims (including pecuniary and non-pecuniary claims) from 20 or more consumers involved in the subject product liability incident in order for it to litigate in its own name. Consumers may revoke such assignment of the rights of claims before the close of oral arguments, in which case they shall notify the court.

In the above scenario, if the number of beneficiaries (ie, the consumers) is reduced to less than 20 as a result of the revocation of such assignment, the consumer protection group's standing as the plaintiff will not be affected.

At the end of the class action, the consumer protection group shall distribute the compensation awarded by the court less necessary expenses for the litigation, and lawyer fees to those beneficiary consumers. Consumer protection groups are not entitled to receive any reward from the consumers for conducting the class action.

5. LITIGATION FUNDING

5.1 Is litigation funding by third parties permissible in your country? If so, is it common?

No. However, legal aid is available under the Legal Aid Act and may be provided via the Legal Aid Foundation. Legal aid includes legal consultation, mediation and settlement, the drafting of legal documents, acting as a representative of the defendant in litigation or arbitration, necessary assistance in respect of services and fees incurred from other legal matters, and other resolutions reached by the Foundation. In addition, for a class action initiated by the consumer protection group in accordance with the CPA, the court fees for the portion of the claim exceeding NT$600,000 shall be waived.

5.2 Are contingency fee or 'no win no fee' arrangements permissible?

There is no statutory limitation under local laws on cost/fee arrangements for legal services. In principle, a client is allowed to agree on a cost arrangement with its lawyers, which can either be a fixed fee arrangement, an hourly charge arrangement or a contingency fee arrangement (a fixed fee plus a fee contingent on success). Those arrangements are acceptable under local ethics rules. However, a 'no win no deal' arrangement might be deemed contrary to ethics rules since it may violate the restriction on solicitation for business.

Local bar associations have promulgated a set of service fee guidelines listing the maximum amount for every kind of legal service that may be charged to a client. Furthermore, the Judicial Yuan of Taiwan has also promulgated restrictions on lawyers' fees at the third instance when the lawyer is appointed by the court in accordance with the TCCP.

6. REMEDIES

6.1 What remedies are available to a party who successfully pursues a product liability claim?

The following remedies are available to the plaintiff consumer(s) who successfully pursues a product liability claim:

(i) Compensation for pecuniary claims: loss and damage resulting from the product liability incident, including medical expenses reimbursement, increased living expenses, and funeral expenses reimbursement, loss of wages, financial support obligations, etc.

(ii) Compensation for non-pecuniary claims: ie, compensation for mental distress suffered as a result of the product liability incident.

(iii) Injunction to discontinue or prohibit a business operator's conduct which has constituted a material violation of the CPA relating to consumer protection.

6.2 How are damages calculated/are there limitations on available damages?

Compensation for pecuniary claims will be determined by the court based on the actual damage and loss suffered as a result of the product liability incident. Compensation for mental distress is usually determined on the basis of, among others, the social and financial background(s) of the tortfeasor(s) (ie, the business operator(s)) and the victim (ie, the consumer(s)), and the severity of the misconduct or negligence.

There is no limitation on available damages discussed above.

6.3 Are punitive or exemplary damages available and in what circumstances?

In a litigation brought in accordance with the CPA, the plaintiff consumer(s) may claim for punitive damages up to three times the amount of actual damages as a result of injuries caused by the wilful misconduct of the defendant business operator(s). However, if such injuries are caused by negligence, a punitive damage of up to one times the amount of the actual damages may be claimed for. For a litigation of product liability concerning food products, in the event of difficulty for the plaintiff consumer(s) to provide or inability to provide evidence to support the actual amount of damages, he/she may request the court to determine the compensation in the amount of between NT$500 and NT$30,000 for each case of damage per person based on the given circumstances.

6.4 Is liability joint and several/how does apportionment of liability work, including where a partially responsible entity is not a party to the proceeding?

According to Article 8 of the CPA, business operators engaging in distribution of goods and services shall be jointly and severally liable for damages with those business operators engaging in the design, production or manufacture of goods or services with respect to personal injury and/or property damage caused by such goods or services.

Among the business operators who are held by a court judgment to be jointly and severally liable for a product liability claim, they shall share the compensation liability equally unless otherwise provided under the law or under their contracts, except for the damages and the costs resulting from facts for which one of the parties/entities shall take up the sole responsibility, who shall in such case, bear the entire liability.

7. ROLE OF REGULATORS

7.1 Please explain the role, responsibilities and powers of the regulators in your country which have jurisdiction over product liability issues.

As specified in the CPA, the competent authorities of consumer protection matters at the central level shall be each of the central authorities having primary jurisdictions over matters of different industries. For example, product inspection matters are governed by the Bureau of Standards,

Metrology and Inspection (BSMI), product liability issues of food, pharmaceutical, cosmetic industries are governed by the Taiwan Food and Drug Administration (TFDA) under the Ministry of Health and Welfare, electronic products are governed by the Ministry of Economic Affairs, and matters relating to financial sectors are governed by the Financial Supervisory Commission. These central competent authorities are responsible for setting product standards for their respective industries and for providing guidance to local authorities.

The competent local authorities of consumer protection matters at are regional governments at the municipal/county level. The regional governments have the authority to investigate into products and services that might endanger the life, body, health or property of consumers and may demand business operators to rectify their violations within a prescribed period of time, and ask them to immediately cease the design, production, manufacture, import, distribution of products and/or services concerned, and may take necessary measures to protect the rights and interests of consumers. For serious violations, the authorities may also publish the names and products of the business operators.

Although the CPC was established shortly after the enactment of the CPA, it only plays the role of a consultant in implementing consumer protection matters. Consumer ombudsmen should be established within the CPC and regional governments; consumer ombudsmen handle consumer complaints and mediation and may file for injunction relief with the court to effectively halt any major violations of the CPA.

7.2 Are there any mandatory reporting requirements related to product safety issues?

The CPA set forth obligations for the immediate recall of products if there are sufficient facts to support the belief that the products of a business operator are likely to result in damaging the safety or health of consumers or if the label provides insufficient or inaccurate information. However, the CPA does not require reporting the incident triggering recall to any authority in charge of consumer protection matters.

Matters relating to the notification of product safety issue to local authority are governed by the Commodity Inspection Act (CIA) and the central authority in charge is the BSMI. The CIA divides commodities into two categories:

- Category I: commodities subject to inspection under the CIA; and
- Category II: commodities not subject to inspection under the CIA.

While local manufacturers or importers of Category I products have a mandatory obligation to report product safety issues to the BSMI, those of Category II products do not have the same mandatory obligation. More specifically, in case of the following events, the local manufacturer or importer of Category I products must notify the BSMI of such events:

(i) ignition, explosion, or fusion of the product that results, or is likely to result, in physical injury or property damage; and
(ii) death or injury that requires hospitalisation caused by use of the product.

7.3 Do the regulators have the power to:

(i) ban certain goods or services?

According to the CPA, competent local authorities have the power to ban goods and services if after investigation, it is determined that such goods and services may endanger the life, body, health, or property of consumers or may be incorrectly or insufficiently labelled. Similar legal basis to ban defective goods in different industries can also be found in other legislations, such as the CIA, the Pharmaceutical Affairs Act (PAA), the FSA, and the Tobacco and Alcohol Control Act (TACA).

(ii) require a supplier to recall a product?

Competent regional authorities may ask business operators to recall defective products within a period of time prescribed by such authorities pursuant to the CPA. Similar legal basis to recall defective goods can also be found in the CIA, the PAA, the FSA, the TACA.

(iii) prescribe standards in respect of certain goods or services and require that the goods or services meet those standards?

It is required under the CIA that Category I products can only be imported or manufactured after such products have passed the inspection required by the CIA unless the BSMI deems that the associated risk of such products is low. The commodities subject to inspection and the inspection procedures and standards are specified in a public notice issued by the BMSI. In addition, it is specified in the Telecommunications Act that for certain controlled telecommunication radio frequency devices, the Chinese national standards (CNS) published by the BSMI must be met.

Furthermore, as required under the FSA, foods, food cleansers, food utensils and food containers or packaging being sold must conform to sanitation, safety and quality standards prescribed by the TFDA, such as the General Food Sanitation Standards, the Dairy Products Sanitation Standards, and the Food Containers Sanitation Standards. On the other hand, although no such standards have been promulgated for pharmaceutical products, such products would need to undergo complicated registration procedures to ensure their safety and quality.

(iv) require production of information without court process?

As long as the competent central and regional authorities consider that certain goods and services are likely to cause damage to consumers, they may initiate an investigation. During such investigation, the CPA grants the authorities with the administrative power to request the investigated business operators to provide information to prove that their goods and/ or services will not cause any harm to consumers. The authorities may also conduct random on-site inspection of the products.

It is also stipulated under the CIA, the FSA, the TACA, the PAA, and many other legislations that their competent authorities may order the obligated entity to provide records of manufacture and other necessary documents for the inspection of the quality of product.

If so, broadly explain the circumstances in which the regulator can exercise the power and any penalties that apply if a supplier fails to comply.

If business operators fail to label their products accurately and sufficiently, to provide proper packages for the products, or to issue written warranty as required under the CPA and fail to rectify their acts within the period of time prescribed by the authorities, the authorities may impose a penalty of NTD20,000 to NTD200,000 (approximately US$670 to US$6,700). If the business operators are uncooperative towards the authorities' investigation, they may be subject to a penalty of NTD30,000 to NTD300,000 (approximately US$1,000 to US$10,000) and further consecutive penalties for continuation of non-cooperation. If the authorities have ordered a business operator to cease its manufacturing, importing, distributing, retrofitting and repackaging of the goods, to rectify its violating acts, to recall or destroy defective products, and/or to publish a notice of urgent handling measures for defective product(s) but the business operator still fails to comply with any of such orders, the authorities may impose a penalty of NTD60,000 to NTD1,500,000 (approximately US$2,000 to US$50,000). For any violations that are deemed serious by the authorities, the business operation of the business operator may be entirely shut down by the authorities.

The CIA provides heavier penalties for violating product labelling, recalling, selling products without passing the required inspection standards, and not cooperating with investigation; a penalty ranging from NTD10,000 to NTD7,500,000 (approximately for US$333 to US$2,500,000) may be imposed depending on the seriousness of the violation and the damages sustained by consumers; consecutive penalty is also available for continuous violations.

8. VOLUNTARY CONDUCT

8.1 Are there regulations pertaining to the voluntary conduct of a product repair or recall by a supplier?

The CPA requires that where there are sufficient facts to suspect the existence of goods or services would endanger the safety and health of consumers, business operators should, at its own initiative, immediately recall such goods or discontinue such services. Similar regulation can also be found in the FSA, the PAA, and other laws that require once the relevant business entities learn about the potential safety or quality issues of the goods, they should immediately recall such goods at their own initiatives. While the CPA does not provide detailed recall procedures for business operators to follow, guidelines relating recall procedures and requirements for food or pharmaceutical related acts are promulgated by the TFDA pursuant to the FSA and the PAA.

9. EMERGING ISSUES AND LAW REFORM

9.1 Are there important developing and emerging issues or trends in product liability law in your country?

Due to the surfacing of dozens of serious food safety scandals in Taiwan over the recent years (such as the illegal use of one plasticiser, DEHP (bis(2-ethylhexyl)phthalate), to substitute palm oil in food and drinks as a clouding agent in 2011 and the illegal use of copper chlorophyllin as a colouring agent for cooking oil in 2013), the FSA was amended substantially in June 2013 and February 2014 to upgrade food regulatory control mechanism.

More specifically, it is now required that an enterprise must certify the safety of all food product ingredients it uses or sells, including all raw materials, semi-products and end products. It must either perform an accreditation testing by itself or commission a certified accreditation laboratory to do so. Any enterprise that is not in compliance with such requirement and fails to correct the violation within the time limit prescribed will be fined ranging between NTD30,000 and NTD3 million (approximately US$1,000 and US$101,300). In addition, the maximum amount of a fine for the adulterated or fraudulent production or sale of food products that are harmful to human health has been raised from NTD10.5 million (US$355,000) to NTD50 million (US$1.7 million). The maximum amount of a fine for labeling, advertisements and promotions that are false, exaggerated or misleading has been raised from NTD200,000 (US$7,000) to NTD4 million (US$135,000). The longest prison sentence for the adulterated or fraudulent use of food additives or additives not authorised by the central government has been raised from three years to five years. Attendant fines for violating legal entities and their representatives have also been increased. Furthermore, a food safety protection fund will be set up to maintain food safety and sanitation standards and safeguard consumers' rights.

9.2 Please describe any proposed important law reform in the area of product liability in your country.

Since the CPA, the dominating legislation for product liability in Taiwan, was last amended in 2005 which is almost a decade ago, a local private foundation, the Consumers' Foundation proposed an amendment bill to the CPA in April 2013. Such foundation also proposed a draft Consumer Protection Fund Act at the same time. These bills aim to introduce more stringent liability upon business operators so as to prevent illegal profiting by adding ingredients that might be damaging to human health and safety and to provide more safeguard for consumers by setting up the Consumer Protection Fund. More specifically, if a business operator is found to have conducted the above-mentioned illegal acts, it should surrender all profit earned from conducting such illegal acts to the public by donating such profit to the Consumer Protection Fund.

10. REGULATORY WEBSITES/INFORMATION

10.1 Please identify any useful regulatory references relating to product liability law in your country, for example, a product safety/consumer law website maintained by the main regulator.

The regulatory references are mostly taken from the Laws and Regulations Database of the Republic of China website (*http://law.moj.gov.tw/Eng/*)

maintained by the Ministry of Justice. Below are some of their links:

- Civil Code: *http://law.moj.gov.tw/Eng/LawClass/LawAll.aspx?PCode=B0000001*
- Consumer Protection Act: *http://law.moj.gov.tw/Eng/LawClass/LawAll.aspx?PCode=J0170001*

Detailed regulations are provided in the websites of the relative regulators:

- Consumer Protection Committee: *www.cpc.ey.gov.tw/cpc_en/Content_List.aspx?n=1680CAE13C36FA16*
- Bureau of Standards, Metrology & Inspection: *www.bsmi.gov.tw/wSite/lp?ctNode=3563&CtUnit=1959&BaseDSD=7&mp=2*
- Food and Drug Administration, Ministry of Health and Welfare: *www.fda.gov.tw/EN/law.aspx*

Turkey

Cerrahoglu Law Firm Sezin Turan & Uraz Canbolat

1. LIABILITY

1.1 What are the principal sources of law and regulation relating to product liability?

There are various laws which may be applied in a product liability case depending on the circumstances of the matter. The main laws are:

- Consumer Protection Law, Law No: 4077 which was published in the Official Gazette dated 08.03.1995 numbered 28835 (Law no: 4077). It should be noted Law no 4077 has been replaced with the new Consumer Protection Law, Law No: 6502 which was published in the Official Gazette dated 28.11.2013 numbered 28835 (Law no: 6502). Law no 6502 shall be in force from 28 May 2014.
- The Law on the Preparation and Implementation of Technical Legislation on Products, Law No: 4703 which was published in the Official Gazette dated 11 July 2001 and numbered 24459 (Law no: 4703).
- The Code of Obligations, Law No: 6098 which was published in the Official Gazette dated 04 February 2011 and numbered 27836 (Law no: 6098)

There are two regulations which were enacted based on Law No: 4077 and Law No: 4703 relating to product liability. These are;

- Regulation on the Liability for Damages due to Defective Products which was enacted based on Law No: 4077 and published in the Official Gazette dated 13 June 2003 and numbered 25137 (Product Liability Regulation).
- Market Surveillance of Products published in the Official Gazette dated 17.01.2002 numbered 24643 (Market Surveillance Regulation)

There are different types of liabilities that may arise due to a defective product. Within the scope of this questionnaire, we are going to focus on civil law liabilities that may arise due to damages incurred because of the defective products. (Furthermore, although there are slight differences between rights of a consumer and a non-consumer in a product liability matter, we do not focus on these differences in this study.)

Article 4 of Law no: 4077 deals with civil law liabilities against consumers and clearly states that the consumer who has been injured because of a defective product has the right to file a lawsuit against the producer (only the producer, not the seller or the importer) and ask for compensation. If the defective product causes death or body injury or damage to other assets (not the defective product itself), then the consumer has the right to benefit from such provision. It should be noted that the whole Product Liability Regulation is based on Article 4 of Law no: 4077. On the other hand, as described above, starting from 28 May 2014, Law no: 4077 will not be in force anymore and the replacing Law no: 6502 does not have any provision regulating liabilities that may arise due to damages incurred because of the defective products, meaning that Product Liability Regulation would not be applicable in practice, starting from 28 May 2014. It should be noted that we have confirmed this with the officers of the relevant Ministry as well. Law no: 4703 will also change in the near future (please see our explanations included under question 8.2 below) and it is expected that the replacement law to Law no: 4703 will include provisions on liabilities that may arise due to damages incurred because of the defective products. Referring to the draft text of the law that will replace Law no: 4703, we understand that the lawmaker's intention is not to change the liability structure but to redefine the location of such liability within the applicable legislation. Therefore, since the liability structure regulated in the Product Liability Regulation will not be changed dramatically, we will continue to refer to the Product Liability Regulation whenever necessary.

Please note that rights regulated in Article 4 of Law no: 4077 are only valid for injured parties that can be characterised as consumers. However, even if the injured party cannot be characterised as a consumer, he/she still has the right to file a lawsuit against the producer and ask for compensation based on general tortious act provisions regulated under Law No. 6098.

1.2 What is required to establish causation under the most common causes of action available?

In principle, under our tortious act law structure, the injured party is required to prove the defect, the damage incurred by him/her, causation link between the defect and the damage incurred and also the defendant's fault. The legislation does not specifically answer what is required to establish causation in product liability cases. However, in one of the well-known decisions of the Court of Appeals, which was a product liability case about an LPG tube, it was concluded that the injured party shall not be required to prove the causation since the production stage of the product is very complicated for the injured party and it is therefore impossible for the injured party to understand the technical details of the product and establish the causation link between the incident and the product. In such case, the Court of Appeals ruled that the producer of the product should prove that the incident and the damage had not occurred as a result of the usage of the product (YHGK, 27.11.1996, E.1996/4-588, K. 1996/831).

1.3 Is strict liability available and, if so, in what circumstances?

Under Turkish Law, strict liability arises only if a law (code, not a regulation) stipulates it. As of now, none of the laws stipulates strict liability for product liability (it is expected that the law that will replace Law no: 4703 will include strict liability for product liability cases) but the Product Liability Regulation does. It imposes strict liability on producers/manufacturers.

In the event that the defective product causes a person's death or injury, or gives damage to a property, the manufacturer/producer is obliged to indemnify such damage irrespective of the negligence of the producer/manufacturer (Article 6, Product Liability Regulation). It should be noted that since the strict liability in product liability cases is regulated in a regulation only and not in a law, it is a controversial matter under Turkish law as to whether there is strict liability for product liability cases or not. The Court of Appeals' view is that there is no strict liability for the producer, but he/she should show much more care for his duties than an ordinary party. Accordingly, the producer is obliged to take every possible precaution in order to eliminate the risks (YHGK, 27.11.1996, E.1996/4-588, K. 1996/831).

1.4 Are guarantees or warranties as to quality implied by law?

Law no. 4703 stipulates that, in principle, a product is deemed safe if it is manufactured according to its technical regulation.

There is a guarantee obligation regulated in Law no. 4077 and also in the new Law no. 6502 for the benefit of consumers. Producers and importers of certain products that are determined by the relevant Ministry are obliged to issue guarantee certificates for each of their products. In general, the guarantee period is determined as two years minimum. During the guarantee period, excluding problems which have occurred as a result of the user's fault, any problems with the product should be fixed without claiming any kinds of fees or costs.

1.5 How is a product 'defect' defined?

There are certain definitions used in Law no: 4077, new Law no: 6502, Law no: 4703, Law no: 6098 and the Product Liability Regulation. According to the definition used in the Product Liability Regulation, a product is defective when it does not provide the safety that a person is entitled to expect, taking into consideration the presentation of the product, the reasonable use and the time when the product is put into circulation.

1.6 Who in the supply chain has obligations or duties for defective products? What obligations or duties do they owe and to whom?

Obligations, responsibilities and duties that may arise due to a defective product have a wide scope. Civil claims, administrative and criminal sanctions can be applied according to the circumstances of the matter. The addressee of these claims and sanctions also differ according to the circumstances of the matter. If we limit the scope to the liability arising from damages incurred because of the defective products, such liability is placed only on the producer/manufacturer of the defective product in Law no: 4077 and the Product Liability Regulation. Once again it should be noted that, contrary to Law no: 4077, the new Law no: 6502 does not contain a special provision about the damages incurred due to the defective products and it just refers to Law no: 6098 for the compensation claims related to the defective products.

Article 4 of the Product Liability Regulation defines the producer/manufacturer as follows:

(i) the manufacturer of a product which is presented to consumers, including public legal entities;
(ii) the producer of raw materials and any component parts of such product;
(iii) a person who puts a product into circulation or imports a product for such purposes by putting his name, trademark or other distinguishing feature.

Furthermore, according to the Product Liability Regulation, where two or more persons are liable for the damage, they shall be jointly liable.

In the event the defective product causes a person's death or injury, or gives damage to a property, the manufacturer/producer is obliged to indemnify such damage based on strict liability principles.

Article 4 of the Product Liability Regulation defines the injured as the consumer who has been injured due to damage caused by the defective product. Similar to Law no: 4077, law No: 6502 defines the consumer as the real or legal persons who are acting for purposes other than commercial or professional purposes. Therefore, it should once again be noted that damages given to a person who acts for commercial or professional purposes shall not be indemnified in accordance with strict liability principles within the scope of Product Liability Regulation. Such injured party would not have the opportunity to benefit from consumer legislation and would have to apply to the general provisions, such as the relevant provisions of Law no: 6098.

1.7 By what means can a supplier limit its liability for defective products?

In accordance with Article 8 of the Product Liability Regulation, any provision set forth in a contract or in any separate document which regulates that the consumer has waived his/her rights under the Product Liability Regulation, or limits or removes the liability of the producer/manufacturer arising from the Product Liability Regulation is invalid.

Therefore, it is not possible for a supplier to limit his/her strict liability arising out of the Product Liability Regulation.

1.8 Are there particular goods or services which have specific obligations or duties attached to them?

We would like to give some general information by referring to Article 71 of Law no: 6098. According to such article, which was not included in our previous Code of Obligations, strict liability principles apply to enterprises possessing significant danger. If it can be concluded that the enterprise is prone to create damages frequently or is prone to create heavy damages even if all the care that should be expected from an expert in such sector is shown, then such enterprise is considered as an enterprise possessing significant danger by the law. According to the same article, if damage occurs as a result of the operations of an enterprise possessing significant danger, both the owner of the enterprise and the operator of the enterprise are held jointly liable based on strict liability principles.

2. DEFENCES

2.1 What are the possible defences to a product liability claim?

The Product Liability Regulation gives us the possible defences that can be used against a product liability claim. According to Article 7 of the Product Liability Regulation, the producer/manufacturer shall not be liable if he proves any of the below:

(i) that he did not put the product into circulation; or
(ii) that the product was not produced for sale or was not manufactured by him in the course of his commercial activities; or
(iii) that, having regard to the circumstances, the defect which caused the damage did not exist at the time when the product was put into circulation by him; or
(iv) that the defect is caused due to the compliance of the product with the relevant technical regulations; or
(v) that the state of scientific and technical knowledge at the time when the product is put into circulation was not such as to enable the existence of the defect to be known.

The producer of a component (an element of the main product) shall not be liable if he proves that the defect is attributable to the design of the product or to the instructions given by the producer/manufacturer of the product.

Furthermore, according to Article 6 of the Product Liability Regulation, the liability of the producer/manufacturer may be reduced or removed, having regard to all the circumstances, if the producer/manufacturer proves that the damage is caused by the consumer or any person for whom the consumer is responsible.

2.2 Is there a limit on the time in which proceedings may be brought (limitations and repose)?

If we limit the answer of this question to the claims arising out of damages incurred due to the defective products, according to Article 4 of Law no: 4077 and Article 9 of the Product Liability Regulation, the injured person must bring proceedings within three years. This term begins on the date the injured person becomes aware or should have become aware of the damage, the defect and the identity of the producer/manufacturer.

Furthermore, according to Article 4 of Law no: 4077 and Article 10 of the Product Liability Regulation, in any case, the claim would be time barred after 10 years have passed since the product which has caused the damage was put into circulation.

On the other hand, as described above, contrary to Law no: 4077, the new Law no: 6502 does not regulate compensation claims related to damages arising out of a defective product and it just refers the matter to the general law, Law no. 6098. Therefore, we believe that once the new Law no: 6502 comes into effect, the prescription periods mentioned above would not be applied. Instead of them, the prescription period regulated in Law no. 6098 for tortious acts would be applicable. Accordingly, the claim should be raised before the courts within two years starting from the date on which claimant learns of the damage and the party responsible for such damage; and in any case, the claim would be time barred 10 years after the incident occurs. Please note that the draft law (please see our explanations included under question 8.2 below), which is expected to replace Law No: 4703 and includes provisions on liabilities that may arise due to damages incurred because of the defective products, also refers to the prescription period regulated in Law no. 6098.

3. LITIGATION OF PRODUCT LIABILITY DISPUTES

3.1 In which courts are product liability proceedings brought?

If the claimant (plaintiff) can be characterised as a consumer under consumer legislation, the liability proceedings should be brought before the consumer courts. If the claimant (plaintiff) cannot be characterised as a consumer, then liability proceedings should be brought before the civil courts (commercial courts). It should be noted that if the claimant (plaintiff) can be characterised as a consumer and the claim amount does not exceed TL3000 (approximately US$1,400), then the proceedings should be brought before the arbitration committee established by the State for the consumers. According to Law no: 4077, it is possible to apply to the arbitration committee even for claims that are higher than the threshold determined in the law (in such case, decisions of the arbitration committee shall not be binding on the parties but serve as an evidence for the trial before consumer courts). However, the replacing new Law no: 6502 clearly restrains applications to the arbitration committee for the amounts higher than the threshold.

3.2 How are proceedings commenced?

The claimant (plaintiff) applies to the court or the arbitration committee with a petition and submits all evidences he/she has. It should be noted that if the claimant (plaintiff) can be characterised as a consumer, the claimant (plaintiff) would be exempted from court fees that are calculated over the claim amount in principle. Furthermore, if the claimant (plaintiff) can be characterised as a consumer, he/she has the right to apply to the court where he/she is domiciled.

3.3 Are disputed issues decided by a judge or a jury?

There is no jury system under Turkish procedural law. Decisions are made by the judge. On the other hand, it should be noted that judges' decisions rely mainly on the expert reports received from the experts appointed by the court.

3.4 Who has the burden of proof and to what standard?

In principle, under Turkey's tortious act law structure, the plaintiff is required to prove the defect, the damage incurred by him/her, causation link between the defect and the damage incurred and also the defendant's fault. However, as described above, in one of the well-known decisions of the Court of Appeals, the Court of Appeals concluded that the injured party shall not be required to prove the causation link since the production stage of the product is very complicated for the injured part and it is therefore impossible for the injured party to understand the technical details of the product and establish the causation link between the incident and the product. Furthermore, in the same decision, the Court of Appeals stated that a producer should show much more care for his duties than an ordinary party and thus concluded that the injured party's obligation to prove the defendant's fault in a product liability case should be diminished.

3.5 How is evidence given in proceedings and are witnesses cross-examined?

If the plaintiff is a consumer and the proceedings are brought before the consumer court, all evidence should be shown at the beginning of the trial while submitting the statement of claim or the response to the statement of claim. If the plaintiff or the defendant possesses the evidence, the evidence should be submitted; if it is not possessed, then the necessary information related to the evidence should be given to the court so that the court conducts the necessary procedures to bring the evidence to the file. On the other hand, if the plaintiff is not a consumer and therefore the proceedings are brought before the civil court, parties have the chance to submit some of their evidence at a later stage. Under Turkish law, there is no cross-examination procedure in civil courts; so witnesses are not cross-examined, only the judge has the right to question witnesses.

3.6 Are the parties able to rely on expert opinion evidence and, if so, are there any special rules or procedures for expert opinion evidence?

For the first time, the new Procedural Law which came into force as of October 2011 regulates expert opinion evidence. Accordingly, both parties are able to rely on expert opinion evidence, but they do not have the right to ask the court to grant additional time just for the purpose of submitting expert opinion evidence. It should be noted that the judge may decide to listen to the expert, who prepared the written opinion, on his own initiative or upon the request of the other party. Experts can be cross-examined by the parties and if the expert does not honour the court's invitation to come to the court, his/her report will not be taken into consideration.

3.7 Is pre-trial discovery permitted? If so, in what circumstances? If not, what other mechanisms, if any, are available for obtaining evidence from a party or a third party?

Pre-trial discovery is not permitted under Turkish law. After the claim is brought before the court, upon the request of any of the parties, the court has the right to force the other party or a third party to submit the evidence in his/her possession. Furthermore, if there is a risk that the evidence may disappear, both parties have the right to apply to the court (prior to the lawsuit being filed or during the trial) for the determination and recording of the relevant evidence. Within the scope of such application, the judge and/ or the expert to be appointed by the judge would have the right to obtain evidence from the other party and/or the third party.

3.8 Is there liability for spoliation of evidence/a remedy for destruction of or failure to preserve evidence (most relevantly, the product)?

There are some regulations in this respect in the Procedural Law regarding documentary evidence. Accordingly, if the party fails to show the court (with the supporting evidence) the reason for his/her failure to present the evidence, then the judge may accept the other party's allegations depending on the circumstances of the matter. We believe that such legal opportunity may also be used for non-documentary evidence such as the product.

3.9 Is interlocutory or interim relief available prior to the full trial of a proceeding?

In principle, yes, interlocutory or interim relief is available prior to the full trial of a proceeding. If the party asking for interim relief almost proves his/her claim and if there is a serious risk that the party asking for interim relief may not reach his/her goal if the interim relief is not granted, then the court may rule for an interim relief. It should be noted that Turkish courts' tendency is not to rule for an interim relief easily.

On the other hand, there is a special interim relief regulated under Law no: 6098 which can apply in product liability cases. According to Article 76 of Law no: 6098, if the injured party submits serious evidence supporting his/her claims and also if he/she is suffering from financial difficulties, then the court may rule that the defendant make temporary payments to the plaintiff. These payments would be deducted from the compensation amount to be ruled by the court at the end of the trial. If the case is dismissed at the end of the trial, the court rules that the defendant return the temporary payments together with the accrued interest.

3.10 Can the winning party recover its costs?

Yes, the winning party recovers its costs, but this does not mean that all actual legal fees paid by the winning party to his/her lawyer would be reimbursed. The amount of legal fees to be reimbursed to the winning party shall be determined according to an official tariff by taking the claim amount into consideration.

3.11 What avenues of appeal are available?

The appeal system adopted by the new Procedural Law is still not in force. Certain conditions must be met by the State to facilitate the new appeal system, thus, it is currently unknown when the new appeal system will start to function. Under the current system, if the claim amount is higher than TL1,890 (approximately US$870), then the local court's decision is appealable before the Court of Appeals. Furthermore, if the claim amount is higher than TL11,530 (approximately US$5,300), it is also possible to apply to the Court of Appeals for the review of Court of Appeals' decision rendered as a result of the appeal.

4. CLASS ACTIONS/REPRESENTATIVE PROCEEDINGS

4.1 Is there a mechanism for class actions or representative proceedings, or coordinated proceedings for product liability claims? If so, what are the basic mechanics?

In general, contrary to the old one, the new Procedural Law contains a framework provision regulating class actions. Furthermore, Law no. 4077 and the new Law no. 6502 have some specific provisions related to class actions or representative proceedings that can be used in product liability matters. In short, consumer organisations, relevant public authorities and the Ministry of Customs and Trade has the right to file a lawsuit for the suspension of production and sale of the defective product and also for the collection of these products from third parties that possess such products for sale. Furthermore, referring to the framework provision included in the new Procedural Law, we believe that especially consumer organisations should have the right to file a lawsuit for the determination of consumer rights or to eliminate the illegal situation or prevention of the breach of consumers' future rights. It should be noted that under the current legal system it is not possible to claim compensation by way of class actions or representative proceedings. Individuals asking for compensation due to product liability should file separate lawsuits.

5. LITIGATION FUNDING

5.1 Is litigation funding by third parties permissible in your country? If so, is it common?

Litigation funding by third parties is not forbidden in our legal system. However, as far as we are aware of, it is not common at all. On the other hand, there are certain rules determined in the Procedural Law regarding litigation funding by the State for people having financial difficulties.

5.2 Are contingency fee or 'no win no fee' arrangements permissible?

It is possible to determine the amount of the legal fee according to a certain ratio of the compensation amount to be ruled by the court. It should be noted that such ratio cannot exceed 25%. On the other hand, 'no win no fee' arrangements are not permissible. At least, the lawyer should be entitled to receive the minimum amount determined in the official tariff for each type of legal services. It should be noted that such minimum amounts determined in the official tariff are significantly low, so, in practice, no win no fee arrangements are almost applicable.

6. REMEDIES

6.1 What remedies are available to a party which successfully pursues a product liability claim?

Various types of claims may arise due to a defective product. If we limit the scope of the claims to damages incurred due to a defective product, the plaintiff can ask compensation both for his/her material and immaterial damages. Within the scope of the material damages; funeral costs, treatment costs, damages incurred and to be incurred as a result of the loss or impairment of the injured party's ability to work and loss of earnings can be claimed. Within the scope of immaterial damages, an appropriate compensation should be ruled by the court considering the circumstances of the matter for the plaintiff's psychological/mental damages. It should be noted that if the injured party dies, certain relatives (such as mother, father, children) can also ask for compensation for their material and immaterial damages.

A consumer also has the right to apply to the court for the determination of the defect in a serial product, suspension of such product's production and sale, elimination of the defect and collection of the product from the market.

6.2 How are damages calculated/are there limitations on available damages?

Damages are calculated by the expert(s) appointed by the court based on the available evidence in the file. There is no mathematical limitation on damages but the compensation amount cannot exceed the plaintiff's actual damage.

6.3 Are punitive or exemplary damages available and in what circumstances?

No, punitive or exemplary damages are not available for product liability cases under Turkish law.

6.4 Is liability joint and several/how does apportionment of liability work, including where a partially responsible entity is not a party to the proceeding?

In general, within the scope of the consumer legislation, producer, importer and seller of the defective product are jointly liable against the consumer for his/her certain claims. However, if we limit the scope of claims to damages incurred due to a defective product, there is no joint liability regulated by the law. The injured party may apply to the seller based on contractual obligations or to the producer based on tortious act principles.

7. ROLE OF REGULATORS

7.1 Please explain the role, responsibilities and powers of the regulators in your country which have jurisdiction over product liability issues.

In general, regulators prepare technical regulations for products and perform market surveillances. Depending on the product type, there are different regulators that are in charge of preparing the technical regulation for each specific product and conducting market surveillances related to those products.

Products supplied to market should meet the necessary criteria determined in the technical regulations. Regulators perform market surveillances in order to ensure that products on the market meet the necessary criteria determined in the technical regulations and that they are safe. It should be noted that although the legislation accepts in principle that a product is deemed safe if it is manufactured according to the applicable technical regulation, it is still possible for a product that is manufactured according to the applicable technical regulation to be unsafe.

During market surveillances, regulators make tests on the products in order to ensure that such products have been produced in line with the applicable technical regulation and that they are safe. Even if the test results are not received and thus, it is not officially determined yet that the product is unsafe, regulators have the right to suspend the supply of the product to the market temporarily if there are concrete indications showing that the product is unsafe. According to the Market Surveillance Regulation, such temporary suspension cannot exceed three days provided that to perform the necessary technical tests does not require more time.

If as a result of the tests performed on the product it is understood that the product is not safe, regulators have the power;

- to ban the supply of the product to the market;
- to provide the collection of all products from the market;
- (if it is possible to fix the product) to notify the producer to fix the product and make it safe within a specific period of time;
- (if it is not possible to fix the product or if the producer fails to fix it) to destroy the products completely or partially;
- to make necessary announcements in two newspapers and two TV channels both of which are distributed and broadcasted countrywide;
- to rule the producer to pay the costs that arise as a result of technical tests and measures described above; and
- to impose administrative monetary fines on the producer.

7.2 Are there any mandatory reporting requirements related to product safety issues?

First of all, producers are obliged to investigate product-related complaints and perform tests on the products that are currently on the market. As a result of such investigations, if the producer determines safety risks on the products on its own, it is obliged to notify the distributors of the products and take necessary precautions such as performing product recalls and destroying the affected products if they cannot be fixed.

The relevant law, Law no: 4703, stays silent about reporting requirements for voluntary product recalls. However, our experience has shown us that the relevant Ministry wants to be informed about the details of the voluntary product recalls. Although the relevant law, Law no: 4703, does not contain specific provisions about voluntary product recalls, an amendment has been made in the Market Surveillance Regulation for Industry Products (this is a sub regulation under the general Market Surveillance Regulation issued by the Ministry of Science, Industry and Technology for only the products that fall in the scope of such Ministry's duty area) recently on 25 February 2014 and certain provisions regarding voluntary product recalls have been incorporated into such regulation.

Accordingly: Article 27/A of the Market Surveillance Regulation for Industry Products regulates voluntary product recalls. It is stated in this article that in the event a producer wishes to conduct a voluntary product recall, such producer is obliged to apply to the Ministry together with all the information and documents with regard to any correction and recall activities before conducting such voluntary recall. It should be noted that there is no specific provision regarding whether the voluntary recall of the same product in another jurisdiction would trigger a reporting obligation in Turkey or not. However, in practice, the Ministry expects the producer to make an application to Turkish authorities for a voluntary product recall if a recall is made outside Turkey for the same product.

7.3 Do the regulators have the power to:
(i) ban certain goods or services?
Yes, as explained under question 7.1 above, they have such power.

(ii) require a supplier to recall a product?
As explained under question 7.1 above, they have the power to require the producer to recall a product. The definition of the producer is broad. Law No. 4703 defines the producer as the producer of the product or any other person presenting himself as the manufacturer by affixing to the product his name, trade mark or other distinctive mark, or the person who reconditions the product, or in the event the producer is outside Turkey, the representative of the producer or the importer of the product, or the real or legal persons in the supply chain whose activities may affect the safety properties of the product.

(iii) prescribe standards in respect of certain goods or services and require that the goods or services meet those standards?
Yes, as explained under question 7.1 above, they have such power.

(iv) require production of information without court process?
Yes, as per the relevant provisions of the Market Surveillance Regulation, regulators have the power to require production of information without court process. This information may include all detailed information related to design and production of the product and also the addresses of the production places and warehouses.

If so, broadly explain the circumstances in which the regulator can exercise the power and any penalties that apply if a supplier fails to comply.
If it is determined that the producer has supplied the market with unsafe products or that the producer has failed to investigate the complaints related to its products and take necessary precautions, regulators have the right to impose administrative monetary fines on the producers.

8. VOLUNTARY CONDUCT

8.1 Are there regulations pertaining to the voluntary conduct of a product repair or recall by a supplier?

As explained under question 7.2 above, the relevant law, Law no: 4703, stays silent about voluntary product recalls. Although the relevant law does not contain specific provisions about voluntary product recalls, an amendment has been made in the Market Surveillance Regulation for Industry Products (this is a sub regulation under the general Market Surveillance Regulation issued by the Ministry of Science, Industry and Technology for only the products that fall in the scope of such Ministry's duty area) recently on 25 February 2014 and certain provisions regarding voluntary product recalls have been incorporated into such regulation.

Accordingly: Article 27/A of the Market Surveillance Regulation for Industry Products regulates voluntary product recalls. It is stated in this article that in the event a producer wishes to conduct a voluntary product recall, such producer is obliged to apply to the Ministry together with all the information and documents with regard to any correction and recall activities before conducting such voluntary recall. It should be noted that there is no specific provision regarding whether the voluntary recall of the same product in another jurisdiction would trigger a reporting obligation in Turkey or not. However, in practice, the Ministry expects the producer to make an application to Turkish authorities for a voluntary product recall if a recall is made outside Turkey for the same product.

Upon the application to the Ministry, the Ministry shall give time to the producer to fulfil its recall activities by taking into consideration the request of the producer, specifications of the product and its market extension. This term cannot be more than one year. In the event voluntary recall activities cannot be fulfilled within one year without the negligence of the producer, the Ministry may give additional time to the producer to complete voluntary recall activities.

The Ministry, if it deems necessary, may request the product to be tested and inspected by a neutral test or inspection institution.

The products which are corrected cannot be put into circulation before being submitted to the review of the Ministry. Therefore, after a voluntary recall, if the producer is willing to put the same product into circulation, the information and documentation with regard to corrective actions must be submitted to the Ministry.

9. EMERGING ISSUES AND LAW REFORM

9.1 Are there important developing and emerging issues or trends in product liability law in your country?

As can be seen in the very recent change in the Market Surveillance Regulation for Industry Products, the State is becoming more interested in product liability matters and especially in voluntary product recalls. Therefore, we believe that compared with the past, producers should be more serious and dedicated in their voluntary product recalls to be performed in Turkey.

9.2 Please describe any proposed important law reform in the area of product liability in your country.

Law No. 4703 was adopted with the purpose of implementing Council Directive 92/59/EC of European Union Legislation into Turkish law and it will be amended in the near future. The draft law, entitled Law on Product Safety and Technical Regulations (Draft Law) that will abrogate Law No. 4703 is published on the website of the Ministry of Economy. The Draft Law is prepared in accordance with the changes in the European Union product safety legislation, particularly: (1) EU Regulation numbered 765/2008/EC; (2) EU Decision numbered 768/2008/EC; (3) EU Directive numbered 2001/95/EC; (4) EU Regulation numbered 764/2008/EC; (5) EU Directive numbered 85/374/EEC; (6) Draft EU Regulation numbered 2013/0048; (7) Draft EU Regulation numbered 2013/0049; (8) Turkey-EU Partnership Council Resolution 1/95, 2/97 and 1/2006; and (9) WTO's Agreement on Technical Obstacles in Trade.

10. REGULATORY WEBSITES/INFORMATION

10.1 Please identify any useful regulatory references relating to product liability law in your country, for example, a product safety/consumer law website maintained by the main regulator.

Although the English version of it is not as satisfactory as the Turkish version, *http://urunguvenligi.ekonomi.gov.tr/ug/* which is a website under the responsibility of the Ministry of Economy, can be a useful reference on the matter.

United States of America

Bradley Arant Boult Cummings LLP
Tripp Haston & Whitt Steineker

1. LIABILITY

In the United States, there are two completely separate court systems; the federal system with a uniform set of laws and procedures and the 50 different state court systems which each have their own state-specific laws and procedures. Often these state laws and procedures vary substantially from each other and from federal laws and procedures. Recognising the wide variety of state laws, this chapter provides an overview of the federal system and a very general discussion of the state system equivalents.

1.1 What are the principal sources of law and regulation relating to product liability?

The principal source of law in product liability actions traditionally has been common law developed in state court systems, as opposed to the federal system, by judges through the years. Approximately 30 states, however, have enacted statutes governing product liability actions. Laws passed by state and/or federal legislatures and rules and regulations promulgated by state and/or federal regulatory agencies have also begun to play an increased role in product liability actions.

1.2 What is required to establish causation under the most common causes of action available?

In any product liability case, the plaintiff must prove that the allegedly defective product or wrongful conduct by the defendant caused the plaintiff's injury. In most jurisdictions, the defect or conduct does not have to be the sole cause of the injury, but it must have been both a direct and proximate cause of the injury. See, eg, *Rife v Hitachi Constr. Mach. Co.*, 609 S.E.2d 565, 569 (S.C. Ct. App. 2005).

For direct causation, or cause-in-fact, most jurisdictions employ either the 'but for' test or the 'substantial factor test'. The 'but for' test is satisfied if the injury would not have occurred but for the defect and/or defendant's actions. See, eg, *James v Arms Tech., Inc.*, 820 A.2d 27, 39 (N.J. Super. Ct. App. Div 2003). The substantial factor test asks if the defect and/or defendant's conduct was a substantial factor in causing the plaintiff's injury. See, eg, *Mitchell v Gonzales*, 819 P.2d 872, 876 (Cal. 1991).

While cause-in-fact focuses on the direct relationship between the defendant's conduct and the plaintiff's injury, proximate causation looks more broadly to the logical proximity of the defendant's conduct to the injury. If the relationship between the two is too remote, the proximate causation requirement is not met. Factors to be considered when determining if the plaintiff has proven proximate causation include whether it was foreseeable that the result would occur from the defendant's conduct and whether, despite the defendant's conduct, there were unforeseeable intervening forces that acted as the superseding cause of the injury. See *Palsgraf v Long Island R. R. Co.,* 162 N.E. 99 (N.Y. 1928).

1.3 Is strict liability available and, if so, in what circumstances?

Strict liability or modified strict liability is available in nearly every state either as a matter of statute or common law. The few states that have rejected traditional strict liability typically have adopted a substitute doctrine (such as an expansive implied warranty) which leads to the same practical result as strict liability. See, eg, *DeWitt v Eveready Battery Co., Inc.,* 565 S.E.2d 140, 147 (N.C. 2002). Strict liability typically is available when there is a manufacturing defect, a design defect, or a failure to warn regarding danger in the use of the product or failure to provide adequate instruction for safely using the product.

1.4 Are guarantees or warranties as to quality implied by law?

In most jurisdictions, warranties of merchantability and fitness for a particular purpose are implied in the sale of goods. See eg, *Hyundai Motor Am., Inc. v Goodin,* 822 N.E.2d 947, 951 (Ind. 2005).

The implied warranty of merchantability generally warrants that the goods sold 'are fit for the ordinary purposes for which such goods are used.' Uniform Commercial Code (UCC) § 2-314(2)(c). The warranty, however, neither requires that the goods be perfect nor incapable of harming a person.

The implied warranty of fitness for a particular purpose warrants that the goods will be fit for the particular purpose for which they were bought. UCC § 2-315. This warranty applies when both:

(i) a seller has reason to know the particular purpose for which the goods are bought; and

(ii) the buyer is relying on the seller's ability to provide appropriate goods. *Id.*

1.5 How is a product 'defect' defined?

Product defects fall into three general categories: manufacturing defects, design defects, or defects due to inadequate instructions or warnings. The defect, regardless of the type, must exist when the product leaves the defendant's possession.

A manufacturing defect is characterised by a deviation in a product from the quality or characteristics of other products of the same design. *Wheeler v Ho Sports, Inc.,* 232 F.3d 754, 757 (10th Cir. 2000).

When evaluating design defect claims, some courts employ the 'consumer expectations' test, which looks to whether the product is more dangerous than the ordinary consumer would expect the product to be when using it in an intended or foreseeable way. See, eg, *Brochu v Ortho Pharm. Corp.*, 642 F.2d 652, 655 (1st Cir. 1981). Other courts look to the 'reasonable alternative design' test, which asks whether a reasonable alternative design could have reduced the harm caused by the product. See, eg, *Wright v Brooke Group Ltd.*, 652 N.W.2d 159, 169 (Iowa 2002); Restatement Third, Torts: Products Liability § 2(b).

An inadequate instruction or warning is one that fails to render a product reasonably safe for its intended use. In other words, an instruction or warning must warn of the scope possible dangers in an understandable way. See, eg, *Bituminous v Black & Decker Mfg. Co.*, 518 S.W.2d 868, 872-73 (Tex. Civ App. 1974).

1.6 Who in the supply chain has obligations or duties for defective products? What obligations or duties do they owe and to whom?

Generally, all parties in a supply chain for a product (including manufacturers, sellers, wholesalers and distributors) owe a duty of reasonable care with respect to the product. *Willey v Fyrogas Co.*, 251 S.W.2d 635 (Mo. 1952). However, certain states have statutes limiting liability for certain members of the supply chain. See, eg, Ala. Code § 6-5-521 (generally limiting product liability claims to the manufacturer rather than the distributor, wholesaler, dealer, retailer, or seller of a product).

1.7 By what means can a supplier limit their liability for defective products?

In nearly every state, a supplier can limit or disclaim a warranty by including specific language in a disclaimer at the time of the sale. See UCC § 2-316(2). A supplier typically cannot disclaim liability for negligence or strict liability.

1.8 Are there particular goods or services which have specific obligations or duties attached to them?

Certain goods or services are regulated by standards, some of which are mandatory and some of which set minimum requirements. See, eg, 15 USC § 2063. For example, the federal Food, Drug and Cosmetic Act requires approval of all new drugs before they are introduced into interstate commerce. 21 USC § 355. Similarly, the Food & Drug Administration (FDA) requires that all advertisements for prescription medications be accurate and not misleading.

2. DEFENCES

2.1 What are the possible defences to a product liability claim?

Defences to product liability claims include, but are not limited to:

- Contributory negligence, whereby some portion of a party's injury was caused by his or her own negligence. In some states, contributory negligence is a complete defence. See, eg, *Lafarge North America, Inc. v Nord*, 86 So.3d 326, 336 (Ala. 2011).
- Comparative negligence, whereby a party's recovery is limited in

proportion to that party's responsibility for his or her own injury.

- Assumption of risk, which applies when a party voluntarily and knowingly assumed the risks inherent to a dangerous activity.
- Misuse or alteration of the product, whereby liability can be extinguished if the product at issue has been altered from its original condition or where the product has been used in a way that was not reasonably foreseeable to the manufacturer.
- State-of-the-art-defence, whereby a defendant establishes *prima facie* defence to negligence by establishing that he or she complied with the state of the art.

Some states have codified these defences in their product liability statutes. See, eg, N.C. Gen. Stat. Ann. § 99B-4. These defences typically are raised either in a motion to dismiss or an answer to the initial complaint. The party asserting the affirmative defence has the burden of proving the defence to a preponderance of the evidence.

2.2 Is there a limit on the time in which proceedings may be brought (limitations and repose)?

The statutes of limitations applicable to product liability actions vary among jurisdictions, typically ranging from one to six years. See eg, Ky. Rev Stat. Ann. § 413.14D(1)(a) (2013); Me. Rev Stat. Ann. tit. 14, § 752 (six years). Under certain circumstances, such as mental infirmity, incarceration, or incapacitation, the statute of limitations may be tolled. See, eg, *Anson v American Motors Corp.*, 747 P.2d 581, 583, 589 (Ariz. Ct. App. 1987). The discovery rule, available in many states, prevents a cause of action from accruing until the plaintiff should have discovered his or her claim. See, eg, Or. Rev Stat. Ann. § 30.905(1) (West 2010). This rule frequently applies in toxic exposure cases.

Certain states have enacted statutes of repose, which require a plaintiff to bring his or her product liability claim within a certain time period of the product's sale, regardless of when any injury occurred or when a plaintiff learned of the basis for a claim. See, eg, Tenn. Code. Ann. § 29-28-103(a) (1993). A statute of repose focuses on the age of the product at issue and not on the plaintiff's knowledge of the cause of action.

3. LITIGATION OF PRODUCT LIABILITY DISPUTES

3.1 In which courts are product liability proceedings brought?

Product liability cases can be brought in any state court that has jurisdiction over the defendant and where venue is proper. Typically this is where the injury occurred or where the defendant is incorporated or maintains its principal place of business.

A product liability case can also be brought initially in federal court if:

(i) the parties are citizens of different states and the amount of damages in controversy exceeds $75,000; or

(ii) the complaint raises an issue of federal law as opposed to simply product liability claims, which are traditionally issues of state law. 28 USC §§ 1331, 1332 (2012).

Under certain conditions, a defendant can remove a case from state court to federal court if the case could have been brought initially in federal court. Typically, a removal must occur within 30 days of receipt of the complaint, but in any event no more than one year after receipt of the complaint. *Id.* § 1441.

3.2 How are proceedings commenced?

A plaintiff typically initiates a proceeding by filing a copy of a complaint with the clerk of the court and then serving a copy of the complaint on each defendant with a summons directing the defendant to respond to the complaint within a specified period of time. A defendant's response is due 20-30 days from the date of receipt of the complaint.

3.3 Are disputed issues decided by a judge or a jury?

Questions of law are usually decided by judges. Questions of fact (including the credibility of witnesses and the resolution of disputed facts) are usually decided by juries. If no party requests a jury, all of the issues can be decided by a judge.

If there is no dispute of material fact as to any particular issue, and the question between the parties is solely one of law, a judge can decide the issue and issue a summary judgment that disposes of the case without need for a trial.

3.4 Who has the burden of proof and to what standard?

A plaintiff in a product liability case has the burden of proving her case to a preponderance of the evidence. This means that the plaintiff must prove that it is more likely than not that the defendant is liable for the plaintiff's injuries.

The burden of proof is higher if the plaintiff seeks to recover punitive damages. In such cases, the plaintiff must establish her entitlement to punitive damages by clear and convincing evidence, which is a more demanding standard than the preponderance of the evidence standard.

3.5 How is evidence given in proceedings and are witnesses cross-examined?

Whenever possible, evidence is provided by live, in-court testimony from witnesses with first-hand knowledge of the relevant facts. Out-of-court statements are admissible under limited conditions when in-court testimony is not feasible. In-court witnesses are subject to cross-examination.

3.6 Are the parties able to rely on expert opinion evidence and, if so, are there any special rules or procedures for expert opinion evidence?

Expert witness testimony often is necessary when the products at issue are sufficiently complex that jurors cannot infer that the product's defect caused the alleged injuries. *Robinson v Ford Motor Co.,* 967 F. Supp 482 (M.D. Ala. 1997). Parties are generally permitted to rely on the opinions of qualified expert witnesses provided that the principles and techniques upon which the expert founded his opinion are sufficiently reliable.

A small minority of jurisdictions follow the 'general acceptance' rule outlined in *Frye v United States,* 293 F. 1013 (D.C. Cir. 1923). Under that rule, expert opinions are admissible if they are based on scientific theories or techniques that are 'generally accepted' in the relevant field. *Id.*

The majority of states and all federal courts follow the test outlined by the United States Supreme Court in *Daubert v Merrell Dow Pharmaceuticals, Inc*. See *Lohmeier v Hammer*, 148 P.3d 101 (Ariz. Ct. App. 2006). Under Daubert, expert testimony is admissible if it is based on reliable principles and techniques. In determining whether the principles and techniques are reliable, courts typically consider:

(i) whether the methodology has been subjected to scientific testing;
(ii) whether the methodology has been peer reviewed or published;
(iii) the known or potential rate of error;
(iv) the existence of standards that govern the methodology's operation; and
(v) the rate at which the pertinent scientific community accepts the methodology.

Expert testimony is subject to various procedural rules to which a party must adhere if the expert testimony is to be admitted. Typically, these rules require advanced disclosure of expert's identity and other pertinent information, such as the witness's opinions, the information that was relied upon in forming the opinions, supporting exhibits, and the expert's qualifications. See Fed. R. Civ P. 26.

3.7 Is pre-trial discovery permitted? If so, in what circumstances? If not, what other mechanisms, if any, are available for obtaining evidence from a party or a third party?

Pre-trial discovery is permitted in product liability actions. As a general rule, the parties to a product liability case may seek all relevant information from other parties through the use of depositions, requests for production of documents, requests for admission and written interrogatories. See Fed. R. Civ P. 30-36. The information requested from another party need not be admissible at trial; rather, discovery need only be reasonably calculated to lead to the discovery of admissible evidence. As a practical matter, depositions often have a broad scope and the subject matter is often not confined to matters which would be admissible at trial.

Discovery is available from third parties on a more limited basis, including requests for permission and depositions, provided that the information requested is not overly burdensome and is reasonably calculated to the discovery of admissible evidence. See Fed. R. Civ P. 45.

3.8 Is there liability for spoliation of evidence/a remedy for destruction of or failure to preserve evidence (most relevantly, the product)?

Each party owes a duty to take reasonable measures to preserve relevant evidence in pending or reasonably foreseeable litigation. *West v Goodyear Tire & Rubber Co.,* 167 F.3d 776 (2d Cir. 1999). When evidence has been spoliated, sanctions may be imposed which proportionately correspond to the culpability of the party responsible for the spoliation and to the prejudice that results to the opposing party. *Tabacco v Spray Products Corp.*, No. 9304961, 1994 WL 683379 (E.D. Pa. Nov 30, 1994).

Sanctions may include:

(i) a jury instruction permitting the jury to assume that the destroyed evidence would have been unfavourable to the spoliating party;
(ii) the exclusion of competing evidence offered by the spoliating party;
(iii) the dismissal of claims by the spoliating party; or
(iv) a directed verdict against the spoliating party.

3.9 Is interlocutory or interim relief available prior to the full trial of a proceeding?

In federal court, interlocutory review is permitted by statute for certain categories of orders that are thought to present special justification for immediate appeal, such as orders relating to injunctions. 28 USC § 1292(a)(1) (2012). Other matters are subject to interlocutory review either:

(i) upon permission of both the district court and the court of appeals; or
(ii) when an issue is independent from the merits of the case, irreparable harm is likely to occur if review is delayed, and the issue is 'too important to deny review.' *Id.* § 1291.

Certain state courts have similar procedures for interim appeal. For example, certain states allow for immediate appeal an order granting injunctive relief. R.I. Gen Laws § 9-24-7 (2013). Other states allow for immediate appeal to an appellate court in the event of a clear error by a trial court. Ala. Code § 12-22-6 (2013).

3.10 Can the winning party recover its costs?

Litigants traditionally bear their own litigation expenses, regardless of the outcome of the case. Certain jurisdictions, however, permit the prevailing party to recover reasonable and necessary litigation costs. *Cooley v Lincoln Elec. Co.*, 776 F. Supp. 511 (N.D. Ohio 2011); Idaho R. Civ P. 54(d)(1). Certain jurisdictions also recognise an independent claim for groundless or frivolous lawsuits. See, eg, Ala. Code § 12-19-270 *et seq.*

3.11 What avenues of appeal are available?

In federal civil cases, final orders of a district court are appealable to one of 13 federal courts of appeals. 28 USC § 1291 (2012). Once the issue is decided by the court of appeals, the case may be reviewed by the United States Supreme Court, although review in the Supreme Court is discretionary and a small fraction of petitions for review are granted.

State courts operate in much the same way. A losing party at the trial court level typically may appeal to an intermediate appellate court or, in certain limited circumstances, directly to the state's highest court. The state's highest court typically has the discretion to review decisions of the intermediate appellate court, although sometimes review in the highest court is provided as a matter of right.

The United States Supreme Court has the discretion to review final decisions of a state's highest court on questions of federal law. *Virginia v Imperial Coal Sales Co.,* 293 U.S. 15, 16-17 (1934).

4. CLASS ACTIONS/REPRESENTATIVE PROCEEDINGS

4.1 Is there a mechanism for class actions or representative proceedings, or coordinated proceedings for product liability claims? If so, what are the basic mechanics?

Class actions may be brought in state or federal court provided that certain requirements are met. In federal court, product liability class actions are governed by Federal Rule of Civil Procedure 23 and the Class Action Fairness Act of 2005 (CAFA). Many states have adopted rules similar to the federal rules on class actions, while others, such as California, have procedures that differ significantly from the federal rules.

Under CAFA, federal district courts have original jurisdiction, with certain exceptions, over cases where the amount in controversy exceeds $5 million, there are 100 or more class members, and at least one plaintiff is a citizen of a different state than any defendant. 28 USCA § 1332(d)(2), (5)(B).

Federal Rule of Civil Procedure 23(a) sets forth the prerequisites for members of a class to sue on behalf of a class in a product liability action. This requires that:

(i) the class is so numerous that joinder of all members is impracticable;
(ii) there are questions of law or fact common to the class;
(iii) the claims or defences of the representative parties are typical of the claims of defences of the class; and
(iv) the representative parties will fairly and adequately protect the interests of the class. Fed. R. Civ P. 23(a)(1)-(4).

An increasingly popular alternative to class actions is a federal coordinating mechanism known as multidistrict litigation. When civil actions involving one or more common questions of fact are pending in different federal districts, they may be transferred to a single district for consolidated pretrial proceedings. 28 USCA § 1407(a). Transfer is not appropriate, however, where common questions of fact will not predominate over individual questions or where significant individual factual questions are involved.

5. LITIGATION FUNDING

5.1 Is litigation funding by third parties permissible in your country? If so, is it common?

Third-party funding agreements are permitted in a minority of jurisdictions, and even then only under specific conditions. See eg, *Anglo-Dutch Petroleum Int'l, Inc. v Haskell,* 193 S.W. 3d 87 (Tex. Ct. App. 2006). In some states, all such arrangements constitute criminal offences. Me. Rev Stat. tit. 17-A, § 516 (1976). In other states, these arrangements are statutorily prohibited or declared void and unenforceable. GA. Code Ann. § 13-8-2(a)(5) (2011).

Conflict of interest issues arise when a third party interferes with the attorney's ability to render independent legal advice to the client. An attorney may not permit the third-party funder to direct the litigation or otherwise interfere with the attorney's duty to his client. Model R. Prof. Conduct 5.4(c). Nor may the attorney disclose confidential information to a third-party funder without the client's informed consent. Model R. Prof. Conduct 1.7, Comment 13.

5.2 Are contingency fee or 'no win no fee' arrangements permissible?

Contingency fees are permitted in most jurisdictions in product liability cases. A 'fee may be contingent on the outcome of the matter for which the service is rendered,' except where prohibited. Model R. Prof. Conduct 1.5(c). Contingent fee agreements must be in writing signed by the client and shall state clearly the method by which the fee is to be determined. *Id.*

6. REMEDIES

6.1 What remedies are available to a party who successfully pursues a product liability claim?

A plaintiff is entitled to monetary damages for harm caused by a defective product, although the types of damages available vary based on the type of action and often by state law. When a case is based on strict liability or negligence, common tort damages are generally available to put the plaintiff in the position she was in before the injury. For breaches of warranty, plaintiffs can recover general damages available under the Uniform Commercial Code. UCC §§ 2-711 to 2-721.

Compensatory damages may include both economic damages such as medical bills and lost wages, as well as non-economic damages such as mental anguish and pain and suffering.

6.2 How are damages calculated/are there limitations on available damages?

Damages are intended to restore the plaintiff to the position she would occupy had she not been injured by the defective product. *Tabieros v Clark Equip. Co.*, 944 P.2d 1279 (Haw. 1997). Other states statutorily define what the measure of damages will be. See, eg, Cal. Civ Code § 3333. Many states have capped noneconomic damages in personal injury or wrongful death actions to a certain sum or a multiple of the economic loss. See, eg, Okla. Stat. tit. 23 § 61.2 (2011); Idaho Code Ann. § 6-1603 (2003).

Experts are often necessary to determine the extent of a plaintiff's damages.

6.3 Are punitive or exemplary damages available and in what circumstances?

Punitive damages often are permitted in product liability actions, provided that the plaintiff makes a sufficient showing of entitlement to such damages. See eg, *Wangen v Ford Motor Co.*, 294 N.W.2d 437 (Wis. 1980). A plaintiff usually must show outrageous, gross or reckless conduct by the defendant to justify punitive damages. See, eg, *Roginsky v Richardson-Merrell, Inc.*, 378 F.2d

832 (2d Cir. 1967). Some states disallow any recovery of punitive damages unless explicitly granted by statute. See, eg, N.H. Rev State Ann. § 507:16. Other states have provided caps on the recovery of punitive damages, either as an absolute amount or as a multiple of compensatory damages. See, eg, Ala. Code § 6-11-21 (2013).

6.4 Is liability joint and several/how does apportionment of liability work, including where a partially responsible entity is not a party to the proceeding?

Many states permit joint and several liability so that a plaintiff can recover the full amount of damages from any one defendant jointly and severally liable for the plaintiff's injury. *Holcim (US), Inc. v Ohio. Cas. Ins. Co.,* 38 So.3d 722 (Ala. 2009). Other states have adopted pure several liability so that a defendant is only charged his portion of the damages. See, eg, ALASKA STAT. § 09.17.080 (1997). Still other states are somewhere in the middle, allowing joint and several liability in specific types of actions. *Allard v Liberty Oil Equip. Co. Inc.,* 756 A.2d 237 (Conn. 2000) (actions in negligence mandate several liability, while other actions retain joint and several liability).

7. ROLE OF REGULATORS

7.1 Please explain the role, responsibilities and powers of the regulators in your country which have jurisdiction over product liability issues.

Product liability issues are regulated in part by set standards that must be followed for products sold in the United States. Product standards may come from various sources such as the Government, industry groups, or organisations whose sole purpose is to craft standards. One governmental agency that sets such standards is the Occupational Safety and Health Administration. See 29 USC §§ 651, 655 (2012). Some of these standards, such as federal regulations, are mandatory, while other standards regulate the industry by providing a minimum baseline for consumer expectations in this country.

7.2 Are there any mandatory reporting requirements related to product safety issues?

The federal Government can require mandatory reporting for information related to product safety. One example is mandatory dairy product information reporting under 7 USC § 1637(b). Under the Federal Food, Drug, and Cosmetic Act, there is a mandatory reporting requirement for adverse events associated with non-prescription drugs and dietary supplements. 21 USC §§ 379aa, 379aa-1 (2012). States, too, have imposed mandatory reporting requirements for adverse events involving the medical care of an individual that results in death or injury. D.C. CODE § 7-161 (2009).

7.3 Do the regulators have the power to:

(i) ban certain goods or services?

Laws such the Consumer Product Safety Act allow the federal Government to ban a wide range of consumer goods and services. 15 USC §§ 2051-2089 (2012).

(ii) require a supplier to recall a product?

The federal Government has mandatory recall authority under acts such as the Federal Food, Drug, and Cosmetic Act. 21 USC § 350l (2012). The Consumer Product Safety Commission also has the authority to direct the recall of consumer products.

(iii) prescribe standards in respect of certain goods or services and require that the goods or services meet those standards?

The Government also requires compliance with standards for consumer products like toys and furniture. See, eg, 15 USC §§ 2056(b) (2013). For example, the FDA and Consumer Product Safety Commission have rules in place to ensure that consumer products and medication meet minimum specifications.

(iv) require production of information without court process?

The FDA and Consumer Product Safety Commission require the reporting of certain adverse events. For example, the manufacturer of prescription medication must report any reports the manufacturer receives from prescribers or the general public regarding adverse events experienced while using the medication.

8. VOLUNTARY CONDUCT

8.1 Are there regulations pertaining to the voluntary conduct of a product repair or recall by a supplier?

Once a product is voluntarily recalled, a supplier incurs a duty to 'act as a reasonable person in recalling the product.' Restatement (Third) of Torts: Products Liability § 11 (1998). How the supplier executes the recall process is governed by various federal regulations, depending on the type of product at issue. See, eg, 21 CFR § 7 (2013) (regulations for recall of products monitored by the FDA).

9. EMERGING ISSUES AND LAW REFORM

9.1 Are there important developing and emerging issues or trends in product liability law in your country?

The federal Government has begun to play an increasing role in the realm of product liability law. Product liability actions traditionally involved the application of a particular state's law. Nevertheless, the federal government's control over certain aspects of product safety through federal statutes and regulations has increased in recent years.

For example, the Consumer Products Safety Improvement Act, enacted in 2008, significantly expanded the Consumer Product Safety Commission's authority to regulate the sale of consumer products within the United States. See 15 USC § 2064 *et seq.* (2012). Additionally, in the Food Safety Modernization Act was passed in 2011, which provided the Food and Drug

Administration new authority to ensure regulatory compliance among both domestic and international food products. See 21 USC § 2201 *et seq.* (2012).

If a state's law conflicts with federal law, the federal law pre-empts the state law and the federal law applies. In 2011, the United States Supreme Court held a failure to warn claim under state law was pre-empted by FDA regulations, which had been promulgated pursuant to the Food, Drug and Cosmetics Act. See *Pliva, Inc. v Mensing,* 131 S.Ct. 2567 (2011). This pre-emption also applies to certain design defect claims under a state law that also conflicted with FDA regulations. See *Mut. Pharm. Co. v Bartlett,* 133 S. Ct. 2466 (2013).

9.2 Please describe any proposed important law reform in the area of product liability in your country.

A growing number of lawsuits – primarily in the realm of prescription medications – allege that a manufacturer is liable under the so-called 'innovator-liability theory' for the activities of other manufacturers which manufacture the same or similar products. The premise is that it is 'foreseeable' that a warning about a brand-name drug product could influence the prescription or ingestion of a generic drug product because the FDA requires generic drug labelling to mirror the brand-name labelling. Thus, the theory goes, it is appropriate to hold the brand-name manufacturer liable for warning-related injuries, even if the consumer took only a generic version of the product manufactured, sold and distributed by the brand-name manufacturer's competitors. To date, proponents of the theory have been largely unsuccessful, but it is possible that the theory will spread to other areas of product liability law.

10. REGULATORY WEBSITES/INFORMATION

10.1 Please identify any useful regulatory references relating to product liability law in your country, for example, a product safety/consumer law website maintained by the main regulator.

- Consumer safety: *www.cpsc.gov/en/*
- Occupational safety and health: *https://www.osha.gov/*
- Air, water, and pesticide standards: *www.epa.gov/*
- Food, drug,and medical devices: *www.fda.gov/*
- Transportation: *www.nhtsa.gov/; www.fhwa.dot.gov/; www.uscg.mil/*

Contact details

GENERAL EDITORS

Annette Hughes
Corrs Chambers Westgarth
Level 36
Bourke Place
600 Bourke Street
Melbourne
VIC 3000
Australia
T: +61 3 9672 3506
F: +61 3 9672 3010
E: Annette.hughes@corrs.com.au
Web: www.corrs.com.au

Rod Freeman
Hogan Lovells International LLP
Atlantic House
Holborn Viaduct
London EC1A 2FG
United Kingdom
T: +44 20 7296 2000
F: +44 20 7296 2001
E: rod.freeman@hoganlovells.com
Web: www.hoganlovells.com

ARGENTINA

Leandro M. Castelli
& Alejo M. Gascón
Marval, O'Farrell & Mairal
Av. Leandro N. Alem 928, 7th floor,
Buenos Aires, Argentina
T: +54 11 4310 0100
F: +54 11 4310 0200
E: lmc@marval.com.ar
aga@marval.com.ar
Web: www.marval.com

AUSTRALIA

Annette Hughes
Corrs Chambers Westgarth
Level 36
Bourke Place
600 Bourke Street
Melbourne
VIC 3000
Australia
T: +61 3 9672 3506
F: +61 3 9672 3010
E: Annette.hughes@corrs.com.au
Web: www.corrs.com.au

BRAZIL

Leopoldo Pagotto & Marina Esposito
Zingales & Pagotto Sociedade de Advogados
Rua Estados Unidos n. 475,
Jardim América
São Paulo (SP),
01427-000
Brasil
T: +55 (11) 2501 7889
F: +55 (11) 4421 1124
E: pagotto@zisplaw.com.br
marina@zisplaw.com.br
Web: www.zisplaw.com.br

CANADA

Peter Pliszka, Michael Parrish, Enrico Forlini & Robin Roddey
Fasken Martineau DuMoulin LLP
333 Bay Street, Suite 2400
Bay Adelaide Centre, Box 20
Toronto, ON M5H 2T6
Canada
T: +1 416 366 8381
F: +1 416 364 7813
E: ppliszka@fasken.com
mparrish@fasken.com
eforlini@fasken.com
rroddey@fasken.com
Web: www.fasken.com

CHINA

Wu Feng
Beijing Dacheng Law Offices
7/F, Parkview Green Building D
No.9, Dongdaqiao Road
Chaoyang Dist
Beijing
China
T: +86 10 58137289
F: +86 10 58137779
E: feng.wu@dachenglaw.com
Web: www.dachenglaw.com

CROATIA

Nina Iličić & Olga Bogdanović
Bogdanović, Dolički & Partners
Attorneys at Law
Miramarska 24
HR-10000 Zagreb
Croatia
T: +385 1/600 56 56
F: +385 1/600 56 57
E: nina.ilicic@odbd.hr
olga.bogdanovic@odbd.hr
Web: www.hoganlovells.com

DENMARK

Jens Rostock-Jensen
& Jakob Dahl Mikkelsen
Kromann Reumert
Sundkrogsgade 5
2100 Copenhagen East
Denmark
T: +45 70 12 12 11
F: +45 70 12 13 11
E: jrj@kromannreumert.com
jdm@kromannreumert.com
Web: en.kromannreumert.com

ENGLAND & WALES

Rod Freeman & Anthea Davies
Hogan Lovells International LLP
Atlantic House
Holborn Viaduct
London EC1A 2FG
United Kingdom
T: +44 20 7296 2000
F: +44 20 7296 2001
E: rod.freeman@hoganlovells.com
anthea.davies@hoganlovells.com
Web: www.hoganlovells.com

EUROPEAN UNION

Rod Freeman & Anthea Davies
Hogan Lovells International LLP
Atlantic House
Holborn Viaduct
London EC1A 2FG
United Kingdom
T: +44 20 7296 2000
F: +44 20 7296 2001
E: rod.freeman@hoganlovells.com
anthea.davies@hoganlovells.com
Web: www.hoganlovells.com

FRANCE

Emmanuèle Lutfalla, partner,
Goulwen Pennec, associate &
Edouard Dufour, associate
SCP Soulié & Coste-Floret
20 Boulevard Masséna
75013 Paris
France
T: +33 (0)1 44 23 53 00
F: +33 (0)1 44 23 17 17/18
E: e.lutfalla@coste-floret.com
g.pennec@coste-floret.com
e.dufour@coste-floret.com
Web: www.coste-floret.com

GERMANY

Dr. Anton G. Maurer, LL.M.
& Klaus-Dieter Schick
CMS Hasche Sigle
Schöttlestraße 8
70597 Stuttgart,
Germany
T: +49 711 9764 181
+49 711 9764 285
F: +49 711 97 64 900
E: anton.maurer@cms-hs.com
klaus-dieter.schick@cms-hs.com
Web: www.cms-hs.com

GREECE

Dimitris Emvalomenos, partner
Bahas, Gramatidis & Partners LLP
26 Filellinon Street,
105 58, Athens
Greece
T: +30 210 3318170
F: +30 210 3318171
E: d.emvalomenos@bahagram.com
Web: www.bahagram.com

INDIA

Zia Mody & Vivek Bajaj
AZB & Partners
23rd Floor, Express Tower
Nariman Point
Mumbai
Maharashtra
400021
India
T: +91 22 6639 6880
F: +91 22 5639 6888
E: zia.mody@azbpartners.com
vivek.bajaj@azbpartners.com
Web: www.azbpartners.com

INDONESIA

Pheo M. Hutabarat
Partner
Hutabarat, Halim & Rekan – Lawyers
DBS Bank Tower
20th Floor (Ciputra World 1),
Jl. Prof. DR. Satrio Kav. 3-5
Jakarta 12940
Indonesia
T: +6221 2988 5988
F: +6221 2988 5989
E: pheo.hutabarat@hhrlawyers.com
Web: www.hhrlawyers.com

ITALY

Alessandro P. Giorgetti
& Prof. Giovanni Iorio
Studio Legale Giorgetti
Via Fontana, 28 - 20122
Milano
Italy
T: +39 02 54 57 734
F: +39 02.55.18.02.82
E: giorgetti@giorgettilex.com
Web: www.giorgettilex.com

JAPAN

Shinji Kusakabe & Aoi Inoue
Anderson Mori & Tomotsune
Akasaka K-Tower, 2-7,
Motoakasaka 1-chome,
Minato-ku,
Tokyo 107-0051,
Japan
T: +81 3 6888 1062
+81 3 6888 5802
F: +81 3 6888 3062
+81 3 6888 6802
E: shinji.kusakabe@amt-law.com
aoi.inoue@amt-law.com
Web: www.amt-law.com

NEW ZEALAND

Robert Gapes
Simpson Grierson
Level 27 Lumley Centre
88 Shortland Street
Private Bag 92518
Auckland 1141
New Zealand
T: +64 9 977 5076
F: +64 9 307 0331
E: robert.gapes@simpsongrierson.com
Web: www.simpsongrierson.com

PORTUGAL

Daniel Reis & Juliana Marcondes
PLMJ, Sociedade de Advogados, RL
Av. da Liberdade, 224
Edifício Eurolex
1250-148 Lisboa
Portugal
T: +351 21 319 73 00
F: +351 21 319 74 00
E: daniel.reis@plmj.pt
juliana.marcondes@plmj.pt
Web: www.plmj.com/en

REPUBLIC OF IRELAND

Isabel Foley, Orla Clayton
& Domhnall Breatnach
Arthur Cox
Earlsfort Centre
Earlsfort Terrace
Dublin 2
Ireland
T: +353 1 618 0000
F: +353 1 618 0618
E: isabel.foley@arthurcox.com
orla.clayton@arthurcox.com
domhnall.breatnach@arthurcox.com
Web: www.arthurcox.com

SOUTH KOREA

Sung Jin Kim, Jay J. Kim
& Brian C. Oh
Kim & Chang
39, Sajik-ro 8-gil,
Jongno-gu
Seoul 110-720
Korea
T: +82 2 3703 1114
F: +82 2 737 9091/9092
E: sjkim@kimchang.com
jjkim@kimchang.com
brian.oh@kimchang.com
Web: www.kimchang.com

SWEDEN

Susanna Norelid, Christer A. Holm
& Fredrik Seemann
Advokatfirman NorelidHolm
Visiting address: Birger Jarlsgatan 15
Box 7394
SE-103 91
Stockholm
Sweden
T: +46 8 463 04 60
F: +46 8 463 04 70
E: info@norelidholm.com
Web: www.norelidholm.com/en/

SWITZERLAND

Stefano Codoni
Walder Wyss Ltd
Via F. Pelli 7
PO Box 5162
6901 Lugano
Switzerland
T: +41 91 911 80 00
F: +41 91 911 80 08
E: stefano.codoni@walderwyss.com
Web: www.walderwyss.com

Dieter Hofmann
Walder Wyss Ltd
Seefeldstrasse 123
PO Box 1236
8034 Zurich
Switzerland
E: dieter.hofmann@walderwyss.com
Web: www.walderwyss.com

TAIWAN

Jill Niu & Katherine Juang
Lee and Li, Attorneys at Law
7F, 201 Tun Hua N. Road,
Taipei 10508,
Taiwan, R.O.C.
T: +886 2 2715 3300 Ext 2457
F: +886 2 2713 3966
E: jillniu@leeandli.com
Web: www.leeandli.com

TURKEY

Sezin Turan & Uraz Canbolat
Cerrahoglu Law Firm
Barbaros Bulvarı
Mustafa İzzet Efendi Sokak,
No:11 Cerrahoğlu Binası
Balmumcu, Beşiktaş
34349 İstanbul,
Turkey
T: +90 212 355 30 00
F: +90 212 266 39 00
E: sezin.turan@cerrahoglu.av.tr
uraz.canbolat@cerrahoglu.av.tr
Web: www.cerrahoglu.av.tr

USA

Tripp Haston & Whitt Steineker
Bradley Arant Boult Cummings LLP
One Federal Place
1819 Fifth Avenue North
Birmingham, AL 35203
USA
T: +1 205 521 8000
F: +1 205 521 8800
E: thaston@babc.com
wsteineker@babc.com
Web: www.babc.com